MATTHEW

ABINGDON NEW TESTAMENT COMMENTARIES

MATTHEW

DONALD SENIOR

Abingdon Press
Nashville

ABINGDON NEW TESTAMENT COMMENTARIES:
MATTHEW

This book is printed on recycled, acid-free, elemental-chlorine–free paper.

Library of Congress Cataloging-in-Publication Data

Senior, Donald.
    Matthew / Donald Senior.
        p. cm. — (Abingdon New Testament commentaries)
    Includes bibliographical references and index.
    ISBN 0-687-05766-3 (pbk. : alk. paper)
    1. Bible. N.T. Matthew—Commentaries. I. Title. II. Series
BS2575.3.S47   1998
226'.207—dc21   98-13827
                                                                   CIP
ISBN 13: 978-0-687-05766-5

08 09 10 11 12 13—10 9 8 7 6 5 4

MANUFACTURED IN THE UNITED STATES OF AMERICA

*Gratefully dedicated to the students, faculty, and staff
of Catholic Theological Union,
my intellectual and spiritual home
for twenty-five years.*

CONTENTS

FOREWORD

The *Abingdon New Testament Commentaries* series provides compact, critical commentaries on the writings of the New Testament. These commentaries are written with special attention to the needs and interests of theological students, but they will also be useful for students in upper-level college or university settings, as well as for pastors and other church leaders. In addition to providing basic information about the New Testament texts and insights into their meanings, these commentaries are intended to exemplify the tasks and procedures of careful, critical biblical exegesis.

The authors who have contributed to this series come from a wide range of ecclesiastical affiliations and confessional stances. All are seasoned, respected scholars and experienced classroom teachers. They take full account of the most important current scholarship and secondary literature, but do not attempt to summarize that literature or to engage in technical academic debate. Their fundamental concern is to analyze the literary, socio-historical, theological, and ethical dimensions of the biblical texts themselves. Although all of the commentaries in this series have been written on the basis of the Greek texts, the authors do not presuppose any knowledge of the biblical languages on the part of the reader. When some awareness of a grammatical, syntactical, or philological issue is necessary for an adequate understanding of a particular text, they explain the matter clearly and concisely.

The introduction of each volume ordinarily includes subdivisions dealing with the *key issues* addressed and/or raised by the New Testament writing under consideration; its *literary genre, structure, and character;* its *occasion and situational context,* including its wider social, historical, and religious contexts; and its *theological and ethical significance* within these several contexts.

In each volume, the *commentary* is organized according to literary units rather than verse by verse. Generally, each of these units is the subject of three types of analysis. First, the *literary analysis* attends to the unit's genre, most important stylistic features, and overall structure. Second, the *exegetical analysis* considers the aim and leading ideas of the unit, deals with any especially important textual variants, and discusses the meanings of important words, phrases, and images. It also takes note of the particular historical and social situations of the writer and original readers, and of the wider cultural and religious contexts of the book as a whole. Finally, the *theological and ethical analysis* discusses the theological and ethical matters with which the unit deals or to which it points, focusing on the theological and ethical significance of the text within its original setting.

Each volume also includes a *select bibliography*, thereby providing guidance to other major commentaries and important scholarly works, and a brief *subject index*. The New Revised Standard Version of the Bible is the principal translation of reference for the series, but the authors draw on all of the major modern English versions, and when necessary provide their own original translations of difficult terms or phrases.

The fundamental aim of this series will have been attained if readers are assisted, not only to understand more about the origins, character, and meaning of the New Testament writings, but also to enter into their own informed and critical engagement with the texts themselves.

Victor Paul Furnish
General Editor

PREFACE

From the very beginning, the Gospel of Matthew has had a profound influence on the life of the church. Its powerful and ordered narrative of Jesus' life, starting with his origins in the history of Israel and stretching out into the mission of the post-Easter community, its majestic discourses that capture Jesus' teaching and give the Gospel a strong ethical bent, its effective use of the Hebrew Scriptures—all of these traits made Matthew's Gospel the most quoted in the apostolic church and situated it at the head of the New Testament canon.

Today Matthew's Gospel remains at the heart of the Christian Scriptures and the focus of renewed study. Of particular interest for scholarship is the relationship of Matthew's community to first-century Judaism. Matthew explicitly situates the life of Jesus in the context of the Jewish Scriptures and Jewish history. At the same time, Matthew's Gospel exhibits what appear to be anti-Jewish traits, particularly the unrelenting negative portrayal of the Jewish leaders. Christian scholarship has become much more nuanced in its understanding of first-century Judaism. This is due in part to advances in archaeology and to more refined methods of assessing Jewish texts and the cultural context of the first-century world in general. But another important motivation for a more objective view of first-century Judaism has been the calamity of the Holocaust and its roots in Christian anti-Semitism. No longer can Christianity afford a biased view of its Jewish heritage. Matthew's Gospel is a key text for understanding those roots.

In two recent publications I had the opportunity to assess biblical scholarship on Matthew's Gospel. *What Are They Saying About Matthew?* (Senior 1996) offers a fairly comprehensive survey of publications that have appeared in the past thirty years. And in Abingdon's *Interpreting Biblical Texts* series, my volume on *The Gospel of Matthew* examines the contributions of recent scholarship to the task of interpreting the Gospel for the life of the church (Senior 1997).

The task of a commentary, however, is to focus not directly on scholarly discussion, but first and foremost on the biblical text itself. My goal is to serve as an informed guide for the reader of the Gospel, explaining key terms, alerting the reader to the probable social and historical context of the Gospel, and tracking the literary contours of the narrative. Matthew's text comes from another time, language, and culture, and therefore today's readers need a certain amount of information to read the text with full comprehension. Here, of course, the data and perspectives accumulated through biblical scholarship make an important contribution. I hope that the assessment of that scholarship I offered in the volumes mentioned above, as well as the literature I have cited throughout the commentary, will equip the reader to understand Matthew's text more readily.

This commentary is not designed to be a demonstration of one particular method or approach to the biblical text. Instead, I draw on a number of methods. Using the insights of literary criticism, the commentary alerts the reader to the literary structure and texture of the passage under consideration. As a true author, the evangelist was shaping the characters in the Gospel as well as giving a particular pace and tone to the overall story or narrative that makes up the Gospel. Redaction criticism focuses on the evangelist's use of source material in the shaping of the narrative. A working assumption of this commentary is that Matthew depended on Mark as his primary source while also absorbing a collection of sayings and brief narratives (called "Q," from the German word *Quelle,* meaning "source") that Matthew holds in common with Luke (although independently of each other). Matthew's reshaping of this traditional material and the way he deploys it in his narrative also contribute to the particular tone and content of the Gospel. Awareness of the social context of the Gospel gives leads as to how the experience of Matthew's community—particularly its setting within the developments of first-century Judaism—may have influenced the text. Explanations of events, people, and places in Matthew's story also call for reference to historical information not found directly in the Gospel itself but which provides important insight into things assumed by the evangelist and his original readers. However, the main focus of this commentary is not on the history behind the text but the intended message of the text itself as presented by its first-century author. No reader has privileged access to the mind and heart of the original author, nor is there likely to be one single interpretation of a text as rich and profound as Matthew's Gospel. Yet careful reading of the Gospel done with awareness of its original context and in dialogue with other thoughtful interpretations can lead to a more responsible understanding of the message of the Gospel. That is the goal of this commentary.

As I complete this work, I want to thank my editors, Vernon K. Robbins and Victor Paul Furnish, for their superb and patient guidance. The call to return to a major administrative responsibility as president of Catholic Theological Union delayed the completion of the manuscript several weeks beyond its deadline. The graciousness of Abingdon Press under these circumstances is deeply appreciated. I also want to thank Lissa Romell for her expert preparation of the manuscript and for her many helpful suggestions as the first reader to see this commentary emerge into the light.

At several points in my work as a student of the Bible I have had the opportunity to turn to Matthew's Gospel and every turn was life-giving—including this one. For that I remain grateful beyond words.

Donald Senior, C.P.

List of Abbreviations

1-2-3 Enoch	Ethiopic, Slavonic, Hebrew *Enoch*
1QH	*Hôdâyôt (Thanksgiving Hymns)* from Qumran Cave 1
1QS	*Serek hayyahad (Rule of Community, Manual of Discipline)*
1QSa	Appendix A *(Rule of the Congregation)* to *1QS*
2 Bar	2 Baruch
'Abot.	*'Abot* Sayings of the Fathers; Tractate of the Mishnah
Ant.	Josephus, *The Antiquities of the Jews*
b.	*Babylonian Talmud*
BETL	Bibliotheca ephemeridum theologicarum lovaniensium
CBQ	*Catholic Biblical Quarterly*
CD	Cairo (Genizah text of the) *Damascus (Document)*
De Ben.	Seneca, *De beneficiis*
Did.	*Didache*
ETL	*Ephemerides theologicae lovanienses*
Gos. Thom.	*Gospel of Thomas*
IBT	Interpreting Biblical Texts
Int	*Interpretation*
JBL	*Journal of Biblical Literature*
JSNT	*Journal for the Study of the New Testament*
JSNTSup	Journal for the Study of the New Testament— Supplement Series
JSOT	*Journal for the Study of the Old Testament*
JSOTSup	Journal for the Study of the Old Testament— Supplement Series
Jub.	*Jubilees*

J.W.	Josephus, *The Jewish War*
Ketub.	*Ketubot*
m.	*Mishnah*
Mart. Isa.	*Martyrdom of Isaiah*
NRSV	New Revised Standard Version
NTabh	Newtestamentliche Abhandlungen
Num. Rab.	*Numbers Rabbah*
OBT	Overtures to Biblical Theology
Prot. James	*Protevangelium of James*
Pss. Sol.	*Psalms of Solomon*
Sabb.	*Šabbot*
Sanh.	*Sanhedrin*
SBL	Society of Biblical Literature
SBLDS	SBL Dissertation Series
SNTSMS	Society for New Testament Studies Monograph Series
STANT	Studien zum Alten und Neuen Testament
T. Naph.	*Targum Naphtali*
TS	*Theological Studies*

INTRODUCTION

This brief introduction will discuss some essential background information on the Gospel of Matthew and a few of its most characteristic features. For more extensive introduction to the Gospel, the reader may consult the works listed in the bibliography.

THE EVANGELIST AND THE CONTEXT OF THE GOSPEL

Although we have no direct evidence about the context of Matthew's Gospel and must deduce it from indications in the Gospel itself or draw on other sources for reconstructing the history of the period, there is considerable agreement, if not unanimity, about certain features of that context. Most interpreters assume that the Gospel of Matthew was written in the final quarter of the first century by a Greek-speaking Jewish-Christian author. The evangelist and his community were probably located in Syria, quite possibly in the city of Antioch. A majority of Matthew's community were Jewish Christians, as was the evangelist himself, but a growing number of Gentile converts were beginning to swell its membership.

Tradition assigns this Gospel to "Matthew," the tax collector of Capernaum whom Jesus called to discipleship and who is listed as a member of the twelve apostles (9:9; 10:3). Papias, a bishop of Hierapolis who lived in the early second century, is quoted by Eusebius (a bishop of Caesarea Maritima who lived 260–340 CE) as providing the information that the Gospel was written by the apostle Matthew. However, the reliability of Papias's testimony has been questioned on this and other points (even Eusebius seems hesitant about Papias!). And internal evidence is hard to reconcile with apostolic authorship: (1) Matthew's Gospel depends on Mark rather than being a firsthand account; (2) it is written in good Koine Greek and does not appear to be a translation from Aramaic; and (3) if the Gospel was written sometime in the last quarter of the first century, it is likely that Matthew the apostle would already have died.

While it may be unlikely that the tax collector Matthew is the direct author of the Gospel, this does not rule out the possibility that this apostle had some traditional connection with the community from which the Gospel eventually emerged. If Matthew's Gospel were written from Antioch in Syria, the community could have been in fairly close contact with Palestinian Judaism and the earliest traditions and personages of the Jesus movement. Accordingly, when using the term *Matthew* in connection with the evangelist and his perspective, the commentary is not referring to the apostle Matthew as such but to the anonymous author of the Gospel whose identity is no longer known to us except through the pages of his text.

Matthew's community still lived out of a thoroughly Jewish perspective, considering the "Old Testament" their primary Scriptures, faithfully adhering to the demands of the Jewish law concerning diet, Sabbath, and other regulations. These Jewish Christians saw their faith in Jesus as the Messiah and Son of God not as a rejection of their Jewish heritage but as the God-intended fulfillment of it. This is a key statement made by the Matthean Jesus at the beginning of the Sermon on the Mount: "Do not think that I have come to abolish the law or the prophets; I have come not to abolish but to fulfill" (5:17). To "fulfill"—a key concept in Matthew—did not mean that the community's Jewish heritage was superfluous, but that Jesus brought to full expression all of the promise God had given to Israel in the course of its history. As will be pointed out in the commentary, none of the Gospels are more thoroughly Jewish in perspective than Matthew.

Yet Matthew's Gospel also contains material that appears to be anti-Jewish. He portrays the Jewish religious leaders as relentlessly hostile to Jesus, even beyond his death (see chaps. 27–28). The

Gospel condemns the leaders as "hypocrites" and "blind guides," responsible not only for rejecting Jesus but for leading the people astray as well (see especially chap. 23). Matthew appears to interpret the terrors of the Jewish revolt against Rome and the eventual destruction of the temple in 70 CE as God's punishment for this rejection (see 21:41; 22:7).

How can one reconcile these divergent currents in the Gospel? For some authors such as W. D. Davies and more recently Ulrich Luz, Matthew and his community no longer saw themselves within a Jewish context (Davies 1964; Luz 1989). The relative failure of the Christian mission to Israel, the tensions that resulted from consolidation on the part of both Judaism and early Christianity in the wake of Jerusalem's destruction in 70 CE, and especially radically divergent understandings of Jesus' identity and authority had resulted in a definitive break between mainstream Judaism and Matthew's Jewish-Christian community. While still marked by its Jewish heritage, Matthew's community now identified itself as Christian rather than Jewish. Davies believes that the polemical material in Matthew is evidence that Matthew's community was in fact shaped by sharp conflicts still raging between the Jewish Christians and the rabbinic leadership of post-70 Judaism.

Other interpreters draw different conclusions from the same evidence. Recent scholarship has emphasized that first-century Palestinian Judaism was not monolithic but quite diverse, with various factions often in tension with one another. Even though Matthew's Jewish-Christian community held views quite divergent from other Jewish groups, this did not mean it was "outside" Judaism. Anthony J. Saldarini, for example, has used sociological categories to describe Matthew's community as a "deviant" group, still within the boundaries of Judaism, yet holding views not supported by the dominant majority and attempting to claim its legitimacy in the face of this opposition. Thus Matthew and his Christians would think of themselves as "Christian Jews" (Saldarini 1994; similarly Overman 1990). Thus some of the problems facing Matthew's community may have included not only disputes with other Jewish groups but concern about what stance to take in relation to the Gentiles.

Earlier in this century, Reinhart Hummel had proposed a "two-front" hypothesis—that is, Matthew's community was engulfed on one front by tensions with rabbinic Judaism and, on the other, by disputes within the community about the future of the Gentile mission (Hummel 1963). Although Hummel's hypothesis has not been fully accepted, there is evidence in the Gospel that Matthew was concerned about the Gentile mission. Even though Jesus initially restricts the mission of his disciples to "the lost sheep of the house of Israel" (10:5; 15:24), the Risen Christ will send his missionaries to "all nations" (28:19). And at several points in the Gospel, Gentiles exhibit exemplary faith that is contrasted with the lack of faith on the part of the religious leaders (see, e.g., 8:10; 15:28; cf. also the magi in contrast to Herod and his Jerusalem court, 2:1-12).

Pinning down the exact circumstances of Matthew's community, therefore, remains elusive. The viewpoint of this commentary is that Matthew and his community stand precisely at a transition moment in the history of the early church. While they were still rooted in Judaism and viewing Jesus as the fulfillment of the God-given promises to Israel, the faith Matthew and his community placed in Jesus as Messiah and Son of God and the divergent viewpoints and practices that were beginning to emerge from that faith were pulling Matthew's Jewish-Christian community in a different direction from the dominant groups within Judaism. At the same time, increasing numbers of Gentiles were entering the Christian community, a movement that was probably welcomed by some as fidelity to the mission of Jesus and greeted by others with anxiety about the long-term consequences. Thus Matthew's Christians were not only concerned about their connection to their Jewish roots but also anxious about their future.

Matthew's Gospel may be intended in large part to address this moment of transition in the history of the early community. As the text of a "scribe . . . trained for the kingdom of heaven," Matthew's Gospel brings from its "treasure what is new and what is old" (13:52) in order to give perspective and clarity. From Matthew's vantage point, Jesus and his mission ensure both continuity with the past and direction for the future.

THE SOURCES OF THE GOSPEL

Matthew did not compose this Gospel on his own, but depended on earlier sources. Primary among these is the Gospel of Mark. Although the relationships among the synoptic Gospels continue to be debated, most interpreters of Matthew consider the so-called "two-source hypothesis" to be the best explanation of the evidence. In composing his Gospel Matthew used as his primary sources both Mark's Gospel and Q. Luke, independent of Matthew, also used Mark and Q as the major sources of his Gospel (on the general issue of synoptic relationships, see Neirynck 1990, 587-95).

Matthew, therefore, drew the basic story line and much of the content of his narrative from Mark. The baptism of Jesus at the Jordan, the concentration of most of his ministry of teaching and healing in Galilee, the fateful journey to Jerusalem, the climactic events in the temple area and the Passion story itself, followed by the discovery of the empty tomb and the proclamation of the resurrection are the fundamental elements of Matthew's story that are drawn from Mark.

As the commentary will indicate, however, Matthew is a "creative editor," freely recasting Mark's material and leaving his own characteristic literary style and theological perspective on the material. Matthew particularly rearranges Mark's material in the earlier chapters of the Gospel, especially through the insertion of the Sermon on the Mount (chaps. 5–7), the grouping of the miracle stories in chapters 8–9, the addition to the mission discourse (chap. 10), and the controversy material in chapters 11–12. After the parable discourse of chapter 13, Matthew follows more closely the sequence of events in Mark's narrative.

Matthew's access to Q also leaves an indelible stamp on the Gospel. Most of this Q material is sayings of Jesus that Matthew combines with Markan material and shapes into discourses of Jesus that appear throughout his narrative. The most important is, of course, the first discourse of Jesus, the famed Sermon on the Mount (chaps. 5–7), which serves as a foundation for all the rest of Jesus' teaching. The other discourses are the mission discourse (chap. 10), the parable discourse (chap. 13), the community discourse (chap.

18), and the apocalyptic discourse (chaps. 24–25). The fact that there are five of these great discourses led some interpreters of the Gospel to propose that Matthew was shaping his Gospel in the form of the Pentateuch, or five great books of the Law, as a way of comparing Jesus to Moses. But this suggestion has not been persuasive to most biblical scholars since it gives undue emphasis to the discourses alone as the organizing principle of Matthew's Gospel (Senior 1996, 25-28). In fact there are more than five discourses in Matthew's Gospel, if one counts the soliloquy in 11:1-30 or the condemnation of the scribes and Pharisees in 23:1-39. Yet the great discourses of Matthew's Gospel remain one of its most characteristic features and enhance Matthew's portrait of Jesus as the great teacher and authoritative interpreter of the law.

Matthew's Gospel also contains a significant amount of material that has no parallel in any other Gospel, most notably the infancy narrative of chapters 1–2 and the events that follow the discovery of the empty tomb (28:9-20; also 27:62-66). This material generally reflects Matthew's own literary style and theological perspective, and it is likely that most of it originated with Matthew, in some cases expanding on leads already within Mark or Q or, in others, elaborating on Old Testament stories or motifs or giving literary expression to traditions that may have circulated in Matthew's own community (Senior 1987, 272-94).

Whatever the sources of Matthew's Gospel, the evangelist has shaped his narrative into a coherent and effective literary whole. While the commentary will note Matthew's interaction with his sources where it helps illumine the meaning of Matthew's text, the most important goal is a close reading of Matthew's Gospel as it now stands on its own.

SOME CHARACTERISTIC ISSUES OF MATTHEW'S GOSPEL

Christology

As suggested above, Matthew wrote his Gospel to give his community members a reliable perspective or vantage point from which to understand the profound historical transition they were experiencing. That vantage point for Matthew was based on the community's faith in the person and teaching of Jesus. When all is said and done, the most fundamental characteristic of Matthew's Gospel is its robust Christology. From the opening lines of the Gospel Matthew affirms for his readers that Jesus is the promised Messiah or "Christ" sent by God to restore and renew Israel, the royal "Son of God," who enjoys extraordinary intimacy with God and reveals God's will, the Son of Man who suffers humiliation and rejection yet will come in glory to judge all peoples at the end of time, the "Savior" who takes away the sin and burdens of the people (a role revealed in the very name "Jesus"; see 1:21), the authoritative teacher greater than Moses whose interpretation of the law brings to fulfillment its God-intended purpose, the compassionate "Son of David" whose healing touch embodies and anticipates the reign of God, the "Emmanuel" or God-with-us who will abide with the community until the end of the age.

These and other titles and roles assigned to Jesus assure Matthew's readers of Jesus' roots in Israel's sacred past and provide guidance for the future. Because Jesus is the promised Messiah, for example, Matthew reads all of Israel's history and its Scriptures as finding their ultimate meaning in Jesus. This is the theological basis for Matthew's extensive use of the Old Testament, particularly his characteristic "fulfillment quotations" that appear throughout the Gospel, but with greater frequency at the beginning of the narrative as Matthew orients the reader to the story of Jesus (see, e.g., 1:22-23; 2:15, 17-18, 23; 4:14-16). Matthew introduces these key quotations with a typical introductory formula that binds the quotation to specific aspects of Jesus' life, making explicit what is implicit in the many other biblical allusions that lie right below the surface of Matthew's narrative—namely, that Jesus' mission is in full harmony with the will of God expressed in Scripture and indeed brings it to its full expression.

Therefore the Christians of Matthew's community were reminded of the reliability and authority of Jesus' teaching, despite the assault by the normative teachers of the rest of the Jewish community. In following Jesus and his teaching as expressed in Matthew's Gospel, therefore, the Matthean Christians were not abandoning their Jewish faith but being most faithful to it.

At the same time, Jesus' actions during his ministry and his explicit instructions following his resurrection would help the Matthean community face their uncertain future, particularly as increasing numbers of Gentiles sought to enter the community. Homage to Jesus by marginal Jews and by Gentiles within the body of the Gospel and Jesus' own words of praise for such people prepared the community to look beyond the boundaries of Israel.

Ethics

Matthew's emphasis on Jesus' role as teacher and interpreter of the Jewish law also gives this Gospel a strong ethical tone. Here, too, Matthew's Jewish heritage, with its emphasis on obedience to the law and attention to covenant responsibilities, is evident. The Matthean Jesus challenges his disciples to lead lives of "righteousness" or justice that should exceed the flawed virtue of the religious leaders (5:19-20). Jesus, for example, lays before his disciples bold teaching that demands near heroic reconciliation in the face of enmity and violence (5:21-48; 18:21-35). Matthew's Gospel strongly emphasizes virtuous action as an essential quality of discipleship. The authentic disciple is one who "does the will of the Father in heaven" as proclaimed by Jesus (7:21); saying the right words or having the right status are insufficient (e.g., 21:28-32). Jesus himself is the exemplar of authentic righteousness (see 3:15); he is the obedient Son of God who is attentive to God's word and carries it out in his life, even to the point of death (4:1-11; 26:36-46). By contrast, Matthew portrays the religious leaders as hypocrites because "they do not practice what they teach" (23:3). At the end of the narrative when the eleven are commissioned to carry the gospel message to the ends of the earth, they are told to make disciples and to teach them "to obey everything that I have commanded you" (28:20).

A Theology of History

A curious feature of Matthew's Gospel is that during his public ministry Jesus restricts his mission and that of the disciples to the "lost sheep of the house of Israel" and explicitly instructs them not to go to Gentiles or to the Samaritans (see 10:5; 15:24). At the end of the Gospel, however, the Risen Jesus sends his apostles on a mission to "all nations" (28:19). This shift is symptomatic of a deeper perspective at work in Matthew's Gospel—Jesus and his mission form the decisive turning point in the history of salvation.

While authors have debated the precise contours and demarcations of Matthew's historical perspective, there is no doubt that he sees Jesus as the fulfillment of God's past promises to Israel and as the inaugurator of the "kingdom of heaven" (4:14-17). When Matthew describes the death and resurrection of Jesus he includes elements such as earthquakes, opening of tombs, and other apocalyptic signs that color these as events ushering in the end time (27:51-53; 28:2). The Risen Christ who appears in triumph in the final scene of the Gospel will remain with the community until its mission is complete and the world has arrived at "the end of the age" (28:20).

This theological perspective on history may enable Matthew to help his community come to grips with the opening to the Gentiles and other difficult pastoral issues that faced them in a time of radical transition. While during Jesus' lifetime the mission was properly restricted to Israel, with the advent of the new age the boundaries of that mission could open to include the nations. If in the past age certain traditional restrictions of the law were properly applicable, in the new and decisive age of salvation other possibilities for interpreting the law were now within reach.

Matthew's theology of history—like virtually everything else in the Gospel—rests ultimately on his Christology. Because Jesus was the Messiah and the authoritative Son of God, he becomes the fulcrum of history and the one who would lead the community to the end of the age.

Matthew and Anti-Judaism

As noted in the preface, Matthew's Gospel is something of a paradox on the issue of its relationship to Judaism. On the one hand, Matthew's Gospel is thoroughly Jewish in tone and language. He lovingly mines the Hebrew Scriptures and other extracanonical Jewish traditions and applies them to Jesus. There is clear evidence that Matthew's Christians still maintained the diet (see the discussion of 15:18), tithing (23:23), Sabbath observance (24:20), and other practices prescribed by the Jewish law such as prayer, fasting, and almsgiving (see 6:1-18). Matthew also tells the readers to respect the position of authority held by the Pharisees (23:2). Yet Matthew is relentless in his criticism of the Jewish leaders and portrays them as hypocritical and evil. Eventually, Matthew sees not just the leaders but, because of their treacherous leadership, the "people as a whole" turning against Jesus (27:24-25). This perspective results in a saying that has been a rallying cry of anti-Semitism throughout the centuries: "His blood be on us and on our children!" (27:25).

It is difficult to know what Matthew's final estimation about the fate of Judaism is. He roundly condemns the leaders of Jesus' generation and may imply that the entire people of that generation who fell under their sway along with their children (i.e., the next generation) would be punished by God through the terrors of the Jewish war of 66–70 CE and its culmination in the destruction of the city and its great temple (see 21:41; 22:7). Certainly he believes that Israel alone no longer holds elect status but that God's plan of salvation now embraces the Gentiles as well (8:5-13; 21:43; 28:29). Some interpreters believe that Matthew sees a definitive turn from Israel to the Gentiles, with Israel now excluded from God's plan. But there is still significant ambivalence in Matthew on this point. At the conclusion of his severe condemnation of the Pharisees and scribes in the discourse of chapter 23, the Matthean Jesus seems to foresee a day when the Messiah would return to Israel and be greeted with cries of acclamation (23:39).

It is important that modern interpreters of Matthew have a sure understanding of this feature of the Gospel. First of all, much of the sharp edge of polemic found in Matthew's portrayal of the Jewish leaders results from the wrenching separation between Matthew's Jewish-Christian community and the rest of Judaism that was then in progress, if not yet come to term. Second, Matthew (unlike John's Gospel) generally attacks specific leadership groups and does not speak of the "Jews" in a generic fashion. Matthew's debate is still an intra-Jewish argument and cannot be labeled as "anti-Semitic" or even "anti-Jewish" in the strict sense. The evangelist himself and probably the majority of his community were, after all, themselves Jewish. Sharp and inflated language roundly condemning what are judged to be failures or excesses on the part of one's opponents was characteristic of such intra-Jewish debate and has precedents in the Bible and in extracanonical Jewish texts of this epoch. Third, the point for most of these passages where the Matthean Jesus condemns the religious leaders is not to attack these figures once again but to serve as a negative example for the Christian reader of the Gospel. In other words, warnings about hypocrisy, about misguided interpretation of the law, or failure to act in accord with the gospel are appeals and warnings meant for the Christian of Matthew's community, not for its non-Christian Jewish opponents.

It is a different matter, of course, when this Gospel is read by another generation that is mainly Gentile and from another culture that does not understand the ground rules of such rhetoric. Add to this the calamitous history of Christian prejudice against a Jewish minority, and the potential of this material in Matthew's Gospel becomes dangerous—as history itself has demonstrated. The modern reader of the Gospel, therefore, has a responsibility to understand the original context of the Gospel and its language and to interpret these passages accordingly.

In these and other issues raised by Matthew's Gospel, the reader must be alert not only to the original context of the Gospel as best one can construct it, but also to the interplay between the Gospel and our own time and place. In the nexus between these two worlds of experience, the message of the Gospel comes alive and takes on new meaning.

COMMENTARY

THE TITLE OF THE GOSPEL (1:1)

Matthew begins his narrative with a title that translates literally as "book of the origin of Jesus Christ, Son of David, Son of Abraham." This opening line introduces a series of events that traces the origin of Jesus from his roots in the history of Israel (1:2-17) through the turbulent and mysterious circumstances of his birth (1:18–2:23), into the beginning of his public ministry with the baptism at the Jordan (3:1-13), and the testing by Satan in the desert (4:1-11). Only after these events does the transition passage 4:12-17 describe Jesus himself initiating his ministry in the arena of Galilee. These events introduce the Matthean Jesus to the reader and preview major motifs that dominate the Gospel as a whole. Each scene has a distinct literary form and function within Matthew's narrative, and in each case the evangelist constructs his material from a distinct blend of sources and his own composition.

◊ ◊ ◊ ◊

Interpreters debate whether the opening line of the Gospel should be understood simply as a statement that leads into the genealogy of 1:2-17 (with possible extension to the conception and naming of Jesus in 1:18-25), as an introduction to the infancy narrative of chapters 1–2, or as an opening for all the events that lead up to the beginning of Jesus' public ministry (4:17). Or is it the title for Matthew's entire narrative (Davies and Allison 1988, 149-54)? The term *biblos* usually means a "book" or "account." The key term is "genesis," translated by the NRSV as "genealogy" but which, in its root sense, is capable of having a broader range of meanings such as "birth" or "origin" or "existence." In 1:18 the same term is used to refer to the "birth" of Jesus, but even here Matthew describes not just the birth but the whole ensemble of circumstances surrounding the beginning of Jesus' life (see 1:18-25). In the Septuagint (Greek) version of Gen 2:4 the identical phrase "book of the origin" *(biblos geneseōs)* is used to summarize the preceding creation account and again in Gen 5:1 to initiate the list of Adam's descendants. Although Matthew may have patterned his opening phrase after these texts, the position it holds as the very first words of his narrative suggests a broader application—namely, a reference not simply to the immediately following passages about his family tree and birth but to the whole history of Jesus that Matthew intends to present to the reader.

This wider scope of the title is confirmed by the remaining contents of the verse: the book of the origin of "Jesus Christ, the son of David, the son of Abraham." The titles for Jesus appear in reverse order from the order of descent in the genealogy—tracking Jesus' origin back through his Davidic ancestry to the inauguration of Israel's saga with Abraham. Each of these designations will prove crucial for Matthew's narrative. Only Matthew contains an explanation of the redemptive significance of the name "Jesus" (1:21). And the messianic identity of Jesus (i.e., as "Christ") is a fundamental assertion of the Gospel as a whole, confirmed for Matthew particularly in Jesus' authoritative teaching and works of healing and exorcism (see 11:4-5, and so on). One of the major purposes of the infancy narrative is to assert the Davidic royal status of Jesus. In accord with this focus the title "Son of David" appears in Matthew more frequently than in any of the other Gospels, particularly to emphasize the distinctive humility and compassionate healing ministry of Jesus (see below, 9:27; 12:23; and so forth). The generic term "Son of Abraham" also has special connotations for Matthew's portrayal of Jesus. In the Hebrew Scriptures and in later Jewish tradition, Abraham was portrayed as "ancestor of a multitude of nations" (Gen 17:5; see also 12:3; 15:5) and the first of the Gentile proselytes. Paul appealed to Abraham as an example of faith prior to the law and therefore as a prefigurement and justification of the Gentile mission (Rom 4:1-25; Gal 3:6-9). Matthew seems to evoke a similar perspective here. Amazement at the faith of the Gentile centurion at Capernaum prompts the Matthean Jesus to envision the nations coming "from east and west" to eat at table with Abraham and the patriarchs (see 8:5-13).

Thus the opening line of Matthew's narrative signals to the reader the scope and fundamental motifs of the entire narrative. The forthcoming story traces Jesus' origin not only back to the sacred history of Israel, its memories of Abraham and David, and its hopes of a renewed and enduring messianic kingdom of God, but also back to the promises God made to Abraham and the multitude of his descendants among the nations. Through his messianic mission Jesus fulfills the promises entrusted to Israel and remains in essential continuity with that sacred history. But at the same time, the unexpected currents of God's providence also prove that Jesus is Son of Abraham, opening the way of salvation to multitudes beyond the boundaries of Israel. The unfolding of this drama, embracing both continuity and unexpected rupture, dominates the pages of Matthew's story.

THE ORIGINS OF JESUS AND HIS MISSION (1:2–4:11)

The Infancy Narrative 1:2–2:23

Matthew begins his story of Jesus by describing the wondrous and turbulent circumstances of his birth and early childhood. Matthew tracks Jesus' Davidic ancestry (1:2-17), describes the mysterious incidents surrounding his conception and naming (1:18-25), and then in the second half of the infancy narrative he describes the mixture of honor and murderous threats that greet Jesus' arrival (2:1-12), and the tortuous journey of the family as they experience exile, return, and displacement before settling providentially in Nazareth of Galilee (2:13-23). In numerous ways, Matthew affirms the strongly Jewish character of Jesus by wrapping Jesus in the mantle of Moses and David, introducing several "fulfillment quotations" that stress harmony with the promises of Scripture, and having Jesus and his family recapitulate the defining experiences of exile, exodus, and displacement. At the same time, through the arrival of the Magi and the murderous threats of Herod, Matthew also signals some of the unexpected turns the Gospel story will later take and the sharp conflicts that will drive it toward the Passion.

In composing this part of the Gospel, Matthew draws on material that has no direct parallel in Mark or Q. Some fundamental aspects of the story coincide with Luke's version, such as the location of Jesus' birth in Bethlehem, the identification of Mary and Joseph, the affirmation of a virginal conception, and the dating of the event to the reign of Herod. Yet the two versions differ significantly in their overall tone and structure. Luke builds his account around the parallel annunciation, birth, and circumcision stories of John the Baptist and Jesus. Matthew, on the other hand, focuses solely on the origin of Jesus and the turbulent events that surround his birth. Joseph's initial misunderstanding about the nature of Mary's pregnancy, the murderous hostility of Herod, and the displacement that it causes the family of Jesus give Matthew's account a more sober tone than that of Luke.

Similar to Luke, Matthew's account is a blend of artful storytelling and subtle use of Old Testament reflection and typology, blended with anticipation of events and motifs drawn from the public ministry of Jesus. The common ground with Luke's account, however, suggests that the evangelist also drew on some traditions that already had wide circulation in the early community prior to Matthew.

The Genealogy of Jesus (1:2-17)

Matthew opens the infancy narrative with a genealogical table that traces Jesus' Jewish and Davidic ancestry from its origin in Abraham down through the descendants to Joseph and Mary. Biblical genealogies were not intended simply as archival records but as basic accounts of events and personages in a broader context of history. In composing Jesus' genealogy, Matthew draws in part from the tables in 1 Chr 1:28-42; 3:5-24; and Ruth 4:12-22. However, the names in the last segment from Abiud to Jacob (Matt 1:13-15) are more difficult. Some are cited in the Bible but not found in the genealogical lists Matthew uses as a source (e.g., "Abihu" in Exod 6:23; 1 Chr 6:3; and so forth; "Eliakim" in 2 Kgs 18:18; 2 Chr 36:4; "Azor" in Neh 3:19; Jer 28:1; "Elihu" in 1 Chr

12:20; "Eleazar" in 2 Sam 23:9-10; "Mattan" in 2 Chr 23:17). Matthew clearly shapes the genealogy to serve his purpose of introducing the reader to the story of Jesus, once again affirming continuity with the history and promises of Israel but also signaling discontinuity and change.

◊ ◊ ◊ ◊

Matthew informs the reader about the structure of the genealogy in verse 17. He intends to trace the ancestry of Jesus through three decisive periods of Israel's history: (1) from its remote origins in Abraham and the patriarchs to its zenith under David (1:2-6a); (2) from the high point in David to the depths of the Babylonian exile (1:6b-11); and (3) from the rupture of exile through to the birth of the Messiah (1:12-16). Matthew calls attention to the symmetry of this condensed history: Each segment contains "fourteen generations." The symbolism intended here has been the subject of much debate (Brown 1977, 74-84). For some the number fourteen is symbolic of the name "David," whose Hebrew characters form the number fourteen. Others consider this to be overly subtle and believe that Matthew was simply pointing to the symmetry of fourteen as a multiple of "seven," which in Semitic gematria (in which Hebrew characters are also numbers) conveyed perfection or completion. The matter is further complicated by Matthew's count. Each of the first two segments of the genealogy do contain fourteen generations, from Abraham to David and again from David to the Exile. However, the last segment contains only thirteen generations. Some interpreters solve the problem by suggesting that "Jesus" and "the Christ" should be counted as two generations in verse 16. If some of the details remain enigmatic, the overall intent of Matthew's genealogy is clear. His distillation of Israel's history brings attention successively to Abraham and patriarchal history, to the image of David the king, to the shattering experience of exile, and to the renewal of hope through the Messiah.

Most of the genealogy is linear, that is, tracking not the various offshoots of Jesus' family tree but only the direct line of successive generations, father to son. One exception to this format occurs in verse 2, which mentions "Judah and his brothers," hinting at the broader expansion of the patriarchal history. But the reassuring rhythm of successive generations—father begets son—is dramatically ruptured by the inclusion of four women in the period from Abraham through David: Tamar (v. 3); Rahab and Ruth (v. 5); and the allusion to Bathsheba (v. 6). Here again the precise significance of these intrusions is debated but some aspects are quite clear. These women are not the great figures that claim attention in biblical history, such as Sarah or Rachel or Rebecca. In each case, the women are either non-Israelites or, in the case of Bathsheba, at least associated with a non-Israelite: Tamar and Rahab are both Canaanites, Ruth is a Moabite, and Bathsheba is the wife of Uriah the Hittite. And in each case their incorporation into the lineage of Israel is through unusual, even startling circumstances: Tamar offsets the injustice of Judah by posing as a prostitute (Gen 38); Rahab, a prostitute of Jericho, shelters the spies who reconnoiter the land prior to the conquest (Josh 2); Ruth, a Moabite servant, wins Boaz with the assistance of Naomi (Ruth); and Bathsheba is the victim not only of David's lust but also of his murderous treachery when he arranges the death of her husband, Uriah (2 Sam 11–12).

Calling attention to the presence of "outsiders" in the messianic lineage of Jesus and to the unusual nature of the circumstances through which they became part of that line has the immediate purpose of preparing the reader for Matthew's account of the conception of Jesus (1:18-25). Here, too, under circumstances that appear discontinuous and even scandalous (to Joseph at first), God's guiding spirit directs the history of Israel and brings it to its fulfillment, not through the patriarchal line of Joseph but solely through Mary. As the story unfolds, the reader learns that Joseph is the legal but not the physical father of Jesus. This is signaled in verse 16 of the genealogy, as Matthew again disrupts the rhythm of the linear genealogy to introduce Joseph as "the husband of Mary, of whom Jesus was born, who is called the Christ." At the same time, the circumstances of Jesus' conception also point to historic discontinuities yet to come in the rejection of Jesus by Israel and the unexpected advent of the Gentiles. The focus of Jesus' mission on Israel alone (10:5; 15:24) will, after the death and resurrection of Jesus, give way to a mission to the nations (28:16-20).

◊ ◊ ◊ ◊

Thus, far from being a lifeless list of names, the genealogy that inaugurates Matthew's story is saturated with his theological perspective. Jesus emerges from a history of Israel that originates in Abraham and unfolds with unexpected turns, finding its most expansive expression in the figure of King David (without forgetting his failure), experiencing the shattered hopes of exile and the renewal of the return, and culminating in the advent of Jesus the Messiah. Through this genealogy, therefore, Matthew alerts the reader to the Gospel's understanding of history, one in which God fulfills the promises given to Israel in often startling and unexpected ways.

The Birth and Naming of Jesus (1:18-25)

To a certain extent, these verses amplify and explain the cryptic reference in verse 16 concerning Joseph and Mary, but they also introduce the reader to fundamental motifs of Matthew's Christology. The focus on Joseph in this segment is characteristic of Matthew's infancy gospel as a whole and is another point of contrast with Luke's account where, to a certain extent, Mary is the lead character. Matthew has Joseph receive the announcement of the birth and name the child. The spotlight falls on the divine origin of Jesus, on his Davidic lineage through Joseph's adoption, and on Jesus' God-given destiny as Savior and Messiah. The first of Matthew's formula quotations anchors the entire event ("all this . . .") in scriptural fulfillment.

◊ ◊ ◊ ◊

Matthew repeats the term "genesis" in verse 18 (see 1:1) but here again it does not mean simply the "birth" of Jesus but the broader set of circumstances surrounding his advent. Matthew's narration has a dual perspective: On the surface human level, Joseph at first confronts scandal and disruption, but from the divine vantage point, shared with the reader and only later with Joseph, things are not what they seem.

The reader learns (v. 18) of crucial information that will be revealed to Joseph in a dream only after some anguish: The child within Mary's womb is "from the Holy Spirit." In ancient Judaism a fairly extended period of formal betrothal preceded the actual marriage. An initial formal agreement between the families would set the terms of the dowry, but the engaged woman remained in her father's house for many months or even years before her spouse would take her to his own family. It is during this interim that Matthew sets the drama of Mary's pregnancy. Before he is illumined in a dream, Joseph assumes that Mary has had relations with another man. Deuteronomy 22:23-25 commanded that if an engaged woman who lived in a town (where neighbors would have heard her cry for help if she had intended to ward off the man) became pregnant, both the man and the woman were to be stoned to death. Although this severe punishment may not have been literally applied in the first century, it does indicate the atmosphere of tension and scandal that Matthew wants to inject into this scene. Joseph is a "just" (*dikaios;* NRSV: "righteous") man and therefore plans to divorce his fiancée quietly rather than expose her as the law permitted (v. 19). This is the first reference in Matthew to a quality that has capital importance for this Gospel (see below, 3:15). While being "just" presumably means adherence to the law, here it also implies that Joseph is compassionate and does not intend to publicly humiliate Mary. Matthew anticipates here the emphasis on interpreting the law with compassion that will be a hallmark of his Gospel (see, e.g., 9:13 and 12:7-8).

The true nature of what is happening is revealed to Joseph through an angelic messenger in a dream (v. 20). Dreams as a medium of divine revelation are a common device in the Bible as well as in other Jewish and Greco-Roman literature, and Matthew uses dreams to underscore the divine guidance of events throughout the infancy narrative (see also 27:19 where Pilate's wife learns about Jesus the "just" man in a dream). The angel's message provides three points of crucial information Matthew wants to give the reader. First, Joseph should not hesitate to accept Mary as his wife, thereby ensuring the legal Davidic ancestry of Jesus (already indicated in v. 16 of the genealogy). Paradoxically, Davidic ancestry does not belong to Jesus through bloodlines but through Joseph's acceptance of Mary as his wife and, therefore, his acceptance of Jesus as his descendant through "adoption." Through this device the Matthean Jesus shares in the "outsider" status of the women in the genealogy, a possible subtle anticipation of the status of the Gentiles. Second, the conception of this child comes through the power of the Holy Spirit and not through human means. There is no hint here that Matthew portrays the Holy Spirit as the sexual agent for the conception of Jesus in the manner of some Greek mythologies. Rather, the virginal conception, which Matthew assumes, underscores the traditional biblical conviction that God initiates major events in the drama of salvation. Therefore, as the opening title indicated, while Matthew wants to portray Jesus as "Son of David" and "Messiah," his Gospel also strongly affirms Jesus as "Son of God," a title that holds for Matthew not only traditional messianic connotations but stresses the unique bond between God and Jesus. In the body of his Gospel Matthew refers sparingly to the Spirit (see 3:16-17; 28:19). The Spirit's role here at the origin of Jesus' life is reminiscent of the function of the Spirit in Genesis at the beginning of creation (Gen 1:1-2) and it may be that Matthew wishes to suggest thereby that the advent of Jesus is a new moment in history. Third, the name "Jesus" reveals the nature of his messianic mission. Matthew is the only New Testament writer to dwell on the significance of the name "Jesus" and he will use Jesus' name more explicitly than the other evangelists (some eighty times). A common first-century Jewish name, it is a derivative of Joshua (in Hebrew, *Yeshua* or *Yeshu*), which literally means "God's help" but was also translated to mean "God's salvation." Jesus bears this name because he will "save his people from their sins" (v. 21). This is a way of characterizing the entire messianic mission of Jesus. At the Last Supper the Matthean Jesus will interpret his death as forgiving sins (26:28) and Matthew understands Jesus' healings as lifting away the burden imposed by sin (see 9:2-8; also 8:17).

The first of Matthew's formula quotations (vv. 22-23) places the entire circumstances of Jesus' birth in the context of scriptural fulfillment, a centerpiece of Matthew's theology (see introduction, p. 27). As he does with most of the quotations, Matthew adapts the text of Isa 7:14 to the context of the Gospel. Although the messianic interpretation attributed to the passage here far exceeds its original intent, several features of the Isaiah passage made it apt for Matthew's purposes: (1) The ambiguity surrounding the sign given by the prophet to King Ahaz concerning a child being born and coming to maturity in the face of the Assyrian threat is now interpreted by Matthew as a clear sign of hope realized in the birth of Jesus the Messiah come for the deliverance of Israel; (2) Isaiah's oracle was addressed to "the House of David," coinciding with Matthew's stress on the Davidic descent of Jesus; (3) whereas the Hebrew version used the term *almah* or "young woman," the Septuagint translates this as *parthenos* or "virgin," fitting with Matthew's conviction of the virginal conception of Jesus as Son of God; (4) the symbolic name "Emmanuel" ("God-with-us"), emphasizing Jesus' abiding presence in the community, becomes a centerpiece of Matthew's Christology amplified in his identification with the "least" members (25:31-46) and reaffirmed in the community discourse (18:20) and, especially, in the concluding verse of the Gospel: "I am with you always, to the end of the age" (28:20).

The segment concludes with Joseph's exemplary response to the revelation he has received. Upon awakening from his dream he immediately carries out everything the Lord commanded: He accepts Mary as his wife, refrains from sexual relations (thereby respecting the divine origin of this child), and he bestows on the child his destined name, Jesus.

◊ ◊ ◊ ◊

In this opening scene of his narrative, Matthew begins to orient the reader to his portrayal of Jesus and his mission. One strong focus is Christology: Jesus is the Christ, the Davidic Messiah who fulfills the hopes of Israel expressed in the Hebrew Scriptures; Jesus is the Son of God, uniquely created by God and bearing the name of Emmanuel; Jesus is the Savior who will lift away the burden of sin. In the figure of Joseph, Matthew introduces another focal point: Joseph is a "just" man, attentive to God's will and faithfully obedient. These will be the hallmarks of Matthew's portrayal of discipleship and reflect the strong ethical emphasis of this Gospel (see 7:21-27).

From Bethlehem to Nazareth (2:1-23)

If in the first half of the infancy narrative Matthew focuses on the identity of Jesus, this section seems to track responses to the child Messiah as well as the movement of Jesus and his family from his birthplace in Bethlehem to his home in Nazareth of Galilee, the staging area for his public ministry (Stendahl 1968).

The literary structure of this section consists of a series of interlocking events. The first scene (2:1-12), introducing Herod and the Magi and sharply contrasting their reactions to the news of Jesus' birth, sets the stage for all the rest. One consequence of Herod's hostility is described in 2:13-15, as Joseph is warned to take the child and his mother and find refuge in Egypt. Another result is Herod's rage at being outwitted by the magi and his decision to kill the children of Bethlehem (2:16-18). The conclusion comes with Herod's death and the return of the holy family to Israel and finally to Nazareth (2:19-23).

Matthew's interplay with scripture is apparent throughout this section. There are three formula quotations relating to the movement of the story from Bethlehem to Egypt to Nazareth (2:15, 17-18, 23) and another explicit quotation identifying Bethlehem as the location for the Messiah's birth (2:5-6). In addition, the threat to Jesus from King Herod and his court, the divinely guided rescue of the child, his exile, and his eventual return are all reminiscent of the stories surrounding Moses' birth as described in Exod 1–2 and the embellished stories in later popular Jewish traditions exhibited in the first-century writers Philo and Josephus. The role of the Magi and the star that guides them to the child also recall the story of Balaam and Balak in Num 22–24. The portrayal of Joseph also suggests the influence of biblical typology: His description as a "just" man, his reception of divine guidance through dreams, and his protection of the messianic family through refuge in Egypt are all reminiscent of the Joseph stories of Gen 37–50.

◊ ◊ ◊ ◊

Herod and the Magi (2:1-12): Herod the Great, who reigned from 37 to 4 BCE, was a shrewd and determined ruler as well as a master builder and orchestrator of public works projects, including the reconstruction of the Jerusalem temple (Richardson 1996). Matthew's Gospel, however, dwells only on his ruthlessness and paranoia concerning potential rivals, another historically attested dimension of his character. Portraying Herod as cunning and cruel sets up the various contrasts Matthew wishes to make here. Herod, joined by "all Jerusalem" and then by "the chief priests and scribes of the people" (v. 3), is disturbed at news of the Messiah's birth and, subsequently, will attempt to destroy Jesus, even by means of infanticide ("all Jerusalem" will also be disturbed when Jesus enters Jerusalem at the end of the Gospel story, 21:10). Herod's apparent interest in the child is deceitful, because he intends to destroy Jesus, not pay homage to him. This response is in stark contrast to that of the Magi, Gentiles "from the East" who earnestly seek the child and, when they find him, offer worship and lavish gifts. Similarly, the story draws a contrast between the despot Herod, who mobilizes his power to pursue and destroy the Messiah, and Joseph, Mary, and the child, who are the victims of his murderous intent and must flee, yet are also given divine guidance to frustrate the power of evil. And, finally, there is the starkest of contrasts between "King" Herod and the one who is born "King of the Jews." The caricature of corrupt power exemplified by Herod throws into relief the essentially different power that will characterize the Son of David (Bauer 1995, 306-23).

The Magi are the first of several characters in the Gospel, such as the centurion (8:5-13) and the Canaanite woman (15:21-28), who point to the Gentile mission. Historically "magi" were of Persian origin, a priestly caste able to interpret dreams and portents. Matthew describes them generically as coming "from the East" and following the guidance of a star. Although Judaism and early

Christianity were wary of astrology and magic, Matthew seems to view the Magi in a positive light, in the manner of the "righteous Gentiles" who had the capacity to draw close to God through good deeds and reflection on nature (e.g., Rom 1:19-20). The star that attracts them, however, is not just any star but "his star," a special divine sign pointing to Jesus. There has been much speculation in commentaries about a possible historical basis for this incident, whether the appearance of Halley's Comet (dated to 12–11 BCE), the convergence of Jupiter and Saturn (dated to 7–6 BCE), or some other astral phenomenon (see Brown 1977, 170-73). It is more likely that Matthew's story is influenced by the popular expectation in the ancient world that royal births were often accompanied by natural portents such as this and by reflection on the story of Balaam in Num 22–24. Although there are obvious contrasts between the Balaam story and Matthew's account, nevertheless some of the essential elements are similar. The attempt of Balak, king of Moab, to have Balaam, a sorcerer from the east, place a curse on Moses and the Israelites is thwarted by divine intervention. This in turn leads to Balaam's oracle, including the prediction in Num 24:17, "a star shall come out of Jacob, and a scepter shall rise out of Israel."

Following the star, the Magi come to Jerusalem to find the "King of the Jews." Their journey may be reminiscent of the pilgrimage of the nations, a biblical motif that anticipated that the nations would ultimately come to Israel either as captives or willing pilgrims intent on offering homage to the God of Israel (see Matt 8:11). The Magi's status as Gentiles is clear from the designation they use (i.e., "King of the Jews" rather than "King of Israel," see 27:11, 29, 37) and from the fact that they must come to Jerusalem and those entrusted with the Scriptures to find the whereabouts of the Messiah's birth. Matthew inserts here a biblical quotation confirming Bethlehem as the place of the Messiah's birth (vv. 5-6). Although its introduction is similar to the formula quotations, it lacks the emphasis on purposeful fulfillment that is essential ("in order to fulfill"). Also in contrast to the other quotations that are observations of the narrator, this quotation is placed on the lips of the priests and scribes. The quotation itself is a composite of Mic 5:1, 3 and 2 Sam 5:2 and shows Matthew's typical adaptation of the text to the Gospel context. Because it is the birthplace of Jesus, Bethlehem is no longer "one of the little clans of Judah" as in the original, but "by no means least." And the segment from 2 Sam 5:2 that concludes the quotation, "who shall be shepherd of my people Israel," recalls the intent of his name "Jesus" (1:21: "he will save his people from their sins") and introduces an image that Matthew will repeat later in the Gospel to stress Jesus' compassion and his mission of gathering the lost and straying (9:36; 26:31).

When Herod learns of the Magi's quest, he summons them to his court to find out the exact time the star had appeared and then treacherously sends them on their way with the request to find the child and let him know "so that I may also go and pay him homage" (2:8). Learning that the Messiah is to be born in Bethlehem, the Magi resume their journey guided by the star until they find the child. Their response is exemplary: They are "overwhelmed with joy" as the star leads to the very place they seek, and upon seeing the child and his mother, they fall down and "pay him homage" (v. 11). The verb *proskyneo*, typical of Matthew, indicates an attitude of profound homage (see, e.g., 4:10; 14:33; 15:25; 28:9, 17). They also offer exotic and expensive gifts befitting the royal status of Jesus. Although later interpreters would delight in finding various meanings in the gold, frankincense, and myrrh, it is likely that Matthew simply thought of these as exotic gifts worthy for a king. As a final indication of the favor in which the Magi are held by the Gospel, they, too, are guided by a dream not to return to Herod (v. 12). Matthew introduces here an ironic contrast that will be a refrain of his Gospel and will come to term in the Passion story. The leaders of Israel react with hostility to Jesus, while Gentiles and sinners respond with faith and devotion (see, e.g., 8:10-12; 21:43). At the same time, there is the paradoxical respect that Matthew, as a Jewish Christian, pays to his Jewish heritage: However astute they may be, the Magi must come to Jerusalem and its Scriptures to learn of God's ways, and even though their own response to Jesus will be negative, the religious leaders have been entrusted with the Scriptures and teach their meaning (see 23:1-2).

The Flight into Egypt (2:13-15): The departure of the Magi turns the spotlight back to Joseph and his family. Once again an "angel of the Lord" intervenes to guide Joseph, instructing him to flee with the child and his mother to Egypt. With the literal obedience that earned him the title "just," Joseph carries out the angel's command exactly, waiting with his family in Egypt until after the death of Herod.

The "flight into Egypt" is another feature of Matthew's story that captured the imagination of later interpreters, despite the fact that the Gospel provides virtually no information about the circumstances of this journey (see Brown 1977, 225-28). In the world of the Bible, Egypt was not only the place of enslavement for Israel but a traditional place of refuge in time of threat or famine (1 Kgs 11:40; 2 Kgs 25:26; Jer 26:21; 41:16-18; 43:1-7; *Ant.* 12.9.7; *J. W.* 7.10.1 and so on). Legends of threats to the royal child are fairly common in ancient literature and Matthew's account fits this pattern (Luz 1989, 144). Yet it is likely that biblical typologies form the backdrop for Matthew's account. The rescue of Israel's hopes by going to Egypt and the protective hand of a Joseph can recall the patriarchal saga of Jacob (later to be "Israel") and his clans seeking refuge in Egypt during the time of famine and finding themselves saved by Joseph (Gen 42–48).

Another chapter of Israel's history is recalled by the formula quotation that concludes this segment: "Out of Egypt I have called my son" (v. 15). The quotation is from Hos 11:1, although the introductory formula does not cite the prophet's name. The Old Testament quotation refers to the exodus event and by means of this quotation Matthew aligns Jesus and his family with this paradigmatic experience of Israel.

The Slaughter of the Children (2:16-18): The vile evil of Herod and the ferocity of his attempt to destroy Jesus are measured by his action against the children of Bethlehem. Although the despotic nature of Herod is well attested historically, there is no independent historical record of this incident. Some commentators have noted that Herod's instructions imply there was an interval of two years between Jesus' birth and the arrival of the Magi (therefore setting the date of Jesus' birth more than two years before the death of Herod or sometime before 6 BCE), but it is difficult to know if Matthew had any such information. Once again the biblical precedent of the Exodus probably drives the story, recalling as it does Pharaoh's instructions for killing the male children of the Hebrews (Exod 1:15-22) and the threat this posed for Moses (2:1-10).

Another chapter of Israel's epic story is drawn into play through the formula quotation of Jer 31:15 that concludes this segment (vv. 17-18). Both the quotation itself and the context of Matthew's narrative are adapted to make this work. The original quotation from Jeremiah poignantly places the matriarch Rachel, wife of Jacob, along the route of the Exile, weeping for "her children" as they are taken into exile. Whether Jeremiah refers to the exile of the northern tribes under the Assyrians in 722–721 BCE or, less likely, that of the southern tribes under the Babylonians in 587 or 586 BCE we cannot be sure. Jeremiah can make this poetic leap from the patriarchal period to that of the Exile because of the location at Ramah, on the route between Bethel and Jerusalem. Ramah was situated along the route of the Exile and also near the burial place of Rachel who died on the way from Bethel to Ephrath (see Gen 35:16-21). Matthew can plausibly shift this scene to Bethlehem because, already in a later gloss on the Genesis text, Ephrath was identified as Bethlehem (Gen 35:15), and the traditional site of Rachel's tomb is Bethlehem.

Ingeniously, therefore, the quotation from Jeremiah allows Matthew not only to inject a plaintive mood of loss and mourning into this scene but also to link Jesus with another archetypal experience of Israel's history: the Exile.

From Egypt to Nazareth (2:19-23): The death of Herod signals the final episode in Matthew's infancy narrative. Once again the angel of the Lord appears in a dream to Joseph and instructs him to return to "the land of Israel" (as anticipated in 2:13). The angel's words recall God's instructions to Moses at the conclusion of his exile in Midian, on the eve of the Exodus (Exod 4:19). For Matthew the movement of Jesus and his family from Egypt to the "land of Israel" recapitulates not only the foundational event of exodus but also Israel's deliverance from exile—salvific events deeply embedded in the religious consciousness of Judaism.

Threat, however, still stands on the horizon. Archelaus, one of the three sons of Herod, now rules over the region of Judea. Therefore, Joseph is warned in a dream not to return to his ancestral home in Bethlehem but to take refuge in Nazareth of Galilee. Here again Matthew's story harmonizes with historical reality. After Herod's death, the Romans had divided the unified monarchy among his three sons, each of whom became an "ethnarch" or local ruler. Archelaus was charged with Judea and Samaria, but his cruelty and incompetence led the Romans to depose him in 6 CE. Thereafter, the Romans would directly rule Judea and Samaria under a procurator stationed at Caesarea Maritima (thus setting the stage for the encounter between the procurator Pilate and Jesus in the Passion story). Most of lower (western and southern) Galilee and Perea (a district on the eastern bank of the Jordan) was entrusted to Herod Antipas, who appears in Matthew's account as the persecutor of John the Baptist (see 14:1-12). The remaining brother, Herod Philip, was given the region of upper Galilee to the north and east. His region with its capital city of Caesarea Philippi would become the site of the transfiguration (see 16:13).

The story is punctuated with a formula quotation, perhaps the most enigmatic in the Gospel (v. 23). Matthew's citation is generic— "spoken through the prophets"—and the quotation, "He will be called a Nazorean," is not in the Old Testament. Some commentators suggest Matthew has no specific biblical text in mind, but simply wants to assert that the entire journey of Jesus and his family from Bethlehem to Nazareth is in accord with general biblical prophecy. More likely, however, Matthew intends a play on the word "Nazorean" in connection with specific biblical antecedents. There are two likely possibilities. One would involve the Hebrew word *nāzîr*, meaning one whose life was dedicated to God, as in the case of Samson: "A razor has never come upon my head; for I have been a nazirite to God from my mother's womb" (Judg 16:17). Matthew might have made this connection through Isa 4:3, "Whoever is left in Zion and remains in Jerusalem will be called holy." In this instance the Hebrew word for "holy" is *qadosh* and the

Septuagint translates it as *hagios*. Yet Matthew was probably also aware that sometimes the Septuagint used the words *naziraios* and *hagios* interchangeably. Thus, various versions of the Septuagint translate the passage from Judg 16:17 either as "I have been a *naziraios* from birth" or "I have been holy *[hagios]* from birth." The other likely possibility is the Hebrew word *neser*, meaning "branch" or "sprig." This term is used in Isa 11:1, "A shoot *[neser]* shall come out from the stump of Jesse, and a branch shall grow out of his roots," a passage interpreted messianically in other New Testament traditions (see Rom 15:12; 1 Pet 4:14; Rev 5:5). Coming as it does on the heels of the Immanuel passage in Isa 7:14, Matthew may have understood this later Isaiah passage as also referring to the Messiah and therefore applicable to Jesus. The mood of Isa 11:1 fits well into Matthew's account. From the stump of Jesse, ruptured through exile, comes the hope of a renewed people. Jesus, born of the stock of Jesse (1:6) and himself experiencing the wrenching pain of exile, is also Israel's hope.

These two possible allusions need not be alternatives: The very fact that Matthew has not identified a prophetic source in the introductory formula and the play on the name of Nazareth allow the evangelist to indulge both possibilities. Jesus is indeed dedicated to God from birth as the events of the baptism (3:1-17) and desert test (4:1-11) will soon illustrate, and he is indeed the blossoming of messianic hope for Israel.

Once again the Gospel narrative works on two levels, both of which are visible to the reader but not always to the characters in the narrative world of the text. The death of Herod and the threat posed by Archelaus are the surface events that lead Jesus and his family to return from Egypt and locate in Nazareth of Galilee. But the dream instructions and the formula quotations reveal another, more fundamental, story just beneath the surface. God is the one protecting the child and it is God's plan that the dawn of salvation will begin in Galilee (see Matt 4:13-16).

◊ ◊ ◊ ◊

The infancy narrative serves as an overture to the Gospel as a whole. Here Matthew sounds those themes that he orchestrates into full melodies in the body of the Gospel. Christology remains a dominant emphasis. As the title of the Gospel (1:1) proclaimed, Jesus is the Christ and Son of David—one whose genealogy reaches back into the history of Israel, one born in the city of David, and one whose royal identity challenges the throne of Herod and draws the homage of the nations in the persons of the Magi. From the first moments of his life, this Son of David and Immanuel is deeply entwined with the history and profound experiences of God's people: threatened by a despot, driven into exile, called by God out of Egypt into the land of Israel, and returned from exile yet still experiencing displacement and danger.

At the same time Matthew underscores Jesus' Jewish roots, he signals another fundamental theme of the Gospel, the mission to the Gentiles. The unexpected turns in salvation history represented by the women of the genealogy and the startling mode of Jesus' conception already alert the reader to the unexpected and the discontinuous. The pilgrimage of the Magi to offer homage—in sharp contrast with the fear and hostility of the Jewish king and his entourage—previews the failure of the mission to Israel and the subsequent turn to the Gentiles that will be a leitmotif of Matthew's Gospel.

The reference to the Hebrew Scriptures is remarkable in these opening chapters, not only the several explicit quotations but also the numerous allusions and typologies. The four formula quotations bring out the underlying theology of this entire appeal to the Scriptures: Matthew wants to affirm that Jesus indeed fulfills the plan of God proclaimed in the Scriptures and that every feature of his life and destiny is in accord with God's will.

Finally, Matthew begins to sketch his understanding of discipleship. Joseph is a prototype: a "just" man who applies the law with compassion and who fully obeys the will of God. The Jewish leaders, on the other hand, become the negative foil for authentic discipleship: Even though they are privileged bearers of the Scriptures, they fail to recognize Jesus or put their faith in him.

Baptism at the Jordan (3:1-17)

The introduction of John the Baptist and the desert location signal a new scene in Matthew's narrative.

For the first time, Matthew links up with the story line of the Gospel of Mark and introduces material he adapts from Q, the two main literary sources for his Gospel (see introduction, pp. 25-26). Matthew absorbs most of the baptism scene from Mark (1:2-11), but his editing of Mark's account and the blending in of Q material (3:7-10 [Luke 3:7-9]; 3:11*b*-12 [Luke 3:16*b*-17]) highlight aspects characteristic of Matthew's own theological perspective.

The scene has two phases: (1) the presentation of John and his mission (3:1-12), and (2) the introduction of Jesus (3:13-17). In the course of this narrative Matthew announces key themes of his Gospel: the reign of heaven, eschatological judgment, the call to repentance and good deeds, and the notion of "righteousness" or justice. And the christological focus on Jesus as Messiah and unique Son of God is strongly reinforced by John's testimony and by the revelation at the moment of the baptism.

◊ ◊ ◊ ◊

Matthew ushers John onto the Gospel stage with the time reference, "in those days" (3:1). This somewhat vague phrase ties the appearances of John with the whole series of astounding events that the reader has witnessed from the outset. Even though it is obvious that years have elapsed in real time from the birth until the baptism, these inaugural events are all part of "those days," of the new era that marks the origin of Jesus and his mission. Just as the first two chapters of Matthew's story had recalled Israel's great epic of salvation by noting key geographical locations (Bethlehem, Egypt, Ramah), here the "wilderness of Judea" becomes the setting, sounding motifs of repentance and renewal and recalling Israel's own desert sojourn prior to its history in the land.

Matthew adapts from Mark the quotation of Isa 40:3 that underscores precisely this theme: "The voice of one crying out in the wilderness: 'Prepare the way of the Lord, make his paths straight,' " (Matt 3:3). But, equally significant, he puts at the very beginning of the scene John's keynote message of repentance triggered by the approaching reign of heaven (reversing Mark's order; see Mark 1:2-4). The formulation "reign of heaven" is characteristic of Matthew with the euphemism "heaven" rather than

"God" probably reflecting the Jewish sensitivities of his community. The Jewish motif of the "reign of God" is a key metaphor of Matthew's Gospel, particularly its ethical emphasis on transformation of one's life in response to the advent of God's salvation. Both John and Jesus proclaim the same fundamental message (see 4:17)—announcing the coming of God's eschatological reign and calling for repentance in view of this decisive event. Note that, unlike Mark, Matthew omits any reference to "forgiveness of sins" in conjunction with John's baptism (contrast Matt 3:2; Mark 1:4). For Matthew, forgiveness of sins is a consequence of Jesus' mission alone (1:21; 9:6; 26:28).

The eschatological tone of this scene is further emphasized by the portrayal of John as Elijah returned. His clothing of camel hair and a leather belt recalls the description of the prophet in 2 Kgs 1:8. Elijah's return as a messenger prior to the end time was a popular Jewish motif (see Mal 3:1; 4:5-6; Sir 48:10-11) and, following Mark's lead, Matthew will explicitly identify John with this expectation (see Matt 11:10, 14; 17:11-13).

The surge of response to John's message provides Matthew with an opportunity to cast the religious leaders in a negative light, something that is characteristic of his Gospel as a whole (3:5-10). Crowds come to John from all the areas of Israel (to this end Matthew adds "all the region along the Jordan" in 3:5b) and accept his baptism of repentance. Many "Pharisees and Sadducees" come as well, but John stops them short with a blistering attack. The leaders exhibit the vices that are detested by this Gospel. They attempt to perform a religious ritual but have not shown "fruit worthy of repentance," the very "hypocrisy" that the Matthean Jesus will condemn (see 23:2-7). They also presume upon their status as children of Abraham and here, too, the Gospel will more than once contrast the authentic response of Gentiles and those on the perimeter with the failures of those at the center of the community (see 8:10-12; 21:28-32). For Matthew's theology, one's standing within the family of God is determined by doing the will of God (see 12:46-50), an axiom with deep roots in Jewish ethical tradition but one that also provides Matthew's community with a theological opening to the inclusion of the Gentiles. Failure to respond to the reign of God brings judgment (3:10). Judgment as a divine sanction against hypocrisy and evil deeds is a recurring theme of Matthew's Gospel and will be the subject of its final great discourse (see chaps. 24–25; Marguerat 1981).

The wedge Matthew places between the crowds, on the one hand, and the religious leaders, on the other, will also continue through most of the Gospel story. The crowds generally react favorably to Jesus' teaching (7:28-29) and healing (9:33-34) while the leaders are consistently hostile. Only in the Passion narrative, and there under the inspiration of the leaders, do the crowds turn against Jesus (see 27:24-25). Here in 3:7 Matthew identifies the leaders as "Pharisees and Sadducees." In Matthew, Pharisees, usually coupled with the "scribes," are a consistent part of the leadership opposed to Jesus and their prominence may reflect the contemporary experience of Matthew's own community (see introduction, pp. 21-24). The Sadducees appear less frequently (see, e.g., 16:1-12; 22:23-34). Matthew casts these leadership groups as opponents of Jesus in a generalized and stereotyped fashion (e.g., the Pharisees and Sadducees were not allies), but to some extent historical circumstances have left an impact on the tradition so that the "priests and elders," for example, are confined to the parts of the story that take place in Jerusalem, where the Pharisees play a minimal role. The presence of the Sadducees in the baptismal scene may also be explained by their proximity to Jerusalem (Luz 1989, 170; on the little that is known about the Sadducees, see Saldarini 1988).

Having stressed the complementarity of John's and Jesus' message, Matthew now introduces the difference between them (3:11-12): John is the prophetic messenger preparing for Jesus the Messiah and Jesus is the "more powerful" one whose sandals John is not worthy to carry; John's baptism is a sign of repentance and the baptism of Jesus brings the power of the Spirit and the moment of eschatological judgment. Matthew uses the image of the harvest to reinforce the threat of judgment, as will be the case in the parable discourse when the weeds and the wheat will be sorted at the final judgment (13:24-30, 36-43). The reference to baptism with "fire" is probably also a reference to judgment (see 25:41), although some consider it a symbol of the Spirit. The baptizing activity of Jesus referred to here should be thought of as a metaphor for the entire mission of Jesus, not just the ritual of baptizing itself.

With verses 13-17 Matthew brings Jesus himself into the spotlight of the narrative, as Jesus comes "from Galilee" to be baptized by John. As Matthew's narrative has unfolded, Judea, with its capital city Jerusalem, has been identified as a place of threat and hostility. Galilee, on the other hand, is the place to which God led Jesus and where his ministry will unfold.

Matthew alone among the synoptic evangelists presents a dialogue between John and Jesus at this moment (vv. 14-15). John reinforces the contrast between himself and Jesus as he protests his unworthiness to baptize Jesus. Only when Jesus has permitted him to do so will John actually administer his ritual. In this way, Matthew's text answers those in the early community who may have questioned the subordination of John to Jesus because of the fact that Jesus had submitted to John's baptism.

More important for Matthew are the first words of Jesus in the Gospel: "Let it be so now; for it is proper for us in this way to fulfill all righteousness" (3:15). The verb "fulfill" *(pleroō)* is a crucial concept for Matthew's theology, as its use in the formula quotations attests. Linked to "righteousness," in this verse it has the immediate sense of "carry out" or "act in accord with," but there may be a deeper sense in which Matthew uses this verb here, implying a sense of "prophetic fulfillment" (Meier 1979). Jesus "brings to completion" or "brings to its intended purpose and goal" that which God has ordained. The verb is used in this sense in the formula quotations as well as in the keynote text of 5:17, "Do not think that I have come to abolish the law or the prophets; I have come not to abolish but to fulfill." The term "righteousness" *(dikaiosyne)* is another key Matthean concept (Przybylski 1980). "Righteousness" or "justice" is a divine attribute, signifying God's fidelity and right relationship to Israel. It also characterizes proper human response to God, implying faithfulness, obedience, and ethical integrity. "Righteousness" exceeding that of the scribes and Pharisees is to be the hallmark of the disciple (5:20).

Matthew does not focus on the actual moment of Jesus' baptism by John (contrast Mark 1:9*b*), but on the revelatory moment that follows it. Jesus' ascent from the water is met with the opening of the heavens and the descent of the Spirit on him (v. 16). With his characteristic emphatic phrase—"and behold" (NRSV: "suddenly")—Matthew introduces the "voice from heaven" that declares, "This is my Son, the Beloved, with whom I am well pleased" (v. 17). This declaration of Jesus' identity as Son of God is drawn from Isa 42:1 ("Here is my servant, whom I uphold, my chosen, in whom my soul delights . . .") and the royal enthronement in Ps 2:7 ("You are my son . . ."). This combined text is already present in Mark (1:11) and probably derived from Christian reflection prior to Mark's Gospel. For Matthew this declaration, coming as it does from the voice of God, harmonizes with the perspective of the infancy narrative where the mysterious and unique origin of Jesus as Son of God is repeatedly affirmed, particularly through the virginal conception (see above, 1:18-25). At the baptismal scene this declaration is now made publicly. In contrast to Mark's formulation, *"You* are my beloved son . . . ,"* Matthew has the voice address the bystanders—and the reader—*"This* is my beloved son. . . ."

Placing Jesus' dialogue with John immediately prior to the declaration of Jesus' sonship adds another important Matthean nuance to the Son of God designation. Jesus is Son of God not only because of his mysterious divine origin from God but also because of his commitment "to fulfill all righteousness" (v. 15). Through his obedience, the Matthean Jesus demonstrates that he is truly God's Son.

◊ ◊ ◊ ◊

The baptismal scene serves both Matthew's Christology and his ethical concerns. The encounter with the Baptist prepares the reader for the fundamental motif of Jesus' messianic mission, namely the advent of the reign of God. At the same time, the subordination of John to Jesus and the divine declaration of Jesus as God's beloved Son contribute to his high Christology.

At the same time, Matthew attends to the ethical perspective of his Gospel. In contrast to the Pharisees and Sadducees, Jesus is dedicated to fulfilling all "righteousness." Jesus' acceptance of John's ritual of repentance is symbolic of his commitment to do both God's will and "deeds of repentance."

John's baptizing was distinct from what we know of Jewish practice in that it was not meant as a periodic ritual cleansing but as a onetime symbol of renewal, making it closer to the meaning of sacramental baptism (Harrington 1991, 57-60). The donation of the Spirit and the designation of sonship at Jesus' baptism add other dimensions that will be amplified in Christian theology. To what extent this theology was already developed in Matthew's community is not clear, although the baptismal formula in 28:19 suggests that practice was already well advanced.

The Wilderness Test (4:1-11)

This mythical scene of Jesus' encounter with Satan in the wilderness continues Matthew's overture to the public ministry of Jesus. It is a blend of Mark's cryptic account of Jesus' desert test (1:12-13) and the more elaborate dialogue with Satan drawn from Q (cf. Luke 4:1-13). The wilderness setting, the reference to the Spirit (v. 1), and the emphasis on Jesus' fidelity as God's Son are all strong links to the preceding baptism scene.

Mark's material, which describes Jesus being driven into the wilderness to be tested by Satan (1:12) and afterward being ministered to by angels (1:13), now serves as the beginning and conclusion of Matthew's passage (4:1, 11). Mark's enigmatic reference to the presence of the "wild beasts" (1:13, which may be an allusion to the messianic reconciliation with nature as in Isa 11:6-9) is replaced by the threefold dialogue with the "tempter" (Matt 4:3). In Matthew's version, the various tests intensify from the first exchange in the wilderness itself (vv. 3-4), then to the "holy city" and "the pinnacle of the temple" (vv. 5-6), and finally to a "very high mountain" (vv. 8-10). Luke's order places the temple encounter last (Luke 4:9-12). It is difficult to determine which version is more original since each arrangement fits the perspective of the particular Gospel.

The scene takes its inspiration from Deut 6–8 where Moses reviews the wilderness test of Israel prior to its entry into the promised land (Gerhardsson 1966). This serves Matthew's style and purpose well. Standing as this scene does on the brink of Jesus' public ministry, its parallel to Israel's moment of test before the entry into the land ties Jesus once again to paradigmatic moments of Israel's sacred history. Demonstrating Jesus' fidelity to God's word (in contrast to the failure of Israel) also presents Jesus as fulfilling the biblical promise. Embedded in this section of Deuteronomy is Israel's great creed or the "Shema" ("Hear, O Israel . . . ," Deut 6:4-9) whose emphasis on wholehearted obedience to God is a distillation of Deuteronomy's theology and has strong resonance with Matthew's perspective (Frankemölle 1974).

◊ ◊ ◊ ◊

The introductory verses (4:1-2) recall not only Israel's wilderness wandering but the "forty days and forty nights" of Moses' fasting during his sojourn on Mount Sinai (Exod 34:28; Deut 9:9, 18) as well as that of Elijah on his way to Mount Horeb (1 Kgs 19:8).

The tempter begins each of the first two temptations with the phrase, "If you are the Son of God. . . ." This phrase will be repeated on the lips of those who mock the crucified Jesus at the moment of his death when Matthew will again stress the fidelity of Jesus as Son of God (see 27:39-43). This is a key to the meaning of this entire scene for Matthew's Gospel. The focus is on the nature of Jesus' identity as "Son of God" rather than on the specific allurements offered by Satan. As was the case in the baptism scene, Jesus' identity as Son of God is demonstrated by his unwavering fidelity to God (3:15). Therefore Jesus refuses to exercise his power at Satan's command but relies solely on the word that comes "from the mouth of God" (Jesus' response is from Deut 8:3). Each of the temptations also projects out into the Gospel. As the narrative unfolds, Jesus will miraculously provide bread for the multitudes (14:13-21; 15:32-39), but this is done out of his compassion for the crowds and in response to the mission God has given him (9:35-38).

For the second test, the "devil" brings Jesus to the "holy city" (cf. Luke 4:9, "Jerusalem") and puts him on the "pinnacle" or literally the "wing" of the temple (Matt 4:5-7). This probably referred to some high tower or promontory on the temple building. It could have been so named in a wordplay with Ps 91:4, "he will cover you with his pinions, and under his wings you will find refuge" and therefore could have been the inspiration for the reference to Ps 91 in the Q passage about the angels' protection (Matt 4:6-7; Harrington 1991, 66-67; Davies and Allison 1988, 365). The devil wants Jesus to test God's promise of protection, but Jesus rebuffs his lure with a quotation from Deut 6:16: "Do not put the Lord your God to the test" (v. 7). The original Deuteronomy quotation also alluded to the famous incident at Massah when Moses was commanded to strike the rock for water after Israel's complaint ("as you tested him [God] at Massah"; see Exod 17:1-7). Although Matthew does not include this latter part of the quotation in Jesus' response, the reference to "testing" God surely recalled for the biblically literate reader Israel's own failure under the wilderness test.

As in the case of the first temptation, the entry into Jerusalem projects the reader into the Gospel story when Jesus will again enter that city and its temple (21:1-27). In contrast to the allurements of the devil, Jesus enters humbly, in obedient fulfillment of God's word (see Matt 21:4-5).

The final test is on a "very high mountain" where the devil shows Jesus "all the kingdoms of the world and their splendor" (vv. 8-10). Here the underlying issue of the temptations is in full view: to either worship Satan or worship God alone. The term "worship" (proskyneō) is characteristic of Matthew and is used in several key texts to describe the homage given to Jesus himself (see, e.g., 2:2, 8, 11; 14:33). Jesus' response is unwavering: "Away with you, Satan!" (The same words will be addressed to Peter at Caesarea Philippi when he protests Jesus' prediction of the Passion; see 16:23.) In words drawn from Deut 6:13, the Matthean Jesus proclaims the driving commitment of his life: "Worship the Lord your God, and serve only him."

The mountain setting for this scene, the enticement of all the kingdoms of the world, and the fact that Matthew has placed this temptation last in the series all suggest that the Gospel links this incident with the climactic scene of the narrative in 28:16-20. There on a mountain in Galilee, the Risen Jesus will declare that God has given to him "all authority in heaven and on earth." Only God has such authority and it will be given to the Risen Jesus. Matthew favors mountains as places for dramatic revelation: This will be the case for the Sermon on the Mount (chaps. 5–7), the compelling magnetism of Jesus' healings (15:29-31), the transfiguration (17:1-8), and the finale of the Gospel (28:16-20; see, further, Donaldson 1985). This final temptation is also a revelation in Matthew, reaffirming in dramatic fashion Jesus' identity as the unique and faithful Son of God.

◊ ◊ ◊ ◊

The face-to-face encounter with Satan and the fantastic settings for the temptations give this scene a mythical texture unlike any other part of the Gospel. As Jesus' mission gets under way, his encounters with the demonic are in the arena of human suffering where, through his power, Jesus will liberate human beings from the grip of evil. Matthew may also be suggesting that Satan lurks behind the hostility of Jesus' opponents, as at the moment of Jesus' death when they will use the devil's own words to taunt him ("if you are the Son of God . . .").

Interpreters of this scene have given much attention to the moral significance of the threefold temptations, suggesting, for example, that Jesus rejects, in turn, self-gratification, arrogance, and corruption of power. While Matthew may intend to present Jesus as a model for rejecting such allurements, the primary focus of the entire scene is christological. The tempter's assaults only make more explicit the spirit that animates Jesus: He lives by God's word alone. Israel was tested in the wilderness and wavered; this Son of Abraham and Son of God proves to be completely faithful.

JESUS: MESSIAH IN WORD AND DEED (4:12–11:1)

Having completed the prelude to Jesus' public ministry (1:2–4:11), Matthew now begins a major new section of his narrative. The introductory scenes of the entry into Galilee (4:12-17), the call of the first disciples (4:18-22), and the majestic summary of Jesus' ministry (4:23-25) all prepare for the major sections that follow—the Sermon on the Mount (5:1–7:29), Jesus' healing activity (8:1–9:35), and the mission discourse (9:36–11:1). In these sections of the Gospel story (and continuing on through chap. 13) Matthew has carefully arranged his material and exhibits the strongest degree of independence from the story line of Mark (Senior 1997a, 24-32).

The Beginning of Jesus' Ministry in Galilee (4:12-25)

Matthew begins his account of Jesus' public ministry with three brief scenes: the entry or return to Galilee (4:12-17); the call of the first disciples (4:18-22); and a majestic summary of Jesus' ministry (4:23-25).

Entry into Galilee (4:12-17)

The description of Jesus' entry into Galilee and the keynote announcement about the reign of heaven (4:12-17) form a critical transition scene for Matthew's story. It draws its content from Mark 1:14-15, but Matthew has enriched the scene, especially with the formula quotation from Isa 8:23–9:1. Some interpreters consider verse 17, with its time reference "From that time . . . ," to be a key to the entire literary structure of Matthew's Gospel, announcing as it does Jesus' ministry of proclaiming the reign of heaven (Kingsbury 1975, 7-25). A similar formula in 16:21 is viewed as initiating another major turning point as the ministry of Jesus begins to focus on the Passion and the journey to Jerusalem. However, rather than lean too heavily on this one verse, it is better to see this *entire scene* (vv. 12-17) as an inaugural piece that launches Jesus' Galilean ministry and sounds a theme that will carry through the whole Gospel.

◊ ◊ ◊ ◊

The sudden announcement of John's arrest (v. 12) establishes continuity with the baptism scene at the Jordan (3:1-17) and warns the reader about Jesus' own fate (the word used for "arrest," literally "handed over," will be repeatedly used to describe Jesus' own deliverance into the hands of his enemies: e.g., in 17:22; 20:18;

26:2; and so forth). The ominous arrest of John also leads Jesus to "withdraw" from Judea to Galilee. Threat had driven Joseph to bring the child and his mother to Nazareth (2:22-23) and by his choice of verb Matthew may wish to imply that once again an aura of threat hangs over Jesus as he returns to Galilee.

Matthew gives particular attention to Jesus' entry on the stage of his public ministry. Geography continues to provide clues to Matthew's theological perspective, as it did in so many scenes of the prelude. Jesus leaves Nazareth and goes to "Capernaum by the sea, in the territory of Zebulun and Naphtali" (cf. Mark 1:21), where much of Jesus' ministry will take place and which the Gospel will call Jesus' "own town" (9:1). From Matthew's perspective, Jesus goes to Capernaum not by accident or for any particular strategic purpose, but solely because it is in accord with God's plan expressed in the Scriptures. The citation is from Isa 9:1-2, but Matthew has worked on both the quotation and the narrative context of the Gospel to make a fit. He introduces Capernaum as being in the "territory of Zebulun and Naphtali" (v. 13), the first two of the northern tribes to be deported in the Assyrian invasion of 721 BCE, thus providing the entry point for the quotation. The Isaiah quotation does not correspond to either the Hebrew or Septuagint versions, but has been condensed and edited to match the Gospel context. The "sea" in the original quotation refers to the Mediterranean, but in Matthew's context it refers to the Sea of Galilee. The light that falls on those in darkness is described as having "shined" in the original quotation but aptly has "dawned" in Matthew's version to fit the beginning moment of Jesus' ministry.

Isaiah's reference to "Galilee of the nations" provides Matthew with a key phrase. Although Jesus' ministry in Galilee will intentionally focus on Israel alone (10:5; 15:24), the Gospel once again anticipates the breakout of the mission to the nations (28:16-20). The homage of the Magi was already one instance that anticipated the Gentile mission, as will be encountered with other extraordinary Gentiles such as the centurion (in Capernaum; 8:5-13) and the Canaanite woman (15:21-28). From Matthew's perspective, therefore, the turn to the Gentiles was not a historical accident, nor solely a result of Israel's rejection of Jesus (although Matthew will see this as a consequence; see 21:43), but was preordained by God.

The content of the quotation also harmonizes with Matthew's view of Jesus' mission. The remembrance of the lost tribes of Zebulun and Naphtali evokes Israel's hopes for restoration and renewal in the end time. Through the advent of Jesus, light dawns for those who are "in darkness" and under the "shadow of death" (v. 16). The summary of Jesus' ministry that follows (4:23-25) and the whole narrative of the Gospel will illustrate the meaning of this text. The Matthean Jesus saves both Jew and Gentile from the burden of sin (1:21).

The keynote of Jesus' ministry is proclaimed in verse 17: "Repent, for the kingdom of heaven has come near." Matthew's formulation makes Jesus' message identical to that of John the precursor (3:2). Expectation of the "kingdom of heaven" is a metaphor grounded in Jewish conviction about God's sovereignty and the people's enduring hope for unending peace (Meier 1994, 237-88). Some commentators suggest that the typical Matthean formulation "of heaven" (rather than "of God") is not only a euphemistic reference to deity but emphasizes the transcendence and sovereignty of God (Garland 1993, 47-48). The Lord's Prayer will ask that God's will be done on earth "as it is in heaven," a petition equivalent to hope for the coming of the kingdom of heaven (6:10). In any case, this phrase serves in Matthew—as it does in the synoptic Gospels in general—as an umbrella concept for the entire mission of Jesus. Through his teaching (see particularly the parables of chap. 13) and his healing ministry (12:28), Jesus both announces and actualizes the reality of God's reign.

As was the case with John's message, so here Jesus puts first the emphatic command, "Repent" (see 3:2; 4:17). For Matthew, a spirit of repentance that issues in right action is both the proper attitude for reception of God's reign and the sign of its effective presence.

The Call of the First Disciples (4:18-22)

Matthew's story about the call of the first disciples is virtually identical with Mark's version (1:16-20). The story emphasizes the authority of Jesus who calls the two sets of brothers without any introduction and wins their immediate and complete response (the term "immediately" is repeated by Matthew in v. 22). Simon, "who is called Peter" (v. 18), is named first, a prominence that will be reinforced by the attention Matthew's Gospel gives this leading figure among the disciples (see below, 4:14, 16).

At the same time, Matthew clearly presents this scene as instruction for the community. The disciples' immediate and complete obedience is exemplary and harmonizes with Jesus' instructions on discipleship that will occur later in the Gospel (e.g., 8:18-22; 19:27-30). They "follow" *(akoloutheō)* Jesus—a term that will be synonymous with Christian discipleship. They leave behind family and possessions, as the radical demands of Jesus will require (see especially, 19:16-30), and they are called to be "fishers of people" (see v. 19). The latter metaphor for Jesus' own ministry obviously reflects the seaside location of the story (see vv. 13, 18) and may be an allusion to Jer 16:16, which refers to the snaring of fish from the chaotic sea. Several dramatic scenes of Jesus' own Galilean ministry will also take place on and around the Sea of Galilee (e.g., 8:23–9:1; 14:22-36; 15:29-31). This exemplary pattern of call and response will be repeated in the summary of Jesus' ministry that immediately follows; there the multitudes who are touched by Jesus' teaching and healing "followed him" (4:23, 25).

The placement of this call story is also strategic. In a sense, the very first action of the Matthean Jesus is to gather the community of disciples. The words and actions of Jesus that will follow in the narrative are intended to instruct and form the community. These same disciples will be among those who are called to be the twelve (10:2) and therefore are part of the "eleven" who will receive Jesus' final commission (28:16-20). They are to "make disciples" and will be "teaching" these future disciples "to obey everything that I have commanded you" (28:19-20). The disciples in the Gospel, therefore, are a bridge between the narrative world of the Gospel and the disciples of Matthew's own community (Howell 1990, 229-36).

The Summary of Jesus' Galilean Ministry (4:23-25)

With Jesus poised to begin his mission, Matthew gives the reader a sweeping preview of Jesus' itinerant ministry in Galilee, first with a summary of that ministry in 4:23 and then with a description of its dramatic impact on crowds from every quarter of Israel (4:24-25).

The summary statement of 4:23 is virtually identical with that of 9:35 and provides a key to the way Matthew has organized these crucial opening chapters of his Gospel. The dual activity of "teaching . . . and proclaiming the good news of the kingdom" and "curing every disease and every sickness" sets the agenda for the following sections, which include the Sermon on the Mount (chaps. 5–7) and the collection of healing stories (chaps. 8–9). The repetition of the summary in 9:35 also provides a lead into the mission discourse of chapter 10. Matthew composes this material from summaries found in Mark 1:39 and 3:7-12 but freely adapts them in his usual manner.

◊ ◊ ◊ ◊

By placing this material here at the very beginning of Jesus' public ministry, Matthew anticipates the entire span of the Galilean ministry and indicates what he considers its essential features. Jesus' mission is an itinerant one "throughout Galilee" and consists, first of all, of "teaching" and "proclaiming the good news of the kingdom." It is difficult to know if Matthew intended some distinction between the two actions of "teaching" *(didaskein)* and "proclaiming" *(keryssein)*. "Proclaiming" seems to accent the initial announcement while "teaching" may have a more explanatory emphasis, but Matthew does not develop this distinction. The phrase "good news [literally, "gospel"] of the kingdom" is unique to Matthew and captures well the full scope of Jesus' message, which through word and action both announces and embodies the reality of God's reign. Matthew situates this teaching and proclaiming "in their synagogues" (see also 9:35; 10:17; 12:9; 13:54; 23:34), a formulation that implies some distance between the vantage point of Matthew's Gospel and the Jewish community (note, however, it is not clear whether "their synagogues" suggests that the Jewish Christians had their own synagogues—i.e., "our synagogues"—or no longer gathered in synagogues at all).

While "teaching" is often considered a characteristic emphasis of Matthew's Gospel, the evangelist also underscores Jesus' role as healer. This aspect of the summary statement ("curing every disease and every sickness among the people") will, in fact, command the next two verses. A similar concentration on healing characterizes Jesus' mission instruction for the disciples in 10:1, 5-8.

The remaining two verses (24-25) describe the impact of Jesus' mission, which draws crowds of people from virtually every point on the compass who are seeking healing and are intent on following him. As in the previous chapters, Matthew's geographical references are significant. He first notes that Jesus' fame spread "throughout all Syria" (v. 24). "Syria," probably referring to what would be the Roman province of Syria extending to the north and east of Galilee, is not on Mark's list and might be an indicator of the Matthean community's own vantage point (see introduction, p. 21). The "great crowds" come to Jesus from every direction: "Galilee" (the region around the lake and extending west beyond Nazareth); the "Decapolis" (the league of ten cities on the eastern and southern shores of the Sea of Galilee); "Jerusalem" (the capital city); "Judea" (the great province to the south); and "beyond the Jordan" (presumably the east bank of the Jordan). Not included are "Tyre and Sidon" (Jesus will go up to the border of this Gentile area in 15:21) or Samaria (off limits for Jews). Matthew's primary focus is on Israel, which is the focal point for his messianic mission (10:5; 15:24). Yet as has already happened with the Magi (2:1-12), echoes of Jesus' mission reach across the boundaries to Syria and the Decapolis, regions usually associated with Gentile territory.

The list of illnesses (v. 24) anticipates the healings and exorcisms that will occur later in the narrative. This procession of the sick converging on Jesus as if drawn to some magnetic force reflects the Gospel's Christology with its emphasis on Jesus as the one who would save God's people from the burden of sin (1:21; see also 8:17; 12:15-21; 15:30-31).

◊ ◊ ◊ ◊

Even though brief, these summary verses play an important role in Matthew's Gospel, providing the reader with a picture of Jesus' entire Galilean ministry and reinforcing the Gospel's portrayal of Jesus as the Messiah, the Savior of Israel, and the inaugurator of

God's eschatological reign. At the same time, the response of the crowds in coming to Jesus for healing and "following" him also reflects the dynamics of discipleship (see 4:18, 22). This majestic scene also puts in proper context the ethical imperatives of Matthew's Gospel that will soon follow in the Sermon on the Mount. True "righteousness" is a response to the free gift of God's grace signified in Jesus' proclamation of the good news and in his healing touch (Luz 1995, 46-51).

The Sermon on the Mount (5:1–7:29)

The Sermon on the Mount is the first of the five great discourses in the Gospel and the foundation for all that follows. The Sermon presents Jesus as the teacher par excellence, in the manner of Moses, but, for Matthew, far exceeding the great lawgiver and Savior of Israel.

Matthew draws the core content of the Sermon from Q (see Luke 6:20-49) but expands it with other scattered Q sayings and material unique to Matthew. The strong Jewish-Christian flavor of this traditional material, as well as its presence in a sermon format in both Luke and Matthew, suggests that it may have originated as a compendium of Jesus' sayings intended for Christian instruction. Hans Dieter Betz, in a major commentary on the Sermon, proposes that it originated as an "epitome," or collection, of the essential teachings of Jesus. Such a literary form was known in antiquity, both in Greco-Roman and Jewish culture. Betz speculates that the original purpose of the Sermon was to instruct Jewish converts to the community on the teachings of Jesus, relating those teachings to the converts' Jewish background (by contrast, Luke's "Sermon on the Plain" explains the teachings of Jesus in relationship to a Greek background; see Betz 1995, 70-88).

Whatever the original form and function of the Sermon, Matthew's careful editing of this material, its correspondence with the surrounding structure of 4:23–9:35, and its resonance with Matthean motifs throughout the Gospel now make it an integral part of Matthew's narrative.

Determining a coherent structure for the Sermon as a whole has generated a lot of discussion. Ulrich Luz, for example, has proposed a "ring like" structure with the Lord's Prayer (6:7-15) as its center (Luz 1989, 211-13). From this core radiates a series of parallel passages based on both thematic and formal similarities. For example, the sections immediately before and after the Lord's Prayer have a similar theme of "righteousness before God" (6:1-6 and 6:16-18); the materials in the next "ring" (5:21-48 and 6:19–7:11) have a formal similarity in that each has fifty-nine lines; the next ring (5:17-20 and 7:12) has a parallel reference to the "law and the prophets"; and the outer ring (5:3-16 and 7:13-27) serves as introduction and conclusion to the Sermon. Proposals such as this are enticing but extraordinarily subtle and often depend on subjective judgments about what constitutes a "parallel."

Some features of the Sermon's structure are more evident. Most of the material has clear demarcations by content: the introduction and Beatitudes (5:1-16); the keynote principle of fulfilling the law and the prophets illustrated by six antitheses (5:17-48); teaching about almsgiving, prayer, and fasting (6:1-18); and the concluding exhortation (7:13-29). The segment in 6:19–7:12 has less evident thematic or formal unity but certainly reflects the typical motifs of the Sermon as a whole. Another characteristic to note is the emphasis on fulfillment of the "law and the prophets" that is explicitly stated in both 5:17 and 7:12, forming a clear bracket around the body of the Sermon and highlighting a fundamental theme of the Sermon as a whole. Typical groupings of three are also detectable such as in the ordering of the Beatitudes (5:3-10, 11-12, 13-16), the three acts of piety (6:1-18), and the three sets of exhortations that conclude the Sermon (7:13-14, 15-23, 24-27). This preference for "three" may also command the overall structure of the Sermon into three major sections: the introduction (5:1-16), the ethical instructions (5:17–7:12), and the concluding exhortations (7:13-29). M. E. Boring suggests that here Matthew follows the original three-part division of the Sermon found in Q, which is still detectable in Luke's version (Boring 1995, 171-73).

Based on these features a probable structure for the Sermon is as follows:

1. Introduction and proclamation of the Beatitudes (5:1-16)
2. The fulfillment of the Law (5:17-48)

3. Authentic piety and right action (6:1–7:12)

4. Exhortation and conclusion (7:13-29)

Thus the format of the Sermon is both linear and progressive. It begins with the Beatitudes, which provide a strong eschatological tone and serve as prelude to the Sermon as a whole. Then it turns to the fundamental theme of fulfillment of the law and the "greater righteousness" demanded of the disciple. A series of six "antitheses" or contrasts illustrates this theme initially, then instructions on key aspects of piety and one's fidelity to God further illustrate this theme. The discourse concludes with warnings of judgment and corresponding calls for action on the part of those who receive Jesus' words. Parallels, catchwords, and inclusions arch back and forth across this linear structure, giving the discourse both formal and thematic cohesion.

Setting the Stage (5:1-2)

The first two verses (5:1-2) are transitional, connecting the discourse to the preceding epic summary of Jesus' ministry (4:23-25) and setting the stage for the Sermon that follows. Prompted by the vast "crowds" who come to him, bringing their sick and afflicted with them, Jesus goes up a mountain with his disciples, sits down in the manner of the synagogue teacher (see Matt 23:2, seat of Moses; Luke 4:20), and "opening his mouth" (NRSV: "he began to speak") begins to teach.

◊ ◊ ◊ ◊

Matthew favors mountain settings as places where dramatic revelations take place (see 4:8; 15:29-31; 17:1-8; 28:16-20; see Donaldson 1985). In this context it is likely that Matthew also intends to wrap Jesus in the mantle of Moses and the revelation on Sinai (Exod 19:3, 12; 24:15, 18; 34:1-2, 4; Allison 1993). The discourse will be directed to the "disciples" but the "crowds" are not abandoned. At the end of the discourse, the "crowds" reappear and are "astounded at his teaching" (7:28). The relationship of the "crowds" and "disciples" in Matthew is not clearly defined. For most of Jesus' ministry the crowds seem to be a neutral entity and often respond favorably to Jesus. Their role will take a decisive turn, however, in the Passion narrative (see 27:20-26). While the "disciples" are explicitly called to follow Jesus (4:18-22) and have the benefit of witnessing his mission and hearing his words, the "crowds," too, are the object of Jesus' ministry and seem to represent the wider community, first of all Israel and ultimately all those to whom he is sent. The Sermon, therefore, is not intended solely for an elite group but is directed to the world (Luz 1995, 42-45).

◊ ◊ ◊ ◊

The Beatitudes of the Kingdom of Heaven (5:3-16)

The Beatitudes (5:3-10) and the related sayings on discipleship (5:11-16) serve as a prelude to the Sermon. They underscore the eschatological perspective of Jesus' mission, lifting up those virtues, attitudes, and characteristic actions that define authentic discipleship as taught by Jesus. The first eight Beatitudes are stated in the third person (vv. 1-10); the ninth beatitude is in the second person and leads into direct instructions for the disciples (vv. 11-16). The literary form, declaring "blessed" those who exhibit a particular behavior or disposition, has biblical precedents, particularly in the Wisdom and prophetic literature (see, e.g., Sir 25:7-9; 48:1-11; Isa 30:18; 32:20). Similar literary forms can be traced far back in hellenistic literature such as the *Homeric Hymn to Demeter* and particularly in some expressions of the Egyptian cult of Isis (Betz 1995, 97-105). The Beatitudes in the Sermon are closer (but not identical) to the prophetic perspective whereby those are declared blessed whose present circumstances will be reversed by God in the end time. Standing at the beginning of the discourse, the Beatitudes give the Sermon a strong eschatological flavor, declaring "blessed" now those who, because of their experience, virtues, and commitments, will fully experience the reign of God in the end time.

Matthew draws some of this material from Q (5:3, cf. Luke 6:20; 5:4, cf. Luke 6:21; 5:6, cf. Luke 6:21; 5:11-12, cf. Luke 6:22-23) and Mark (5:13, cf. Mark 9:49-50; 5:14-16, cf. Mark 4:21). In Luke's version the Beatitudes are directly linked to corresponding "woes" but Matthew has only Beatitudes, seeming to reserve "woes" for Jesus' sharp attack on the Pharisees and scribes in 23:13-23. Several of Matthew's Beatitudes (5:5, 7-10) have no parallel in Luke and are reflective of traditional biblical virtues that have particular force for Matthew.

The "kingdom of heaven" is mentioned in the first (5:3) and the eighth (5:10) Beatitudes, framing these core declarations and linking them to the fundamental motif of the kingdom announced in preceding scenes (4:17, 23). Another key Matthean motif—"righteousness"—is cited in the fourth and eighth Beatitudes, providing another link to opening scenes of the Gospel (3:15) and anticipating Jesus' teaching in 5:20. The sayings on discipleship that conclude this section (5:11-16) have a transitional function, moving the reader from the magisterial declarations of the Beatitudes to focus on Jesus' instruction of the disciples in the body of the Sermon.

◊ ◊ ◊ ◊

The situations, actions, and virtues blessed in these verses all have strong roots in biblical tradition and reflect Matthew's ethical perspective. The formulation "poor in spirit" (in contrast to Luke's straightforward "poor") in the first Beatitude (v. 3) evokes not only the traditional theme of God's care for the poor (see, e.g., Exod 22:25-27; 23:11; Lev 19:9-10; Deut 15:7-11; Isa 61:1), but emphasizes the ethical disposition of trust and dependence on God. "Those who mourn" is a generalized reference to those who have suffered loss or oppression and is strongly reminiscent of Isa 61:1-3 where God promises to vindicate and comfort those who mourn in Zion. The blessing of the "meek" stresses an ethical stance of humility, a virtue that will describe Jesus himself in Matthew's Gospel (see 11:29; 21:5); the promise that they will "inherit the earth" echoes Ps 37:11 (see also Isa 60:21; *Jub.* 22:14; 32:19). The designation "hunger and thirst *for righteousness*" (emphasis added; contrast Luke 6:21, "you who are hungry now") again reflects Matthew's abiding ethical interest: Those who strive for righteousness are in accord with Jesus' own commitment (3:15) and with his fundamental teaching (5:20). "Mercy" is also a consistent Matthean emphasis illustrated in Jesus' own compassionate ministry (see, e.g., 9:13; 12:7); by contrast, the Pharisees are excoriated for neglecting it (23:23). Experiencing judgment from God in accord with exactly what one practices is also typical of Matthew (see, e.g., the parable of 18:23-35 and the Lord's Prayer in 6:12, 14-15). To be "pure in heart" implies single-minded devotion to God; echoing Ps 24, such obedience is characteristic of those "who seek the face of the God of Jacob" and will be vindicated (Ps 24:3-6; also Pss 51:10; 73:1). The blessing on the "peacemakers" will be amplified in the Sermon (5:21-26, 43-48) and is in accord with Matthew's strong emphasis on reconciliation. The peacemakers will be called "children of God" because they act in accord with God's own reconciling love and thus prove to be God's sons and daughters (5:45). The kingdom of heaven belongs to those "persecuted for righteousness' sake" (v. 10); warnings of persecution from both Gentile and Jewish authorities are given to the disciples in the mission discourse (see 10:16-31) and the eschatological discourse (24:9; see also 23:34).

The shift to the discipleship sayings of verses 11-16 begins with a restatement of the preceding Beatitude on persecution and then moves into themes of witness and mission. The sayings on "salt" (v. 13) used to give "taste" (thus emphasizing its qualities as seasoning and not as a catalyst for burning, as some suggest), and "light," which illumines "all in the house" (vv. 14-15), stress not only the impact the disciples are to have on others but the wide horizon of their mission: They are to be salt "of the earth" and light "of the world." Thereby Matthew anticipates the final commission of 28:16-20 and shows that Jesus' teaching in the Sermon itself is directed far beyond the narrow circle of the disciples themselves. The ultimate purpose is that those who witness the "good works" of the disciples will "give glory to your Father in heaven" (v. 16; see also 6:9; 11:25).

◊ ◊ ◊ ◊

This opening segment forms a portrait of authentic discipleship for Matthew and thereby prepares for the specific instructions of the Sermon to follow. At the same time, the eschatological tone set by the Beatitudes illustrates the underpinnings of Matthew's ethical perspective. These virtues and commitments blessed by Jesus anticipate the full life of God's kingdom and lead to it. The disciple, in effect, is to live now the life that is to be realized fully at the end time, yet, through Jesus, is already breaking into the world. Consistent with his Jewish heritage, Matthew is not afraid to speak of the rewards for good deeds. At the same time, he is conscious that authentic discipleship is possible only in response to Jesus' mission as teacher, healer, and Savior.

The Fulfillment of the Law (5:17-48)

With these verses one enters the conceptual center of Matthew's theology: Jesus has come to "fulfill" the law and the prophets, and to instruct the disciples in the way of true righteousness. The section falls into two clear divisions: (1) 5:17-20 is a programmatic statement about Jesus' relationship to the law and the fidelity required of his disciples; and (2) 5:21-48 is a series of six illustrations or "antitheses" that illustrate what it means to "fulfill" the law.

The programmatic statement of 5:17-20 contains four sayings of Jesus. Although there are echoes of Matt 5:17-18 in Luke 16:16-17, most of the language harmonizes with Matthew's characteristic style and is probably a restatement of traditional material and convictions held by his Jewish-Christian community. Verse 20 recapitulates the emphasis on fidelity to law expressed in verses 17-19 and serves as a transition to the antitheses where exemplary cases of "greater righteousness" are spelled out (note the emphatic "I tell you . . ." at the beginning of v. 20 that is repeated in vv. 22, 28, 32, 34, 39, 44).

The material in 5:21-48 contains six illustrations of Jesus' teaching about "greater righteousness," each introduced by the phrase "you have heard that it was said . . ." (vv. 21, 27, 31 ["it was also said . . ."], 33, 38, 43) and followed by Jesus' own magisterial statement, "but I say to you. . . ." Since the time of Marcion (d. 154 CE) the term "antitheses" has been traditionally used to label this section, implying that Jesus' teachings are in some fashion contradictory to either aspects of the law itself or traditional interpretation of it. However, Matthew's language here (using the Greek disjunctive "de") does not have a strong adversative sense and, as the introductory verses 17-20 imply, the evangelist may have understood Jesus' teaching not as running contrary to the law but as a contrast only in the sense that this teaching was an intensification of the law's claims and a definitive clarification of its meaning. Some of this material is drawn from Q but some portions, as in the case of the sayings on anger (5:21-26) and on oaths (5:33-37), are unique to Matthew.

Attempts to detect a rationale for the order of the so-called "antitheses" or contrasts based, for example, on the order of the Pentateuch or in relation to the Beatitudes, have not been successful (see Betz 1995, 201-5). It is clear, however, that the first (5:21-26) and the last (5:43-48) set, with their teaching about reconciliation and avoidance of retaliation, frame this entire section with a principle fundamental to Matthew's theology. Also, the final contrast on love of enemies serves as the climax of the section, concluding with Jesus' saying about being "perfect" as God is perfect (5:48). The series of antitheses or contrasts is also bound together in other ways: Each deals with human relationships and each calls for a more exacting fidelity to the law on the level of both actions and interior disposition.

◊ ◊ ◊ ◊

5:17-20: Verse 20 expresses Matthew's fundamental understanding of how the teaching and ministry of Jesus relate to the Jewish law. The emphatic "I have come" in verse 17 and the placement of this saying immediately after the Beatitudes and at the beginning of the Sermon give it a keynote quality. Jesus has not come to "abolish" the "law or the prophets" (Matthew's characteristic way of referring to the Jewish Scriptures: see 7:12; 11:13; 22:40) but to "fulfill" them. Used in reference to the Jewish law, the term *plēroō* can have the meaning of "keeping" the law, underscoring Jesus' obedience. However, when this same verb is used by Matthew to introduce an Old Testament citation, as in the fulfillment quotations (see introduction, p. 27), it takes on a "prophetic" nuance. Thus the connotation in verse 17 would be that Jesus has come not to invalidate the law and the prophets but to bring them to their intended purpose. Matthew seems to use the word here in this more comprehensive sense. The words and actions of Jesus the Messiah are not only completely in accord with the law but reveal its God-given intent and bring its purpose to completion, particularly through centering the law on the love command (see 22:34-40).

Relating the strict sayings of verses 18 and 19 to this generic principle has been a challenge for many interpreters. In the view of some, the seemingly unqualified endorsement of even the least commands of the law, including "one letter" or even "one stroke of a letter," are hard to reconcile with Jesus' own liberal interpretation of the law in the series of contrasts in 5:21-48 and in other parts of the Gospel. However, Matthew and his community may have seen no contradiction at all, considering Jesus' interpretations on such issues as sabbath observance and acceptance of sinners as "fulfillment" of the law (see 9:13; 12:7). There are indications in the Gospel that Matthew's community continued to accept the law, including its cultic requirements (see, e.g., 23:23, 26 and the omission of Mark's unqualified abrogation of the kosher laws; Matt 15:17 [cf. Mark 7:19]; as well as the added reference to the sabbath in 24:20).

The precise meaning of the temporal references in verse 18 is difficult to determine. Does Matthew suggest that the Torah remains valid until the end of the world ("until heaven and earth pass away"), as some Jewish traditions speculated, or is this simply a way of saying "never" (similar to the saying about the enduring validity of Jesus' own words in 24:35)? And does the second phrase—"until all is accomplished"—imply restatement of that end of the world time limit? Or, as others have suggested, does Matthew consider the Jewish law valid only until the beginning of the new age that starts with Jesus' own death and resurrection when "all is accomplished" and therefore Jesus' own teaching supplants the law (Matthew will surround the moment of Jesus' death with eschatological signs; see below, 27:51-53)? In fact, the coherence of these verses suggests that Matthew views the Jewish law, as definitively taught by Jesus and embodied in his exemplary practice, as remaining valid for all time and offering the way to true righteousness before God.

The meaning of verse 19 is also problematic. Characteristically Matthew insists on the integrity of teaching and action and will condemn the religious leaders for failing on this very point (see 23:3). Evaluating the "weightier" and "lighter" demands of the law was a refrain of rabbinic tradition and has echoes here. What is curious is the notion that those who fail to teach with integrity will be given a lower place in the kingdom of heaven. The idea of "rankings" in the kingdom of heaven reappears at other points in the Gospel (see 11:11; 18:1, 4; 20:21).

Verse 20 completes this segment of the Gospel and orients the reader to the "antitheses" that follow. The key terms "righteousness" (*dikaiosynē*, see 3:15; 5:6, 10) and "kingdom of heaven" (3:2; 4:17; 5:3, 10) come back into play. In order to enter the kingdom of heaven, the righteousness of the follower of Jesus must exceed that of the scribes and Pharisees. The reference to the religious leaders anticipates their stereotyped role in the remainder of the Gospel as negative examples of those whose teaching is corrosive and whose actions lack integrity. By contrast, the teaching of Jesus points the way to true righteousness before God.

5:21-48: Through a series of six "antitheses" or contrasts, the Matthean Jesus illustrates what "fulfillment" of the law (5:17) and "greater righteousness" (5:20) mean. Although the material finds most of its inspiration in Q and occasionally in Mark (e.g., the sayings on scandal; cf. Matt 5:30 and Mark 9:43), Matthew has shaped the material into its present format. What Jesus teaches in these antitheses is not a direct confrontation between the Jewish law and Christian teaching or interpretation (sometimes caricatured as the contrast between "law and gospel"). Virtually all of Jesus' teaching here has echoes in Jewish ethical tradition found either in the Hebrew Scriptures or in rabbinical teachings. This should not be surprising since Matthew considers Jesus as the one who fulfills the law and teaches its God-given intent. What is fresh and "contrasting" about Jesus' teaching is rather its cumulative intensity, its consistent drive for complete and radical obedience to God's commands, and its reach not only to the level of action but to the intentions and dispositions that lead to action. At the same time, the framing of the series of antitheses or contrasts with the instructions on reconciliation (5:21-26, 43-48) and love of enemies (5:43-48) show that for Matthew this is not a loose collection of various teachings, each with equal weight. Rather, the focal center for Jesus' interpretation of the law is the love command; everything else finds its ultimate coherence here (see also 7:12; 22:33-40).

Each of these contrasts deals with human relationships, first citing a command of the law or common interpretation of it and then Jesus' own teaching coupled with concrete illustrations. The terms "brother" and "sister" (the NRSV's more inclusive translation of the original "brother" or *adelphos*) are used throughout many of these antitheses. Although Matthew may be thinking first of all relationships within the community, the term can also have a broader meaning of all those one encounters (see 5:45).

The first contrast (5:21-26) cites the sixth commandment ("You shall not murder . . ."; see Exod 21:12; Lev 24:17; Num 35:16-18); Jesus' contrasting teaching first extends that prohibition to the kind of anger and insults that can lead to violence and then calls for active steps of reconciliation. The text cites an Aramaic term, *raka* (translated in the NRSV generically as "insult"), which probably meant "empty head" or "stupid," and a Greek term, *mōre*, meaning "fool" (v. 22). Neither is particularly vicious, but they can be the path to more deadly enmity and are therefore condemned. So urgent is the command to reconcile that one should leave a gift at the altar and go first to be reconciled with an aggrieved brother or sister (v. 23). The priority of ethical integrity over the obligations of the cult was also a Jewish conviction (see, e.g., Isa 1; and frequently in the Wisdom tradition, e.g., Prov 15:8; 21:3, 27; Sir 34:21-27; 35:1-4). The final saying about settling one's accounts (presumably situations of alienation and enmity) on the way to court probably refers to the threat of God's judgment ("your accuser") against those who steadfastly choose enmity over reconciliation (see a similar thought in Matt 18:35).

The second segment on adultery and lust sets the stage for the third one that follows on divorce (5:27-30, 31-32). Jesus cites the law condemning adultery (see Exod 20:14; Deut 5:18) and then goes on to warn against the lustful glance. In this context the term "woman" (Gk. *gynē*) refers most directly to a married woman. Jewish law, too, found it morally abhorrent to look at a married woman with the intent to commit adultery (see Exod 20:17). The vivid sayings about mutilating oneself rather than commit such a violation underscore the intensity of Jesus' command.

The prohibition against divorce (5:31-32) is one of the Sermon's most challenging and extensively debated passages. Matthew provides further teaching on divorce in 19:3-9, a passage parallel to Mark 10:2-12. Jesus first cites Deut 24:1, which permitted a writ of divorce; the circumstances that justified such a step were debated in Jewish tradition. Jesus' own teaching appears to render Deut 24:1 unnecessary because he forbids even the possibility of divorce. The discussion in 19:3-10 elaborates on this in Jesus' appeal to God's original intention expressed in Genesis that the couple become "one flesh"; thus the procedure in Deut 24:1 was only a "concession," not really an expression of God's will. In the Sermon, however, we have no explanation but simply the prohibition and its consequences. To divorce a woman is tantamount to causing her to commit adultery; likewise, to marry a divorced woman is to commit adultery. This rigorous demand of Jesus (which Mark will present as without exception; Mark 10:11-12) seems to be somewhat mitigated in Matthew's version by the phrase "except on the ground of unchastity" (5:32). The precise meaning of the term *porneia* (NRSV: "unchastity") is the focal point of the debate. It can mean some act of sexual misconduct, probably adultery (as implied by the previous antithesis), which in Jewish tradition was considered so grave a violation that it destroyed the marriage and reconciliation should not even be attempted; or it can also refer to marriage within forbidden boundaries of kinship, which rendered a marriage invalid (see Lev 18:6-18). In the former case, the exception clause would imply that Matthew's community had mitigated Jesus' rigorous saying in favor of the Jewish tradition that considered adultery so serious that continuance of a marriage in such circumstances was inconceivable. This stance would align Matthew with the rabbinic school of Shammai, which restricted the grounds for divorce to such cases. If a reference to marriage within forbidden kinship lines is the meaning of the term *porneia* in

Matthew's text, then the so-called "exception" would probably apply mainly to Gentile converts entering the community who had contracted marriages considered invalid in the eyes of the community (and Jewish tradition); in effect, this would be no "exception" at all to Jesus' prohibition of divorce and the contrast with Deut 24:1 would remain.

The fourth segment concerning oaths is another instance in which Jesus' teaching goes beyond specific commands of the law and makes them unnecessary. It is no longer a matter of the law having to command that one respect an oath that has been taken (see, e.g., Lev 19:12). Rather, a disciple's word is to be so honest and reliable that no oath is to be made. Another motivation at work here seems to be Jesus' extraordinary reverence for God's name; the divine name or euphemisms for it (such as "heaven," the "earth," or "Jerusalem") should never be used to certify the truth of what one says. This also reflects Jewish tradition that was concerned about frivolous oaths. For Matthew the prohibition against oaths was a serious command of Jesus; later in the Gospel both Herod (14:7) and Peter (26:72) will take oaths with disastrous consequences.

The fifth segment returns to the theme of violence and reconciliation. The "law of talion" ("an eye for an eye . . .") apparently was intended to moderate vengeance and make it at least proportionate to the offense—that is, take only an eye and no more if one has endured such a loss from an enemy (see especially, Lev 24:19-20; also Exod 21:23-25; Deut 19:21; Betz 1995, 275-76). Jesus, however, not only forbids all resistance or retaliation for evil but commands that response to an offense be disproportionate in graciousness. Thus if someone strikes you on the "right" cheek (perhaps implying that it was a left-handed slap, an insult in Semitic culture), turn the other cheek as well; if someone takes your coat (literally the tunic or inner garment), give your cloak as well (a much more valuable garment that provided warmth and protection from the elements; see the command in Exod 22:26-27 about a creditor's obligation to return a pawned cloak to a poor man before nightfall); if someone (a Roman soldier?) impounds you to go one mile, go two; anyone who begs or borrows is not to be refused (see a similar thought in Deut 15:7-11).

The final contrast (5:43-48) amplifies this theme of disproportionate graciousness and carries it to the ultimate level. The command to "love your enemies" is often cited as the most radical and characteristic of Jesus' teachings (Klassen 1984; Piper 1979; Swartley 1992). Matthew gives it the climactic position in the series of antitheses: More than anything else, love of enemies defines what fulfillment of the law means. The contrast is set with the command of Lev 19:18 to "love your neighbor"; the addition "and hate your enemy" is not found in the Hebrew Scriptures but probably reflects the kind of sectarian perspective that does emerge, for example, in Qumran where members of the community are warned to "hate" the ungodly (see 1QS:10; ix 21). Love of one's own and antipathy toward the threatening outsider is a common human stance that cuts across time and culture. Matthew's text does not define who the "enemy" is, although the instruction to "pray for those who persecute you" suggests that the primary examples of "enemy" were the opponents of Matthew's community (see the warnings about persecution in chaps. 10; 24).

Judaism, as well as Stoic philosophy, counseled against retaliation toward enemies, but no real parallels have been found for Jesus' teaching to *love* an enemy, so this saying does have a distinctive, if not an absolutely unique, flavor. Equally important, however, is the *motivation* for such a radical teaching (5:45-47). In loving the enemy the disciple acts as God acts, when God lavishes the sun and rain on both good and bad, just and unjust. This kind of metaphor was also used in Greco-Roman literature to describe God's beneficence expressed in creation that is experienced by both good and bad. Seneca, for example, says, "If you are imitating the gods, . . . then bestow benefits also upon the ungrateful; for the sun rises also upon the wicked and the sea lies open also to Pirates" (Seneca, *De Ben.* 4.26.1; see, further, Best 1995, 317; Piper 1979, 20-25). In the context of the Sermon, however, the sun and rainfall become metaphors for God's indiscriminate and radically gracious love that envelops even the enemy. This kind of radically gracious love becomes the guiding principle for authentic righteousness.

Reciprocity, whereby one loves those who love you, is a normal human response of which even the "tax collectors" and "Gentiles" are capable.

The final saying (v. 48) sums up all that Jesus teaches here and leads into the next segment of the Sermon. By loving the enemy, the disciple becomes "perfect . . . as your heavenly Father is perfect." The Greek term for "perfect" is *teleios,* from the root word *telos* or "goal." The connotation is that of "completion" rather than a static sense that the English term "perfect" can imply. The word *teleios*—"complete" or "perfect"—is used in the Septuagint to translate the Hebrew term *tamim* or also *shalom,* both of which connote "wholeness" (e.g., 1 Chr 28:9; on the term *teleios,* see also Davies and Allison 1988, 561-63; Betz 1995, 322-24). Matthew will use the same word in 19:21 where the rich young man is invited to sell his possessions and follow Jesus, "if you wish to be *perfect [teleios].*" Holiness in imitation of God was an ideal of the Hebrew Scriptures (Lev 19:2; 20:26; 21:8) and for Matthew that desire is now fulfilled by following the teaching and the example of Jesus.

◊ ◊ ◊ ◊

This entire opening section of the Sermon on the Mount (5:17-48) is fundamental for Matthew's theology. Here he situates the Jewish law in relationship to Jesus, affirming for his Jewish-Christian readers that Jesus does not destroy the sacred heritage of Judaism but, as the Son of God and Messiah, "fulfills" the law by revealing its ultimate intent and purpose. The six "antitheses," or contrasts, illustrate what fulfillment of the law means for the disciple of Jesus. In each instance Jesus' teaching opens for the disciple the way to "greater righteousness" before God. All of these commands cohere in the teachings on compassion and radical love that frame the entire set of contrasts and bring them to their climax. Only because one has first experienced God's own reconciling and indiscriminate graciousness revealed in Jesus' own healings and proclamation of God's reign (see above, 4:23-24) is it possible to love the enemy. Here, as in other parts of the Sermon, the eschatological dimension evoked by the Beatitudes is also present. In the concrete instances taught by Jesus, the disciple learns the kind of responses and actions that lead one in the direction of God's future reign and, at the same time, are symptomatic of its presence even now breaking into history.

Authentic Piety and Right Action (6:1–7:12)

The main body of the Sermon continues to define Jesus' teaching on "greater righteousness," but with increasing emphasis on the interior attitudes and dispositions that are to inform authentic action.

A first section (6:1-18) takes up three classical expressions of Jewish piety: almsgiving, prayer, and fasting. In each instance, Jesus' words probe the spirit and intent that must inform authentic piety. The Lord's Prayer, framed by further sayings on prayer and forgiveness, stands at the heart of this segment and reinforces its message (6:7-15). The organization of the remaining material (6:19–7:12) is less clearly defined. In the proverbial style of Wisdom literature, the Sermon strings together a number of Jesus' sayings on concern for possessions (6:19-34), on judging others (7:1-5), on reverence for what is holy (7:6), and on confident prayer (7:7-11). The body of the Sermon closes with the "Golden Rule" (7:12), which reprises the fundamental theme of 5:17-48.

The first section on authentic piety (6:1-18) is unique to Matthew, except for the Lord's Prayer, which parallels Luke's briefer version of the Prayer (Luke 11:1-4). Some have suggested that for this section Matthew may have had access to a preexisting literary piece. However, it is just as likely that Matthew himself is responsible for the present format, drawing on traditions and teachings within his own Jewish-Christian community. The material is steeped in Jewish practice and the sayings have the tang of Jesus' own teaching style. In the final segment (6:19–7:12) Matthew draws mainly on Q, with virtually all of the material finding parallels in Luke.

◊ ◊ ◊ ◊

6:1-18: The opening verse sets the tone and content for the entire section. Jesus warns the disciples not to perform acts of piety before others in order to be seen. The word translated here as "piety" is actually "righteousness" *(dikaiosynē),* the key motif that runs like a powerful current through the entire Sermon (see 5:20; also 3:15; 5:6, 10). Here "righteousness" is defined as acts of piety, revered by Judaism and surely also by Matthew's own community. Matthew's concern is that such action be truly an expression of one's interior communion with God. Another key term in this verse is "your Father in heaven," which will be cited throughout the following passage (see 6:4, 6, 8, 9, 14, 15, 18). Typical of Matthew, this designation affirms both God's loving presence ("Father") and awesome transcendence ("in heaven") and will find full expression in the Lord's Prayer (6:9-13).

The fundamental principle expressed in verse 1 sets up the contrasts that run through Jesus' teaching on all three categories of piety: a contrast between actions that are done in public and those that are hidden; a contrast between actions done to be seen by people and those done to be seen by God; a contrast between an immediate reward and a future reward. What is at stake here is not really the question of favoring "private" over "public" forms of piety but the guiding intention and spirit of all religious acts.

Thus almsgiving (6:2-4) was not to be done in order to "be praised by others." The biting edge of Matthew's critique of the religious leaders begins to emerge by identifying as negative examples the "hypocrites . . . in the synagogues and in the streets." "Hypocrites" (a Greek term meaning an "actor" but in this context obviously implying a false facade of behavior) is a label Jesus will apply to the scribes and Pharisees (see 23:13, 15, 23, 25, 27, 29). Rather than sounding a trumpet to draw attention and reap praise, the disciple should give alms "in secret" so that only God will know and give the true reward. The notion that God would reward the just in the end time was a staple of Jewish eschatology and is a theme of several Matthean parables (see, e.g., 25:14-30, 31-46).

Nor is prayer (6:5-6) to be done for public display but in secret, in an inner room of the house where only God can see one pray. This intriguing emphasis on prayer in secret with God will find an echo later in the Gospel when Jesus himself goes to pray alone (14:23). The "reward" for such prayer is not human admiration but the response that God alone can give (7:11).

Likewise, one's fasting (6:16-17) is not to be broadcast by external signs and looking gloomy. (Perhaps by heaping ashes on one's head? The word "disfigure" used by Matthew here is undefined.) Instead disciples who fast should put oil on their heads and wash their faces (i.e., no ashes or distinguishing signs of a fast)—in other words look normal or even festive. The text does not speak of the motivation for fasting (as 9:14-15) but assumes it is a worthwhile act of devotion and therefore should be directed to God alone.

To the segment on prayer, Matthew adds his centerpiece, the Lord's Prayer (6:9-13), which the evangelist presents as a model prayer and one that breathes the spirit of authentic "righteousness" (Kiley 1994, 2-27). No New Testament passage has had a greater impact on Christian piety than this, thereby fulfilling Jesus' directive "pray then in this way . . ." (v. 9). At the same time, because of its depth and directness, its eloquent yet unadorned statement of human need before God, the Lord's Prayer is also the most ecumenical of prayers, appealing even beyond the boundaries of the Christian community.

Matthew frames the Lord's Prayer with related sayings. Verses 7-8 provide an introduction by warning the disciples not to "heap up empty phrases" (the Greek term *battalogeō* probably means "babble") and "many words" like Gentiles do. Here "Gentiles" are the negative examples (as in 5:47). The text may have in mind the incantations or magical formulae of some Greco-Roman cults in which names or phrases were repeated, or it may simply be stereotyping the Gentiles as non-Jews who naturally would not know how to pray properly. The notion that God already knows what one needs (and therefore does not need a lot of words) echoes Isa 65:24 and accords with the spirit of Jesus' teaching in 6:32 and 7:7-11. Likewise, verses 14-15 on forgiveness echo a key petition of the Prayer and one of importance for Matthew's Gospel (see 5:23-26, 43-48; 18:21-35).

Luke's version of the Prayer (Luke 11:2-4) is briefer than Matthew's. To Luke's direct address "Father" (perhaps echoing the Aramaic *abba,* a term of affection and respect that may have been typical of Jesus' address for God in prayer), Matthew adds the pronoun "our" and his typical designation "in heaven." Matthew has also expanded the number of petitions, making a set of three "your" petitions (adding "your will be done, on earth as it is in heaven") and three "we" petitions (adding "rescue us from the evil one").

Matthew's text breathes the spirit of Jewish piety found in such synagogue prayers as the Kaddish and parts of the Eighteen Benedictions, as well as expressing characteristic themes of Jesus' teaching in the Gospel. Such Jewish prayers characteristically begin with praise of God in the manner of the Lord's Prayer, express the desire that God's will be done, pray for the coming of the kingdom, and add succinct petitions (Petuchowski and Brocke 1978; Charlesworth 1994). At the same time, there is no reason to doubt that the peculiar form and content of the Prayer should be attributed to Jesus himself (Betz 1995, 372-73). Matthew's version probably reflects the form this prayer had taken in his community, with its symmetry and greater solemnity harmonizing with its use in public prayer. Even with its Matthean expansions, the Lord's Prayer is terse and pointed. There is no need to contrast its brevity with supposedly longer prayers of Judaism; in fact Jewish piety, too, appreciated prayers that could be brief (Matthew complains about long *Gentile,* not Jewish, prayers).

More recent interpretation of the Prayer has emphasized its eschatological tone (Harner 1975; Brown 1965, 217-53; for extensive bibliography, see Betz 1995, 382-86; and especially Charlesworth 1994, 101-57). As is true of Matthew's theology in general, the expectation of the future advent of God's reign leads to present ethical imperatives. This spirit sweeps through the prayer. The disciple prays, "Our Father," conscious of God's abiding love and nearness to the community; yet, at the same time, God is "in heaven," fully to be revealed only at the end time. The "you" petitions also echo this perspective. The Christian prays that God's name would be "hallowed" (see Lev 22:32; Deut 32:51; Isa 8:13; 29:23)—this is something that ultimately God alone will ensure, but reverence for God's name is also a commitment of the disciple now. The disciple prays that God's "kingdom" will come fully in the future while aware that one is to live now in accord with the vision of God's reign. Similarly, God's will is to be done here and now on earth by the obedient disciple as it is done completely in heaven.

The "we" petitions express the practical and urgent needs of the disciple who lives in a world that is not yet fully conformed to God's will. The exact meaning of the petition for "bread" is debated. The Greek term translated in the NRSV as "daily" is *epiousian,* found only here in the New Testament (and in Luke's parallel, 11:3). Its most likely derivation is from the Greek root *epienai* ("to come") and therefore literally meaning the "bread that is coming" or the "bread for tomorrow." Some, therefore, give this petition an eschatological interpretation: One prays for the bread of the future heavenly banquet. Others (reflected in the NRSV translation "daily") see a more practical and urgent sense of the bread one needs for sustenance in the day that looms ahead, making this a prayer of those who live in need day by day.

As with the "you" petitions, it may be best not to set up a sharp cleavage between these alternatives but to make room for both eschatological and present ethical concerns. This seems to be the case with the remaining petitions. The disciple who prays for God's forgiveness from "debts" (Matthew uses the more Jewish term "debt" over Luke's "sins") is also committed to forgiving others, thereby the Prayer links present action with eschatological judgment (as in Matthew's parable of the unforgiving servant, 18:23-35). Likewise, the disciple asks God not to be led into "the test" and to be delivered from "evil" (the NRSV translates this as the "evil one," although the word can also be neuter). Both words, "test" *(peirasmos)* and "evil" or "evil one" *(poneros),* have a strong eschatological flavor referring to the ultimate test of the final days and the assault of the demonic, but can also be attached to those incursions of threat and evil in the present age, which are, in a sense, anticipations of the final test (as in Jesus' own desert "test," in 4:1-11, and his exorcisms, e.g., in 9:28-34, note especially 9:29).

6:19–7:12: This segment of the Sermon continues Jesus' illustration of authentic righteousness. As noted earlier, this section has a less definable structure, grouping various sayings (almost all of them from Q) around basic motifs. Several strong prohibitions mark the material: "Do not store up . . ." (6:19); "Do not worry . . ." (6:25); "Do not judge . . ." (7:1); "Do not give . . ." (7:6).

1. *On possessions* (6:19-34). A series of proverbial sayings forcefully illustrates the way the disciples of Jesus are to deal with possessions. "Treasures" are to be "stored up" (literally, "treasured") in heaven where they are permanent, rather than on earth where they are vulnerable to decay and loss. Storing up earthly possessions is critiqued because "where your treasure is, there your heart will be also" (v. 21). Matthew uses "treasure" as a metaphor for that which commands the allegiance of one's "heart" (see, e.g., the parable of 13:44 and the description of the "scribe who has been trained for the kingdom of heaven," 13:52). The critique of possessions as a competing allegiance for one's devotion to God's will is typically Jewish and is reaffirmed in the saying in verse 24 about serving God or *mammon* (an Aramaic word probably meaning wealth or possessions; on the NT view of possessions see Wheeler 1995).

The sayings about the "healthy" and "unhealthy" eye (vv. 22-23) are more difficult to decipher but, in the context of this segment on possessions, they are probably to be understood in a metaphorical sense. Building on the popular assumption that the eye is the window to one's inner life and values, common Jewish metaphors spoke of the "healthy" eye as a sign of one who is generous; conversely, the "unhealthy" eye was symbolic of one who is possessive or stingy.

The famous passage that begins with the admonition "do not worry about your life . . ." finds its fundamental meaning and its thematic link to the Sermon as a whole in the concluding saying: "But strive first for the kingdom of God and his righteousness, and all these things will be given to you as well" (v. 33). Jesus' sayings on not worrying about the necessities of life such as food or clothing are not naive or romantic statements that overlook the life-and-death struggle for existence many face. Rather, even the acquiring of such necessities must be related to the overwhelming reality of God's reign and one's commitment to it. Therefore, "worrying" in this context is not to be defined as ordinary concern, but a debilitating anxiety that is antithetical to trust in God. In this Q passage Matthew finds a term he will use repeatedly to describe the disciples: "little faith" (v. 30; cf. Luke 12:28; the same word will be used by Matthew in 8:26; 14:31; 16:8; cf. 17:20). In contrast to the "Gentiles" (i.e., the nonbelievers) who are consumed in striving for possessions—the equivalent of "worrying"—the disciples are to exercise their faith. The enigmatic saying that concludes the section ("So do not worry about tomorrow . . ." [v. 34]) may be understood in this same sense: The disciples are to focus their attention and energy on the urgent demands of God's reign; the future (a veiled reference to future judgment?) will bring its own concerns.

2. *On not judging* (7:1-5). Similar to the exhortations on forgiveness, the prohibition not to judge others is linked to what one can expect from God (see, e.g., 6:14-15). The point of the memorable image about first taking the log out of one's own eye before attempting to remove a speck from your neighbor's eye (literally, your "brother's," i.e., first and foremost another member of the community) actually leaves open the possibility of judging another but turns the focus to the question of one's own integrity before God as a prerequisite for any judgment of others.

3. *The saying on holiness* (7:6). The precise meaning of this verse, unique to Matthew, is very difficult to determine. It may be placed here to counterbalance the prohibition on judging, in the sense that Jesus' words in 7:1-5 should not be taken by members of the community as condoning laxity (so Davies and Allison 1988, 674). Dogs were not treated as household pets but were considered wild and dangerous; swine were, of course, unclean animals. Therefore one should not give what is "holy" (the community's teachings? membership in the community?) to those who would desecrate or attack it.

4. *On bold and confident prayer* (7:7-11). The triad of verbs in verses 7-8—"ask," "search," "knock"—sets the tone for this segment on praying confidently, knowing that God will respond. Once again the spirit of the Lord's Prayer permeates this section (note especially the image of asking for "bread"). As in the teaching on love of enemies, the motivation for the disciple's action (there, love

for the enemy; here, radical trust in prayer) finds its taproot in God's graciousness. If a human parent, even though weak and capable of evil, is inclined to respond positively to a child's trusting request, what can one expect of the "Father in heaven"?

5. *The "Golden Rule"* (7:12). The main body of the Sermon concludes with Matthew's version of the "Golden Rule" to which is appended the phrase, "this is the law and the prophets" (see 5:17). The exhortation to "do to others as you would have them do to you" finds numerous analogies in both Jewish and Greco-Roman ethical teaching (Harrington 1991, 105; and the extensive discussion in Betz 1995, 508-16). Although usually formulated negatively—"Do not do to others what you do not want them to do to you"—even the positive formulation of Jesus' saying cannot claim to be unique. However, placed here as a conclusion to the body of Jesus' teaching and forming an obvious bracket or inclusion with the fundamental text of 5:17, this ethical maxim takes on new meaning. *What* one does to others has been defined by Jesus' teaching in the body of the Sermon, particularly the radical graciousness called for in the antitheses of 5:21-48. Actions that spring from love of God and love of neighbor fulfill the "law and the prophets" for Matthew (see also 22:40) and define authentic "righteousness."

Exhortation and Conclusion (7:13-29)

As is the case with other discourses in the Gospel, Matthew concludes the Sermon with warnings of final judgment for those who do not put Jesus' teaching into practice (see, e.g., 13:36-43, 47-50; 18:23-35; 24:37–25:46). Virtually all of the material is drawn from Q, enriched by Matthew with traditional Jewish ethical imagery.

A series of contrasting images dominates the passage: the narrow gate and the difficult way compared to the wide gate and the easy way (7:13-14); the good tree that bears good fruit and the bad tree that bears bad fruit (7:17-20); the wise man who builds his house on rock and the foolish man who built his house on sand (7:24-27). Woven into this series are warnings about false prophets (7:15-16, 21-23). The key word "doing" *(poieō)* dominates the section and reveals Matthew's characteristic emphasis on praxis (see 7:17, 18, 19, 21, 22, 24, 26; cf. 7:12). The section concludes with a transition formula that will find echoes at the conclusion of each of the discourses (7:28-29; cf. 11:1; 13:53; 19:1; 26:1).

◊ ◊ ◊ ◊

The entire section contrasts those who, on the one hand, not only hear Jesus' words but put them into practice with those who, on the other, fail to act on Jesus' teaching and may even attempt to mask their failure by saying the right words or by inauthentic action.

The opening series of images about the two gates and the two ways (7:13-14) evokes the journey image that will reemerge later in the Gospel (John came "in the way of righteousness," 21:32; "we know that you . . . teach the way of God," 22:16). Matthew has added this traditional image to the Q material (cf. Luke 13:23-24; see also *Did.* 1:2–5:2; this image is already found in the OT, e.g., Jer 21:8). That "way" has been illustrated in the specific teaching of the Sermon and now the disciples (and through them, the community and the world) are exhorted to set out on this way that is difficult but leads ultimately to "life."

The disciples are warned of "false prophets" who are wolves in sheep's clothing (7:15-20) and are offered a typically Matthean criterion for judgment—they will be known by their "fruits." This introduces the next set of contrasting images, the good and bad trees (7:16-20), and leads into additional warnings about the stern fate that awaits those who do not act in accord with God's will. They say the right words ("Lord, Lord") and appear to prophesy and perform impressive miracles (v. 22), but their plaintive cries on the day of judgment will not offset their failure to do "the will of my Father in heaven." The eschatological vantage point of Matthew breaks into the clear as the Jesus of the Gospel now speaks plainly as the judge of the end time: "I will declare to them, 'I never knew you; go way from me, you evildoers' " (v. 23). There has been much speculation about the identity of these "false prophets" and workers of mighty deeds: Does Matthew refer to non-Christians? To Jewish opponents of the community? Or to problems internal to the Christian community? As other early Christian texts indicate, there were problems in the early church with charismatics who exploited their extraordinary powers for personal gain (*Did.* 11:4-6; 12:1-5, e.g., warns about prophets who overextend their stay in the community) or were the source of false teaching (the Pastoral Epistles warn against "false teachers"; e.g., 1 Tim 4:1-5; 2 Tim 3:1-9; 4:1-5). Matthew may be referring to such people whom he brands as "evildoers" (v. 23), literally those who do "lawlessness" (*anomia;* see also 13:41; 23:28; 24:12). The parallel to 24:10-12 is particularly illuminating. There Jesus warns the disciples that, in the end time, false prophets would "lead many astray" and, because of "lawlessness, the love of many will grow cold."

The final set of images is in the form of a parable about two housebuilders (7:24-27). In contrast to the foolish man who built his house on sand only to have it swept away in the wind and floods of the rainy season, the wise man builds on rock and his dwelling endures. The application of the parable drives home Matthew's emphatic and consistent message: "Everyone who hears these words of mine and does not act on them" will be liable to judgment (v. 26). The phrase "these words of mine" refers to the entire Sermon, which for Matthew is a distillation of Jesus' teaching.

The Sermon concludes with the transitional formula of 7:28-29. The Sermon had begun with Jesus addressing the "disciples" (5:1); at its conclusion the "crowds" are "astounded" at his teaching. The crowds first came into the picture in Matthew's dramatic summary of Jesus' Galilean ministry as they had converged on Jesus from every corner of Israel, bringing their sick for healing (4:24-25). That epic scene is evoked here at the end of the Sermon and will come into play again immediately before the mission discourse (see 9:35-36). For Matthew, the Sermon is not addressed solely to the disciples or the community but to all those in need of salvation. The response of the crowd is favorable and they contrast the "authority" of Jesus with that of the "scribes" (7:29). For Matthew, Jesus speaks with the authority of the Messiah and Son of God, one whose teaching fulfills the law and the prophets (5:17). The "scribes," by contrast, begin to fulfill their stereotypical role in the

Gospel as those in opposition to Jesus and whose teaching and actions are inauthentic.

The major players of Matthew's Gospel drama are now on stage and are taking up their characteristic roles: Jesus as the authoritative teacher and healer; the disciples forming the core community of Jesus and believing in him even if their faith is weak ("little faith"); the scribes and Pharisees who along with others among the Jewish leaders play the role of opposition and serve as negative examples; the crowds taking a neutral and often favorable response to Jesus (at least until the Passion).

◊ ◊ ◊ ◊

The Sermon on the Mount is not only the first of the Gospel's five great discourses but also its most fundamental. Several conclusions can be drawn about its meaning in the context of Matthew's overall theology:

1. In the history of interpretation of the Sermon there has been constant debate about its intended audience and the moral authority of its provisions (see the discussions in Betz 1995, 5-44; Carter 1994a, 103-29; Luz 1989, 218-23; Senior 1997a, 108-10). Some later interpreters understood the teaching of the Sermon as intended only for those seeking a life of perfection, such as monastics, or for those individuals or sectarian groups who did not have to face the compromises of public life. For others, the eschatological assumptions of the Sermon made it effectively an "emergency ethic," applicable only to the original audience who may have lived in a context of a foreshortened history when heroic virtue might be expected but now, in view of subsequent Christian historical experience, no longer has moral force.

Yet there is no real evidence that Matthew intended the Sermon for only a portion of the Christian community. In the narrative context of Matthew, Jesus speaks directly to the disciples (5:1) but the "crowds" form an outer ring and respond with amazement at the authority of Jesus' teaching at the conclusion of the Sermon (7:28-29). At no point in the Sermon are the commands of Jesus presented in a "conditional" manner related to a particular audience or a particular time; the text seems to clearly assume that Jesus is teaching the normative way of authentic righteousness for all disciples, indeed for all who seek to do God's will.

2. The content of the Sermon provides the reader with the heart of Matthean theology, that is, as the evangelist and his community interpreted the teaching of Jesus. That teaching reflected in the Sermon includes the following fundamental points:

a.) The Sermon expresses a theological vision: The God of Israel is close to his children and to creation itself, attentive to human need, gracious with forgiveness, and intent on bringing humanity to its destiny. This pattern of God's "righteousness" is to be the pattern and norm for all human action.

b.) Matthew's Christology is apparent in the context and content of the Sermon. As Messiah and God's Son, Jesus fulfills God's plan of salvation revealed in the Old Testament. Jesus proclaims the advent of God's reign and through his words and deeds begins to enact the reality of that eschatological kingdom of God in present history. Thus the Sermon has a strong eschatological tone, first announced in the Beatitudes but sustained throughout the body of the Sermon. The disciples are taught to be imbued with those dispositions and to act in such a manner that reflects now the future reality of God's reign. Being compassionate, using honest speech, refraining from judging others, continuing unbroken marital fidelity, and demonstrating acts of reconciliation even with the enemy are the kinds of actions and commitments that reflect God's own justice or "righteousness" and will be characteristic of life within the reign of God.

c.) Within the array of dispositions and actions commended by Jesus in the Sermon, reconciliation, forgiveness, and love even of the enemy stand at the center and provide orientation for all the rest. For Matthew's Jesus, all interpretation of the law and all human actions and relationships are to be ruled by the love command; this, ultimately, fulfills the law and the prophets.

d.) Despite the Sermon's consistent emphasis on action as the guarantee of genuine faith and the criterion of final judgment, Matthew's theology is not a "works" theology. Jesus' proclamation of the kingdom of God and the dramatic summary of his healing ministry that preface the Sermon (4:23-25), as well as the emphasis on prayer that stands at its center (6:5-15), show that God's enabling grace is a fundamental assumption for faith in Jesus and for the disciples' ability to follow the way of righteousness.

These theological perspectives should guide interpretation of the Sermon. The teachings of Jesus in the Sermon, though calling for heroic response, are not intended to be "impossible ideals" even though complete fulfillment of these demands may be apparent only in the final age. Nor are they meant to underscore human sinfulness, even though the Gospel is aware that the disciples are of "little faith" and capable of only partial response to Jesus' commands. Nor does the specificity and concreteness of Jesus' teaching disqualify these teachings as ethical norms even though they require thoughtful interpretation. Rather, the concreteness of Jesus' demands ("turn the other cheek," "leave your gift at the altar," "do not judge," and so on) may be best understood as "ethics by example" (Luz 1995, 54-55) or "focal instances" (Cahill 1987, 144-56) indicating how the teachings of Jesus are to be carried out. Jesus' teachings often stand in deliberate tension with the way we usually live and think. The directions in the Sermon prompt the reader to extend the examples in Jesus' teachings to other circumstances and actions. Even while recognizing that the array of moral actions available to an individual or community at any given time may be limited, the moral force of Jesus' teaching guides the disciple toward that course of action that is most in accord with God's will.

Jesus the Healer (8:1–9:35)

With the Sermon on the Mount concluded, Matthew now turns to the other fundamental dimension of his portrayal of Jesus signaled in the summary of 4:23: his work as healer. The crowds, who already experienced Jesus' extraordinary healing power at the beginning of the Sermon (4:24-25) and have been amazed at his words (7:28), are now in view again as Jesus descends the mountain (8:1). The evangelist will narrate ten miracle stories in these two chapters to illustrate Jesus' extraordinary power and authority; at the same time, a related emphasis on discipleship also begins to emerge.

All but one of the miracle stories are in parallel with Mark. The story of the healing of the centurion's servant (8:5-13; cf. Luke 7:1-10) as well as the material on discipleship (8:18-22; cf. Luke 9:57-62) are from Q. Although showing contact with the Markan order in these stories, Matthew sets out his own distinctive arrangement. In the cluster of stories taken from Mark's account of Jesus' first day of healing in Capernaum (1:21-45), Matthew makes the dramatic cure of the leper the first of Jesus' actions instead of the last (cf. Mark 1:40-45 and Matt 8:1-4). Matthew resumes Mark's sequence in the next group of stories that parallel Mark 4–5 (cf. Matt 8:23-34 and Mark 4:35–5:20). The series of narratives and sayings in Matt 9:1-17 parallels Mark 2:1-22. The next segment of material—the story of the woman with the hemorrhage and the raising of Jairus's daughter—picks up the remaining material in chapter 5 of Mark (cf. Matt 9:18-26 and Mark 5:21-43). The final story in Matthew's last series of three (Matt 9:27-31) is a version of Mark 10:46-52. The concluding incident of the cure of a mute demoniac (Matt 9:32-33) seems to be a doublet of 12:22-24 (see also Luke 11:14-15) and is less a full-blown miracle story than a peg on which to hang the contrasting reactions of the leaders and the crowds.

The thesis of H. J. Held continues to be influential in that Matthew arranged the stories in three groups of three, each with a dominant motif. The motif of Christology seems to dominate the first segment of three miracles (8:1-17), climaxing in the formula citation of 8:17. In the next section, 8:18–9:17, motifs of discipleship are key. And in the final segment, 9:18-34, emphasis falls on the issue of "praying faith." Held stressed, however, that these themes cannot be taken in a mutually exclusive sense because they "not only overlap in actual content but they occur in each single story overlapping each other in some way or other" (Held 1963, 169). This caution is important, for while Matthew's focus on the authority of Jesus is particularly evident in 8:1-17, it remains strong throughout both chapters of this section. Likewise, motifs of discipleship (with its essential relationship to faith in Jesus) and mission weave throughout the material.

Matthew also substantially reduces the narrative detail in the healing stories. As I will note in the commentary below, this is not haphazard editing, but rather focuses the stories on christological concerns.

At the outset Matthew sets the scene in Capernaum, the town in Galilee that is the center point of Jesus' ministry (4:13). Jesus appears to be on his way to Capernaum as the first story, the cure of the leper, takes place (see 8:5). As he enters the town he is confronted by the centurion (8:5-13) and then enters Peter's house where he cures the apostle's mother-in-law (8:14-16). Jesus leaves Capernaum to go "to the other side" of the sea for the healing of the Gadarenes (8:18) but immediately returns again to "his own town" (9:1). Matthew gives the reader the impression that the next several incidents—the cure of the paralytic, the call of Matthew, the discussion about fasting, the cure of the woman with the hemorrhage, and the raising of Jairus's daughter—all take place in Capernaum, too, although the geographical references are vague. Only in 9:27 are we informed that Jesus "went on from there," implying that he was leaving his hometown, a point made explicit in the summary of 9:35: "Then Jesus went about all the cities and villages."

For the time being, therefore, Matthew portrays Jesus exercising his mission of healing only to Israel and within the confines of his "hometown." The excursion across the sea to the land of the Gadarenes is the only exception and, as we will note below, even here Matthew mutes this journey of Jesus into Gentile territory. Yet this incident, and particularly the encounter with the centurion, are enough to remind the reader that Jesus' mission will one day no longer be confined to the "lost sheep of the house of Israel."

◊ ◊ ◊ ◊

Jesus the Healing Servant (8:1-17)

Three healing stories, concluding with a summary and a fulfillment quotation, make up this first segment. Perhaps taking his cue from Mark (1:21-34), Matthew presents this as a full day of healing, beginning with Jesus' descent from the mountain (8:1) and concluding in the evening with a number of exorcisms (8:16). The thrust of Matthew's presentation is clearly to emphasize Jesus' power to heal and yet, with the exception of Simon's mother-in-law, the sick or those associated with them also take initiative to seek out Jesus.

Matthew may have moved the story of the leper (8:1-4) to first place in the series because of the significance of leprosy as an illness within the purity laws (see Lev 13–14). Apparently some kind of serious skin disease (different from modern leprosy or Hansen's disease), the contagion and highly visible impact of biblical leprosy gave it a potent symbolic dimension, the aura of death itself. To avoid contamination, therefore, the leper was banned from social contact and, in the event of a cure, had to undergo elaborate verification by the priests before being allowed back into the community. This backdrop is not elaborated on by Matthew's version of the story, but would be evident to the biblically literate reader and raises the stakes in the healing story. Matthew emphasizes the reverential approach of the leper in a way that will characterize a number of this Gospel's healing stories (e.g., 9:18; 15:25): He came forward and "knelt" (*proskynein,* a characteristic Matthean word implying profound homage; see, e.g., 14:33) in front of Jesus and addressed him as "Lord" (*kyrie,* a title emphasizing the authority of Jesus). The leper's request is also deferential: "If you choose, you can make me clean" (8:2).

Jesus' response is direct and powerful (the extraordinary emotional response in Mark 1:41, *splangchnistheis* [literally, "his bowels churned"] is omitted). Jesus extends his hands in a gesture of authority, touches the man (touch was a typical healing gesture in the ancient world), and declares: "I do choose. Be made clean!" (8:3). Instantly the man is cleansed of his leprosy. Following the lead in Mark's story, Matthew has Jesus send the man directly to the priests to certify that his healing complied with the commands of Lev 14. This detail meshes well with Matthew's perspective in that it illustrates that Jesus acts in accord with the law (as Matthew will emphasize in later stories, such as in 12:1-8). Although the leper's bold action in approaching Jesus, as well as Jesus' touching the leper, might be interpreted as contrary to the stipulations of Leviticus, Matthew's story does not make these points.

The healing of the centurion's servant is from Q (Matt 8:5-13; Luke 7:1-10, with echoes in John 4:46-54). In Luke's version, Jewish elders act as intermediaries on behalf of a righteous Gentile who has been a generous benefactor to the community. And even when the centurion wants to communicate directly with Jesus he does so through "friends" (Luke 7:6). But in Matthew's version Jesus directly interacts with the Gentile centurion who appeals on behalf of his servant who is "at home" paralyzed. Here, too, issues of cultic purity lurk just beneath the surface and heighten the drama of the story. In this case the purity issue would be that of entering a Gentile dwelling and touching an ill Gentile. Whether or not Matthew intends to direct the reader's attention to this issue depends in part on whether one interprets his words to the centurion as a question or a statement—both of which are possible in the Greek. If the former ("Am I to come and cure him?"), the story may suggest Jesus' hesitation or perhaps even annoyance at such a request. If, as most commentators assume, Jesus' words are a statement ("I will come and cure him"), then the focus shifts to the extraordinary faith of the centurion and Jesus' ability to heal at a distance with a mere word.

The centurion's response is fully respectful of Jesus' authority: He addresses Jesus as "Lord" (just as the leper had done), confesses his own unworthiness, and states his conviction that Jesus can heal his servant with only a word. The centurion's comparison with his own role as a commander makes Matthew's point. The centurion is "under authority" (the Greek term *exousia,* used frequently in healing stories, means "power" or "authority"—the phrase "under authority" may mean he is "authorized" to command) and therefore able to give commands to his soldiers and presume their obedience. Jesus has the same power over illness and evil spirits.

The faith of this Gentile centurion exceeds that which Jesus has experienced in Israel (8:10). Here Matthew seems to anticipate later parts of the Gospel narrative. Although Jesus had urged the disciples to go beyond the "righteousness" of the scribes and Pharisees (5:20) and criticized the false piety of the "hypocrites" (6:1-18), the leaders had not yet expressly rejected Jesus (see, however, 9:3). But the faith of this Gentile centurion triggers in Jesus a vision of a future that involves both Israel's rejection of Jesus and the inclusion of Gentiles. Matthew appends to the healing story the Q sayings of verses 11-13 (see Luke 13:28-29), which foresee the nations coming "from east and west" and sitting at table "with Abraham and Isaac and Jacob in the kingdom of heaven." The procession of the nations to Israel, either as captives or in docile reverence, was a motif of the prophetic literature promising Israel's vindication in the end time (e.g., Isa 2:2-4; Mic 4:1-4; Zech 8:20-23). A similar motif is the gathering of the scattered Israelites from the "east and west" (i.e., the Diaspora), a theme sometimes coupled with the notion of the messianic banquet (Isa 25:6 speaks of the banquet on Zion to which all peoples stream; Ps 107:3 refers to a gathering from the four points of the compass; similarly Isa 43:5-6). While the original context of these Q sayings may have implied that the scattered Diaspora Israelites would reply to the gospel more readily than those privileged to live in the land ("the sons of the kingdom"; see Davies and Allison 1991, 27-28), the present context in Matthew's Gospel applies this contrast to the inclusion of the Gentiles. Those in Israel who reject Jesus will experience judgment; the notion of being thrown into the "outer darkness" and the image of "weeping and gnashing of teeth" are typical judgment metaphors in Matthew (see 13:42, 50; 22:13; 24:51; 25:30). This conviction of Matthew will become clear as the Gospel unfolds.

The conclusion of the story reaffirms the fundamental motifs of this part of the Gospel by illustrating both the extraordinary power of Jesus to heal, both with a word and at a distance, and the exemplary faith of the centurion (8:13).

The third story in this section, the cure of Simon's mother-in-law (8:14-15), fixes its attention on Jesus' power to heal. As in the centurion story, Matthew's editing screens out intermediaries; no longer do "they" (presumably in Mark, Simon, Andrew, James, and John; see Mark 1:29-30) tell Jesus about the woman but Jesus himself "sees" her (Matt 8:14). He "touched her hand" and the fever left her. Now cured, she "got up" (the term *ēgerthē* is reminiscent of resurrection vocabulary; see 28:6, 7 and elsewhere) and "began to serve him." In Mark the cured woman serves "them" (1:31). Coupled with the verb "to serve" *(diakonein)*, Matthew's formulation implies an attitude of reverent homage and service directed at Jesus (see, e.g., 4:11; 20:28; 25:44; 27:55), which is more than ordinary hospitality. Thus the faith that drove the leper and the centurion to approach Jesus for healing in the first two stories is matched here by the faithful response of Simon's mother-in-law to the experience of healing.

This segment closes with a summary (8:16) and a fulfillment quotation (8:17). Matthew's summary is terse (cf. Mark 1:32-34), indicating that the three previous stories are only samples of much more extensive healings and exorcisms carried out by Jesus, including ones done "with a word" as in the case of the centurion's servant. The recapitulation of Jesus' healing activity leads into the fulfillment quotation from Isa 53:4. The typical introductory formula stresses that Jesus' healing activity "fulfills" the Scriptures. Here the implied "narrator" of the Gospel enters the text to underscore this fundamental Matthean perspective. The formula cites Isaiah, the prophet who proclaimed salvation to Israel and who is a favored source of Matthean citations. Typical of many of the fulfillment quotations in Matthew, this citation is identical to neither the Septuagint (Greek) nor the Masoretic (Hebrew) texts known to us. It is likely that Matthew has freely quoted the passage to harmonize it with the immediate context of the Gospel. Thus the first half of the quotation emphasizes the healing activity just narrated: Jesus "takes away" (not simply "has borne") "our physical illnesses" (the specific sense of the word *astheneias* used by Matthew). The second phrase, "and bore our diseases," moves more in the direction of the vicarious suffering exemplified in the servant motif. In Matthew's perspective, the identification of Jesus with the sufferings of the community is a recurring motif (see, e.g., 10:24-25, 40-42; 25:31-46, as well as the recapitulation of Israel's sufferings experienced by the infant Jesus in chap. 2). This portrayal of Jesus as the servant who bears the sufferings of the community may also be a hint of the Passion that Jesus will yet endure.

Healings Around the Sea (8:18–9:8)

A second set of three healings takes place in the context of Jesus' journey across the Sea of Galilee. Held pointed to the motif of discipleship as dominant in this section, but Matthew's focus on Christology and mission also continues.

The press of the crowds (8:18; a motif probably drawn from Mark's summary in 1:32-33) prompts Jesus to journey to the other side of the lake. At this point Matthew interjects some Q sayings about discipleship that give a new context to the story of the stilling of the storm that will immediately follow (8:19-22; cf. Luke 9:57-62). Two would-be disciples approach Jesus before the departure to the other side and in response Jesus makes strong declarations on the demands of following him. The first to approach, a scribe, perhaps unwittingly lays out the issue: "Teacher, I will follow you wherever you go." Jesus' response emphasizes the itinerant life of the "Son of Man" who has "nowhere to lay his head." The second to approach is already a "disciple" who makes what seems a most appropriate request (addressing Jesus properly as "Lord"), to first go and bury his father, a primary obligation of Jewish piety (see, e.g., Tob 1:16-20). The prophet Elisha had requested of his mentor Elijah to be able to "kiss my father and my mother" before leaving them and the request was granted (1 Kgs 19:20). Jesus' response, "Let the dead bury their own dead," is somewhat enigmatic (i.e., who are the "dead"?) but its basic thrust is clear—even such a profound familial obligation cannot take preference over the call to discipleship. In Matthew the itinerant life of Jesus and his disciples, who for the sake of the gospel travel unburdened by possessions or family ties, remained a compelling ideal (see 4:18-22; 10:9-11; 19:16-22).

The rigors of discipleship implied in Jesus' sayings begin to be illustrated in the sea story that immediately follows (8:23-27). At the same time, Matthew's focus on Christology is clearly on display. Matthew's rendition of this story makes it a nearly allegorical portrayal of Jesus' protection of the community in travail (cf. Mark 4:35-41 for whom this story is another instance of the disciples' inability to understand Jesus). As Jesus enters the boat, Matthew notes that "his disciples followed him" (8:23). Once at sea, a "great earthquake" (the literal meaning of *seismos megas* translated by the NRSV as "a windstorm") breaks out and threatens the boat (8:24) while Jesus sleeps tranquilly. Calling the storm an "earthquake" may imply that this turbulence is akin to the cataclysms that will accompany the end time (see 24:7; 27:51; 28:2). Matthew treats the disciples' peril as a kind of healing story: They "approach" Jesus as the leper and the centurion had done and cry out with a terrified prayer of supplication, "Lord, save us! We are perishing!" (8:25). Jesus' response is both a reassurance and a reproach expressed in typical Matthean terms—"Why are you afraid, you of little faith?" (8:26). "Fear" and "little faith" are virtually synonymous in Matthew (see also 14:31; Matthew uses the term "little faith" repeatedly: see 6:30; 16:8; 17:20). Jesus then stands up and in a manner similar to an exorcism "rebukes" the winds and the sea, bringing about a "dead calm" (8:26).

The story ends with the amazed question: "What sort of man is this, that even the winds and the sea obey him?" (8:27). While this stops short of the dramatic confession of Jesus the disciples will make at the end of a later sea story (14:33), Matthew's formulation—*what sort of* man is this . . . ?—guides the biblically literate reader to the story's point. Within the biblical world, the fearsome power of the sea was associated with demonic forces. To exert power over the sea was, therefore, a symptom of the divine presence (see, e.g., the famous passage in Ps 107:23-32; likewise Pss 74:12-14; 89:9-12; Job, and so on; Isa 51:9-10 calls upon God to "awake" and overcome the sea as at the moment of creation and at the crossing of the sea during the Exodus). The so-called "nature" miracles here and in 14:23-33 enable Matthew to portray Jesus in profound christological tones and to anticipate what this Gospel sees as the abiding relationship between the Risen Christ and the community in the period leading up to the consummation of the age (see 28:16-20; cf. 24:1-31).

For the first and perhaps the only time in Matthew's Gospel, Jesus and his disciples venture into Gentile territory, crossing the sea to the "country of the Gadarenes" (8:28-34; in 15:21 Jesus approaches the district of Tyre and Sidon but does not seem to cross over into this Gentile region). Although this was an area where both Jews and Gentiles lived, Matthew and Mark present it as a Gentile region by locating it in the Decapolis, a loose confederation of hellenistic cities originally founded in the wake of Alexander's conquest of the region, and by including the reference to a herd of pigs, animals considered unclean in Jewish law and therefore obviously associated with Gentiles. Even though the journey to this "foreign" shore is a significant step, Matthew seems hesitant to exploit it (cf. Mark 5:18-20 omitted by Matthew). While undoubtedly Matthew views this as an incursion into Gentile territory, it is still only a preview of the later mission. The demons themselves sense this as they ask of Jesus, "Have you come here to torment us *before the time?*" (Matt 8:29, emphasis added).

Matthew's version of the story is much shorter than Mark's and keeps its focus on the power of Jesus. (In Mark there is a single tormented demoniac who lived in the tombs; Matthew has "two"; see a similar tendency to double in 20:29-34; cf. Mark 10:46-52.) At the conclusion of the story the crowds come out "to meet Jesus" (in Mark's version they come to see "what . . . had happened") and when they see him they ask him to leave their territory, possibly a reaction of awe and fear at his power. Note, too, that Matthew locates this story differently than Mark. Even though there are a number of variants in the manuscripts, Mark seems to identify the location as Gerasa (5:1), a Decapolis city several miles from the Sea of Galilee and therefore a location hard to reconcile with the details of the story. Matthew, on the other hand, seems better informed about the geography, locating the story more plausibly at Gadara, which is closer to the lake, and thus covers the problem of the herd's plunge into the sea by situating them "at some distance" from Gadara itself.

Jesus and his disciples cross back over the sea to Capernaum ("his own town," 9:1) where Jesus will encounter the paralytic, the final healing in this series of three (9:1-8). As in the previous story, Matthew's version is far leaner than Mark's, omitting all of the colorful details about the friends of the paralytic lowering the pallet to Jesus through the roof (cf. Mark 2:1-12). Now the focus is on Jesus' cure of the paralytic, and the conflict that follows, the first of many in the Gospel. While in previous stories the initiative is from the sick, in this instance the *friends* of the paralytic bring him to Jesus. Their active faith is what moves Jesus to care for the paralytic, first forgiving his sins and then healing him ("[seeing]

their faith," 9:2). As in Mark's story, healing and forgiveness of sin are interwoven. The biblical world saw sickness and even death itself as somehow symptomatic of evil. Sickness, in this view, was not necessarily the fault of the person afflicted, but ultimately all sickness and death could be traced to the noxious power of evil. "Sin" in this sense is broader and deeper than an individual's culpable acts; it is a mortal condition that holds all human beings in its grip and only the power of God can overcome it. Jesus, therefore, first moves to forgive the man's sins. Matthew had already prepared the reader for this power of Jesus, indeed the very name "Jesus" designated him as one sent to "save his people from their sins" (1:21) and at the Last Supper Jesus declares that his shedding of blood is "for the forgiveness of sins" (26:28). But some "scribes," the first of Jesus' opponents to emerge, interpret this as "blaspheming," that is, appropriating for himself authority that belonged to God alone (Mark 2:7, in a detail omitted by Matthew, explains "blasphemy" in precisely this way: "Who can forgive sins but God alone?"). Jesus, "perceiving their thoughts," challenges their disbelief and heals the paralytic as a demonstration of his authority both to forgive sins and to heal (9:5). The "Son of Man" has authority on earth to forgive sins. This enigmatic title will be used by Matthew to describe the humiliations and sufferings of Jesus (e.g., 8:21; 17:12; 20:18, 28; 26:2, 45) and to depict his triumphant return at the End of time (e.g., 16:27; 24:27, 30, 37, 39, 44; 25:31; 26:64). In this instance, Jesus exhibits now the divine power that will be manifestly his in his final exaltation (see 28:16-20).

The story ends in triumph. The paralytic obeys Jesus' command, by standing up, healed, and then returning to his home (a form of *egeirein*, again reminiscent of resurrection vocabulary; see above, 8:15), while the "crowds" are filled with "awe" and "glorified God, who had given such authority to human beings" (9:8). By "human beings" Matthew may mean a collective reference to the power given to Jesus, but the implication is more likely that the community itself is now entrusted with the power to forgive as well as heal (see, e.g., the power of "binding and loosing" given to Peter and the community in 16:19; 18:19).

Healings in Capernaum and Beyond (9:9-35)

Held considers "praying faith" the dominant motif of this final triad, as illustrated, for example, in the story of the woman with the hemorrhage (9:18-26; see Held 1963, 165-299), but the story of the call of Matthew (9:9-13) and the question about fasting and its aftermath (9:14-17) prevent this section from being reduced to any single motif.

Matthew's version of the call of Matthew the tax collector and its aftermath is close to that of Mark (see Mark 2:13-17), but has its own twists. Just as the protests of the scribes about Jesus' forgiving the sins of the paralytic led to a programmatic statement of his mission, so here, too, the protests of the Pharisees about Jesus' association with "tax collectors and sinners" results in an affirmation of his fundamental mission to the unrighteous.

The initial call of Matthew is told in the same absolute terms that marked that of the first disciples by the sea (4:18-22): At Jesus' compelling invitation, Matthew "follows" him without hesitation (the word for "follow" is *akolouthein,* a near technical term for discipleship in the synoptic Gospels). The new disciple is named "Matthew" (versus "Levi" in Mark). The reason for this is not certain. Perhaps the evangelist thereby signaled the association of the apostle Matthew with this Gospel or at least the community that produced it (see the introduction), or perhaps he wanted the character in this story to be one of the twelve and the list available to him included no "Levi" but did have a "Matthew" (the "tax collector"; see Matt 10:3).

As exemplary as this call story may be, the main interest of the passage comes in the subsequent verses. Jesus' dining with many "tax collectors and sinners" brings a protest from the Pharisees about such association with the unclean. Capernaum at the time of Jesus was, in fact, a border town between the areas ruled by Herod Antipas and Herod Philip, so the location of a tax (or more likely a toll) collector there has verisimilitude. Because of their role as agents of the rulers, and ultimately of the Romans whose vassals the rulers were, and also because of their necessary interaction with Gentiles and Gentile baggage and goods, tax collectors were considered to be among those who were chronically unobservant of the law and thus to be identified with the generic "sinners." The historical Jesus' compassionate association with non-observant Jews, including dining with them, was one of the hallmarks of his ministry and a source of conflict with his opponents, as this story reflects.

The protest of the Pharisees about Jesus' behavior is addressed to his disciples (in Matthew the Pharisees refer to Jesus as "teacher"), but Jesus himself responds with a pointed aphorism: "Those who are well have no need of a physician, but those who are sick" (9:12). This saying links the call of Matthew and its aftermath with the surrounding context of Jesus' healings. Even though in this instance a physical cure is not at stake, Jesus' association with sinners and inclusion of them in his mission is treated as equivalent to the salvation brought through his healing. Underlying this connection is a keen awareness in ancient medicine of the social implications of both illness and healing. As the stories of the leper and the Gadarene demoniacs already indicated, illness and demonic possession often meant isolation and exclusion while healing involved reconnection with the community through the mediation of the healer or exorcist.

Jesus' final words to the Pharisees are found only in Matthew and are of critical importance to this Gospel's perspective. Jesus tells the leaders, "Go and learn what this means, 'I desire mercy, not sacrifice.' For I have come to call not the righteous but sinners" (9:13). The citation is based on Hos 6:6 (it will be repeated in Matt 12:7) and implies that cultic impurity, while retaining its importance, is subordinate to the demands of mercy and compassion (see an explicit statement of this principle applied to the tithe in Matt 23:23). Therefore, Jesus' actions of calling Matthew and associating with tax collectors and sinners are not contrary to the law but in accord with it. By having Jesus teach this to the religious leaders ("Go and learn what this means . . .") Matthew illustrates that it is Jesus (and by implication, his community) and not his opponents who exemplify authentic obedience to the law.

The somewhat enigmatic exchange between John's disciples and Jesus over the issue of fasting was already connected to this section in Mark (see 2:18-22). Matthew edits the material and turns in the direction of his own perspective. Presumably Matthew's community continued the traditional Jewish practice of fasting (see, e.g., Lev 16:1-34), as the instructions in 6:1-18 imply. This is reflected in Matthew's nuanced phrasing of the question: "Why do we and the Pharisees fast *often* . . . ?" (9:14). By implication the issue is now the intensity and motivation for fasting, not fasting as such. And while fasting is under discussion here, it is really the identity of Jesus as the "bridegroom" that is at stake. The eschatological banquet was a biblical metaphor for the fulfillment of Israel's hopes (see, e.g., Isa 25:6-10 and similarly in 2 Bar 29:3-8; *1 Enoch* 62:14), and marriage imagery was applied to the relationship of God and Israel (see especially Hos 1–3; Isa 62:5). Now Jesus is portrayed as the "bridegroom" of that messianic banquet (see also the parables of Matt 22:1-14; 25:1-13).

Mark's account had already interpreted fasting as an act of mourning in the absence of Jesus (see 2:20). Matthew carries this over into Jesus' reply: "The wedding guests cannot *mourn* as long as the bridegroom is with them, can they?" (9:15, emphasis added). The days will come when Jesus is "taken away." Then the disciples ("the guests" at the wedding feast) can fast—another reminder of Jesus' impending death. For Matthew the "absence" of Jesus from the community through his death is actually brief, since the Risen Christ returns to his community at the conclusion of the Gospel and promises to remain with his disciples until the End of time (28:16-20).

The sayings about the cloth and the wineskins (9:16-17) are only loosely attached to the question of fasting, but the impact of Jesus as the Messiah moves through all of these images. Matthew's concern (different from Mark's version of the same material; see Mark 2:21-22) is that in each instance the old need not be conserved, but must make way for the new. Thus patching new and unshrunken cloth on an old garment risks making a worse tear, and putting new wine into old wineskins risks having the skins burst and be destroyed. But when "new wine is put into fresh wineskins . . . *both are preserved*" (9:17, emphasis added). Although Matthew struggles with the limits of these metaphors, the underlying thought of accepting the new while not destroying the old has echoes in other key texts (see 5:17; 13:52) and reflects a fundamental concern to portray Jesus as in continuity with Israel while bringing Israel to new and decisive fulfillment.

As in Mark, the stories of the ruler's daughter and the woman with the hemorrhage are entwined (9:18-26). The ruler approaches Jesus reverently, "kneeling" before him (see the same action of the leper in 8:2 and the Canaanite woman in 15:25). Matthew anticipates the climax of the story and thereby intensifies its drama—the ruler's daughter is not simply "at the point of death" (as in Mark 5:23), but is already dead. Even so, the man believes that Jesus can touch her and bring her back to life, a strong demonstration of his faith. As Jesus leaves with his disciples to follow the ruler to his house, there is another demonstration of suppliant faith. A woman suffering from a hemorrhage for twelve years comes up behind Jesus and touches the "fringe" of his cloak (a detail not found in Mark's version [5:27, but see 6:56] that reveals Matthew's awareness of Jewish customs; see Num 15:38-39; Deut 22:12; and the reference to such tassels in Matt 23:5). Matthew's version omits the colorful details found in Mark about Jesus' sensing that power had streamed out from him yet not knowing who had touched him, and the fearful reaction of the woman as she comes forward to confess that she was the one (Mark 5:29-33). In Matthew, the exchange between the woman and Jesus is untroubled and Jesus is fully in control of what is happening. The healing takes place only after Jesus' endorsement of her act of faith (9:22).

Once at the ruler's house, Jesus moves swiftly to raise the ruler's daughter from the dead. Yet another detail gives a Jewish flavor to Matthew's story—the flute (or clarinet) was an instrument played at times of mourning (see *J. W.* 3.437; *m. Ketub* 4.4). Matthew notes that there were "flute players" among the mourners at the house (9:23). The skepticism of the crowd ("they laughed at him") only underscores the awesome power of Jesus that Matthew describes with an economy of words: "He . . . took her by her hand, and the girl got up" (the verb *egertheis*, "to rise," associated with resurrection, is once again used by Matthew in healing contexts; see above, 8:15).

The final healing in this third triad of stories is a cure of two blind men (9:27-31). This is a near carbon copy of the story in Matt 20:29-34, which in turn is inspired by Mark 10:46-52. Once again Matthew screens out details to focus on the essential action of the story. The two blind men plead with Jesus for mercy, addressing him as "Son of David." This messianic title favored by Matthew and already cited in the opening verse of the Gospel (1:1) is used several times in healing contexts (see 12:23; 15:22; 20:30, 31) as well as to acclaim Jesus as he enters Jerusalem in a humble manner (21:9, 15). Thus the narrative contexts in which Jesus is described as "Son of David" define his messianic power as that of compassion and humility (a point made by Matthew's fulfillment quotation in 21:4-5). Matthew also retains his focus on faith in this story. He situates the cure in a house (9:28, perhaps also wanting to identify the location as still in Capernaum; see 8:14) and, in typical fashion for healing stories in Matthew, they "approach" Jesus. Jesus' question to them as well as his final words concentrate on the issue of their faith in Jesus' power to heal: "Do you believe that I am able to do this?" Their response is perfect: "Yes, Lord" (kyrie, a title used repeatedly in Matthew to express reverent homage in contexts of healing or rescue; see 8:2, 6, 8, 25; 14:28, 30; 15:22, 25, 27; 17:15; 20:31, 33). And in accord with their faith they are healed (9:29).

The story ends with Jesus attempting in vain to suppress report of the miracle (9:30-31, a theme taken over from Mark; see, e.g., 1:45; 3:12; 5:43). By this device Matthew highlights the widening impact of Jesus' mission (9:26, 31) and prepares for the conclusion of this entire section of the Gospel. One more healing is cited, that of a mute demoniac (see Luke 11:14-15 and a doublet in Matt 12:22-24), but Matthew shows little interest in the story itself except to further reinforce the contrasting reactions of the crowds and the Pharisees. The crowds marvel that "never has anything like this been seen in Israel"—an acclamation that reflects the strong christological tones of Matthew's narrative—but the Pharisees take a diametrically opposed interpretation, that Jesus is in league with the "ruler of the demons" (see the same phrase in Mark 3:22).

In 9:35 Matthew repeats the summary, first stated in 4:23, which serves as the keynote for the entire portrayal of Jesus' mission in chapters 5 through 9. Jesus' teaching on the mountain and his healing activity in the environs of Capernaum described in these chapters are only samples of his messianic mission taken to "all the cities and villages."

◊ ◊ ◊ ◊

Chapters 8 and 9 demonstrate that, for Matthew's Gospel, healing is an essential dimension of Jesus' messianic ministry, on a par with his authoritative teaching. Through his teaching Jesus fulfilled the law and the prophets (5:17), revealing that the intent and guiding principle of the Torah is the love command. Through his healings Jesus embodied the mercy and compassion that characterized his teaching and fulfilled the law (8:17; 9:13). The mission discourse of chapter 10 will further illustrate the importance of healing as an expression of the Christian ministry.

In this section Matthew keeps his focus on Christology and discipleship. Jesus' profound authority and power extend even to the stilling of the demonic power of the sea and the raising of the dead. An amazing array of titles appears in the section and further defines the depths of Jesus' identity for Matthew: As Son of David Jesus exerts his royal power with compassion and mercy; as Son of Man he is endowed with the authority to forgive sins; the sick appeal to him with reverence, kneeling and addressing him as "Lord"; the Gadarene demoniacs defer to him as "Son of God" and acknowledge his power over the demonic; the fulfillment quotation of 8:17 portrays him as God's servant liberating people from their infirmities and bearing their illnesses; and the sayings of 9:15 present Jesus as the "bridegroom" of the eschatological wedding feast.

The proper response to such an awesome presence is also stressed by Matthew. The question the dazed disciples ask in the aftermath of the stilling of the storm is an underlying question of this entire section: "What sort of a man is this?" (8:27). As many of the sick do, one is to approach Jesus in reverent homage, kneeling in supplication and crying out in prayer, and be animated by tenacious, determined faith in the power of Jesus to save one from evil. This kind of faith characterizes the sick who come to Jesus, including the Gentile centurion whose response amazes Jesus (8:10). The crowds, too, are amazed at Jesus' power (9:8) and acclaim that "never has anything like this been seen in Israel" (9:33).

But Matthew warns the reader that not all respond with firm faith. The would-be disciples who approach Jesus before crossing the lake apparently underestimate the cost of discipleship. And the scribes and Pharisees play the role of implacable opposition to Jesus, going so far as to interpret his healings as a symptom of his covenant with Satan (9:34).

The Mission Discourse (9:36–11:1)

The mission discourse serves as the conclusion to Matthew's epic portrayal of Jesus' mission that began in 4:23. Jesus' call of the twelve and his mission charge to them extend Jesus' ministry to the "lost sheep of the house of Israel." What had been implicit in these previous chapters now becomes explicit: The words and deeds of Jesus are intended as model and instruction for the community.

The formal call of the twelve and part of their mission instruction are drawn from Mark 3:13-19 and 6:8-11. The warnings about suffering and persecution are transposed from Mark's apocalyptic discourse where they describe the future opposition the community would face as it carried out its mission in the period before the coming of the Son of Man (Matt 10:17-25; Mark 13:9-13). Other sayings come from Q, such as the exhortations not to fear and assurances about God's provident care for the missionaries (Matt 10:26-33; Luke 12:2-9), the warnings about family divisions (Matt 10:34-36; Luke 12:51-53), and the primacy of discipleship over family ties (Matt 10:37-39; Luke 14:25-27; 17:33).

Although he draws on traditional material for most of its content, Matthew gives the discourse its overall structure and suffuses it with his perspective. A narrative segment (9:36–10:4) serves as a transition from the previous section on Jesus' healing ministry and, with the call of the twelve, sets the stage for the discourse proper. The discourse itself is rather loosely structured, with sayings clustered around dominant motifs. "Amen" sayings (10:15, 23, 42) punctuate major sections and may provide a formal basis for dividing the discourse into three parts (see Weaver 1990, 73-74): (1) basic instructions for the mission to Israel, 10:5-15; (2) warnings about persecutions and divisions, 10:16-23; and (3) exhortations based on trust in God and loyalty to Jesus, 10:24-42. Matthew's characteristic formula (11:1) bridges the transition from the discourse to the narrative that follows.

◊ ◊ ◊ ◊

The Plight of the People and the Call of the Twelve (9:36–10:4)

Matthew had concluded the previous section with a summary of Jesus' mission of teaching and healing throughout all the cities and towns of Israel (9:35). Now the stage is set for channeling that mission to the disciples whose ministry will be presented as an extension of Jesus' own.

Jesus' compassion for the crowds who are "harassed and helpless, like sheep without a shepherd" leads him ultimately to summon the twelve for mission (9:36). Matthew is quite consistent with this. The Sermon on the Mount had also been prompted by the sight of the crowds who had come from all over Israel and beyond its borders seeking healing (4:24–5:1). The presence of the crowds was also noted at the beginning of Jesus' healing ministry in 8:1 and the crowds acclaimed Jesus at the conclusion of his healing work in 9:33. The verb "moved with compassion" (Gk. *esplangchnisthē;* a verb already used in Mark 1:41 to describe Jesus' response to the leper) is quite vivid, literally meaning the stirring of one's bowels, which were considered the source of emotions. Jesus' being "moved with compassion" for the crowds is a recurring motif in Matthew (see 14:14; 15:32; also his reaction to the blind men in 20:34; the same verb describes the king's compassion for the indebted servant in a parable unique to Matthew, 18:27).

Matthew uses two traditional images to describe the plight of the crowds—"sheep without a shepherd" and the ready "harvest."

The image of "sheep without a shepherd" is applied in the Old Testament to Israel bereft of leadership as in Num 27:17 (see also 1 Kgs 22:17; 2 Chr 18:16; Zech 13:7). The classic text of Ezek 34 is an indictment of the leaders of Israel as shepherds who leave the sheep abandoned and vulnerable. Matthew, drawing on Mark 14:31, will later cite Zech 13:7 to apply the same image to the condition of the disciples once Jesus has been "struck" (see Matt 26:31), and the parable of the lost sheep who is sought out by the shepherd echoes the same note (18:12-14). Through this image, therefore, Matthew portrays the people of Israel (the "crowds") as scattered and aimless, a description that may also be an implicit critique of the religious leaders who are meant to be their "shepherds."

The abundant and ready "harvest" (9:37) is also a traditional biblical image for the eschatological judgment (see Isa 18:4; 24:13; 27:12; Jer 51:53; Hos 6:11; Joel 3:13). Matthew will define it precisely in this way in the parable of the wheat and the weeds (see 13:30, 39). Thus the mission of the disciples, like that of Jesus himself who announced that the kingdom of heaven was imminent (4:17), is connected with the eschaton. Importing material from Mark 13 into the body of the discourse will add further eschatological color and urgency to the discourse proper (see 10:17-25). Despite the abundant harvest, the "laborers" are few and therefore Jesus urges his disciples to pray to the "Lord of the harvest" to send out laborers for the harvest. The counsel to turn to prayer for this urgent need harmonizes with his instructions to them in the Sermon on the Mount (7:7-11).

In a masterly fashion, Jesus calls his "twelve disciples" and gives them authority to perform exorcisms and healings (10:1). This is the first time in the Gospel that Matthew has used this number to refer to the band of disciples and it has obvious symbolic reference to the "twelve tribes" of Israel (see 19:28). The numeration of the founding tribes now scattered through deportation evokes the ideal of a reassembled Israel, itself another eschatological hope. This reveals Matthew's underlying vision of Jesus' primary mission: He is sent to the "lost sheep" of the house of Israel (10:6; 15:24) who are bereft of leadership and therefore "harassed and helpless." His twelve apostles will participate in this messianic mission, sent to "all the towns of Israel" (10:23) in the time remaining before the eschaton, and eventually will share even in the final judgment of the reassembled tribes (19:28).

The twelve disciples are given the "authority" to cast out unclean spirits (the Greek word *exousia* used here implies authority in the sense of power) and "to cure every disease and every sickness"—the exact phrase used by Matthew to summarize Jesus' own healing ministry (4:23; 9:35). Matthew's emphasis here on the actions of exorcism and healing without mentioning teaching is intriguing, particularly in view of the attention given to Jesus' teaching in chapters 5–7. Only in 28:20 will the "eleven" be commissioned to "teach." Whether or not Matthew has deliberately suspended this dimension of the Christian mission until the disciples have completed their time with Jesus is difficult to determine.

A list of the "twelve apostles" follows—the only time in the Gospel that Matthew uses this formal designation. The change in term from "disciples" *(mathētai)* to "apostles" (*apostoloi*, meaning ones "sent") is appropriate in this mission context. Matthew's list is drawn from Mark 3:13-19 but adds some characteristic touches. Matthew orders the list in six pairs (pairing Andrew with Peter and identifying him as his brother [see 4:18] and omitting the information about the surname "Boanerges" for James and John; see Mark 3:17). The apostle Matthew is identified as "the tax collector" in line with the story of 9:9.

Although the "twelve" will be mentioned later in Matthew's narrative (see, e.g., 11:1; 20:17; 26:14, 20, 47; and especially 19:28), this entity does not seem to have major significance for Matthew other than as a way of designating Jesus' followers in a manner that evokes the symbolism of the gathered tribes of Israel. In 28:16, for example, Matthew refers to those who remain after Judas's death as "the eleven" (in contrast with Luke who makes the restoration of the "twelve" one of the first activities of the post-Easter community; see Acts 1:15-26). Apparently more significant for Matthew is the term "disciple" as a designation for the followers of Jesus in this Gospel, that is, one who learns and obeys what Jesus has taught (see 28:19-20; cf. 13:52).

Instructions for the Mission to Israel (10:5-15)

The first segment of the discourse, based in part on Mark 6:8-11, is Jesus' mission charge to the apostles. The specific emphasis of Matthew and one that has challenged interpreters is the instruction "Go nowhere among the Gentiles, and enter no town of the Samaritans, but go rather to the lost sheep of the house of Israel" (10:5). This restriction to Israel, and its repeated assertion in 15:24, stands in sharp contrast with the conclusion of the Gospel when the Risen Christ will send the "eleven" to make disciples "of all nations" (28:19). But from the perspective of Matthew's Gospel there is no real contradiction. Jesus' mission is to Israel in fulfillment of God's promise in the Scriptures. A few noteworthy Gentiles cross the screen of the Gospel—the Magi, the centurion in Capernaum, the Gadarene demoniacs, and later the Canaanite woman—but they are only hints of the still unfolding future. Jesus' mission of teaching and healing is first directed to the people of Israel and it is theirs to accept or reject. So, too, would be the mission of the apostles whose ministry is presented as the extension of Jesus' own.

The phrase "lost sheep of the house of Israel" is also significant. It picks up the image of the people as lost sheep who are harassed and helpless as already mentioned in 9:36. The designation "lost sheep" is Matthew's way of referring not to a specific group among the people but to the plight of the entire nation, bereft of leadership and subject to perils of evil.

Matthew leaves no doubt that the apostles' mission mirrors that of Jesus (10:7-8). Thus they are to proclaim the advent of the "kingdom of heaven" (as both John the Baptist and Jesus had; see 3:2; 4:17), and to "cure the sick, raise the dead, cleanse the lepers, [and] cast out demons" (a summation of Jesus' healing activity in chaps. 8–9; see also 11:5-6). As in 10:1, Matthew continues to place singular emphasis on the work of healing and exorcisms in these descriptions of the Christian mission.

The subsequent material describes the manner in which the apostles are to carry out their mission. There is no reason to doubt that these instructions were originally intended as practical guidelines for the itinerant missionaries of Matthew's community. These commands not only portray the missionaries in terms that reflect

Jesus' own style of life, but also serve as a check on potential abuses. The strictures applied to wandering prophets in the *Didache,* a late first-century Christian text (i.e., their stay in any one place, for example, was limited to three days, see *Did.* 12), and Matthew's own warnings about "false prophets" (7:15-23), indicate that charismatic Christians who imitated the itinerant and ascetic life-style of Jesus and preached and healed in his name were not only a source of vitality and inspiration for the early community but in some instances a problem.

The instructions, therefore, forbid payment for the mission; the apostles' own call was a "gift" so they should offer their ministry as a gift (10:8). They are to be equipped with no resources other than the clothes on their back: "no gold, or silver, or copper" (NRSV: "money"; Matthew adds "gold or silver" to Mark's original "copper" coin; cf. Mark 6:8). While Mark's version permits wearing sandals, Matthew's does not (10:10; cf. Mark 6:9). Matthew also makes explicit what is probably implied in Mark, namely that the apostles have a right to be supported with food and hospitality in the communities they visit—"laborers [see 9:37-38] deserve their food." The apostle Paul cites this same expectation, although he himself preferred to maintain his own craft to avoid dependence on anyone (see 1 Cor 9:3-18; 2 Cor 11:7-11; 1 Thess 2:9; 2 Thess 3:7-8).

The support owed the missionary by the communities they visit is not simply a matter of hospitality but is based on the inherent worth of the mission (10:11-15). The missionary is commissioned by Jesus, and as Jesus' representative the missionary embodies Jesus' presence (10:40-42). When entering a town or village, therefore, the missionary should seek out a household that is "worthy" and stay there. As the missionary enters such a household he should bring a greeting (probably to be understood as the customary Jewish greeting of *"shalom,"* or "peace"; see 10:13). The blessing brought to the household is spoken of in almost physical terms: If the house is worthy, peace is given to it; if not, the peace is taken away. Rejection of the missionary will have dire consequences, just as Matthew predicts for those who reject Jesus himself (10:14-15). The apostle is told to "shake off the dust from your feet" when faced with such a household or town and leave (a dramatic gesture used by Jewish travelers when returning from outside Israel). This segment concludes with a solemn warning of coming judgment (10:15). Based on the incidents in Genesis 19, "Sodom and Gomorrah" were biblical stereotypes for places of corruption and sin punished by God (see, e.g., Deut 29:23; Isa 1:9; 13:19; Jer 49:18; 50:40). Those who reject Jesus can expect an even worse punishment (similarly 11:23-24).

Warnings About Sufferings and Divisions in the Course of the Mission (10:16-23)

The prospect of rejection mentioned in 10:14 is amplified in this section that alerts the apostles to the sufferings they will have to endure, suffering resulting from persecution from the outside as well as divisions within the community itself. Matthew draws most of this material from Mark's apocalyptic discourse (see Mark 13:9-13) in which Jesus warns his disciples of the hardships they can expect as they await the coming of the Son of Man. The eschatological tone of this material is retained in Matthew's version and reveals the dual temporal levels of this discourse. On one level, within the framework of Matthew's narrative world, it is a mission instruction to the apostles as they continue Jesus' historic mission to Israel and, therefore, has a certain anachronistic flavor (e.g., directed only to Israel) even though its essential content has enduring validity. On another level, however, this discourse is projected into the world of the community that receives the gospel, that is, to those who live in the meantime between the earthly ministry of Jesus and his coming in triumph as the Son of Man (24:30-31). For these latter missionaries the restriction to Israel no longer holds (28:19-20) and they are expected to give witness to Gentiles as well as Jews (10:18). The circumstances described in 10:16-23 reflect that post-Easter experience of the Matthean community.

Jesus sends his apostles out as "sheep into the midst of wolves," a self-evident metaphor that continues the pastoral imagery used earlier in the discourse (9:36; 10:6; the classic visions of eschatological peace in Isa 11:6 and 66:25 depict the sheep and wolf living in harmony). The serpent was thought of as cunning and shrewd (see, e.g., Gen 3:1). In the face of the travails they would have to face, the missionaries would need to combine some assets of both the sheep and the serpent: They needed to be both innocent and resourceful.

A series of warnings and exhortations follows. They are to beware of those who would deliver them up to "councils" (probably gatherings of elders in various towns and villages), flog them in "their synagogues" (an expression Matthew uses several times, implying a sense of separation between "their" synagogues and those of his community; see 4:23; 9:35; 12:9; 13:54; 23:34 ["*your* synagogues"]), and drag them before "governors" (the title *hēgemōn* was used for Roman provincial governors or prefects such as Pilate in Judea) and "kings" (probably the different members of the Herodian dynasty who ruled regions of Israel in various configurations during the first century CE). In all of these hostile forums, the missionaries are to give "testimony" or "witness" to "them [presumably the Jewish authorities] and the Gentiles" (10:18). Matthew undoubtedly has in mind giving "testimony" not simply in a legal sense but as a fearless profession of their faith in Jesus. It is "because of me [Jesus]" that they are brought before the authorities (10:18) and it is the Spirit who will empower them to speak (10:20).

The apostles are not to be anxious about what they are to say in these harrowing circumstances. Consistent with Jesus' teaching in the Sermon on the Mount, God's provident love will guide them (see 6:25-34 where the same verb "worry" or "be anxious" is used five times). Mark's version refers to the "Holy Spirit" who will speak through the apostles at that moment (13:11); Matthew's phrase, "the Spirit of your Father," reflects this Gospel's stronger emphasis on God as provident "father" (see 6:26, 32-34, and the entire spirit of the Lord's Prayer, 6:8-13).

Another source of apostolic suffering comes from within, as betrayal and strife break out within the household (10:21-22). Family divisions were often part of the general turmoil in apocalyptic scenarios (see, e.g., Mic 7:6, which speaks of "contempt" and divisions between parents and children and among in-laws), but these verses in Matthew are particularly bitter, speaking of denunciations that lead to death and universal hatred. He also speaks of "brother will betray brother to death." The term "brother" is used by Matthew as a typical designation for members of the community (*adelphos;* the term is masculine but is used in a generic sense; see 5:22, 23, 24, 47; 7:3, 4, 5; 12:49-50; 18:15, 21, 35; 23:8; 25:40; 28:10). Use of the term here implies that the divisions are not just within families but in the Christian community itself with the threat of persecution causing apostasy and betrayal.

The missionaries are counseled to flee persecution and not let their ministry be checked, continuing to move from one town to the next. Jesus solemnly promises that the Son of Man will come before they have "gone through all the towns of Israel" (10:23). At first glance, this enigmatic saying appears to mean that the apostles will not have completed their circuit of the towns in Israel before the *parousia* of the Son of Man arrives. But such an interpretation raises not only the doctrinal question of an erroneous prediction ascribed to Jesus but also asks why Matthew would have included such a prediction in his Gospel. Some interpreters suggest that "all the towns of Israel" is intended in a very broad sense, including not only the towns in Israel proper but all the places in the Diaspora where Jews have gathered—thus extending the mission to incorporate the circumstances of Matthew's own day. For others, the "coming of the Son of Man" refers to Jesus' death and resurrection, which Matthew interprets in an apocalyptic sense (see, e.g., the apocalyptic signs of 27:51-53 and 28:2). The appearance of the Risen Christ to the eleven in Galilee in 28:16-20 would, therefore, be a "proleptic *parousia*" and make Jesus' words in the mission discourse true. The rejection of Jesus, coupled with the new age inaugurated by his death and resurrection, curtails the exclusive mission to Israel and opens the way to the Gentiles.

Whether this is, in fact, the rationale for 10:23 remains elusive. What is clear, however, is the conviction of the discourse that the mission entails persecution, betrayal, and division, and the follower of Jesus must be prepared to endure such sufferings for the sake of the gospel. How accurately this reflects the actual historical experience of the early community is another question. Given the struggles of both formative Judaism and Jewish Christianity to define their identity in this period, it is not surprising that sharp tensions and conflict would develop between these groups (see the introduction). Conflicting allegiances also led to bitter rifts among family members. And probably there were also heated debates within the Christian community over many issues, as tensions mounted over what practices and stances were appropriate to the followers of Jesus. Did this strife go so far as to lead to floggings, imprisonment, legal trials, and even death? Paul's letters in which he confesses his initial opposition to the Christian movement and his own later apostolic sufferings as a missionary suggest that in some circumstances the struggles were bitter and deadly (see, e.g., Rom 8:31-39; 1 Cor 4:8-13; 2 Cor 11:23-27; Gal 1:13-14). However, the exhortatory rhetoric of the mission discourse may be somewhat inflated and there is no evidence that the earliest missionaries experienced general persecution from Jewish or Roman authorities (see Hare 1967).

Trust in God and Loyalty to Jesus (10:24–11:1)

The final section begins and ends with sayings that reveal the underlying principle of the entire discourse: The disciple is to be like the master (10:24-25, 40-42). The identification of the messenger or representative with the one who sends them, or the idea of agency, was a concept known to the ancient world (the notion of Jesus as the "one sent" by God is a special emphasis of Johannine Christology; see, e.g., John 12:49-50; 20:21). Likewise, the master/disciple relationship expected that the disciple would depend on and imitate the master. These notions merge in the mission discourse. The identification of Jesus with the apostles sent in his name is both the basis of their authority and power and the guarantee of their suffering. Just as the religious leaders would accuse Jesus of being in league with Beelzebul (the "ruler of the demons," see Matt 12:24), so the disciples should expect the same condemnation.

A series of sayings introduced by variants of the phrase "do not fear" (10:26, 28, 31) expresses the utter confidence the apostles should have in carrying out their mission. They are not to fear those who oppose them because the gospel message cannot be "covered" or made "secret." What Jesus tells them in the darkness is to be spoken in the light (see also 5:14-16); what they hear whispered is to be proclaimed from the housetops. Nor should the apostles fear those who threaten their bodies but cannot claim their "souls"; rather they should fear (10:26-33) God who is sovereign over the entire being, body and soul, and can inflict eternal judgment (10:28).

God's provident care is stressed by two captivating images: Not even sparrows, birds sold cheaply as food for the poor, "fall to the ground" apart from God's will and even the hairs of the disciples' heads are numbered by God (10:29-31). This mode of reflection, which first asserts God's all-encompassing will in relation to nature and then uses it as a lever to affirm God's care for human beings, is identical to the exhortations against anxiety in 6:25-34.

The exhortations about not fearing give way to a stress on loyalty (10:32-39). Those who publicly "confess" Jesus (a translation that may more accurately capture the force of the Greek verb *homologein* used in 10:32) will be publicly acknowledged by Jesus before the Father in heaven while those who "deny" Jesus will be denied before God in heaven. This note of judgment, which couples earthly behavior with divine response, is typical of Matthew (see, e.g., 6:14-15; 18:35; cf. 6:10, "Your will be done, on earth as it is in heaven"). The example of Peter's threefold denial during the trial of Jesus will exemplify just such failure (the identical phrase "deny before others" is used in both passages, 10:33 and 26:70).

The prediction of family division is repeated (10:35-36; see 10:21), but this time as illustration of Jesus' warning that he has "not come to bring peace, but a sword" (10:34). Given the prohibitions about retaliation and violence in 5:21-26, 38-39, 43-47, as well as the command not to use the sword at the moment of the arrest (26:52), the word "sword" here is a metaphor for division that comes because of allegiance to Jesus (see the parallel in Luke 12:51, "Do you think that I have come to bring peace to the earth? No, I tell you, but rather division!"). The following sayings in 10:37-39 make precisely that point. Anyone who subordinates the demands of discipleship to family ties is "not worthy" of Jesus, the same stark assertion of primary allegiance that confronted the would-be disciple in 8:21-22.

For the first time in the Gospel the word "cross" is used. Discipleship is defined as "taking up the cross" and following Jesus (10:38). Similarly, those who "find their life" will lose it, while those who "lose their life for [Jesus'] sake will find it" (10:39). In contrast to the saying in 10:28 that used the term *psyche* to mean "soul" as distinct from "body"—reflecting a hellenistic anthropology—here the same word is used in more Semitic fashion to refer to the entire human body/spirit (and aptly translated in the NRSV as "life"). These sayings will be repeated in 16:24-26 following the first Passion prediction.

The final set of sayings returns to the notion of agency and the identification of Jesus with those sent in his name (see 10:24-25, 11-15). Whoever welcomes the apostles welcomes Jesus and, therefore, ultimately welcomes the God who has sent Jesus. This fundamental principle is affirmed in a series of mounting propositions—those who welcome a prophet because he is (the meaning of the Semitic expression "who comes in the name of") a prophet receive a prophet's reward; those who welcome a "righteous" person because he is righteous receive a righteous person's reward; and, finally, those who give even a cup of cold water to "one of these little ones" are emphatically assured (Gk. "Amen I tell you . . .") that they will not lose their reward (10:42). "Prophets" or wandering charismatics who taught in Jesus' name were certainly revered in the early community even though Matthew's Gospel also seems to be somewhat leery of them (see above, 7:15-20). And being "righteous" or "just" is central for Matthew's notion of discipleship (see 5:21). These are not really different categories of persons, but rather highlight different qualities or roles. But pride of place is reserved for the "little ones." This affectionate description can be used in a more generic fashion to refer to someone who has low standing and is liable to be despised (see 18:6-10). In the mission discourse, however, it describes the missionaries who are likely to suffer rejection, hatred, and even the threat of death because they come in Jesus' name. To offer hospitality to one of them will be rewarded because in so doing one receives Jesus himself. This is very similar to the judgment parable of 25:31-46 where those who treat kindly the "least" (the superlative form of the term *mikros* used in 10:42) also are rewarded.

Matthew's transition formula concludes the discourse and orients the reader back to the narrative of Jesus' ongoing ministry, in which Jesus went on to "teach and proclaim his message in their cities," a phrase that hints at the conflicts to come in chapter 11 (note the tension implied in the phrase "*their* cities"; see especially 11:20-24).

◊ ◊ ◊ ◊

Along with its portrayal of Jesus' mission to Israel, the mission discourse also asserts several fundamental principles that shape Matthew's understanding of the community's ongoing mission: (1) The mission of the community is ultimately a gift from God, rooted in the authority of Jesus who was sent in God's name; (2) the content and character of the community's mission are patterned on that of Jesus himself; (3) the mission of the community shares in the eschatological urgency of Jesus' mission and is a preface to the final consummation of the world; (4) because they are sent by Jesus and act in his name, the disciples will experience what Jesus experienced; (5) in the midst of persecution and divisions those who proclaim the gospel can depend on the empowerment of the Spirit of the Father and God's all-encompassing providence; and (6) despite suffering and apparent rejection, the mission will ultimately be successfully proclaimed to the world.

RESPONDING TO JESUS: REJECTION AND UNDERSTANDING (11:2–16:12)

Jesus' ministry of teaching and healing, which commanded the contents of the previous section (4:12–11:1), will continue in the chapters that follow. But now another motif surfaces, that of response to Jesus' message. With increasing intensity, Matthew will portray the religious leaders as intransigent and utterly opposed to Jesus. The crowds continue to react favorably, but the disciples now move closer to center stage. Even though fearful, hesitant, and often baffled, they ultimately show they are capable of understanding the mystery of Jesus' person and the meaning of his mission.

Typical of Matthew, this section is a blend of materials from Mark, Q, and the evangelist's own editorial contributions. With the parable discourse of chapter 13, Matthew will bring to a close the long stretch of narrative that began in 4:23 where he is most independent from the sequence of Mark's story line. From chapter 14 to the end of the Gospel, with very few exceptions, Matthew follows closely the sequence of Mark's Gospel and incorporates virtually all of its content even as he gives it his characteristic editing.

This section of Matthew's Gospel does not have the kind of clear topical markers such as the two major discourses (chaps. 5–7 and 10) and the collection of miracle stories (chaps. 8–9) that made the major structure of chapters 4:23–11:1 fairly easy to detect. Jesus continues to center his mission of teaching and healing in Capernaum, but he also moves further about Galilee and will venture out on the sea again and travel to the borders of Tyre and Sidon. The flow of this ministry is interrupted by several speeches or discourses. In the opening scene Jesus speaks to the crowds prompted by the question of John's disciples (11:2-30). There is a fairly long exchange with the leaders in 12:24-45 and again in 15:1-20. Finally, this section includes the third great discourse of the Gospel, the parable discourse of chapter 13.

John and Jesus: Response to God's Messengers (11:2-30)

This entire segment is presented as a soliloquy of Jesus, reflecting on his own mission and that of John and the reception they both receive. Segments of the discourse are marked by slight shifts in focus: (1) In 11:2-15 the spotlight is on the messianic works of Jesus and the prophetic role of John, triggered by the question brought by John's disciples; (2) the text of 11:16-24 turns to judgment motifs in the wake of the rejection experienced by both figures; and (3) the segment concludes on a rich christological note with Jesus' prayer of thanksgiving and his wisdomlike invitation to those weary and burdened (11:24-30).

Most of the material is drawn from Q, although Matthew has probably altered the original order of the materials. The encounter with John's disciples and the recitation of messianic works in

11:2-15, as well as the assessment of John's place in salvation history, find a parallel in Luke 7:24-28, but Matthew injects the saying about violence and the kingdom of heaven, adjusting the saying to his own perspective (cf. Matt 11:12-15; with Luke 16:16). The judgment material of 11:16-19 returns to what was the probable order in Q (see Luke 7:31-35), but Matthew adds the woes against the Galilean cities (11:20-24; cf. Luke 10:12-15 where it is found in the mission instruction to the seventy disciples). Jesus' hymn of thanksgiving in 11:25-27 is also drawn from Q (see Luke 10:21-22), but the final wisdom sayings (11:28-30) are unique to Matthew.

◊ ◊ ◊ ◊

John and Jesus (11:2-19)

The reintroduction of the figure of John recalls the inauguration of Jesus' mission at the Jordan with his baptism by John (3:1-17) and the ominous note about John's arrest as Jesus had withdrawn to Galilee (4:12). Matthew carries forward that narrative thread by locating John still in prison (11:2; Josephus [*Ant.* 18:116-19] reports that John was imprisoned at Herod's fortified palace at Machaerus on the eastern bank of the Jordan, but Matthew's narrative gives no hint of the location). Later the reader will learn of John's martyrdom at the hands of Herod Antipas (see 14:1-12). Yet there is a certain dissonance with the earlier material: John's question about Jesus' identity seems much less confident than his deferential first encounter with Jesus (3:14). Matthew's interest, however, is not really in John's frame of mind but in using the Baptist's question as a means of reviewing Jesus' messianic credentials. This is signaled in the opening verse of the section: In prison John hears "what the Messiah was doing" (11:2; see also 11:19, "wisdom is vindicated by her deeds"); "Christ" in this context is not a quasi-proper name for Jesus, but is used in a titular sense as the "Messiah."

John's question, "Are you the one who is to come?" echoes his words in 3:11, "One who is more powerful than I is coming after me." In the context of the baptismal scene John's words could be interpreted as referring to Elijah, who is to come in preparation for the end time (see the application of Mal 3:1 to Elijah in 11:10 and the exchange between the disciples and Jesus in 17:10-11: " 'Why, then, do the scribes say that Elijah must come first?' He replied, 'Elijah is indeed coming and will restore all things . . .' "). But Matthew clearly identifies John himself as fulfilling the role of "Elijah" in preparing for the Messiah (17:12, "But I tell you that Elijah has already come, and they did not recognize him, but they did to him whatever they pleased") so that in the context of chapter 11, John's own reference to the "one who is to come" refers to Jesus' role as the Messiah. As such this may be a messianic interpretation of Ps 118:26, "Blessed is the one who comes in the name of the LORD."

Jesus' response (11:4-6) echoes the list of works associated with God's redemption of Israel in Isa 35:5-6 (see also a reference to the raising of the dead in Isa 26:19), but more immediately summarizes the ministry of Jesus narrated in the earlier chapters of the Gospel. The disciples of John are to report what they "hear"—that is, Jesus' proclamation of the good news to the poor (see 4:23; 9:35; and the teaching material in 5:1–7:29)—and what they "see"—"the blind receive their sight" (9:27-31), "the lame walk" (9:2-8), "the lepers are cleansed" (8:1-4), "the deaf hear" (8:32-33), and "the dead are raised" (9:18-26). As is typical of Matthew's perspective, Jesus, through his ministry, both "fulfills" the scriptural promise expressed in a text such as Isa 35:5-6 and, at the same time, gives new meaning to the manner of God's salvation of Israel.

The review of Jesus' messianic deeds concludes with an ominous Beatitude: "Blessed is anyone who takes no offense at me" (11:6). Here Matthew anticipates the motif of rejection that will dominate the next few chapters. The term "take offense" translates the Greek verb *skandalizomai,* and implies finding Jesus an "obstacle." Jesus' own townspeople "take offense" at him when he visits Nazareth (13:57) and the Pharisees will "take offense" at his words about defilement (15:12). At the Last Supper Jesus predicts that the disciples themselves will "take offense" at him (26:31, 33; see also in the explanation of the parable of the sower where some who hear the word "take offense" when trouble or persecution arises [13:21]).

When John's disciples leave, presumably to report back to their master, Jesus turns to the crowds and speaks about John and his role in salvation history (11:7-15). Jesus' words praise John but also reaffirm his subordinate role to that of the Messiah. A series of rhetorical questions addressed to the crowds probes John's identity and manner of life and recall his mission of reform set in the Judean wilderness: "What did you go out into the wilderness to look at?" (11:7-9; see 3:1-6 where the crowds stream out into the wilderness to be baptized and confess their sins).

The "reed shaken by the wind" (11:7) probably refers to the tall marsh reeds that still thrive in the moisture along the banks of the Jordan. Some commentators suggest that this image, in combination with that of the "soft robes" worn in "royal palaces" (11:8), are subtle allusions to Herod Antipas and his court, the monarch who would put John to death (see 14:1-12). A reed was used as a symbol on coins minted during Herod Antipas's reign and the "soft robes" imply the corruption of Herod's court, reflected as well in the dissolute manner in which the king cedes to John's execution. Even on their surface level the image of a reed easily shaken by the wind and the finery of royal garb contrast effectively with Matthew's portrayal of John as the sturdy prophet who dressed in camel hair and unflinchingly challenged the authorities who ventured into the wilderness to hear him (3:4, 7-10).

John is even "more than a prophet" because he assumes the role of precursor for Jesus the Messiah (11:9). Here, following the lead of Q, Matthew utilizes the citation from Mal 3:1 that he omitted in the baptismal scene (cf. Matt 3:3 and Mark 1:2-3). This text is now interpreted messianically and John is the one who prepares for the Messiah's advent. Because of this unique role John is solemnly praised: "Among those born of women no one has arisen greater than John the Baptist." Yet John belongs to the period of preparation for the inbreaking of the reign of God and, therefore, "the least in the kingdom of heaven is greater than he" (11:11).

Matthew continues this line of thinking in the enigmatic saying about violence, which is a Q saying that the evangelist substantially recasts (cf. Matt 11:12-15 and Luke 16:16). Continuing the theme of response to both John and Jesus, the saying considers the time "from the days of John the Baptist until now" (i.e., Jesus' own ministry) as a period when "the kingdom of heaven has suffered violence, and the violent take it by force" (11:12). Some ancient manuscripts read that the kingdom "comes violently," but the reading chosen by the NRSV is preferable. John's arrest and imprisonment are evidence of this violence and there have already been indications that Jesus and his disciples will suffer a similar fate (see 10:16-31). The opponents of John and Jesus, not to mention the demonic forces Jesus contended with in his exorcisms and healings, are the "violent" who attempt to overpower God's reign. Similar to the warning about scandal in 11:6, the emphatic counsel to "listen" (11:15) underscores the sober warning implied in John's fate.

"All the prophets and the law have prophesied until John came"—this is a neat summary of Matthew's fulfillment theology, which views the entire Scriptures and all of Israel's history as coming to fulfillment in Jesus (cf. 5:17). Therefore John is in the line of this prophetic tradition. But because John is the prophet who introduces Jesus into the arena of salvation history, he has a unique and towering role; he is, in fact, "Elijah" preparing the way of the Messiah (11:13).

Both John and Jesus are rejected by "this generation," a point made in the enticing metaphor of the children playing in the marketplace (11:16-19). Jesus repeatedly uses the designation "this generation" to refer to his opponents as unbelieving (see 12:39-42, 45; 16:4; 17:17; 23:36; 24:34). The metaphor portrays children at play, annoyed at their unresponsive companions who do not dance when they play the flute and do not mourn when they try a funeral wail. The failure to respond to the lure of either the flute or the wail aptly describes the opponents' attitude to John and Jesus, as well as the contrasting roles each figure plays in salvation history. John comes as the ascetical prophet announcing the end time, "neither eating nor drinking," and he is judged to have a "demon" (Jesus himself will be accused of being in league with Satan; see 12:24). Jesus, the messianic bridegroom who makes fasting impossible

(9:14-15) and whose mission is to "call sinners" (9:10-13), is accused of being "a glutton and a drunkard, a friend of tax collectors and sinners!" These sayings of Jesus, which have the smack of authenticity, capture in a remarkable way the spirit of Jesus' mission even as they reflect the hostility of his opponents.

The saying that closes this segment repeats the emphasis on "the deeds" of Jesus cited at the beginning (see 11:2, "what the Messiah was doing") and reveals another dimension of Matthew's Christology by portraying Jesus as "wisdom" (11:19). Luke's parallel speaks of "wisdom's children," suggesting that Jesus is a child of wisdom (Luke 7:35). For Matthew, however, Jesus' messianic works are the deeds of wisdom itself, implying Jesus' identification with wisdom. Such an identification carries over into 11:25-27, in which Jesus, similar to Wisdom, speaks of himself as the revealer of God, and into 11:28-30, where Jesus invites refreshment in the manner of wisdom. Wisdom speculation in Judaism presented "wisdom" as a poetic metaphor, embodying God's revelation to Israel through nature and proverbial experience (see, e.g., Prov 8). "Wisdom," the first of God's works, is present at creation, comes into the world to reveal God, and experiences both rejection and acceptance. Johannine theology makes use of such wisdom reflection in its portrayal of Jesus as the Word incarnate who enters the world to reveal God (see especially John 1:1-18). Matthew also taps into wisdom traditions to present Jesus as the unique revealer of God through his words and actions, yet also as one who experiences rejection.

Judgment on the Cities of Galilee (11:20-24)

In the manner of a prophet, Jesus reproaches for their lack of repentance three Galilean cities where he had done his "deeds of power" (in Luke 10:12-15 these Q sayings are part of the mission discourse to the seventy disciples). The term "deeds of power" (Gk. *dynameis*) picks up a term used in the following judgment sayings (11:21, 23) and elsewhere in the Gospel to refer to Jesus' acts of healing and exorcism (13:54; 14:2; in 7:22 the term refers to the deeds done by others in Jesus' name). By prefacing the judgment sayings with this reference to Jesus' actions, Matthew ties this material into the previously described ministry of Jesus (especially chaps. 8–9) as well as the summary of his ministry in 11:4-5. The deeds of Jesus have the ultimate purpose of revealing the presence of God's reign and therefore should lead to repentance (see 7:17; also 3:2).

The three cities mentioned are all located in the northwestern area of the Sea of Galilee near to Capernaum, Jesus' "hometown" and the place where Matthew situates much of Jesus' activity (9:1). Chorazin was a small village about two miles to the north of Capernaum. Bethsaida was a fishing village to the east of Capernaum on the northern shore near the point where the Jordan empties into the sea. Matthew does not report any visits of Jesus to Chorazin or Bethsaida (for Bethsaida see Mark 6:45; 8:22; Luke 9:10; John identifies Bethsaida as the village of Philip, Andrew, and Peter; see John 1:44; 12:21; Chorazin is not mentioned anywhere else in the NT). The image of Capernaum being not "exalted to heaven" but "brought down to Hades" plays upon the taunts against the king of Babylon in Isa 14:12-20 ("You said in your heart, 'I will ascend to heaven' . . . but you are brought down to Sheol"). Even Sodom, the notorious condemned city of Gen 19, would have fared better (and "would have remained until this day") if it had had the benefit of the mighty deeds witnessed by unrepentant Capernaum.

The coastal cities of Tyre and Sidon are often the targets of prophetic condemnation as places outside the realm of Israel, corrupted by idolatry and destined for destruction (see Isa 23:1-12; Jer 25:22; Ezek 28:11-23; Joel 3:4; Zech 9:1-4). Yet if Tyre and Sidon had experienced the deeds Jesus performed in Chorazin and Bethsaida, those pagan cities would have repented and put on "sack cloth" and "ashes"—both signs of public repentance (see the reaction of the king of Nineveh to Jonah's preaching in Jonah 3:5, an incident Matthew will cite in 12:41). The woe directed to Capernaum alone is more severe. The crowds in that city had been filled with awe and "glorified God" in response to Jesus' cure of the paralytic (9:8). Yet in his first miracle in Capernaum, Jesus had contrasted the faith of the centurion with that of Israel ("in no one in Israel have I found such faith" [8:5-13]) and in this same town he would first encounter the hostility of the religious leaders (9:3, 11).

The rhetorical contrasts between these unrepentant Galilean (and Jewish) cities with such prominent examples of supposed Gentile wickedness, such as Tyre and Sidon and Sodom, fit a pattern characteristic of Matthew's perspective. After experiencing the faith of the centurion, Jesus had predicted that many would come from east and west to eat at the table of the patriarchs while "the heirs of the kingdom" would be thrown into the outer darkness (8:11-12). In the mission discourse Jesus had warned that it would be more tolerable for Sodom and Gomorrah on the day of judgment than for the cities of Israel that rejected those sent on mission (10:15). The "people of Nineveh" and the "queen of the South" will rise up in judgment over "this generation" for its failure to repent (12:41-42). In the parable of the two sons, Jesus tells the leaders that "tax collectors and the prostitutes are going into the kingdom of God ahead of [them]" (21:31) and in the subsequent parable of the vineyard, the owner will take away the vineyard from the tenants and give it to the Gentiles who will produce the fruits of the kingdom (21:43). One of the basic rationales for the opening of the mission to the Gentiles in Matthew is the simple fact that they, in contrast to many in Israel, prove more receptive to the gospel.

Jesus the Revealer (11:25-30)

Cast in the form of a thanksgiving prayer of Jesus, this segment picks up the wisdom motifs that emerged earlier in this chapter (11:19). In the manner of wisdom, Jesus is the unique revealer of the Father, and the weary and burdened are invited to be refreshed in him. The prayer itself is Q material (11:25-27; see Luke 10:21-22), but the concluding invitation is found only in Matthew (11:28-30). In Luke's narrative, Jesus' prayer of thanksgiving is a response to the triumphant return of the seventy disciples from their mission and their triumph over the demonic forces (see Luke 10:17, 21-22). Matthew, however, links this prayer of Jesus to the preceding material on rejection and judgment. A literal translation of the editorial linking phrase Matthew uses would be "at that time Jesus *responding,* said . . ." (11:25). This seems to imply that Jesus' declaration is triggered by the previous material. Jesus' unique bond with God and his role as the revealer of God are the foundation for Jesus' messianic deeds and the reason why response to Jesus is imperative.

The form and content of the prayer are thoroughly Jewish and also harmonize with deep currents of Matthew's theology. Hymns of thanksgiving similar in form have been found among the Qumran materials (see *1 QH* iv 9, 17, 26; x 20, 31). The address "Father, Lord of heaven and earth" captures the same blend of intimacy and reverence expressed in the Lord's Prayer (see above 6:9-13). Wariness about the "wise" and "intelligent" whose learning feeds their arrogance and becomes an obstacle to piety was also a recurring motif in Jewish reflection. Paul makes a similar contrast between the "wise" and the "foolish" in 1 Cor 1:18-31 and cites Isa 29:14, a text that may also influence this Q passage: "The wisdom of their wise shall perish, and the discernment of the discerning shall be hidden."

At the same time, there is a certain novelty in Jesus' sayings. "Wisdom" was viewed as God's endowment on the "wise" rather than the "foolish" (see, e.g., Dan 2:20-21: "Blessed be the name of God from age to age, for wisdom and power are his. . . . He gives wisdom to the wise and knowledge to those who have understanding"; similarly 4 Ezra 12:35-38). So there is an air of prophetic reversal in the assertion that God's revelation is given to "infants" rather than to the "wise and the intelligent," not unlike the jarring contrasts between the Galilean and Gentile cities noted previously (see 11:20-24) or Matthew's attention to the "little ones" and the "least" (see 10:42; 18; 25). Within the context of Matthew's story, one has to think, as well, of the contrasting responses of the religious leaders who are hostile to Jesus, and the crowds and disciples who respond favorably.

While the saying in verse 27 may be a proverbial comparison to the special relationship of father and son in the setting of a traditional culture, within the context of the Gospel this relationship has a more radical christological significance. Jesus' identity as the "Son" has been affirmed from the outset of the story in the promises to Joseph (1:21, 23), in the fulfillment quotation of 2:15, in the solemn declaration of the divine voice from heaven at the moment of the baptism (3:17), and in the fact that Satan had taunted Jesus' identity as "Son of God" in the temptation scene (4:3, 6). Likewise Jesus himself had addressed God as "our Father" (6:9) or "my Father in heaven" (7:21; 10:32-33; 12:50; 15:13; 16:17; 18:10, 19; 20:23; 25:34; 26:29, 39, 42, 53; also as "your Father" in addressing the disciples; see 5:16, 45; 6:1, 4, 6, 8, 14-15, 18, 26, 32; 7:11; 10:29; 18:14).

The passage is an exceptional assertion of Jesus' authority based on his identity as Son of God. Jesus declares that "all things" have been handed over to him by the Father. The term "all things" is somewhat vague, but probably refers to Jesus' God-given power and authority expressed in his teaching and healing (see the "deeds of power" ignored by the unrepentant Galilean cities: 11:20, 21, 23). Jesus alone knows the Father just as the Father alone knows Jesus. Jesus' recurring emphasis on the "will of the Father" (see, e.g., 7:21; 12:50; 18:14; 21:31; 26:42) also finds its rationale here. Because he alone knows God's will, so Jesus' teaching can uniquely reveal God's will to those to whom Jesus chooses to reveal it.

The passage ends with an invitation to those who are "weary" and carry "heavy burdens" (11:28-30). These words may be directed most immediately to those both inside and outside the community who are still under the influence of the scribes and Pharisees who "tie up heavy burdens, hard to bear, and lay them on the shoulders of others" (23:4). But it also has a more encompassing intent, inviting the disciples to submit to the "yoke" of Jesus' teaching. "Yoke" was used in Jewish tradition as a metaphor for teaching or instruction and in Sir 51:26 is extended to the image of wisdom. This Old Testament (Apocrypha) passage surely influenced the formulation of Matt 11:28-30. Wisdom speaks, inviting the "uneducated" to "draw near to me" (Sir 51:23). Wisdom urges them, "Put your neck under her yoke, and let your souls receive instruction. . . . See with your own eyes that I have labored but little and found for myself much serenity" (Sir 51:26-27). Now Matthew presents Jesus as the personification of Wisdom who invites the disciple to accept his teaching ("Take my yoke upon you, and learn from me"). Jesus is "gentle" and "humble in heart"; both are significant qualities in Matthew's Gospel. The "gentle" or "meek" are blessed in 5:5 and in 21:5 the formula quotation from Zech 9:9 describes Jesus' entrance into Jerusalem as a king who is "meek" (NRSV: "humble"; the Greek word *praus* used here can also mean "considerate" or "unassuming"). In the community discourse, the disciples are instructed to "humble" themselves as a child in order to enter the kingdom of heaven (the verbal form of the same word, *tapeinos,* is used in 18:4 as in 11:29). Similarly in chapter 23, when Jesus condemns the scribes and Pharisees for the burden of their teaching and their hypocrisy, he declares that "all who exalt themselves will be humbled *[tapeinōthēsetai],* and all who humble themselves will be exalted" (23:12).

Unlike those who reject Jesus and are liable to judgment (see 11:20-24), those who respond and accept Jesus' "yoke" will find "rest for [their] souls" because the yoke of Jesus is "easy" and his burden "light" (11:30). The mood of this passage evokes the compassion of Jesus toward those in need (see especially 9:36). At the same time, Matthew has also portrayed Jesus' teaching as demanding, requiring greater "righteousness" than that exhibited by the scribes and Pharisees (5:20). Matthew apparently saw no contradiction here. Despite Jesus' demands, his teaching was "easy" and not a burden because it was motivated by the command of love (7:12; 22:40) and unerringly revealed the will of God.

◊ ◊ ◊ ◊

Chapter 11 begins and ends with a focus on the authority of Jesus whose deeds confirm he is the Messiah, "the one who is to come," and whose identity as God's Son and Wisdom incarnate make his teaching refreshing and life-giving. The passage in 11:25-27 has been described as a "Johannine meteor" arching unexpectedly across the Matthean sky. Although the formulation of this passage may be somewhat singular for this Gospel, its fundamental theology is not. For Matthew's Gospel, Jesus' identity as Son of God is the foundation for the authority of his interpretation of the law and his power to heal and cast out demons. And, ultimately, this same authority and power will be invested in the Matthean community itself (see 28:16-20).

Christology and ecclesiology are closely linked in Matthew's Gospel. The judgment material in this chapter urges the community to repentance from sin and obedience to Jesus' teaching in order to avoid the fate of the Galilean cities who fail to respond to Jesus. At the same time, there are hints of the future here. Jesus' wager that pagan cities such as Tyre, Sidon, and notorious Sodom would respond more positively to Jesus than their Jewish counterparts alerts the reader to a stunning turn in history yet to unfold within the Gospel drama. Another rhetorical ploy, the enticing invitation of wisdom in 11:28-30, urges those not yet immersed in Jesus' teaching and perhaps still under the thrall of the scribes and Pharisees to take up his yoke and find life.

Conflict on the Sabbath (12:1-21)

Concern in response to Jesus and his mission continues in this section where Matthew presents two conflict stories about Sabbath observance, punctuated with the Gospel's longest fulfillment quotation. Both stories are found in a section of Mark's Gospel where conflict between Jesus and his opponents is a dominant motif (see 2:1–3:6). Matthew had already used some of this material in describing Jesus' healing mission (see Matt 9:1-17; cf. Mark 2:1-22). Now he employs the remaining material here (Matt 12:1-14; cf. Mark 2:23–3:6). The summary of Jesus' healings that introduces the fulfillment quotation also follows Mark's sequence (Matt 12:15-16; cf. Mark 3:7-12).

Matthew's editorial seams tie the material together in a loose fashion. The general framework for Jesus' activity was presented in 11:1: "[Jesus] . . . went on from there to teach and proclaim his message in their cities." That vague geographical framework envelops the next several incidents as Jesus moves "through the grainfields" (12:1), enters "their synagogue" (12:9), teaches in a house (12:46), and tells them parables from a boat offshore (13:1). This combination—a synagogue, a house, and the sea—is reminiscent of the setting around Capernaum where Matthew had situated Jesus' ministry for most of chapters 8 and 9 (see 8:14; 9:1, 10, 18).

◊ ◊ ◊ ◊

Through his initial editorial phrase, "at that time" (12:1), Matthew links the story about the disciples plucking grain on the Sabbath (12:1-8) to the preceding declaration of Jesus about his "easy yoke" (11:28-30). Matthew's editing of the story emphasizes that Jesus' defense of his disciples is not a disregard for the law, but an authoritative interpretation that displays Jesus' characteristic compassion. The disciples are "hungry" and begin to pick ears of grain and eat them. The law permitted an individual who was hungry to pick grain in this manner from another person's field (but not to use a sickle; see Deut 23:25). The point of contention here is that it is done on the Sabbath. Observance of the Sabbath rest in conformity with Exod 34:21 was a constant focus of debate among Jewish teachers long before precise regulations were codified in the Mishnah (third century CE; Harrington 1991, 175-79). The Pharisees in this story observe the behavior of Jesus' disciples and declare it "not lawful," apparently considering the disciples' action as equivalent to reaping on the Sabbath, which was forbidden (12:2).

In defense of his disciples, Jesus cites two biblical examples. The first is the example of David who, when his young men needed food, entered the sanctuary and procured for them the shewbread that had been set aside for the cult. This incident is described in 1 Sam 21:1-6. (Both Matthew and Luke omit Mark's apparently erroneous reference to the high priest Abiathar [see Mark 2:26]; Ahimelech, not Abiathar, is the priest mentioned in 1 Samuel.) The precise point of this comparison is subtle. David's actions were not done on a Sabbath, so they provide no precedent for Jesus' disciples on that score. The point of comparison must be deeper—and even bolder. Matthew interprets David's procuring of the bread for his men as an act of compassion that superseded the regulations of the sanctuary; therefore, just as David the king did for his followers so Jesus could do for his disciples. In other words, it is not only a matter of the priority of human need over cultic observance in both instances, but the royal authority of both David and Jesus as David's Son—and, in Matthew's eyes, one far greater than David (see 22:41-46 and below, 12:23).

The acclaim of Jesus' greater authority, latent in the first example, becomes explicit in the next (12:5-6). Jesus appeals to the law instructing the priests to perform certain duties in the sanctuary on the Sabbath, such as setting out the shewbreads and frankincense as well as performing the prescribed burnt offerings and libations (see Lev 24:8; Num 28:9-10). As in the previous example, the authority of Jesus provides the sanction for his interpretation of the law. The point is driven home in verse 6: "I tell you, something greater than the temple is here." The phrase "something greater" is not defined but it surely refers to Jesus and, by extension, to the reign of God he embodies and the community of disciples who act in his name. Matthew had made a similar defense of the disciples' failure to fast in 9:14-15—the wedding guests (i.e., the disciples) cannot mourn when the bridegroom is present.

This first incident closes plaintively with Jesus' lament about the Pharisees' ignorance of the true spirit of the law (12:7). Matthew cites Hos 6:6, as he had done previously in 9:13—"It is mercy I desire and not sacrifice"—illustrating again the fundamental principle of the Gospel that in giving precedence to human need over cultic commands Jesus did not destroy, but fulfilled the law (5:17; see also 23:23). The concluding verse underscores the authority of Jesus and the grounds for his teaching: "The Son of Man is lord of the sabbath" (12:8). From the vantage point of Matthew's community, Jesus as God's Messiah and privileged revealer of God (11:27) towers over both temple and sabbath. (Matthew omits the Markan saying that preceded it: "The sabbath was made for humankind, and not humankind for the sabbath" [Mark 2:27; also absent in Luke 6:5]. Its assertion that the sabbath was subordinate to humankind [and not just to Jesus as Son of Man] may have seemed too strong, especially if, as is likely, Matthew's community continued to keep sabbath observance.)

The second story also involves a conflict over interpretation of law (12:9-14). On that same sabbath day Jesus enters "their" synagogue and encounters a man with a "withered" hand. What Mark narrates in indirect discourse ("They watched him to see whether he would cure on the sabbath," 3:2), Matthew, as often, casts in direct discourse: "And they asked him, 'Is it lawful to cure on the sabbath?' " At the conclusion of the story we learn that "they" are the Pharisees and their purpose is to entrap Jesus (see

12:14). Jewish tradition permitted action to relieve a life-threatening situation on the sabbath but this man's condition seems chronic and not life-threatening. Matthew's version of the story adds Jesus' argument about the sheep falling into a pit on the sabbath, underscoring that Jesus' action is not an arbitrary violation but a valid and indeed authoritative interpretation of the law (Matt 12:11-12; contrast Mark 3:3-4; Luke 6:8-9). The argument uses a typical rhetorical device called *qal wêḥômer*, which contrasts a lesser with a greater (cf. 6:25, 26, 30; 10:31). If an essential animal could be rescued on the sabbath, how much more a human being. Such cases were apparently a point of debate in first-century Judaism. A discussion in the *Damascus Document* (11:13-14), a text associated with the Qumran group, took a strict stance on this issue and forbade rescue activity on the sabbath. Jesus' interpretation is allied with a more flexible application of the law in cases of urgent human need.

Jesus' interpretation of the law is emphatically stated not just in words but in his resolute healing of the man's hand. The bad faith of Jesus' opponents, already evident in their intent to entrap him (12:10), boils over at the conclusion of the story. The Pharisees (not in concert with the Herodians as in Mark 3:6) begin to conspire "how to destroy him" (12:14). These ominous words measure the intensity of the opposition to Jesus on the part of the leaders and already alert the reader to the Passion of Jesus.

Matthew concludes this segment with a brief summary of Jesus' ministry and a fulfillment quotation (12:15-21). The summary parallels Mark's long summary of Jesus' mission in 3:7-12. Matthew had already mined some of this in his introduction to the Sermon on the Mount (see 4:23-25). Here he is content with a condensed version of the essential points that he adapts to the context of his story. Jesus "departed" from the synagogue and the site of his sabbath controversies because he "became aware" of the leaders' plot against him. Despite the leaders' reaction, "many" of the people still "followed" Jesus and he continues his mission of healing. In Mark 3:12 Jesus silences the demons who reveal his identity as "Son of God"; naming one's opponent (and thereby demonstrating power over them) was a typical element in ancient exorcism stories. In Matthew, Jesus counsels silence on the "many" people he heals so that he can remain hidden from the threat of the leaders.

The fulfillment quotation from Isaiah (12:17-21) interprets this withdrawal on the part of Jesus not simply as a stratagem to foil his enemies but as a manifestation of the humility and gentleness that is his as God's servant. The basic quotation is from Isa 42:1-4 but does not conform to known versions of either the Septuagint or the Hebrew text. As is often the case with the fulfillment quotations, Matthew adapts the quotation to its surrounding context (see the introduction, p. 27). The term "servant" translates the Greek word *pais,* which can also mean "child" or "son" (in contrast to an alternate such as *doulos,* which unequivocally would mean "slave" or "servant"). Matthew may also wish to evoke Jesus' identity as "Son" of God so strongly emphasized in 11:25-27. Matthew also reinforces the intensity of God's election of the servant/son by adding the phrase "my beloved" and using the verb "with whom my soul is well pleased"—both of which recall the divine declaration about Jesus' sonship at the moment of the baptism ("This is my Son, the Beloved, with whom I am well pleased," 3:17) and at the transfiguration ("This is my Son, the Beloved; with him I am well pleased," 17:5). As in the baptism scene, the quotation also emphasizes Jesus' endowment with the Spirit, a point that anticipates the immediately following controversy where Jesus' opponents accuse him of casting out demons through the power of Beelzebul rather than through the power of the Spirit (see 12:24-32).

The Spirit-filled servant will "proclaim justice to the Gentiles" (12:18) and "in his name the Gentiles will hope" (12:21). The latter phrase is not found in the Isaiah passage yet reflects Matthew's theology (see, e.g., Matthew's adaptation of Isa 8:23–9:1 in 3:15-16 and the promise to the centurion in 8:11). The eventual mission to the Gentiles hovers in the background of Matthew's narrative, particularly in contexts where contrast with Israel's rejection is present. The gentle and nonviolent manner of the servant harmonizes with the character of Jesus' messianic authority. He does not "wrangle" or "cry aloud" or lift his voice "in the streets." Nor will he "break a bruised reed." These descriptions bind the quotation to the immediate context where Jesus withdraws in the face of bitter opposition by the leaders and suppresses reports of his healing (12:15-16). For Matthew these are the trademarks of the one who is "gentle and humble in heart" (11:29) and become part of the cumulative portrait of Jesus' distinct messianic identity. A later fulfillment quotation from Zechariah will make this same point (see 21:4-5).

◊ ◊ ◊ ◊

The sabbath controversies illustrate that Jesus' healings are not a violation of the law but valid interpretations that derive from the primacy Jesus gives to the love command, placing urgent human need above other legitimate concerns of the law. Even more crucial for Matthew is the issue of Jesus' authority that runs like a deep current through this entire section. Jesus is "lord of the sabbath" and one "greater than the temple"; he is God's servant and beloved Son whose messianic authority is exercised with gentleness and humility. Matthew's Christology is what ultimately legitimates Jesus' interpretation of the law.

The opposition of the Pharisees to Jesus within the narrative world of Matthew's story may also be a mirror image of a conflict between Matthew's Jewish-Christian community and other factions of Judaism contemporary with Matthew (see the introduction, pp. 22-24). Issues over sabbath observance and other issues regarding the law may have been flash points between these communities. Matthew's response is to show that Jesus, endowed with messianic authority, did not disregard the law but interprets it in ways that fulfilled its God-given intent. In the course of this, Matthew also stereotypes Jesus' opponents and, by implication, delegitimates the opposition of Pharisaic Judaism: they act in bad faith; blindly oppose Jesus; and become intent on destroying him.

This Evil Generation (12:22-50)

The motif of conflict and rejection in 12:1-22 continues in this next segment. An exorcism performed on a man who was blind and mute (12:22) provokes a series of fierce exchanges between Jesus and the Pharisees. Most of the material in this section comes from Q, although Matthew also draws on Mark 3:22-27; all of it receives Matthew's characteristic emphases.

◊ ◊ ◊ ◊

The exorcism that begins this section is virtually a repetition of the story in 9:32-34, although this time the man is blind as well as mute (cf. Luke 11:14-15). In both instances the narrative focuses less on the exorcism itself than on the reactions it triggers. The crowds are amazed and wonder whether Jesus isn't the "Son of David" (the formulation of the question indicates they are still uncertain). This messianic title is used in Matthew in connection with Jesus' healings (see 9:27; 15:22; 20:30, 31). In Jewish tradition, Solomon, David's son, was viewed as an exorcist who had power over evil spirits (both Josephus and Philo, e.g., portray Solomon in this manner), and this connection may be part of the reason this title is applied to Jesus in similar contexts (note that Jesus is declared "something greater than Solomon" in 12:42). By contrast, the reaction of the Pharisees is strongly negative (12:24). They accuse Jesus of being in league with "Beelzebul, the ruler of the demons" (see also 10:25). The etymology of this derogatory term for Satan is unsure, but it originally probably meant the "Lord of the Flies," a contemptuous designation that ridiculed the Philistine god "Baal-zebub" (see 2 Kgs 1:2).

Jesus uses a series of arguments and images to counter the leaders' chilling suggestion that he works in and through the power of Satan. The first argument is that if Jesus casts out evil by the power of evil, as the Pharisees claim, then Satan's kingdom is divided against itself (vv. 25-26). The implication that there are two realms or kingdoms, one belonging to God and the other to Satan, has a strong apocalyptic flavor. Second, Jesus points to the fact that the Pharisees, too, perform exorcisms; if that is the case, then by whose power do they cast out demons (12:27)? Jewish exorcists were not unknown in this period (see, e.g., the story of the seven sons of Sceva, the high priest in Acts 19:11-20; Tobias drives out a demon with the odor of burning fish, Tob 8:2-3).

If, in fact, Jesus is not in league with Satan then the true meaning of his exorcisms becomes clear—they are signs of the reign of God now made present in Jesus' mission: "But if it is by the Spirit of God that I cast out demons, then the kingdom of God has come to you" (12:28). Luke's version of this Q text uses the quaint phrase "by the finger of God" (see Luke 11:20) and is probably more original. However, Matthew's phrase "by the Spirit of God" fits well into this context where the question is raised of whether Jesus works through evil spirits, and with the preceding fulfillment quotation from Isa 42:1 that spoke of Jesus' investment with the Spirit (see 12:18). This programmatic saying reinforces a point already strongly affirmed in the Gospel, namely that Jesus' healing and exorcisms are signs of the advent of God's reign and the guarantee of Jesus' messianic identity (see 11:2-6). The parable of the strong man (12:29; see Mark 3:27) makes the same point: Jesus is the "stronger" one who enters Satan's house, ties him up, and wrests away those under the demon's control (on Jesus as the "stronger one," see 3:11).

Matthew cites a Q saying: Whoever is not with Jesus is against him and whoever does not participate in his mission of "gathering" (this same verb is used elsewhere to describe the gathering of people to Jesus in his ministry: 13:2, 47; 18:20; 22:10) scatters. To identify Jesus with Satan is "blasphemy against the Spirit" and cannot be forgiven (12:31-32). The precise meaning of this ominous saying is not completely clear, but it surely does not refer to some unknown sin that one could unwittingly commit and be condemned—as many Christians have fearfully understood this passage in the past. But to attribute Jesus' power to Satan rather than to the Spirit of God is a "blasphemy" or insult against God so perverted in the eyes of the Gospel and so closed to the truth that it leaves no room for repentance or forgiveness either "in this age or in the age to come."

Another set of imagery is mobilized in 12:33-37 to further condemn the Pharisees for their false interpretation of Jesus. The aphorism about the tree and its fruits recalls a similar metaphor in 7:16-20: The Pharisees' evil actions in falsely accusing Jesus reveal their own evil state. Similarly, the metaphors about speaking from one's "heart" and one's "treasure" recall the saying in 6:21 where both these images are also linked. The warning about idle words in 12:36-37 appears originally to have been a general moral exhortation, but in this context it adds to the condemnation of the Pharisees for their verbal attacks on Jesus.

Another segment of the narrative is introduced by the approach of some "scribes and Pharisees" who ask Jesus for a "sign" (12:38-42; see a similar exchange in 16:1-4). Presumably the kind of "sign" they are looking for is not simply another miracle or exorcism but some extraordinary wonder that would certify Jesus' claims—perhaps in the manner of the great "signs" and wonders that Moses had performed during the Exodus to confound Pharaoh and to claim the people's allegiance. Jesus' response leaves no doubt that the request of the leaders is not to be taken as genuine but as another disbelieving challenge to Jesus. "This generation" is a phrase that occurs repeatedly in Matthew, often with negative adjectives as here, to refer to those in Jesus' day who reject him (see, e.g., 11:16; 12:41, 42, 45; 16:4; 17:17; 23:36; 24:34). The leaders are described as "evil" and "adulterous," the latter a term often used metaphorically in the Bible to refer to infidelity toward God (see especially the extended use of this metaphor in Hos 1–3).

No sign will be given "except the sign of the prophet Jonah" (12:39-41). In Mark's version of this scene (see 8:11-12, which is a closer parallel to Matt 16:1-4), Jesus refuses to give any sign at all to "this generation." For Luke (11:29-32) the sign of Jonah given this "evil generation" is the fact that Jonah became a "sign" to the people of Nineveh just as Jesus is to this generation—an apparent reference to Jesus' mission of mercy to sinners. But for Matthew the "sign of Jonah" is the prophet's strange sojourn in the belly of the sea monster, a harbinger of the death and resurrection of the Son of Man (Matt 12:40). This would be the ultimate sign vindicating Jesus' messianic identity, yet the reader will learn that even this sign can make no impression upon the leaders, confirming the dire prediction of 12:32 (see 27:62; 28:11-15). Matthew also gives a role to the "people of Nineveh" (cf. Luke 11:31-32). They will condemn "this generation" on the day of judgment because they repented in response to Jonah's preaching, but the leaders fail to believe Jesus, one who is "greater than Jonah." And Sheba, the

COMMENTARY

"queen of the South" (see 1 Kgs 10:1-13), will also condemn this generation because she came from the ends of the earth to listen to Solomon's wisdom, yet Jesus is "something greater than Solomon" (12:42). Once again Matthew contrasts favorably the response of outsiders and Gentiles with that of the religious leaders (see similarly in 8:10-12; 11:20-24); all of these are forward glances in the narrative, building a rationale for the Gentile mission. At the same time, Matthew uses every opportunity to assert his fundamental Christology: Jesus is a greater prophet than Jonah and wiser than Solomon, David's son.

The story of the wandering spirit is a dire prediction of what will befall the leaders for their lack of faith in Jesus' mission (12:43-45; cf. Luke 11:29-31). Placed here it serves as a fitting conclusion to the section that began with the exorcism of the blind and mute man (12:22). When an unclean spirit leaves someone, it wanders through the desert (typically in the Bible the abode of Satan; see 4:1-11) in search of a resting place. When it finds none it can come back to its original "house," which is now "empty" and all in order. Not only does it return but it brings seven more evil spirits with it and so the state of that household is worse than before. The final line added by Matthew—"So will it be also with this evil generation"—makes it clear that this story is a commentary on the leaders and the terrible consequences of their sin. Jesus' mission of healing and exorcism has Satan on the defensive but if his mission is not accepted then in due time the evil spirits will return to infest the land.

This whole section closes with the story about Jesus' true family (12:46-50). Along with the similar story of Jesus' visit to his hometown of Nazareth that follows the discourse (13:54-58), this motif of authentic relationship to Jesus serves as a frame around the parable discourse. It also brings to a conclusion the preceding material by reminding the reader what it is that establishes a proper relationship with Jesus: "For whoever does the will of my Father in heaven is my brother and sister and mother" (12:50).

Although this is a story already present in Mark (see 3:31-35), it fits well into Matthew's theology. The preference for discipleship ties over blood or family ties is found in several New Testament passages and will reappear in Matthew (4:18-22; 19:27-30; 23:9; also Luke 11:27-28; see, further, Barton 1994, 178-84). Such teaching was important for the early community to free it from the constraints of a patriarchal familial model. Modeling the community along family lines would have led to a hereditary form of leadership and made membership for non-Jews more difficult. Matthew softens Mark's implicit critique of Jesus' blood family by omitting the reference to their judgment that Jesus is "beside himself" (3:21; NRSV: "has gone out of his mind") and by noting that they wanted "to speak to [Jesus]" rather than to "seize" him as in Mark's version (NRSV: "restrain him"; cf. Matt 12:46-47 with Mark 3:21, 31. Matthew 12:47 seems redundant and is omitted from some ancient manuscripts). Yet the conclusion of the story is firm: Those who do the will of the heavenly Father are Jesus' true family [12:50]. "Doing the will of the heavenly Father" is a motif that runs throughout Matthew's Gospel and is one that reflects the deep Jewish roots of this narrative (see, e.g., 6:10; 7:21; 18:14; 21:31; 26:42).

◊ ◊ ◊ ◊

In this section Matthew strongly affirms his portrayal of Jesus as the Messiah, the "Son of David" whose power to cast out evil and restore human life is a manifestation of the reign of God. Jesus is greater than Jonah the prophet and his death and resurrection are unimpeachable signs that he works with God's favor. Jesus is greater than Solomon, David's son and the paragon of Wisdom, because, as the reader already knows, Jesus is the beloved Son who uniquely reveals God (see 11:25-27).

Matthew continues to present the religious leaders as unalterably opposed to Jesus and his mission. This negative portrayal serves as a foil to Matthew's presentation of Jesus—their opposition and accusations of blasphemy draw from Jesus a sharp defense of his ministry and a declaration that his exorcisms, performed with the power of God's Spirit, make the reign of God present. True kinship with Jesus belongs to those who, like Jesus himself, seek to do God's will. But condemnation of "this evil generation" also serves another purpose. The opposition Jesus experienced threw light on the experience of Matthew's community in its struggles with Pharisaic Judaism. Accusations that Jesus was a sorcerer and a blasphemer were probably echoed in the rhetorical exchanges between Matthew's community and its opponents as both sought to establish the legitimacy of their religious claims. Matthew rebuts those accusations and assures his community that in following Jesus they are assured of a place in God's reign.

The Parable Discourse (13:1-52)

The parable discourse is the third great discourse of the Gospel. This is not the only time in the Gospel that Jesus speaks in parables, but the concentration of them in this discourse rivets the attention of the reader on this mode of Jesus' teaching. The inspiration for this discourse is Mark 4:1-34, which Matthew incorporates almost entirely (the only exception is Mark's parable of the seed growing secretly, Mark 4:26-29, and the sayings in 4:21-24 that Matthew incorporates elsewhere in his Gospel). But typically Matthew carefully edits his source, expanding the discourse with Q material (Matt 13:16-17//Luke 10:23-24; Matt 13:33//Luke 13:20-21) and some parables unique to this Gospel (13:24-30, 36-43, 44-46, 47-50, 51-52), while giving all of it his characteristic stamp.

The placement of the parable discourse in this part of the narrative is most apt. Since the beginning of chapter 11 Matthew has focused on Jesus as the revealer of God's reign and on the varying and often hostile responses to that revelation. By their nature, "parables" fit into the dynamics of both revelation and response. "Parables" are extended metaphors or comparisons designed to draw the hearer into a new awareness of reality as revealed by Jesus, yet their artful nature adds a special twist of paradox and unexpected challenge. C. H. Dodd's classic definition has captured the essential elements of the parable: "At its simplest the parable is a metaphor or simile drawn from nature or common life, arresting the hearer by its vividness or strangeness, and leaving the mind in sufficient doubt about its precise application to tease it into active thought" (Dodd 1961, 5). As Dodd noted, our everyday language is full of "dead metaphors" but Jesus' stories and extended comparisons were not "dead"; their "vividness" and "strangeness" had the capacity to both perplex and challenge the listener—to "tease the mind into active thought."

It is this opaque character of the parables that made them an extension of the mystery of Jesus' own person and helps situate the parable discourse in this section of Matthew's Gospel. The parables help amplify the profound Christology that suffuses Matthew's narrative, namely that in Jesus the reign of God has come. At the same time, the ability to penetrate the meaning of the parables and to "understand" them or, conversely, the refusal or inability to understand the parables separates the disciples from Jesus' chronic opponents.

It may be helpful, first of all, to note the staging Matthew gives the discourse before considering its formal or logical structure. In the immediately preceding scene Jesus was with his disciples and the crowds in a house and had pointed to his disciples as his true family, as those who did "the will of my Father" (12:46-50). At the beginning of the discourse he leaves the house and sits in a boat along the shore in order to address the great crowds that had gathered on the beach (13:1). As the discourse continues, both the "crowds" (13:34) and the "disciples" (13:10) are present. But in 13:36 Jesus moves away from the crowds and back into the house with his disciples, and the remainder of the discourse appears directed exclusively at them. Thus the overall movement of the discourse is from a general interaction with the crowds to a focus on the disciples alone. For some commentators, this is a pivotal moment in the Gospel as a whole (Kingsbury 1969), capping the rejection that Jesus had experienced in the previous chapters of this section and signaling that the remainder of the narrative will focus on discipleship instruction. Making one verse the turning point in the whole Gospel may be too ambitious, but undoubtedly this shift in setting reflects a fundamental change in the atmosphere of the Gospel that will continue to emerge as the narrative develops.

Deciphering the overall structure of the discourse is difficult. There is no compelling evidence that Matthew has grouped the parables around a single consistent theme or central motif; probably more formal arrangements determine the discourse's structure. All of the parables are introduced with the phrase "the kingdom of heaven may be compared to" (13:24) or "the kingdom of heaven is like" (13:31, 33, 44) and most are strung together with linking phrases such as "he put before them another parable" (13:24, 31, 33) or simply "again [he told them]" (13:45, 47). In the opening part of the chapter Matthew clearly follows the structure provided by Mark in which the parable of the sower (13:3-9) is followed first by a discussion of the reasons for speaking in parables (13:10-17) and then by an interpretation of the sower parable (13:18-23; cf. Mark 4:1-24).

This basic pattern of a cluster of parables followed by explanations and assorted sayings may also explain the format for the rest of the discourse. In the next section, 13:24-43, Matthew begins with a cluster of three parables (13:24-33), followed by another explanation of why Jesus speaks in parables (13:34-35), and then by the interpretation of the parable of the weeds (13:36-43). In the concluding section, the pattern is similar but not identical: first a cluster of three parables (13:44-48), followed by the interpretation of the parable of the net (13:49-50), and finally Jesus' interaction with the disciples about understanding the parables (13:51-52). The chapter, therefore, has a threefold structure: (1) 13:1-23; (2) 13:24-43; (3) 13:44-52.

There is some thematic progression as the discourse moves from beginning to end. The first half of the discourse focuses primarily (but not exclusively) on accounting for the mixed reception given Jesus and his message. The latter half turns more to motifs of discipleship, recalling the total commitment demanded by the compelling value of the kingdom, urging tolerance and forbearance in the face of evil within the community, and confidently predicting triumph for the followers of Jesus and punishment for those who are evil.

◊ ◊ ◊ ◊

The Parable of the Sower (13:3-23)

With the audience in place (13:1-2), the discourse begins with the parable of the sower (13:3-9). Right from the beginning of the discourse, emphasis falls on both revelation and response. Sowing of seed was a common image in the Bible and in Jewish literature for God's interaction with Israel (see, e.g., Jer 31:27-28; Ezek 36:9; Hos 2:21-23; 4 Ezra 8:6; 9:31), and the harvest was a stock metaphor for eschatological judgment already used by Matthew (see 9:37). The parable and its subsequent explanation (13:18-23), however, give particular attention to the variety of responses.

Recent interpreters have speculated about the action of the sower in strewing seed without discrimination across a variety of soils. Joachim Jeremias (1963, 11-12) asserted that the parable reflects common Palestinian practice in which the seed was sown prior to plowing and would, therefore, not seem bizarre to its original audience. Others, however, are more skeptical. In any case, the parable itself makes no comment about any subsequent plowing and we cannot be sure that Matthew's audience would have filled in this blank. If not bizarre, the indiscriminate sowing at least gives the impression that the harvest is somewhat precarious and depends in part on reaching good soil despite an array of obstacles.

Matthew subtly alters the conclusion of the parable. In Mark the concluding image is that of an explosive harvest on the good soil, "growing up and increasing and yielding thirty and sixty and a hundredfold" (4:8). Matthew's version, which omits the description "growing up and increasing and yielding . . . ," shifts the focus to the varying yields among the seeds, even of those that fell on the good soil: "*some* a hundredfold, *some* sixty, *some* thirty" (13:8, emphasis added). There is debate whether or not a yield of a "hundredfold" was considered a spectacular harvest in first-century Palestine. The question is less urgent in Matthew since his conclusion describes a variety of successful yields at partial rates rather than a crescendo to the hundredfold.

Matthew considerably edits and expands the explanation for speaking in parables found in Mark (13:10-17; cf. Mark 4:10-12). The disciples' question, "Why do you speak to them in parables?" prompts Jesus' extended response, contrasting the disciples who have been gifted to know the mystery of the kingdom with those who are fated not to understand. The phrase "mysteries of the kingdom of heaven" is inspired by Mark 4:11 ("mystery of the kingdom of God"; in both cases the NRSV translates the Greek word *mystērion* as "secret" or "secrets"), but fits well into Matthew's perspective. Jesus' entire public ministry was a revelation of God's reign (beginning with 4:17), but the Gospel had already emphasized that this revelation was hidden from the "wise and intelligent" and was given only to those to whom the Son chose to reveal it (see 11:25-27). Matthew reinforces this fundamental declaration with a saying that occurs later in Mark's discourse: "To those who have, more will be given, and they will have an abundance; but from those who have nothing, even what they have will be taken away" (13:12; see Mark 14:25).

From an initial emphasis on the grace of "knowing the secrets of the kingdom," which the disciples have received, the discourse turns to the situation of those who do *not* understand. Jesus speaks to them "in parables"—and here the emphasis falls on the opaqueness of the parable as veiled speech—because " 'seeing they do not perceive, and hearing they do not listen, nor do they understand' " (13:13). Matthew, following Mark's lead, introduces here a theology of "hardening" that will be amplified in the subsequent quotation from Isa 6:9-10. But the perspectives of the two Gospels are somewhat different. Mark's discourse underscores the fact that the opponents are taught in parables *in order that* they will not understand *lest* they should turn and be forgiven (4:11-12). Mark, in short, attempts to explain the opposition that Jesus experienced through a kind of "predestination" theology—the rejection of Jesus was foreseen by God and the opponents play their allotted role. In Matthew's version, however, emphasis falls on the *disposition* of the opponents: They are taught in parables or veiled speech *because* they do not understand. The quotation from Isa 6:9-10 that Matthew cites in full restates this: "This people's heart has grown dull . . . *so that*" they do not understand and turn to be healed. Matthew's version, therefore, offers a moral explanation for the opponents' failure to respond to Jesus (Donahue 1988, 64-56).

However, Matthew's explanation still retains some of the predestined character found in Mark. For Matthew the rejection of Jesus expressed in the opponents' failure to understand the parables is a fulfillment of Isaiah's prophecy. Their opposition is not an accidental calamity, therefore, but falls within the foreseen plan of God. It is interesting that Matthew carefully formulates the introduction to the formula quotation in such a way that the opponents' behavior falls under the scope of scriptural fulfillment, yet keeps some distance from full intentionality. Instead of the usual formulation "this was in order to fulfill . . . ," the formula reads, "with them indeed is fulfilled . . ." (13:14; see a similar nuance in 2:27 and 27:11). The quotation from Isa 6:9-10, is used elsewhere in the New Testament to explain the rejection of Jesus or, in Paul's terms, the "hardening" of Israel (Rom 11:25; for Isa 6:9-10, see Mark 8:18; John 12:40; Acts 28:25-27; see further Evans 1989). By means of the quotation Matthew also introduces another key metaphor for Matthew's theology of discipleship, that of "understanding" (*suniēmi*; see Barth 1963, 105-12; Luz 1995, 119-23). The disciple is one who "sees," "hears," and, above all, "understands" Jesus and his word. The Isaian phrase to "understand with their heart" catches the profound and comprehensive sense of "understanding" in this context (see 13:19, 23, 51; 15:10; 16:12; 17:13).

The Beatitude of 13:16-17, drawn from Q (see Luke 10:23-24) and added here by Matthew, further emphasizes this quality of discipleship—the eyes of the disciples are blessed because they see and their ears are blessed because they hear. Many prophets and "righteous people" (a change to Matthew's favored word, *dikaios*, from Luke's "kings") longed in vain to hear and see what the disciples now can experience. These sayings reinforce the privileged position of the disciples as those who witness the dawning of the messianic age (see similar concepts in 9:15; 11:11).

This first segment of the discourse concludes with the explanation of the parable of the sower (13:18-23). Most interpreters assign the origin of this material, with its allegorical explanation of the parable and reference to community experiences, to the proclamation of the early church. Given the role of Jesus as proclaimer of the kingdom, the reader is probably to assume that the sower of "the word of the kingdom" is Jesus (as in the explanation of the parable of the weeds, see 13:37). In Matthew's version all the references are in the singular (in contrast to Mark's plural), so that the focus continues to fall on various types of individual responses.

Four different dispositions or ways of responding to the word are listed. The seed that lands on the path is snatched away by the evil one. The importance of "understanding" as a key virtue of discipleship is evident in the way Matthew casts these opening verses. He omits Mark's reference to the disciples' lack of understanding (cf. 13:18 and Mark 4:13) and, instead, frames the first type of negative response as "*anyone* [who] hears the word of the kingdom and does not understand it" (13:19). The word is sown "in [one's] heart" (contrast Mark 4:15, "in them"), perhaps a reminiscence of the phrase in the previous quotation from Isa 6:10, to "understand with their heart" (see 13:15). The reception of the seed sown on rocky ground (13:20-21) describes what happens when initial enthusiasm for the word gives way because "trouble or persecution arises on account of the word"—a circumstance that surely reflects Matthew's community experience (and one foretold by Jesus in the mission discourse, see 10:16-17; also 5:10-12; 23:34; 24:9, 21, 29). The seed sown among the thorns describes one whose reception of the word is choked off by the "cares of the world and the lure of wealth" (v. 22)—competing values that Jesus had warned about in the Sermon on the Mount (see 6:19-34) and which would discourage the rich young man from becoming a disciple (19:16-26).

The final circumstance is that of the seed sown on good soil. Once again Matthew defines "understanding" as essential to authentic discipleship. The disciple is one "who hears the word and *understands* it," along with "bearing fruit" and yielding a good harvest according to one's capacity—"in one case a hundredfold, in another sixty, and in another thirty" (13:23; cf. Mark 4:20).

The Parables of the Weeds, the Mustard Seed, and the Yeast (13:24-43)

A new segment of the discourse introduces three additional parables whose only thematic link seems to be the notion in each parable of present "hiddenness" or secrecy coupled with future triumph. The first is the parable of the weeds (13:24-30), a parable unique to Matthew but one that bears some similarities to Mark's parable of the seed growing secretly (Mark 4:26-29, omitted by

Matthew). As in the case of the sower parable, the allegorical interpretation comes later (see 13:36-43). The close fit of parable and allegory, as well as its Matthean language and perspective, suggests that the parable itself was composed by the evangelist.

The point of the story is that an enemy ("while everybody was asleep") sows weeds among the wheat, leaving the householder with a dilemma. He instructs his servants not to try to root up the weeds prior to the harvest lest in doing so they also harm the wheat. The parable and its explanation foresee a "mixed" community of both good and bad. Rather than take strong action against the "weeds" planted by Satan, the community should await God's judgment when evil will be dealt with.

The message of this allegorical parable resonates with a number of Matthean motifs. The sober reality of a less than ideal community emerges at several points in the Gospel, including warnings about lawlessness (e.g., 7:21; 23:28; 24:12), predictions of divisions and betrayals (10:21-22; 24:4-8, 21-26), and procedures for handling disputes (18:15-20). The parable urges restraint and tolerance on the part of the community, a stance that harmonizes with Matthew's strong emphasis on not judging and on seeking reconciliation, even with an enemy (5:21-26, 43-48; 7:1-5). God, not human agency, will deal in a decisive way with iniquity. In the meantime, the community should be aware of evil in its midst but not be compelled to uproot or destroy it.

At the same time, the allegory reveals Matthew's view of history and human destiny, extending the horizon of the parable beyond the immediate perimeter of the community to the final judgment of humanity. The mission of the Son of Man is to sow the good seed in the "world" (13:37-38). The world is sorted out between the "children of the kingdom" and "the children of the evil one" who are offspring of the devil (13:38-39). At the end of the age, the Son of Man will send the angels to execute judgment on all "evildoers" (13:41; see 7:23; 24:30-31). They will be condemned to the furnace of fire where there will be "weeping and gnashing of teeth" (13:42; see Matt 8:12; 13:50; 22:13; 24:51; 25:30) while the righteous will "shine like the sun in the kingdom of their Father" (13:43). The expectation of reward for a life of good deeds is a firm part of Matthew's teaching (see 6:2-4; 25:1-30, 31-46).

The other two parables in this triplet are the parable of the mustard seed (13:31-32), which is found in Mark (4:30-32), and that of the leaven, which is from Q (13:33; see Luke 13:18-19). The parable of the mustard seed contrasts small and insignificant beginnings with flourishing conclusions. The "mustard seed" is a tiny seed, probably the black mustard plant, an annual that is common in the Middle East and grows rapidly into a large shrub. As an image of the kingdom of heaven the parable suggests that the mission of Jesus, judged to be insignificant by his opponents, will ultimately triumph. In the context of Matthew's Gospel, the parable may also bear the meaning that Matthew's community, itself under assault by its opponents, will also grow in the manner of the mustard seed into a large and flourishing entity. The assertion that the mustard plant will become a "tree, so that the birds of the air come and make nests in its branches" adds a note of fantasy true to the usually "strange" twist found in Jesus' parables. The mustard plant, in fact, does not become a tree where birds can nest in its branches. The image of a great tree was used in the ancient world as a symbol of a strong and flourishing world kingdom (see, e.g., Judg 9:7-15; Ps 80:8-11; Ezek 17:23; 31:5-6; Dan 4:10-12). Does Matthew see the parable as applicable to the Gentile mission, when the nations would come and nest in the community (see 8:11-12; 21:43; 28:19)?

The parable of the leaven has a similar message, although it is even more enigmatic and starkly brief (13:33). The kingdom of heaven is like the leaven that a woman "hides" in three measures of flour. On the surface it appears that here, too, the contrast is between the apparently innocuous leaven and its comprehensive impact on the flour or meal ("until all of it was leavened"). It is difficult for us to know what the original audience of this parable would assume. The amount of the meal or flour appears to be extraordinarily large, equivalent to approximately four and one-half pecks or fifty pounds—enough to make bread for a hundred people. Yet in some traditional villages, bread making was done communally so that this may not have been an unusual amount

(Schrottroff 1995). And while leaven or fermented dough was a usual ingredient in bread making, it also frequently had a negative connotation as a symbol of corruption. Thus the parable may suggest not only that the kingdom of heaven will grow to complete measure despite its seemingly small beginnings but also that what is judged a "corruption" by Jesus' and the community's opponents will prove to be God's triumphant work (similar to the unlikely claim of the mustard plant to be a tree).

Embedded in this section, not unlike the passage in 13:10-17, is the narrator's comment about the rationale for the parables (13:34-35). In Mark these verses form the conclusion to the discourse (see 4:33-34), but in Matthew they are transformed into a fulfillment quotation, reinforcing the authority of Jesus and his mission and asserting that his preaching in parables fulfills the Scriptures. The quotation is from Ps 78:2, which Matthew freely adapts, forming a translation that is identical with no known Hebrew or Greek versions. The introductory formula identifies this as the words of the "prophet" (13:35); some ancient manuscripts add the name "Isaiah" and it is not impossible this was the original reading since Matthew cites Isaiah several times in this part of the Gospel (see 12:17; 13:14; 15:7). Matthew felt free to adapt the wording of the Old Testament to fit his conviction that Jesus messianically fulfilled God's word to Israel. In this case the words of the psalm are considered "prophetic" since they express the reality that through his words and actions Jesus brought to ultimate expression God's saving action on behalf of Israel. The opening verses of the psalm, in fact, refer to testimony given to coming generations about "the glorious deeds of the LORD, and his might, and the wonders that he has done" (Ps 78:1-4).

Here Matthew emphasizes the revelatory dimension of the "parables" in contrast to the previous quotation from Isa 6:9-10, which dwelt on their opaqueness (see 13:14-15). Jesus speaks to the crowds in parables in order to reveal to them the mystery of God's kingdom that had been hidden since the foundation of the world.

The summation of Jesus' mission in the idiom of the parable also signals a turning point in the narrative where Jesus leaves the crowds and turns his attention to the disciples (13:36). Before he explains the parable of the weeds, he enters a house with his disciples. As discussed earlier, it may be claiming too much to suppose that this verse is the pivot on which the entire Gospel turns. Yet Matthew clearly passes a milestone in his story, as the hostility of the opponents and the vague neutrality of the crowds become fixed and Jesus begins to focus his attention solely on his disciples, instructing them about the meaning of God's kingdom and the cost of discipleship.

The Parables of the Hidden Treasure, the Pearl, and the Net (13:44-52)

Three brief parables (13:44, 45, 47-48, the last coupled to an equally brief explanation, 13:49-50) and a concluding interaction of Jesus with his disciples (13:51-52) constitute the final segment of the discourse. All of this material is unique to Matthew and thoroughly reflects his theology.

The parables of the hidden treasure and the pearl of great value express the wholehearted commitment demanded by the kingdom of heaven. The parable of the hidden treasure has a single-minded focus on the exceeding value of the kingdom, so that anyone who finds it sells every possession in order to buy it. The parable leaves out of consideration questions such as who owned the field, or whether it is immoral to buy the field without first disclosing to the owner the fact that it contained treasure. Some suggest that because of such questions the parable was meant to shock the moral sensibilities of the audience. But, more likely, these parables attend solely to the overwhelming value of the kingdom, which commands allegiance above everything else. This perspective is not foreign to the Gospel, which described the disciples as leaving all to follow Jesus (see 4:18-22) and invited the rich young man to sell his possessions in order to follow Jesus and thereby to store up for himself "treasure in heaven" (19:21; see also 19:27-30). Likewise, Jesus had warned the disciples not to seek corruptible "treasure" that moth or rust could destroy, but "treasures in heaven" (6:19-21; the same word, *thesauros,* is used in each instance). Similarly, the notion of the kingdom as a "hidden" treasure fits with the previous set of parables that emphasized the hidden and unpretentious nature of the reign of God (see 13:24-43).

The parable of the pearl has a similar message (13:45). The discovery of the pearl is not simply a happy accident, as seems to be the case with the discovery of the treasure in the field. Rather, the merchant is in "*search* of fine pearls" and at last finds one "of great value." To procure it he sells all his possessions to purchase it. Again, the fundamental proclamation is clear: The reign of God is of overwhelming value and it is now proximate. A proper response to such a critical reality is illustrated in the merchant's determined search for this supreme good and, once found, his decision to put aside all else in order to give the reign of God his complete commitment.

The concluding parable in the discourse, that of the net (13:47-48, coupled with its explanation, vv. 49-50), opens the horizon once more to the final judgment. Its message is similar to that of the parable of the weeds (13:24-30) but here there is less concern about the scandal of evil and the need for patient tolerance. Rather, the parable draws a confident picture of the final age, assuring the disciples that evil people, such as those who blindly oppose Jesus, will be punished and those who commit themselves to the kingdom of heaven will be saved. The kingdom of heaven is like a "drag net" (the term *sagēnē* refers to the kind of fishing net that dragged beneath the surface), which inevitably gathers a variety of catch, both good and bad. Just as the good and bad fish are sorted out after the net is full and has been brought ashore, so "at the end of the age" (13:49; see 13:40-41) the angels will sort out the evil from the "just" and the evil will be punished. The image of being thrown "into the furnace of fire, where there will be weeping and gnashing of teeth" makes a decidedly mixed metaphor with the fishing imagery of the parable but reflects Matthew's typical way of referring to judgment (see 13:42; also 8:12; 22:13; 24:51; 25:30).

The discourse concludes with a direct exchange between Jesus and his disciples (13:51-52). Jesus asks his disciples if they have "understood all this" and they reply without hesitation "yes" (13:51). This is clearly a Matthean formulation. Presumably "all this" refers to the entire discourse with its revelation of the mystery of the kingdom. To "understand" (Matthew's characteristic *suniēmi,* see above, 13:14) is an essential quality of authentic discipleship. Matthew's portrayal of the disciples as "understanding" contrasts notably with that of Mark who presents them as lacking comprehension (see, e.g., Mark 4:13; 6:52; 7:18; 8:21).

The final verse about the scribe trained for the kingdom of heaven might be considered a "signature" verse in the Gospel. Because he "understands" (the initial phrase of the verse, *dia touto,* "because of this," implies a causal link with the previous exchange), "every scribe who has been trained for the kingdom of heaven is like the master of a household who brings out of his treasure what is new and what is old" (13:52). "Scribe" is a generic term implying one who is learned but, in the Jewish context, often applied specifically to one learned in the law. Matthew often identifies "scribes" (usually linked with the "Pharisees") as stereotyped opponents of Jesus (see, e.g., 5:20; 9:3; 12:38; 15:1; 16:21; 20:18; 21:15; 23:13, 15, 23, 25, 27, 29; 26:57; 27:41). Yet Matthew also refers positively to "scribes," as in this verse, and it is possible that the leadership group within his Jewish-Christian community was a type of Christian scribe, learned in the Scriptures and in the developing traditions of the community (see, e.g., in 23:34 the reference to the "scribes" Jesus will send and who, along with the prophets and sages, will be persecuted by the Jewish "scribes and Pharisees." See further, Orton 1989). Here the scribe is one "trained for the kingdom of heaven." The term for "trained" is Matthew's characteristic word *mathēteuō,* which literally means to be "made a disciple"; this same word will be part of the mission charge to the eleven at the conclusion of the Gospel (28:19) and the noun form, *mathētēs,* is Matthew's characteristic designation for the followers of Jesus. It is likely that the text refers here not simply to disciples in general but to a leadership group within the community. A "scribe who has been trained for the kingdom of heaven" is compared to the "master of a household," implying some authority over the community.

The scribe's leadership is exercised in bringing out of his "treasure what is new and what is old." The term "treasure," *thēsauros,* has already been used by Matthew in the parable chapter and elsewhere to describe that which is most precious and central in one's life (see above, 13:44; also 6:19, 20, 21; 12:35; 19:21). Earlier in his conflict with the Pharisees, Jesus said, "The good person brings good things out of a good treasure, and the evil person brings evil things out of an evil treasure" and this Q saying may well be the inspiration for Matthew's formulation here with the focus shifting from "good" and "evil" to "new and old" (see 12:35; Luke 6:45). Therefore, the scribe brings from out of his deepest commitments and most treasured values "what is new and what is old." Precisely what is "new and old" is not said. Such a formulation may have been part of the Jewish tradition to express the need to retain the old along with innovations, as some later texts indicate (see Davies and Allison 1991, 447). Matthew portrays a Jesus who has come "not to abolish but to fulfill" the law and the prophets (5:17), and the Gospel's entire agenda can be characterized as an attempt to find in Jesus a fulfillment of (and therefore continuity with) the Jewish biblical heritage. At the same time, Matthew sees in Jesus and his message the inbreaking of the kingdom of heaven and the beginning of a new and decisive age of salvation history, one in which new understanding of the law is possible and a new and inclusive perception of the kingdom was imperative. The Christian scribe, therefore, was one who could mediate both dimensions for a community stretched across a turning point in history.

◊ ◊ ◊ ◊

The parable discourse reaffirms the Gospel's profound Christology at a crucial juncture in the narrative when Jesus has been under assault by his opponents. Jesus both teaches and embodies the mystery of the kingdom of heaven, a mystery "hidden from the foundation of the world" (13:35) but now revealed at this dawning of the final age.

The parable discourse explains why, despite Jesus' manifest identity as the Messiah, his opponents do not respond positively to him, or to the community who proclaims him. Their inability to penetrate to the meaning of Jesus and his mission is a result of their obstinate disbelief and dullness of heart, as Isaiah had prophesied

(13:10-15). Thus, for them the parables compound their lack of understanding.

Matthew also reaffirms his theology of discipleship. Unlike the opponents, the disciples do "understand" Jesus and his teaching. This makes them blessed recipients of the mystery of the kingdom, something that the prophets and just ones of old longed to see (13:16-17). In these parables Jesus reminds the disciples of the exceeding value of the kingdom and the necessity of total commitment to it. The disciples are counseled to patiently tolerate the presence of infidelity and evil in the community and in the world, since God will reward the just and punish the evil at the final judgment. Above all, they are to be confident about the destiny of the community. God's power rules the course of history—the power of evil will be destroyed and the "children of the kingdom" will triumph at the end of the age. Those who exercise responsibility for the community are to be like "scribes trained for the kingdom of heaven," following Jesus in his manner of keeping faith with the old while boldly proclaiming the new.

Rejection in Jesus' Hometown (13:53-58)

Matthew's transition formula (13:53; see also 7:28; 11:1; 19:1; 26:1) signals the end of the parable discourse and the resumption of the narrative suspended in 13:1. At this juncture Matthew will rejoin the story line of Mark and follow it virtually unchanged until the end of the Gospel.

The story of Jesus' rejection in Nazareth finds a parallel in Mark 6:1-6 (see another version of the story in Luke 4:16-30 where it serves as the inauguration of Jesus' mission). Matthew had already incorporated the material that followed Mark's parable chapter in his chapters on Jesus' healings (see Mark 4:35–5:43; Matt 8:23-34; 9:18-26). As a result, in Matthew's narrative the end of the parable chapter leads immediately into the Nazareth story. In fact, this serves Matthew's dramatic interests. The encounter with his hometown people of Nazareth, with its reference to the family of Jesus, forms an inclusion with the story of Jesus' true family in 12:46-50, which had served as a transition into the parable discourse. A fundamental motif of the discourse itself was response to the mystery of the kingdom of heaven revealed through Jesus. The Nazareth story demonstrates the lesson of the discourse: Those who do not understand Jesus end up rejecting him.

While Matthew draws this story from Mark, he edits it carefully, simplifying some of Mark's material and giving the story compact symmetry. The astonishment (13:54) and disbelief (13:58) of the townspeople frame the story, while their skeptical questions about Jesus' identity hold its center (13:54b-56; on the structure of this story see Van Segbroeck 1972, 344-72; Davies and Allison 1991, 451-52).

◊ ◊ ◊ ◊

The transition formula of 13:53 concludes the parable discourse and moves the narrative to a new setting. Jesus comes to his "hometown" and begins to teach in "their synagogue." The Greek word translated as "hometown" is *patridis,* which connotes one's place of origin and is therefore distinct from Capernaum, described by Matthew in 9:1 as Jesus' "own town." The reference to Jesus' family (13:55-56) confirms that this is Nazareth where Jesus and his family had taken up residence in Galilee (see 2:23). The designation *"their* synagogue" is also typical of Matthew (see 4:23; 9:35; 10:17; 12:9).

Right from the beginning the people are confounded by Jesus and ask the first of their disbelieving questions: "Where did this man get this wisdom and these deeds of power?" (13:54). Matthew's formulation is reminiscent of 11:1-24, where the narrative reviews Jesus' acts of power (see 11:20 where the same root term *dynamis* is used in reference to Jesus' actions) and presents him as the embodiment of wisdom (see 11:20)—also in a context of rejection by his own people.

Their next series of questions flows from the people's conviction that they already "know" who Jesus is, yet, in the eye of the Gospel, their assertions fail to penetrate to Jesus' true identity. "Is not this the carpenter's son? Is not his mother called Mary? And are not his brothers James and Joseph and Simon and Judas? And are not all his sisters with us? Where then did this man get all this?" (13:55-56). In place of Mark's "the carpenter, the son of Mary" (Mark

6:3), Matthew describes Jesus as the "carpenter's son" and "his mother called Mary." Matthew may have found the phrase "son of Mary" baffling at best, since a son was usually identified in terms of his father. Mark's formulation may have been intended to be an insult on the part of the Nazarenes or, as some have suggested, meant to imply that Mary was a widow, or even as Mark's deference to the tradition of Jesus' virginal conception. In any case Matthew prefers a more ordinary formulation, which also coincides with the reference to Joseph as the husband of Mary in the genealogy (1:15). Since the reader of Matthew's narrative is already informed about the extraordinary manner of Jesus' birth, the surmise of the Nazarenes is further indication that they do not know the origin of Jesus' wisdom and power. Matthew retains the term *tektōn* (which can mean "craftsman," but more frequently was translated as "carpenter"), but now uses it to identify Joseph rather than Jesus. Whether this was a reaction of piety against identifying Jesus as a "carpenter" or, what is more likely, that Matthew simply wanted to use the words "son of" in a different manner cannot be determined.

The Nazarenes assert that they know Jesus' family, including his brothers James and Joseph, Simon and Judas (Matthew substitutes "Joseph" for Mark's abbreviated "Joses" and reverses the order of the latter two brothers, as in 10:4), and his sisters who are "with us." This reference to the brothers and sisters of Jesus has been a debated text in view of the post–New Testament tradition of the perpetual virginity of Mary. In themselves the terms *adelphos* and *adelphē* refer first of all to blood brothers and sisters. However, other interpretations have proposed that in this context the terms refer to Jesus' stepbrothers and stepsisters from an earlier marriage of Joseph who was a widower when he was betrothed to Mary (as in the *Prot. James* 9:2), or to cousins of Jesus, since in clan cultures the term "brother" or "sister" was used of relatives other than siblings (a solution suggested by Jerome). The latter interpretation receives some support within Matthew's own text by the reference to "Mary the mother of James and Joseph" in 27:56. Matthew (following Mark 15:40, "Mary the mother of James . . . and of Joses, and Salome") cannot be referring to the mother of Jesus here and therefore the evangelist himself seems to presume that at least James and Joseph are not blood brothers of Jesus. In any case, Matthew's story itself shows no particular interest in this question and provides no direct information to resolve it.

The final question—"where then did this man get all this?" (13:56)—parallels the opening question of the story (13:54) and underscores the townspeople's lack of understanding. They therefore "took offense" at Jesus; the verb *skandalizomai* forcefully expresses their alienation in that they literally find Jesus an "obstacle," unable to move beyond their supposed familiarity with Jesus and his family to discover the mystery revealed in him (see 11:6, "blessed is anyone who takes no offense at me"). Jesus responds with a proverb, "Prophets are not without honor except in their own country and in their own house" (13:57). Matthew omits the phrase "among their own kin" (Mark 6:4), perhaps to avoid direct criticism of Jesus' relatives (Matthew had also omitted an earlier judgment of the family that Jesus was "out of his mind" in Mark 3:21). But the judgment on the people of Nazareth remains severe: "He did not do many deeds of power [the same phrase as in 13:54] there, because of their unbelief" (13:58). The weakness of the disciples will earn them the label "little faith" (*oligopistoi;* see 6:30; 8:26; 14:31; 16:8; also 17:20); but Jesus' hometown people who completely fail to understand Jesus are plagued with *apistia,* "no faith."

◊ ◊ ◊ ◊

The story at Nazareth continues the motif of revelation and rejection that dominated Matthew's narrative since the beginning of chapter 11 and was forcefully expressed in the parable discourse. Although the focus of this story is on the narrow perimeter of Nazareth, the fact that the Nazarenes are Jesus' countrymen, in such an obvious way makes this incident a harbinger of what will eventually unfold on a much larger scale at the climax of the Gospel, as Matthew presents Jesus rejected by the leaders and the whole people. For the disciples and the reader of the Gospel, the open-ended question of the townspeople hangs in the air: "Where did this man get this wisdom and these deeds of power?"

The Death of the Prophet John (14:1-12)

Jesus' declaration in his hometown of Nazareth that "prophets are not without honor except in their own country" (13:57) is vividly illustrated in the final episode of John the Baptist's prophetic career. Matthew tracks John's ministry with his first appearance at the Jordan baptismal site (3:1-17), then notes his arrest at the beginning of Jesus' mission (4:12), and reports his leading question from prison in 11:2. Throughout, Matthew has clearly identified John as a fearless prophet, one not afraid to confront the powerful (see, e.g., 3:7-10), and now he dies a prophet's death.

Matthew's interest in John remains christological: John's destiny is a preview of Jesus' own destiny. This story is found in Mark 6:17-29, but Matthew has significantly abbreviated his version, reducing many of Mark's more colorful details (and creating some difficulties in the flow of the narrative as a result; see below). The death of John is also reported by Josephus (*Ant.* 18:118-19), but there the emphasis is on Antipas's political motivations; the death of John was a preemptive strike taken before John's prophetic voice could create too many difficulties. Matthew's version follows the lead of Mark and presents a more lurid account of life in Herod's court, perhaps reflecting popular traditions about the circumstances of John's death. At the same time, Matthew tones down Mark's story and places the blame more squarely on Herod, moving his account closer to the tradition reported by Josephus.

◊ ◊ ◊ ◊

The villain of Matthew's story is Herod Antipas, the son of Herod the Great whom Matthew correctly identifies as the "tetrarch," who in the wake of his father's death ruled over the area of lower Galilee, site of most of Jesus' ministry (14:1, contrast Mark 6:14 who calls him "king"; but see also Matt 14:9). Matthew ties this story loosely to the episode in Nazareth through his editorial phrase, "at that time" (14:1). Herod hears reports of Jesus' "powers" (the term *dynameis* also picks up a motif from the previous story; see 13:54, 58) and tells his servants that Jesus is John the Baptist raised from the dead. Given the fact that Herod is the one who killed John, this surmise can only be intended as ominous and immediately links the fate of Jesus with that of John. The belief that Jesus was really John the Baptist returned is also repeated in 16:14.

This deadly interest of Herod in Jesus leads to the flashback that continues in the rest of the story (14:3-12). Herod had arrested John because the prophet had criticized his marriage to Herodias, whom the Gospel identifies as the wife of Herod's brother Philip, the ruler of upper Galilee. In fact, Herodias had been married to another half uncle also named Herod (not Antipas); Salome, the daughter of Herodias and presumably the one who appears unnamed in the story, would become the wife of Philip. In any case, the marriage of Herod to Herodias violated Jewish law forbidding incestuous marriage to the wife of one's (living) brother (see Lev 18:6; 20:21).

Although Matthew says that Herod had imprisoned John "on account of Herodias" (14:3), Matthew's version emphasizes Herod's initiative. It is not Herodias but Herod himself who wants to put John to death and his only hesitation is the crowd's reverence for John as a prophet (14:5; see similarly 21:26; in Mark's account, Herod protects John from Heriodias's wrath; see Mark 6:19-20). Such hesitation is overcome on the occasion of Herod's birthday celebration when the king promises "on oath" to give Salome whatever she asks and the girl, prompted by her mother, asks for the head of John (14:7-8). Matthew's Gospel frowns on the taking of oaths (5:33-37) and both Herod and later Peter (26:72, 74) take oaths with dire consequences. Matthew retains Mark's comment that the king was "grieved" to have to accede to the girl's request—a comment that now makes less sense in Matthew's account since he had already presented Herod as *wanting* to kill John (see 14:5). Matthew has reduced many of Mark's vivid details about the celebration and the machinations of Herodias and her daughter, yet his account still portrays the court as corrupt and murderous. Historians have debated the probable location of the court as told in the story. Herod had a fortified palace at Machaerus in the Jordan valley (a more likely site for John's imprisonment), but his regular court would have been in Tiberias.

Matthew's main interest is in portraying John dying as a prophet martyr at the hands of a cruel and corrupt despot. The reader of the Gospel is aware that this same martyr's death awaits Jesus, a connection poignantly made when the story ends with John's disciples telling Jesus of the prophet's death (14:12), a detail found only in Matthew's account. The parallels between John and Jesus are clear: Each fearlessly proclaims the advent of the kingdom of God (3:1-10); Each experiences rejection (11:18-19); and each ultimately is arrested and unjustly put to death by the ruling powers (a fate also predicted for the disciples; see 10:17-18).

◊ ◊ ◊ ◊

Matthew's typical moral and christological concerns are apparent in this story. Those who oppose John and Jesus are corrupt; they violate the law; they take frivolous oaths; they oppose the prophetic word and end up in violence. John, on the other hand—and by implication, Jesus himself—is presented as heroic proclaimer of the word even in the face of threat and death. Even Herod's erroneous surmise that Jesus is John the Baptist raised from the dead has ironic truth for the reader who knows that violent death will not still the voice of either John or Jesus.

The Feeding of the Multitudes (14:13-21)

This is the first of two stories about the miraculous feeding of the multitudes (see also 15:32-39). This Gospel incident is particularly rich in symbolism and, coming immediately after the rejection of Jesus in Nazareth (13:54-58) and the ominous account of John's martyrdom (14:1-12), shifts the spotlight back to the extraordinary messianic power of Jesus. Matthew also gives attention to the role of the disciples in Jesus' mission, a motif that will intensify as the Gospel continues. Matthew draws this story from Mark 6:32-44 but characteristically abbreviates some of Mark's details and highlights motifs of special interest to the Gospel.

◊ ◊ ◊ ◊

Curiously, Matthew begins this segment with what appears to be an editorial lapse. Because Matthew placed the missioning of the apostles earlier in chapter 10, and because he does not portray the apostles actually engaging in a distinct mission until the end of the Gospel (28:16-20), he cannot use Mark's transition where the apostles return and Jesus invites them to a "deserted place" to rest (see Mark 6:30-31). Matthew has to create a transition from the story of John's death, which he accomplishes by beginning with, "Now when Jesus heard this, he withdrew from there in a boat . . ." (14:13). The reader assumes that "this" refers to the report of the prophet's death brought to Jesus by John's disciples (see 14:12). The problem is that the account of John's death is a "flashback," not part of the real time of the narrative, so Matthew has created a "parenthesis that never ends" (Davies and Allison 1991, 463). It is possible that Matthew intended to refer to Herod's interest in Jesus mentioned in 14:1-2 and this lethal curiosity of Herod's may have prompted Jesus to withdraw, but if this is the case Matthew has still made an awkward transition.

Once under way, however, Matthew's story is trim and cogent. The setting for the story is a "deserted place," obviously near the sea but the word *erēmos* ("desert," "wilderness") may evoke thoughts of the feeding of the multitude with manna during the Exodus, the first of several rich allusions in this account. Despite Jesus' efforts to retreat by himself, the crowds hear of it and are on the shore waiting as Jesus' boat touches land. His response to the crowd is a familiar one in the Gospel: "He had compassion for them and cured their sick" (see also 9:36; 15:32; 20:34; in each case the verb *splangchnizomai* is used in connection with healing). Matthew does not include Mark's reference to teaching nor to the crowds' being like "sheep without a shepherd" (Mark 6:34); that latter description was already used in the important summary text of Matt 9:36.

Several layers of meaning can be detected in this story. First of all, it is another "deed of power" (see 13:54, 58; 14:2) expressing Jesus' messianic mission, this time miraculously feeding a large crowd with meager provisions of five loaves and two fish. Matthew emphasizes the role of the disciples in this miracle. The disciples' suggestion that the crowd be sent away into the surrounding villages to buy food for themselves is countered by Jesus with the direct command: "They need not go away; you give them something to eat" (14:15-16). Unlike Mark where the disciples seem to mock Jesus' suggestion, the Matthean disciples are simply concerned that there are insufficient provisions on hand (cf. Matt 14:17 and Mark 6:37-38). Matthew also underscores the role of the disciples in distributing the food once it has been blessed by Jesus (14:19).

Other layers of meaning reach back into Israel's history, as well as forward into the Gospel narrative and the experience of the community. As already noted, the feeding of hungry multitudes in a "deserted" place recalls the incident of the manna where, through Moses, God fed the Israelites during the wilderness wandering (see Exod 16). Even the combination of bread with fish may find some anticipation in Jewish reflection on the manna as in Wis 19:12, which refers to the manna and to the "quails [that] came up from the sea." Some suggest that Matthew's addition of the phrase "besides women and children" in noting the count of those present, may also be intended to recall the method of counting the Israelites during the Exodus (Matt 14:21; see Exod 12:37; Num 11:21).

The feeding of hungry men with meager provisions more evidently recalls the story of Elisha in 2 Kgs 4:42-44 where the prophet feeds a hundred people with twenty loaves of barley and some ears of grain (see also the story of Elijah feeding the widow and her son with a handful of meal and a jar of oil in 1 Kgs 17:8-16 and Elisha's miraculous multiplication of the oil in 2 Kgs 4:1-4). Matthew presents Jesus as continuing in the line of these great prophetic figures, but doing so in a way that is far more astounding.

Other elements in the story project its symbolic links into the future. The approach of evening (*opsias genomenēs;* 14:15 and 26:20), Jesus' gestures over the provisions ("taking . . . he looked up to heaven . . . blessed and broke the loaves, and gave them to the disciples," 14:19; cf. 26:27), as well as the focus on the loaves and not the fish at the conclusion of the story (14:20; contrast Mark 6:43; the *Didache* uses forms of the same word for "fragments" *[klasmata]* to refer to the eucharistic elements; see *Did.* 11:3-4) all link this feeding story with the Last Supper account in 26:26-29 and ultimately with the community's celebration of the Eucharist. The story's anticipation of the Eucharist may also be one reason Matthew gives the disciples a more positive and prominent role in the feeding story itself.

The symbolic meaning of the story may extend even beyond the community's liturgical experience into the eschaton. The abundance of this banquet, the fact that Jesus the Messiah is its provider and host, and the satisfaction of the multitude's hunger evoke the symbolism of the eschatological banquet, as depicted in a text such as Isa 25:6-9. (This motif was also popular at Qumran; see, e.g., *1QS* vi 4-5; *1QSa* ii 17-22; and in other Jewish texts such as 2 Bar 29:3-8; 4 Ezra 6:52. In the latter texts both bread and fish are included in the messianic feast.)

◊ ◊ ◊ ◊

Attention to the possible liturgical and eschatological symbolism in the miraculous feeding should not detract from the more fundamental levels of meaning the story has within the immediate narrative framework of Matthew. This "powerful deed" is an integral part of Jesus' mission as presented by Matthew and is thereby meant as a paradigm for the community. Jesus has compassion on the multitudes and both heals and feeds them. A large number of people are involved (five thousand men plus women and children), adding to the extraordinary dimensions of this work of Jesus, an action to be repeated in chapter 15. The role of the disciples illustrates that this mission of Jesus is also intended to be mission instruction for the community; instead of sending the hungry crowds away, the disciples are to feed them.

The feeding story also amplifies Matthew's Christology. Jesus is the Messiah whose mission fulfills great signs of the Old Testament, such as the manna in the wilderness and the prophet ministries of Elijah and Elisha. At the same time, Jesus' mission of gathering and feeding the multitude is a pledge of the eschatological peace assured by his inauguration of the kingdom of God. As the community's celebration of the eucharistic meals developed ever more profound significance, it no doubt caught up many of these layers of meaning.

The Walking on the Sea and Healings at Gennesaret (14:22-36)

The extraordinary Christology reflected in the preceding story of the miraculous feeding is intensified in Matthew's account of

Jesus' walking on the water. This story also accelerates Matthew's focus on the disciples, a motif that will continue over the next several chapters. This segment is a particularly vivid illustration of Matthew's reinterpretation of Markan material (cf. Mark 6:45-52). In Mark, Jesus' appearance only underscores the deepening confusion and even the "hard-heartedness" of the disciples (see especially Mark 6:51-52). In Matthew, the accent on Jesus' intent to rescue the disciples is more emphatic and his mysterious appearance on the water leads to their full confession of his identity as "Son of God" (14:33). Along with a completely different conclusion to the story, the other notable difference from Mark's account is Matthew's insertion of the incident about Peter (14:28-31). This story demonstrates Jesus' ability both to empower and to rescue the leading disciple. At the same time, Peter's weak faith, his fear and doubt in the face of the storm, and his crying out to Jesus in prayerful supplication portray the disciples in a manner typical of Matthew's Gospel.

◊ ◊ ◊ ◊

Matthew provides a transition from the feeding story and sets the stage for the encounter on the sea by first separating Jesus and the disciples. Here he follows Mark but adds some nuances (cf. Matt 14:22-23; Mark 6:45-46). Jesus sends the disciples by boat "to the other side," which Mark identifies as "Bethsaida" on the northeastern shore of the sea. Matthew omits the reference to Bethsaida, perhaps because he thought it clashed with the ending of Mark's account where the boat actually comes ashore at "Gennesaret" on the northwestern shore (see Mark 6:53//Matt 14:34). Matthew also stresses that Jesus "went up the mountain" to pray. Given Matthew's penchant for mountain settings as places of revelation (see 4:8; 5:1; 15:29; 17:1; 28:16), it is not impossible he wants to strike that note here. In effect, Jesus prays in preparation for the mighty work of revelation and redemption he is about to enact on behalf of his disciples. Some have suggested that the evangelist may even intend to wrap Jesus in the mantle of Moses at this point, recalling the ascent of Moses to Sinai in the midst of the Exodus (see Davies and Allison 1991, 502). While some Exodus motifs may work beneath the surface of this story, the connection to Moses in this story is very subtle, if present at all.

While Jesus is in prayer, the disciples have traveled some distance on the sea and find themselves in distress. Matthew describes it literally as "many furlongs" from the shore (14:24; a *stadion* was a measurement of approximately two hundred yards) while Mark says they were in the "middle of the sea" (4:47). The boat is battered by the waves and the wind has risen against them. All of this is preparatory for Jesus' mysterious appearance. "Early in the morning" (literally, "during the fourth watch of the night," a Roman measurement of time for approximately three to six A.M.), Jesus approaches the disciples, "walking toward them on the sea" (14:25). By omitting Mark's enigmatic reference—"He intended to pass them by" (6:48b)—Matthew presents Jesus' appearance clearly as an act of both revelation and rescue. Typical of reactions to such theophanies in biblical and Jewish literature, the disciples cry out in terror, "It is a ghost!" (14:26, cast in direct address as is typical of Matthew's style; cf. Mark 6:49). Jesus immediately reassures the disciples, "Take heart, it is I; do not be afraid" (14:27). The Greek phrase *ego eimi* ("I am") points to the depths of Matthew's christological affirmation here. Drawing on the revelation of the divine name in Exod 3:14, this formulation is used repeatedly as a self-designation of God in Isaiah (see Isa 41:4; 43:1-13; 47:8, 10). In Isa 43, the divine name is coupled with reminders of God's redemptive act in rescuing Israel from slavery and exhortations not to fear.

Motifs of divine rescue from storm as well as manifestations of divine power by walking upon the sea occur repeatedly in the Bible and other Jewish literature. Psalm 107, which extols the redemptive power of God toward Israel, provides a classic description of peril at sea and divine rescue: "They mounted up to heaven, they went down to the depths; their courage melted away in their calamity; they reeled and staggered like drunkards, and were at their wits' end. Then they cried to the LORD in their trouble, and he brought them out from their distress; he made the storm be still, and the waves of the sea were hushed" (Ps 107:26-28; see also Job 26:11-12; Pss 65:7; 89:9-10). Walking upon the sea is also depicted as a manifestation of divine power over the chaos of the waters, as in Job 9:8, "[God] who alone stretched out the heavens and trampled the waves of the Sea" (see also Job 38:16; Sir 24:5-6). The dramatic Exodus event where the Israelites march dry-shod through the sea may also be an influence here (see Exod 14:13-31). Psalm 77 reflects on this event in terms reminiscent of the Matthean story: "Your way was through the sea, your path, through the mighty waters; yet your footprints were unseen" (Ps 77:19; see also Isa 43:16; 51:10; Hab 3:15). What is remarkable in the Gospel account is that such divine power is attributed to Jesus.

Matthew "interrupts" the theophany and rescue story with his insertion of the story about Peter (14:28-31). This incident is unique to Matthew's Gospel and most of the vocabulary and motifs it contains are typical of the evangelist. Some have suggested that the story originated as a resurrection appearance story, reminiscent of the encounter with Peter at the sea in John 21, or may have been drawn from a popular story that circulated orally in Matthew's community. It is more likely that Matthew himself composed this story as a kind of homiletic expansion on the Markan account. Attention to Peter as the leader and prime representative of the disciples will be evident from this point on in Matthew's narrative (see below, 15:15; 16:16; 17:4, 24-27; 18:21; 19:27; 26:33, 35). Presenting Peter as weak in faith and in need of rescue in the middle of the sea story retains some of the critical tone in Mark's depiction of the disciples (6:51-52) and, at the same time, frees Matthew to give the overall account another, more positive conclusion.

Peter's words to Jesus—"Lord, is it you?" (AT)—seem to interplay with Jesus' own declaration: "I am." The disciple asks to share in Jesus' power to walk upon the sea and is invited by Jesus to do so. The audacity of Peter's request harmonizes with Matthew's theology of discipleship. In the mission discourse, Jesus had given the disciples a share in his own redemptive mission: proclamation of the kingdom of heaven and the power to "cure the sick, raise the dead, cleanse the lepers, cast out demons" (10:7-8). That redemptive power is now translated into the idiom of walking upon the sea, an expression of divine power over chaos and threat. Peter began to walk upon the "water" toward Jesus but, "when he noticed the strong wind," fear overcame him and he began to sink. Peter's response in the midst of this peril is exemplary—he cries out to Jesus in supplication, "Lord, save me!" a desperate prayer that echoes that of the disciples in the story of the storm at sea (8:25). Crying out to God in the peril of drowning also has biblical echoes. Psalm 69 is particularly eloquent: "Save me, O God, for the waters have come up to my neck" (v. 1); "Do not let the flood sweep over me, or the deep swallow me up. . . . Answer me, O LORD, for your steadfast love is good; according to your abundant mercy, turn to me" (vv. 15-16; see also Pss 18:15-16; 107:28, 30; 144:5-8; Wis 14:2-4). Rescue from drowning as a metaphor for divine redemption is also found in the Qumran and other Jewish literature (see *1QH* iii 6, 12-18; vi 22-25; vii 4-5; *T. Naph.* 6:1-10).

Jesus reaches out and saves Peter, a gesture used in other healing contexts (see 8:3; 12:13). At the same time, Jesus chides Peter for his "little faith" (Matthew's characteristic expression, see 6:30; 8:26; 16:8; 17:20) and asks him, "Why did you doubt?" This same verb is used in the final scene of the Gospel where some or perhaps even all of the eleven apostles "doubt" when confronted with the Risen Christ (28:17). The verb *distazō* can imply "doubt" or even "hesitate," as in the kind of personal confusion or uncertainty that prevents action or commitment. The portrayal of Peter succumbing to fear even though he has the power to walk on water defines what Matthew means by such terms as "little faith" and "doubting."

The story concludes with the calming of the sea as Jesus and Peter enter the boat and the disciples' confession of faith. The rescue first experienced by Peter now extends to the entire band of disciples. They, in turn, "worship" Jesus. Matthew's characteristic verb *proskyneō* literally means to "prostrate" or "reverence," implying an attitude of profound respect in the presence of a deity (see, e.g., 8:2; 15:25 where it is also used with the title "Lord"). They acclaim, "Truly you are the Son of God" (14:33; cf. 16:16; 27:54). Thus the entwined theophany and rescue story concludes appropriately with the safety of the disciples in the boat and with their reverent acknowledgment of Jesus' unique identity and divine power. The contrast with Mark's portrayal is stark (cf. 6:51-52): Instead of confusion and disbelief, the Matthean disciples, even though weak, express their faith in Jesus as Son of God.

A transitional summary (14:34-36) concludes the story and prepares for the conflict story that will follow (15:1-20). Matthew draws upon the Markan summary of 6:53-56 but typically edits it by reducing details and clarifying the focus. When the boat comes ashore at Gennesaret, "men of that place" (reminiscent of Matthew's phrasing in 14:21) recognize Jesus and bring the sick from the surrounding region to Jesus. The sick beseech Jesus even to touch the fringe of his cloak in order to be healed (these are probably the tassels worn by observant Jews as a sign of obedience to the Torah; see Num 15:38-40; Deut 22:12; cf. Matt 9:20-22). This poignant scene, with the sick desperate to touch Jesus, provides a lingering focus on the extraordinary redemptive power that Jesus had displayed upon the sea.

◊ ◊ ◊ ◊

Walking upon the sea and having the power to still the sea and rescue those in its terrible grip are divine attributes in the Bible and other Jewish literature. For Matthew, Jesus' identity as "Son of God" goes beyond the traditional messianic designation, depicting Jesus in numinous terms and as one who bears divine power. This extraordinary communion with the divine was already affirmed in 11:19 where Jesus was identified with Wisdom and especially in 11:25-27, which stressed the unique bond between Father and Son and Jesus' role as revealer of God. The metaphors of storm at sea and rescue from drowning, as well as the revelation of the divine name, "I am," have strong links to the Exodus story as a paradigm of God's saving action on behalf of Israel. As in the preceding story of the loaves, Matthew's narrative is attentive to this Exodus motif.

The insertion of the Peter story enables Matthew to make this also a discipleship story. The disciples' dignity and power are affirmed in that Peter is able to walk on the water when invited by Jesus. The disciples' reverent confession of Jesus as Son of God is also an exemplary expression of faith from Matthew's perspective. At the same time, Matthew refuses to idealize the disciples by noting Peter's "little faith" expressed in fear and "doubt." The community that experiences weakness and fear in the face of threat is reminded of Jesus' divine power. The appropriate response is to cry out in earnest prayer.

A Dispute with the Pharisees and Scribes (15:1-20)

The Gospel's juxtaposition of outright rejection of Jesus by the religious leaders and profound, if still weak, faith on the part of the disciples and those seeking healing continues through the next series of scenes where Jesus clashes sharply with the Pharisees and scribes and then meets unexpected faith from a Gentile woman. Matthew follows the narrative sequence provided by Mark. Following the dramatic encounter on the sea, Jesus and the disciples come ashore at the plains of Gennesaret, on the western side of the lake. It is there, apparently, that the debate with the Pharisees and scribes takes place (15:1). Later, Jesus will leave them to go to the "district of Tyre and Sidon" (15:21), a change of scene that is an implicit comment on the intransigence of the leaders while it also prepares for the contrasting faith of the Canaanite woman. Afterward, Jesus will return again to this same general region around the Sea of Galilee (15:29).

Matthew has made substantial changes in this Markan story (see Mark 7:1-23). Mark's version concentrates on the issue of cultic purity as illustrated in the question of washing one's hands before eating in order to avoid ritual defilement. One of the end results of Jesus' dispute with the Pharisees, according to Mark, is that he declares "all foods clean" (7:19). For Matthew, however, the key issue is not cultic purity as such, but the clash between Jesus' teaching and "the tradition of the elders" as interpreted by the Pharisees and scribes. Their views on "Corban" (i.e., declaring that one's possessions belong to God in order to avoid family obligations) and washing of hands are illustrations of how, from Matthew's point of view, the leaders' interpretation of the tradition runs counter to the intent of God's law.

Matthew achieves this realignment by several editorial changes, the most apparent of which is reversing the order of Mark's account so that the question of "Corban" precedes that of hand washing. Matthew also drops Mark's radical comment about all foods being declared clean (7:19) and suppresses Mark's sweeping critique of Jewish practices (7:13). However, he amplifies the critique of the Pharisees with his additions in 15:12-15.

Matthew retains the basic structure of the story based on a succession of audiences, beginning with a direct confrontation between the religious leaders and Jesus (15:1-9), then Jesus' declaration to the "crowd" (15:10-11), and finally a discussion between Jesus and his disciples (15:12-20). Having Peter pose the question about the meaning of the "parable" in 15:15 narrows the circle even further to a concentration upon discipleship instruction.

◊ ◊ ◊ ◊

Pharisees and scribes from Jerusalem confront Jesus with the fundamental question: "Why do your disciples break the tradition of the elders?" (15:1-2). The "tradition of the elders" was an important concept for the Pharisaic movement, referring to the entire body of regulations and customs that had developed in interpretation of the law in order to apply it to everyday life. Later this "tradition" would be formalized in such codifications as the Mishnah (beginning around 200 CE). But at the time of Jesus the tradition was more fluid. In the spectrum of first-century Jewish life, the Pharisees' use of such tradition in application of the law was considered innovative and was opposed by more conservative groups such as the Sadducees. As this Gospel scene indicates, Matthew's community did not dispute the concept of tradition as such, but the tenor and authority of Pharisaic viewpoints over against those of Jesus.

The Pharisees protest because Jesus' disciples do not wash their hands before eating (15:2b). This was not a matter of sanitation but a strict observance of ritual purity. In treating the issue of contamination incurred by contact with a bodily discharge, Leviticus enjoined the washing of hands for purposes of purification (see Lev 15:11). This probably led to a practice on the part of the very devout to wash their hands routinely before eating as an act of purification. One of the characteristics of the Pharisaic reform was an attempt to extend the level of holiness and ritual purity maintained by the priests into the arena of ordinary lay life.

By having Jesus reply with a fundamental question of his own and then inverting Mark's order, turning first to the matter of "Corban" and only later to the issue of ritual impurity raised by the leaders, Matthew puts the focus of the debate on the tenor of the Pharisees' teaching rather than the validity of the cultic practice (see Matt 15:3-6). "Why do you break the commandment of God for the sake of your tradition?" (15:3). Jesus' example (adapted from Mark 7:9-13) is the practice of declaring one's possessions to be dedicated to God and therefore not available for other use as a ruse for avoiding the obligations of supporting one's parents. There is evidence that such abuses did occur, although it is unlikely that it was typical of all Pharisees (Fitzmyer 1974, 93-100). Note that Matthew has omitted the term "Corban" and its explanation, presumably because this was already well known to his community. Jesus cites the obligation of the Decalogue to honor one's parents (quoting Exod 20:12 and Deut 5:16), introducing it with the phrase "for *God* said . . ." and setting up a contrast with the Pharisees' teaching introduced with "but *you* say . . ." (15:4, 5, emphasis added). Jesus repeats his fundamental accusation against the leaders in 15:6: "So, for the sake of your tradition, you make void the word of God." Despite the severity of this judgment, it is less sweeping than the formulation in Mark 7:13 ("thus making void the word of God *through your tradition that you have handed on. And you do many things like this*" [emphasis added]; Matthew also omits Mark 7:8, perhaps because he judges it is also too inclusive). One senses that Matthew wants to restrict Jesus' critique to particular viewpoints of the Pharisees and not to Jewish tradition and practices as such, probably because Matthew's Jewish-Christian community still maintained Jewish practices, including cultic ones, and saw no incompatibility with the teaching of Jesus on this score.

The first segment of the pericope concludes with a quotation from Isa 29:13, a text particularly suitable because it provides a scriptural grounding for Jesus' challenge to the authenticity of Pharisaic traditions. Matthew adds the biting phrase, "you hypocrites," his typical judgment on what is considered religiously fraudulent (see 6:2, 5, 16; 7:5; 22:18; 23:13, 15, 23, 25, 27, 28, 29).

Jesus turns from the leaders and now addresses the "crowd" (15:10-11). Matthew distinguishes between the religious leaders and the general population. The former are condemned while the latter are instructed. Jesus' words to them take the form of an aphorism stating the priority of moral purity over cultic purity: It is not what goes into the mouth that defiles a person but what comes out (15:11). The importance of purity of heart as the touchstone of authentic worship was a fundamental teaching of the prophets and, as such, is not an innovation of Jesus (see, e.g., Isa 1:12-17). Yet here, as in other parts of Matthew's Gospel, we see a consistent and often emphatic relativizing of cultic observance in favor of moral integrity and compassion, a perspective that undoubtedly was characteristic of Jesus' own teaching.

A new segment begins with the approach of the disciples to Jesus (15:12). Their question and Jesus' response are unique to Matthew and reveal his interests: "Do you know that the Pharisees took offense [literally, "were scandalized"; see 11:6; 13:57] when they heard what you said?" Jesus' reply uses the metaphor of the "plant," probably inspired by Isa 60:21, "They are the shoot that I planted, the work of my hands, so that I might be glorified." In Qumran (see *1QS* viii 5; xi 8; CD i 7) and in other Jewish literature, the symbol of the righteous plant was used to claim God's favor on a particular community and it is not impossible that some Pharisaic groups may also have made this claim. Jesus' words turn this claim on its head, threatening God's judgment ("will be uprooted"). The image of the plant also recalls the parable of the wheat and the tares, which warns the disciples to expect the presence of "weeds" among the seed God has planted (see 13:24-30, 36-43). The Pharisees are also termed "blind guides" whose teaching leads others astray, an indictment that will be repeated in chapter 23 (see 23:16, 17, 19, 26).

Peter, again assuming a leadership role (see above, 14:28), asks for an explanation of the "parable" on behalf of the other disciples ("explain to *us*")—presumably the saying of 15:11 about defilement that has the enigmatic quality of a parable and calls for "understanding" (see 13:13-15). Peter's question is interpreted by Jesus as a sign that he still struggles with full comprehension. Jesus' words provide a vivid explanation: What goes into the mouth passes into the stomach and then into the latrine (15:17). But what comes out of the mouth proceeds from the "heart" and this is what defiles. The "heart" is perceived as virtually the center of consciousness, the place where one's values reside and commitments are made (see 5:8, 28; 6:21; 9:4; 11:29; 12:34; 13:15, 19; 15:8, 19; 18:35; 22:37). It is ultimately from the "heart" that the most grievous human impurity comes (15:19). Matthew's list of impurities is briefer than that of Mark (seven compared to thirteen in Mark 7:21). Besides his penchant for abbreviating Mark, Matthew's selection may also be influenced by the list of capital sins in the Decalogue (e.g., evil thoughts, murder, adultery, theft, false witness).

The concluding verse (15:20) brings the discussion back to the original protest of the Pharisees and scribes (see 15:2). By now, however, Matthew has put Jesus' teaching in a broader perspective. Moral purity—or the cleanliness of one's heart—is far more important than ritual purity, and all religious practice must be informed by the intent of God's law.

◊ ◊ ◊ ◊

Matthew casts the religious leaders as foils for Jesus. Their challenge to Jesus enables Matthew to portray Jesus' teaching as fully in accord with the intent of God's law. Matthew also continues his focus on discipleship instruction: Peter and his companions are reminded that authentic purity begins in the heart, not on the hands. One may also trace here the efforts of Matthew's community to remain true to its Jewish heritage, now informed by the teaching of Jesus. Jesus' words should not be construed as putting aside the cultic laws altogether, nor did Jesus condemn all Jewish practices. The issue was placing purity of heart as the center from which all religious practice should take its proper expression. In directly criticizing some Pharisaic practices and in demonstrating that Jesus' teaching was in accord with the Scriptures, Matthew attempted to bolster the authority of his own community and its tradition.

The Canaanite Woman (15:21-28)

The story of the Canaanite woman is also in Mark (7:24-30), but Matthew's revisions are substantial. Although Matthew does not underscore the point, the contrast is obvious between this Gentile woman's extraordinary faith and the stance of the religious leaders in the preceding story who were condemned for their hypocrisy and erroneous teaching.

This story also plays a significant role in Matthew's view of the Gentile mission, a view that unfolds for the reader as the narrative develops. Previous encounters with Gentiles—such as the visit of the Magi (2:1-12), the healing of the centurion's servant (8:5-13), and the Gadarene exorcism (8:28-34)—as well as the mission instruction of 10:5-6 and the final commission of 28:16-20 all have to be kept in mind to understand the full range of Matthew's perspective. The evangelist's changes in the story of the Canaanite woman intensify the issue by having the woman and Jesus directly confront each other, not twice but three times, and by having Jesus explicitly reaffirm that his mission is only to Israel (15:24). Matthew also gives the disciples a role as they urge Jesus to dismiss the woman (15:23). Without question, this story reflected a crucial debate within Matthew's community.

◊ ◊ ◊ ◊

Matthew subtly alters the setting for this story. Jesus leaves the scene of his confrontation with the Pharisees and scribes and goes "to the district of Tyre and Sidon" (15:21). At the time of Jesus the region of Tyre and Sidon was an extensive area beginning at the Mediterranean coast on the west and extending along the northwestern border of Israel for much of upper Galilee. Within Matthew's story, Tyre and Sidon had already been identified as typical Gentile territory (see 11:22). In contrast to Mark's account, where Jesus goes to the region and enters a house (7:24), Matthew gives the impression that Jesus goes near to the border of Tyre and Sidon but does not actually enter it (the preposition *eis* can mean "to" or "toward"). The Canaanite woman "comes out" to approach him, apparently crossing over into Jewish territory to make her plea on behalf of her daughter (15:22). This setting harmonizes with Jesus' own instructions in the mission discourse: "Go nowhere among the Gentiles, and enter no town of the Samaritans" (10:5). In Matthew's Gospel, Jesus does stay within the boundaries of Israel, with the only exception being the flight to Egypt and the visit to Gadarene territory (where Matthew in fact downplays the Gentile context; see above, Matt 8:28-34). The fact that Matthew identifies her as a "Canaanite" instead of Mark's "a Gentile, of Syrophoenician origin" (7:26) also adds to the picture. The reader thinks of the traditional archenemies of Israel in the biblical saga and the chasm between the pagan world and that of Israel.

The focus in Matthew's story is clearly on the remarkable conversation that will ensue between Jesus and the woman. The woman presents her case insistently and with unshakable faith. Matthew's typical use of direct address throughout the story stokes its intensity. In the opening exchange, which is added by Matthew (15:22-23), the woman begs for healing on behalf of her daughter who is "tormented by a demon." She addresses Jesus with two strong christological titles: "Lord" and "Son of David." The title "Lord" is often used in moments of supplication in Matthew's Gospel (see, e.g., 8:2, 6, 8; 8:25; 14:28, 30; 17:15; 20:30); the Canaanite woman will address Jesus this way three times in this story. Similarly, "Son of David" is a messianic title that is favored by Matthew in contexts of healing (see 9:27; 20:30).

Jesus responds with silence, leading the disciples to urge him to "send her away" (15:23). The verb used here (apoluein, literally to "release" or "dismiss") is somewhat ambiguous—do the disciples want Jesus to heal her daughter and thereby free the woman to leave or, as is more likely, to send her away without the healing? In the feeding story the disciples' response to the needs of the crowds was to advise Jesus to "send them away" (the same verb, apoluein, is used, see 14:15) and that is probably their stance here as well. Jesus answers the disciples (not the woman) that he is "sent only to the lost sheep of the house of Israel" (15:24). This reaffirms his mission instruction to the apostles in 10:5-6. The "lost sheep of the house of Israel" probably refers to the whole community of Israel, not just a particular group with a special claim on Jesus' mission. The term "lost sheep" characterizes Israel as leaderless and in desperate need (see 9:36; 10:6; 18:12). Matthew affirms what in fact was historically most probable: Jesus restricted his mission to Israel and only occasionally encountered Gentiles.

The woman does not accept Jesus' refusal but comes and "kneels" before him. The verb used here is *proskynein,* a word favored by Matthew that connotes an attitude of reverent faith (the same verb is translated as "worship" by the NRSV in 14:33). She addresses him again as "Lord" and pleads for his help in the manner of prayer (reminiscent of other urgent supplicatory prayers as in 8:2, 25; 14:30). Once again Jesus refuses her, this time with a seemingly cruel rebuff: "It is not fair to take the children's food and throw it to the dogs" (15:26). Matthew omits Mark's reference— "let the children be fed first" (Mark 7:27)—which foresees a temporal sequence with priority to Israel and then a place for the Gentiles. In the tension of Matthew's story, no room at all is provided for the Gentiles and the focus remains squarely on the privilege of Israel. The "children's" food is not to be given to "dogs." Even though the word used here is a diminutive, it remains a contemptuous term for the Gentiles and emphasizes the boundary between Jew and Gentile. The story actually uses the term "loaves" (not just "food"), an enticing link with the feeding stories of 14:13-21 and 15:32-39, as well as the preceding story where the Pharisees had protested the eating of "bread" with unwashed hands (15:2).

Even in the face of this stern refusal, the woman's faith remains strong: "Yes, Lord, yet even the dogs eat the crumbs that fall from their masters' table" (15:27). The woman's response is an artful blend of deference—addressing Jesus reverently as "Lord" and conceding the privileged status of Israel—and a clever retort. Even dogs are able to eat the crumbs that fall from the table! Jesus' resistance finally dissolves in the face of the Canaanite woman's extraordinary faith: "Woman, great is your faith! Let it be done for you as you wish" (v. 28). Matthew's formulation emphasizes that it is the woman's profound and tenacious faith that overcomes Jesus' resistance and enables her daughter to be healed (cf. Mark 7:29, "For saying that, you may go—the demon has left your daughter").

◊ ◊ ◊ ◊

This story puts together with acute tension Jesus' affirmation of his exclusive mission to Israel and the insistent faith of a Gentile who makes a claim upon Jesus' mission despite the privilege of Israel. No other Matthean story presents Jesus as reluctant to heal. In the encounter with the centurion at Capernaum, a story with some similarities to this one, Jesus immediately accedes to the request of the Gentile officer who pleads on behalf of his servant (see 8:7, "I will come and cure him"). In the story of the Canaanite woman, Jesus becomes the proponent of an exclusive mission to Israel that does not even leave room for a salvation history sequence in which Gentiles would come later (i.e., Mark's "let the children be fed *first*" is omitted by Matthew). Yet this exclusive stance is challenged and eventually overwhelmed by the profound and tenacious faith of the Gentile woman who recognizes Jesus as "Lord" and "Son of David" and begs for his healing power on behalf of her child.

Several things seem to be stirring in this remarkable story. Certainly the Canaanite woman stands out as an example of faith that is strong, unhesitant, and persistent (a contrast with the weak, fearful, and hesitant faith of Peter in the story of the walking on the water; see 14:28-31). But the story also contributes to Matthew's mission theology. By presenting Jesus as the proponent of an exclusive mission to Israel, Matthew honors the historical dimensions of Jesus' ministry and the viewpoints of those in the community who still hesitated before the prospect of a Gentile mission. Yet by also showing Jesus yielding to the genuine faith of the Canaanite woman, the evangelist counseled his Jewish-Christian community that a mission to the Gentiles was part of God's plan and not incompatible with reverence for Israel's historic privilege, a divine plan that would burst into reality in the postresurrection experience of the community.

Jesus Heals and Feeds the Multitudes (15:29-39)

From his encounter with the Canaanite woman at the border of Tyre and Sidon, Jesus now returns to the lake region. Matthew continues to follow the narrative sequence of Mark but will make significant changes in the next two stories. Matthew recasts the

Markan story of the healing of the deaf mute (Mark 7:31-37) into a magnificent summary of Jesus' healing power. Not unlike the summary of Jesus' healing in 14:13-14, this display of Jesus' extraordinary compassion for the crowds also serves to introduce the feeding of the multitudes.

In Mark's Gospel the second feeding story is clearly situated in Gentile territory (see 7:31), providing a rationale for the doublet, with the first feeding done for Jews and the second for Gentiles (6:34-44; 8:1-10). Matthew, however, presents a different setting for the story. It is unclear whether Matthew thinks of this as having taken place in Gentile territory. True to his own declarations (10:5; 15:24), the Matthean Jesus appears to restrict his mission to Israel, with only rare exceptions. Yet through his subtle editing, Matthew will bring forward other motifs that make this more than a duplication of the previous miraculous feeding.

◊ ◊ ◊ ◊

Jesus the Healer (15:29-31)

Matthew completely transforms Mark's story of the deaf mute (7:37); virtually all that remains are the references to Jesus' healings of those who are "mute" in 15:30-31. Matthew may have found the vivid details of the Markan account excessive (see especially the very detailed description of Jesus' healing technique in Mark 7:33-34). Now the story is subsumed into a magnificent summary of Jesus' healing of the multitudes of sick who are brought to him by the crowds.

Matthew has also changed the setting for this story (and thereby the setting for the feeding story itself that immediately follows). It no longer takes place during a circuitous route deep into Gentile territory (see Mark's somewhat awkward "by way of Sidon towards the Sea of Galilee, in the region of the Decapolis," 7:31) but "along the Sea of Galilee" and on a mountaintop (Matt 15:29). Jesus ascends the mountain and "sits" in a position of authority, reminiscent of the great scene that introduced the Sermon on the Mount (4:23–5:1). Jesus' healing of the sick leads the crowds to be "amazed" (see similarly 8:27) and they ultimately "praised the God of Israel" (15:31; the verb used here is literally to "glorify" as in 9:8; see also 5:16). The particular formulation the "God of *Israel*" might suggest that Matthew thinks of these crowds as Gentiles looking on in admiration at this agent of Israel's God (see Harrington 1991, 240), but, if so, the suggestion remains quite subtle.

It is likely that Isa 35:5-6, with its reference to the healing of the blind, the deaf, the lame, and the mute in the messianic age, already had an influence on Mark's story of the man who was deaf and mute. Matthew's expansion of the list of Jesus' healings to include the blind and the lame (15:30-31) characteristically strengthens the ties to this important Old Testament text (see Davies and Allison 1991, 566-67, who note that Isa 35 is part of a whole motif connected with Mt. Zion). The entire scene becomes a verbal icon proclaiming Jesus' messianic authority expressed in his mission of healing.

The Feeding of the Multitudes (15:32-39)

Similar to the first feeding story in 14:15-21, this second account is one of the Gospel's most profound illustrations of Jesus' messianic mission, retrospectively evoking thoughts of the feeding of Israel with manna in the wilderness and the prophetic missions of Elijah and Elisha as well as prospectively making links with the eucharistic practice of the community and its longing for the eschatological banquet (see the discussion in 14:15-21).

Taking Matthew's story on its own terms, this feeding of the multitudes now takes place on the same mountain where the crowds of sick had gathered in the previous scene. This enhances the story's connection with the motif of the great eschatological banquet on Zion portrayed in Isa 25:6-9. Thus, on the mountain Jesus wipes away the tears of the people (the image used in Isaiah) through his healing and feeds them with the joyous food of the kingdom. Even the expansion of the numbers of those present (four thousand *plus* women and children in Matt 15:38) contributes to the epic atmosphere of the scene. This connection to the Zion motif is not explicit, but lies close to the surface of Matthew's narrative (see above, 15:29-31).

Matthew also has other characteristic touches in his story. As in the previous feeding story, the disciples have an important role. Here they seem to readily grasp their responsibility to feed the crowds (contrast 14:15-16) but do not know how to do so. The use of the term *eucharistēsas* ("giving thanks," 15:36) and the suppression of the blessing and distribution of the fish (note the elimination of Mark 7:7), with the resulting focus on the loaves and the baskets of leftover fragments, underscore the connection of this story to the eucharistic practice of the community.

The story ends with Jesus getting into a boat and going to the region of "Magadan"; Matthew probably thinks of this as somewhere on the eastern shore of the lake, but its location is unknown. Other manuscripts identify this as Magdala (on the northwest corner of the lake) or Dalmanutha (as in Mark 7:10, also to be located somewhere on the northwest corner). In Matthew's version of the story, Jesus is alone at this point; the disciples join him later (16:5; contrast Mark 8:10).

◊ ◊ ◊ ◊

Matthew presents Jesus as a majestic healer whose compassion for the sick and disabled leads the witnessing crowds to glorify God. Those same crowds who stay with Jesus for three days are miraculously fed by him, itself an act of compassion that evokes for the community an array of powerful memories from Israel's history: God's feeding of the people with manna in the desert; the prophetic ministries of Elijah and Elisha; the great visions of future healing and joyous banqueting forged by Isaiah. Those memories are now embodied in Jesus and his mission as well as in the eucharistic celebrations and eschatological hopes of Matthew's community.

Conflict with the Pharisees and Sadducees (16:1-12)

Matthew continues to adhere to Mark's narrative sequence in these two conflict stories, but holds the focus more intently on Jesus' critique of the religious leaders, thus softening Jesus' frustration with his own disciples (a point stressed in Mark 8:14-21) and emphasizing the infidelity of the leaders' teachings. In effect, Matthew crafts one continuing discussion out of what were two distinct scenes in Mark. When Jesus comes ashore in the region of "Magadan" (15:39) he is immediately embroiled in a debate with the Pharisees and Sadducees. He then leaves them and meets his disciples as they, too, reach "the other side" (16:5) and continues his condemnation of the religious leaders (16:6-12).

◊ ◊ ◊ ◊

The first stage is Jesus' encounter with the Pharisees and Sadducees (16:1-4). Except for the scene where Pharisees and Sadducees come to the Jordan for baptism (and are severely condemned by John; see 3:7-10), this is the only episode in the Gospel where Matthew pairs these two groups of leaders. Obviously they serve in Matthew's view as representative of the religious leadership. In 16:6 this pairing replaces Mark's unusual coupling of Pharisees and "Herod" (see Mark 8:15). The leaders' intent is to "test" Jesus by asking for some spectacular sign to certify his messianic identity. Thereby Matthew clearly signals their hostile attitude; the word "test" (the Greek verb *peirazō*) was also used to characterize Satan's efforts to dissuade Jesus in the temptation story (see 4:1, 3).

Some manuscripts omit Jesus' saying about reading the signs of the weather (16:2-3; cf. Luke 12:54-56), but the contrast is apt between the ordinary ability to read nature's signs and the leaders' failure to read the "signs of the times." Jesus rebuffs the test of this "evil and adulterous generation": The only sign to be given is the "sign of Jonah." Matthew's Gospel had already explained this sign as a reference to Jesus' death and resurrection (see 12:38-42).

After rejecting the leaders' hostile test, Jesus leaves them and meets the disciples as they come ashore on "the other side" (16:5-12). Matthew's editing leaves the precise location uncertain here; presumably this is some distance both from Magadan where Jesus encountered the leaders and the location of the feeding story from which the disciples also embarked. Unlike Mark, who situates this conversation in a boat on the sea (8:14-21), Matthew locates it on dry ground.

Matthew also artfully holds the focus on Jesus' criticism of the leaders and their teaching. Mark's enigmatic statement about the disciples having "one loaf with them in the boat" is omitted (8:14), and the string of sharply worded challenges to the disciples' lack of understanding (8:17-20) is reduced and softened. While the Matthean Jesus chides the disciples for their "little faith" (see also 6:30; 8:26; 14:31) and reminds them about the great miracles of the loaves, the main point is a warning about the "leaven" of the Pharisees and Saducees, not, as in Mark, a criticism of the disciples. Leaven or yeast was used in some Jewish texts as a metaphor for corruption or sin (Harrington 1991, 245). Matthew more precisely identifies it as the false teachings of the Pharisees and Sadducees (16:12). The label "adulterous," applied to them in 16:4 and 12:39, has the same connotation. At last the disciples grasp Jesus' warning: "Then they understood . . ." (16:12).

◊ ◊ ◊ ◊

Matthew continues to portray the religious leaders as negative foils in the Gospel. Their piety is hypocritical and their teaching is false and misleading. One suspects that Matthew's community was still embroiled in conflict with other Jewish groups about the identity of Jesus and the validity of Christian interpretation of the law. Surely the Jewish Christians and the authoritative teachers of Judaism held much in common. But in the polemical atmosphere that may have characterized relations between the two groups, the differences became emphasized and the Jewish leaders were portrayed in one-dimensional fashion. For the reader of the Gospel, the leaders exemplify the attitudes and conduct a true follower of Jesus should avoid.

THE JOURNEY TO JERUSALEM (16:13–20:34)

Confession at Caesarea Philippi (16:13-18)

The confession at Caesarea Philippi is a major turning point in Matthew's narrative. Jesus' pointed question to the disciples about his own identity and Peter's response link this scene to what has already unfolded in the Gospel, including Jesus' great messianic works of teaching and healing that have been on display since the end of chapter 4, as well as the recognition of his identity as Messiah and Son of God that has been a strong current in the Gospel (particularly since chap. 11). Now the first explicit Passion prediction directs the reader's attention forward to the death and resurrection of Jesus, the climax of the Gospel drama.

Taking its cues from a pattern in Mark's narrative (8:27–9:1), the scene has three major components: (1) Jesus' dramatic question to the disciples about his identity and Peter's response (16:13-20); (2) Jesus' prediction of his Passion (16:21-23); (3) discipleship instruction in the light of the cross (16:24-28).

Yet Matthew has imposed his own perspective on this scene. Because the disciples have already confessed Jesus as "Son of God" in 14:33 at the conclusion of the walking on the water (contrast Mark 6:51-52), the dramatic impact of Peter's confession is somewhat blunted. Instead the focus shifts to the interchange between Jesus and Peter: The apostle who confesses Jesus as Messiah and Son of the living God is in turn blessed and given authority in Jesus' community. Matthew adds material unique to his Gospel. Peter's role is also more evident in the segment on the Passion prediction: Peter speaks directly to Jesus and Jesus' rebuke to Peter is more stinging than in Mark's version.

The source for Matthew's special material in this scene is debated. Some consider it purely a composition of Matthew, expressing his typical interest in Peter and perhaps reflecting the significant role that the leader of the apostles had played in the Antiochan church. Others, detecting Semitic elements in the language of 16:17-19, assert that this is archaic pre-Matthean tradition, originating perhaps in resurrection appearance traditions where Peter has prominence (similar to 1 Cor 15:5) or even in historical reminiscence (see Davies and Allison 1991, 604-15). In any case, Matthew has adapted this material to the theological perspective of his Gospel as a whole.

◊ ◊ ◊ ◊

The scene takes place in the "district of Caesarea Philippi," in the northernmost reaches of Israel near the slopes of Mount Hermon. Jesus asks his disciples who people say the *"Son of Man"* is (16:13), a self-designation for Jesus already used frequently in reference to Jesus' authority (see 9:6; 12:8; 13:37) and his future coming at the *parousia* (see 10:23; 13:41), as well as to his rejection and suffering (see 8:20; 11:19; 12:32). The initial response of the disciples cites the prophetic figures "John the Baptist," "Elijah," and, unique to Matthew, "Jeremiah." This prophet who thundered against Israel's infidelities and experienced rejection is favored by Matthew, cited explicitly in the fulfillment quotations of 2:17 and 27:9 (on Matthew's use of Jeremiah, see Knowles 1993). Popular estimation of Jesus sees him respectfully but inadequately as one in a line of God's messengers to Israel who preach repentance and judgment.

The probing question—"But who do you say that I am?"—is answered by Peter, who frequently assumes the role of spokesperson or representative in this Gospel (see 14:28; 15:15; 17:4, 24-27; 18:21; 19:27; 26:33). Without hesitation he confesses Jesus as the "Messiah" and as "Son of the living God." Both titles have already been applied to Jesus in Matthew. In the title of the Gospel and in the infancy narrative Jesus was explicitly called the Messiah (1:1, 17, 18), and in response to John's disciples Jesus lists his messianic works (11:2-6). The reverential formulation "Son of the *living* God" will be repeated by Caiaphas when he interrogates Jesus during the Passion (see 26:63) and the title "Son of God" itself is a major christological title in Matthew's Gospel, already applied to Jesus by Satan in the temptation story (4:3, 6), by the Gadarene demoniacs (8:29), and most forcefully by the disciples themselves at the conclusion of the sea story in 14:33.

Jesus' blessing of Peter is unique to Matthew (16:17-19). In Mark's version, Peter's confession of Jesus as the "Messiah" (without the added "Son of God" title) is met immediately with Jesus' admonition to silence, adding an aura of ambivalence to the apostle's confession. But in Matthew, Peter is openly blessed by Jesus because his recognition of Jesus' true identity is no mere human intuition ("flesh and blood"), but a revelation from "my Father in heaven" (16:17). The blessing for such a revelation is reminiscent of 11:25-27 where Jesus had praised God ("Father, Lord of heaven and earth") for revealing "these things" to infants.

The blessing is followed by investiture of Peter with authority in the community of Jesus. He was first addressed in this scene as "Simon son of Jonah," recalling his inaugural call to discipleship in 4:18 ("Simon, who is called Peter"). Simon son of Jonah appears to be the traditional name for Peter, similar to that in John's Gospel where Peter is identified as "son of John" (John 1:42; 21:15). But now Jesus calls Simon by his discipleship name, "Peter," giving him, in effect, a new identity, and promising that on this "rock" he will build his "church" (16:18). The Greek name *petros* allows this play with the word "rock" (*petron;* in fact, a similar play on words can take place in the Aramaic terms for the name "Cephas" [see Gal 2:7-8] and the word for rock, *cepa*). The word *ekklēsia,* meaning "assembly" or "church," is a designation that will be repeated in the community discourse (18:17). The portrayal of Peter as the foundation "rock" on which the community is built evokes the image of Abraham and Sarah as foundation stones of the community of Israel (see Isa 51:1-2). Later in the Gospel Jesus himself will be designated as the rejected stone who becomes the "cornerstone" of a new edifice, drawing on the image of Ps 118:22 (see Matt 21:42; similarly 1 Pet 2:7). Other New Testament traditions speak of the community as a temple with Jesus as the cornerstone and the apostles and prophets as the "foundation" for the edifice (see Eph 2:20; 1 Pet 2:4-5; cf. 1 QH vi 24-28, which speaks of the community in this manner). The community, thus built on "rock," will be secure (see the image in Matt 7:24-25) and the "gates of Sheol," a metaphor for the power of the underworld or the demonic (see Isa 38:10), will not prevail against it, just as Jesus himself had overcome the assaults of the evil one (see 4:1-11).

Furthermore, Jesus gives Peter the "keys of the kingdom of heaven," an image drawn from the story in Isa 22:15-25 where Shebnah, the unfaithful "master of the household," is replaced by Eliakim. Eliakim is given the "key of the house of David" and has the power to open and shut the gates. Peter is invested as the master of the household of Jesus and given the power to "bind and loose" (16:19); his decisions will be ratified by heavenly authority. The terms "binding and loosing" are used in rabbinic literature to cover several functions, including the authority to determine membership, to impose rules and sanctions, and even for the power of exorcism. The same power is given to the community itself in 18:18 where the issue at stake is clearly the authority to determine membership (see above on 18:15-17).

Jesus' blessing of Peter and the donation of authority to him appear to give the apostle the role of "prime minister" or "master of the household" in the community built by Jesus. Perhaps, as many interpreters suggest, Matthew may be thinking of Peter as having an authoritative role in Jesus' "church" as distinct or even over against the role of rabbinic authority in ("their") synagogue, but this contrast is not explicitly drawn in the Gospel.

After speaking to Peter, Jesus now turns to the disciples and orders them not to tell anyone that he is the Messiah, a motif of secrecy more characteristic of Mark. The admonition paves the way for the instruction about the Passion that now enters the picture with the first Passion prediction (16:21). Matthew reinforces the significance of this moment with his emphatic phrase, "from that time on" (see above 4:17), signaling that this entire scene is an important turning point in the narrative. Jesus must go to Jerusalem, "undergo great suffering," and "on the third day" (contrast Mark's less precise "after three days," 8:31) be raised.

Just as Matthew highlights the blessing of Peter, he also underscores the apostle's weakness. In his typical style, Matthew has the apostle directly address Jesus (contrast the indirect address in Mark's version, 8:32). Peter begins to "rebuke" (the same word is used when Jesus "silences" or "rebukes" the stormy sea in 8:26 or those healed in 12:16 and 17:18) Jesus for speaking about his impending suffering, using an exclamation that literally can mean "mercy on you!" and ironically addressing Jesus as "Lord" even while attempting to suppress what Jesus had just predicted. Jesus' words to Peter are also forceful—the apostle is not only called "Satan" because he attempts, as the demon had in 4:1-11, to divert Jesus from his messianic destiny but he is a "stumbling block," the word *skandalon* perhaps playing upon Peter's identity as "rock." In resisting Jesus' words about death and resurrection, Peter thinks in human rather than divine terms and becomes an "obstacle" to

Jesus' mission (see the warnings about being a "stumbling block" for the "little ones" in 18:6-9).

With the Passion in view, Jesus now begins to instruct his disciples (16:24-28). The sayings on following in the way of the cross and losing one's life to save it were already used by Matthew in the mission discourse (10:38-39). The Passion becomes emblematic of the self-transcendence and life-giving service of Jesus himself and therefore the touchstone for authentic discipleship. To the saying about the future coming of the Son of Man at the end time Matthew appends his typical admonition about judgment on the basis of one's actions (16:27; see, e.g., 7:15-27).

The segment concludes with the enigmatic saying about the return of the Son of Man in his kingdom before some of those standing there will see death (16:28). This, too, echoes the mission discourse that predicted that the disciples would not have gone through all of the towns of Israel before the coming of the Son of Man (10:23). The projection of the community and its mission out into the nations and the End of time in 28:16-20 seems to belie the kind of immediacy of the End implied in this saying. Some interpreters suggest that this saying prepares for the glorious vision of Jesus in the transfiguration scene that immediately follows (17:1-8) or to the final episode of the Gospel when the Risen Christ returns triumphantly to meet his disciples on the mountain in Galilee (28:16-20). In the immediate context of 16:24-28, the saying reinforces the authority of Jesus' words as the Son of Man (see 16:13, 27) and underscores the urgency of preparing for judgment by faithful action.

◊ ◊ ◊ ◊

The role of Peter in this scene of the Gospel has long been a source of debate (Brown, Donfried, and Reumann 1973; Kingsbury 1979; Perkins 1994; Wilkins 1995). Peter's confession and Jesus' blessing of the apostle appear to catapult Peter into a position of authority in the community formed by Jesus. He is, in effect, the "prime minister" of the "church," holding the power of the keys and able to make authoritative decisions that will be divinely ratified. These affirmations harmonize with Matthew's Gospel as a whole. The hostility of the Jewish leaders and the distance implicit in the frequently used term "their synagogues" (e.g., 4:23; 9:35; 10:17; 12:9; 13:54; 23:34; see also 6:2, 5; 23:6) contrast with those in the assembly or "church" of Jesus who express their faith in him as Messiah and Son of God, "understand" him, and attempt to live in accord with his teaching.

Yet the precise role of Peter remains a point of controversy. For many Peter is a "representative disciple," exemplifying the qualities and authority that should characterize any member of the community of Jesus (e.g., Kingsbury 1979; Wilkins 1995). This viewpoint seems confirmed by the fact that Matthew will attribute to the community as a whole the power of "binding and loosing" that is given to Peter in this scene (cf. 16:19 and 18:18). Other interpreters believe that Matthew gives prominence to Peter because of his role within salvation history. Peter's role as the first to be called by Jesus (4:18) and as spokesperson for the disciples reflects his preeminence in the resurrection appearance traditions (1 Cor 15:5) and his historic role in the primitive Jerusalem community, as well as his mediation between the Jewish and Gentile sectors of the community (as described in Acts 15:6-11; also 11:1-18; and by implication in Gal 2:11-14 where Paul chides "Cephas" for withdrawing from table fellowship with Gentiles in Antioch). This salvation history role, however, is uniquely fixed in time and should not be construed as an "office" handed on to successors. Still others, especially Roman Catholic interpreters, see the figure of Peter in Matthew as symbolic of an emerging ecclesial order in which Peter represents a position of authority, responsible for the community in Jesus' name and exercising the power of binding and loosing. The prominent role of Peter in Matthew and Luke–Acts, as well as in the later Petrine letters, suggests a developing interest in the figure of Peter in the early community, a trajectory best explained by the apostle's symbolic role as exemplifying unifying leadership within the community.

Whatever choice one makes among these alternate interpretations, it is clear that Matthew also refuses to idealize the figure of Peter, highlighting his weakness and failure alongside his robust faith and his role as spokesperson. If Matthew's Gospel saw an enduring role for Peter as a symbol of leadership within the community, he surely also intended his clear-eyed portrayal of the apostle's need for conversion as part of his message to the church.

The Transfiguration of Jesus, the Coming of Elijah, and the Perils of Weak Faith (17:1-20)

The confession at Caesarea Philippi is followed "six days later" by another dramatic set of three scenes that amplify both Matthew's Christology and his understanding of discipleship. Jesus leads three of his disciples to a high mountain and is transfigured before them (17:1-8). As they descend the mountain, Jesus and his disciples discuss the return of Elijah and the impending sufferings of the Son of Man (17:9-13). At the base of the mountain they encounter the father of an epileptic boy whose illness the disciples have not been able to cure (17:14-20).

Although dependent on Mark for the basic content and sequence of this material, Matthew has significantly altered its focus. In Matthew's version, the transfiguration account is a fusion of Pentateuchal traditions that portray Moses' ascent of Sinai and the dazzling theophanies that accompany the reception of the law (especially Exod 24 and 34) with apocalyptic traditions that anticipate the return of the triumphant Christ at the End of time (drawing especially on the visions of Dan 7 and 8). The discussion about Elijah identifies John the Baptist as the prophet who ushers in the end time, further emphasizing Jesus' rule as the eschatological Son of Man, yet also as one who must suffer before the triumphant End will be realized (17:8-13). Matthew radically edits the story of the epileptic boy, greatly reducing its content and riveting its focus on the weak faith of the disciples (17:14-20).

◊ ◊ ◊ ◊

The Transfiguration (17:1-8)

Matthew notes an explicit time sequence with the previous scene at Caesarea Philippi: "Six days later" Jesus takes Peter, James, and John by themselves to a "high mountain." This may be the first of numerous biblical allusions to the theophanies on Mount Sinai that suffuse this story (see Allison 1993, 243-48). "Six days," for example, may be drawn from Exod 24:8 where the cloud covers Mount Sinai for "six days" and then on the seventh day God appears to Moses. Likewise the three disciples who accompany Jesus may also reflect the scene in Exod 24 when three of Moses' companions (Aaron, Nadab, and Abihu) accompany him as he approaches the Lord (see Exod 24:2). Peter, James, and John were among the first disciples called (see 4:18-22) and they will reappear as privileged companions of Jesus in the Gethsemane scene (26:37). The reference to a "high mountain" also evokes the Sinai stories as well as reflects Matthew's proclivity for mountains as places of revelation (see 4:8; 5:1; 15:29; 28:16; Donaldson 1985).

On the mountaintop the disciples witness a dazzling transfiguration of Jesus. The word used, *metemorphōthē*, implies profound transformation. Jesus' "face shone like the sun," recalling the impact of God's appearance on the countenance of Moses ("the skin of his face shone because he had been talking with God," Exod 34:29) but also anticipating the glory of the exalted Christ at the end time. In the explanation of the parable of the wheat and the weeds, the Matthean Jesus had predicted that in the end time the righteous "will shine like the sun in the kingdom of their Father" (13:43). The bright countenance of Jesus extends to his garments that "became dazzling white." Here, too, is a sign of the final glory where the garments of the blessed are described as dazzling white (see, e.g., Dan 7:9 where the clothing of the "Ancient One" is "white as snow"; cf. *1 Enoch* 14:20; 63:15-16; Rev 3:4-5; 7:9).

Moses and Elijah become part of the vision, talking with the transfigured Jesus. Matthew has altered the order of the names as found in Mark ("Elijah with Moses," Mark 9:4); the phrase "Moses and Elijah"—equivalent to the "law and the prophets"—harmonizes with Matthew's way of referring to the Scriptures (5:17; 7:12; 11:13; 22:40). From Matthew's perspective the full sweep of Israel's salvation history is in view: Moses, Elijah, and the eschatological fulfillment of the Scriptures in Jesus (see especially 5:17). That eschatological note will be underscored in the following scene where Matthew refers to Elijah not only as the exemplar of the prophet (i.e., role), but also as the eschatological precursor of the Messiah, a role embodied in John the Baptist (17:10-13).

In verse 4, as in the previous scene, Peter takes the lead. Typically, Matthew softens Mark's portrayal of the disciple. Peter addresses Jesus with the reverential title "Lord" (see 14:28, 30; 16:22) in contrast to using "rabbi" as in Mark's version (9:5), a title Matthew does not favor (see 23:8; 26:25). And Matthew omits the reference to Peter's confusion (see Mark 9:6). The apostle offers ("if you wish") to set up three "dwellings" (literally, the term is *skēnas*, meaning "tent" or "tabernacle") for each of the three luminaries in the vision. The precise meaning of Peter's gesture is difficult to determine. Perhaps this is intended to recall the Feast of Tabernacles (which also occurs "six days" after the feast of the Atonement; see above 17:1), but the connection with the transfiguration seems tenuous. Peter may simply be offering to construct three commemorative dwellings or tents to honor the three people in the vision.

The vision reaches its zenith with the sudden appearance ("while he was still speaking") of a "bright cloud" that overshadows them, and a voice from the cloud, "This is my Son, the Beloved; with him I am well pleased; listen to him!" (17:5). The remembrance of the Sinai theophany is unmistakable—there, too, a "bright cloud" envelops the Divine Presence (see Exod 24:15-16; cf. Exod 16:10; 19:9; 33:9) and in Exod 34:5, the Lord speaks to Moses from the cloud. A more proximate analogy is found in the Gospel's baptismal scene where a "voice from heaven" acclaims Jesus in the exact words used at the transfiguration (see Matt 3:17). By aligning the words exactly (contrast Mark 9:7), Matthew draws attention to the two moments of theophany. At the inauguration of his public ministry God declared Jesus to be his "Son," using the royal enthronement of Ps 2:7 ("You are my son . . ."), and the "Beloved" in whom God is well pleased, citing the servant text of Isa 42:1 (see also Isa 44:2; the term "Beloved" may also be a reference to Isaac in Gen 22:2). The identity of Jesus as God's Son, as royal Messiah and Servant of God, is reacclaimed on the mountain of transfiguration. Now, however, the divine voice adds the command, "Listen to him." Jesus is revealed to the disciples as the Messiah, the fulfillment of Israel's hopes, and the triumphant Son of Man who will come at the end time.

The disciples fall to the ground, overcome by fear—a typical and appropriate response to a theophany. In Mark's version of the story, the disciples' "fear" was linked to Peter's initial and uncomprehending reaction to the vision of the three figures (9:6). In Matthew, however, their prostration and fear come after the divine message about the identity of Jesus and the injunction to obey him. Appropriately, Matthew also alters the ending of the scene. In a gesture of healing and reassurance, Jesus approaches the disciples, touches them, and soothes their fear (17:7). When the disciples open their eyes they see only Jesus, precisely the focus the Gospel intends.

The Coming of Elijah (17:9-13)

As they are coming down from the mountain, Jesus and the disciples discuss the role of Elijah as the precursor to the Messiah. Jesus' initial warning not to reveal the "vision" to anyone until the Son of Man has been raised from the dead triggers the disciples' question about Elijah. Matthew's version is much clearer than Mark's counterpart (cf. Mark 9:9-13) and he manages to neatly tie the discussion into the major themes of the surrounding context.

First of all, the transfiguration is defined as a "vision" (17:9; contrast Mark 9:9, "what they had seen"), reflecting its nature as an evocation of the Sinai theophany as well as an anticipation of the glorified Jesus of the end time. The reference to the death and resurrection of the Son of Man also orients the disciples and the reader to the Passion, the focus emphatically begun in the previous scene at Caesarea Philippi. In fact, the pattern found in that scene is repeated here: first a confession of Jesus as the Christ and the Son of God and then a reminder of the sufferings and ultimate resurrection of the Son of Man.

The popular Jewish tradition about the return of Elijah at the commencement of the messianic age, a tradition fueled by the mystery surrounding Elijah's death, is reaffirmed (see, e.g., Mal 4:5-6). But Matthew also reasserts what his Gospel has already stated: John the Baptist fulfills the expected role of Elijah *redivivus*. The Gospel signaled this at the baptism when John first appears wearing the desert garments of Elijah (3:4) and his identity as Elijah is explicitly declared by Jesus in 11:14. By emphasizing John's role as Elijah, Matthew, in turn, reaffirms Jesus' identity as the promised Messiah, the eschatological note asserted in the transfiguration scene. At the same time, Matthew ties both John and Jesus to the way of suffering. John himself was not "recognized" (a typical Matthean emphasis on "understanding") and was maltreated—so, too, would be the fate of the Son of Man (17:12).

The Perils of Weak Faith (17:14-20)

The aftermath of the transfiguration concludes as Jesus and his chosen disciples complete their descent of the mountain to meet yet another waiting crowd (see similar scenes in 8:1; 9:36; 14:14; 15:30; 19:2). From the crowd a man "approaches" Jesus and "kneels" before him (both typical Matthean terms, taken from Greek, used to describe supplications to Jesus on the part of the sick or their surrogates) to ask healing on behalf of his epileptic son. The father's words—"Lord, have mercy on my son"—echo other prayerful entreaties in the Gospel that reflect Matthew's strong Christology (see, e.g., 8:2, 5-6, 25; 14:30; 15:22, 25; 20:30-31).

Matthew has radically edited this story, omitting numerous details found in Mark. Mark's version stresses particularly the tenacious hold the evil spirit has over the boy and puts in the foreground the interaction between the halting faith of the boy's father and Jesus' power to cast out a demon that appears to be a shadow of death itself (see 9:25-29). In Matthew, however, the interaction between the father and Jesus nearly disappears. It is no longer a question of an evil spirit too potent for the disciples to cast out, as in Mark's version, but a test case illustrating that even a modicum of faith ("the size of a mustard seed") would, if exercised, be sufficient.

Matthew describes the boy's illness as "epilepsy" (literally, "being moonstruck"), an affliction that caused him great suffering and torment. The father had brought his boy to the disciples, but they were unable to heal him. Matthew's story interprets the disciples' inability as a result of their weak faith. Jesus is exasperated with the disciples and castigates them as a "faithless and perverse generation," words that echo Moses' stern judgment on Israel in Deut 32:5. Without hesitation, Jesus himself silences the demon that grips the boy and cures him (17:18).

In privacy the chastened disciples approach Jesus and ask why they were unable to cast out the demon. Here Matthew drives home the lesson on faith that is the singular point of the story. The disciples failed because of their "little faith" (17:20; see this characteristic phrase in 6:30; 8:26; 14:31; 16:8). Matthew includes a Q saying (cf. Luke 17:6) to secure the point: If the disciples had faith the "size of a mustard seed," they could move a mountain and nothing would be impossible to them. The image of the mustard seed ("the smallest of all seeds") had already appeared in the parable chapter as an image of the reign of God that, once planted, grows to become the greatest of shrubs (see 13:31-32). Now such small but vigorous faith can enlist the divine power to move the mountains and do the impossible. While the disciples' "little faith" may be better than no faith at all, it is not strong enough to carry out the mission Jesus and his disciples face.

This scene is one of Matthew's harshest treatments of the disciples. Throughout this middle section he has presented both the strength and weakness of his followers as demonstrated in the paralyzing fear of Peter and the disciples on the sea (see 14:22-33) or their difficulties in grasping the meaning of his teaching (see 15:16; 16:8-12). They remain the privileged witnesses of Jesus' most urgent teaching and have been entrusted with his mission, yet their weak faith will lead to more failures as Jesus' journey to Jerusalem unfolds. (Note that some manuscript versions include v. 21, "But this kind does not come out except by prayer and fasting"—a text that would push Matthew's story more in the direction of Mark.)

◊ ◊ ◊ ◊

These scenes are a parade example of Matthew's perspective. Jesus stands in the line of Israel's salvation history with Moses and Elijah, but also brings that history to its intended fulfillment. Therefore Jesus evokes the memory of Moses the lawgiver and savior of Israel, but goes beyond Moses. Jesus enacts the prophetic ministry of Elijah, but is far greater than Elijah. The transfiguration story projects the reader forward in history to the consummation of the world when Jesus would come as the triumphant Son of Man, imbued with divine glory. But even now, within the confines of the Gospel story and its narrative of Jesus' earthly mission, that messianic authority is exercised in Jesus' teaching on the meaning of discipleship. Following Jesus to future glory would mean passage through suffering and death. This had been the way of John, the Elijah who pointed the way to the coming of Christ, and it would be the way of the Son of Man and those who would be his disciples.

Jesus Predicts His Passion; the Payment of the Temple Tax (17:22-27)

Following Mark's lead, Matthew presents Jesus again predicting to his disciples his Passion and resurrection as the journey to Jerusalem and the cross continues. The scene about the temple tax appears at first sight to be unconnected to its surrounding context. But, in fact, it continues the focus on Christology and discipleship that has been a leitmotif of this section of the Gospel. And the status of the disciples as sons of the kingdom prepares for the community discourse of chapter 18, which is concerned with the question of what is true greatness in the kingdom of God.

◊ ◊ ◊ ◊

The Passion Prediction (17:22-23)

For the fourth time since Peter's confession at Caesarea Philippi, Jesus tells his disciples that the Son of Man must suffer before being raised from the dead (16:21; 17:9, 12).

This Passion prediction is based on Mark 9:30-32, but Matthew has made some subtle changes. Matthew describes Jesus and his disciples as "gathering" in Galilee, implying a regrouping of the disciples after the transfiguration and the encounter with the epileptic boy (17:1-21). With his community assembled, Jesus again solemnly warns them that the Son of Man will be "betrayed" into human hands. The Greek word used is *paradidōmi,* that is, to be "handed over," a word that takes on almost technical meaning in relation to Jesus' Passion. While it immediately refers to the betrayal of Jesus by human agency (as the NRSV implies), the generic meaning of the Greek term and its passive voice leave room for the mystery of God's own initiative in delivering up Jesus to death. As is frequently the case, the title "Son of Man" is used in connection with the death and resurrection of Jesus. The Son of Man who will come in triumph at the End of time must first experience passage through death to resurrection.

Unlike Mark's version where the disciples typically cannot understand the meaning of Jesus' words and are afraid to ask him (9:32), the Matthean disciples are "greatly distressed" or "saddened" (see the use of the same word in 18:31; 26:22). Understanding of what lies ahead for Jesus now begins to take hold of the disciples (see also 17:13).

The Temple Tax (17:24-27)

This curious story, unique to Matthew's Gospel, is composed of two conversations: one between the tax collectors and Peter, and the other between Peter and Jesus. Matthew situates the story in Capernaum (taking his cue from Mark 9:33), described earlier as Jesus' and Peter's "own town" (see 8:14, which locates Peter's house in Capernaum; and 9:1) and the location of an earlier story about tax collectors (9:9-13).

Collectors of the "didrachma" (the Greek term literally means a double drachma coin or in Jewish terms, a half-shekel) approach Peter and ask him if his teacher does not pay the tax. As most commentators do, the NRSV interprets the "didrachma" as meaning the "temple tax." Prior to 70 CE, while the temple still existed, this "tax" was a donation expected of all male Jews over twenty in accord with the prescription of Exod 30:11-16 (see also Neh 10:32). The proceeds of the tax were for the support of the sanctuary, but the half-shekel tax also had important symbolic meaning as a sign of solidarity of all Jews both in Israel and in the Diaspora. After the destruction of the temple in 70 CE, the Romans continued to levy the tax but this *fiscus Judaicus* or "Jewish tax" was now used for the upkeep of the Jupiter Capitolinus temple in Rome. The story in Matthew is obviously situated in a time when the temple was still standing, so the question raised by the tax collectors is about Jesus' allegiance to the temple and his obligation to support it. Peter responds that Jesus does pay the tax.

The second conversation is between Jesus and Peter. When the apostle comes home, Jesus speaks first. Jesus' words are the heart of this story. He asks Peter whether the "kings of the earth" take toll or tribute from their children or from others. To Peter's response—"from others"—Jesus adds the decisive point: "Then the children are free" (17:26). Jesus' question about "toll or tribute" goes beyond the temple tax itself. "Tolls" (Gk. *telos*) were indirect taxes on goods or for right of passage; "tribute" (*kēnson*, root of the English word "census") was a more direct head or poll tax. The key to Jesus' saying is the interplay between "children" or "others"; an earthly king would not levy a tax on his own family. By implication, Jesus and his disciples are free from the temple tax, because the temple is the house of God and they are the children of the Father. This implicit Son of God theology brings this story into relationship with the surrounding context. Peter had acclaimed Jesus as "Son of the living God" at Caesarea Philippi (16:16), and the disciples' quest for greatness within the "kingdom of heaven" will be the starting point for the following discourse (18:1-5). While Matthew's community used the political term "kingdom," the relationships that characterized that community were based on the love and freedom that existed between God and his children. This, too, would be amplified in the community discourse of chapter 18.

The story concludes with a practical solution to the question of paying the temple tax. To avoid giving offense to "them" (literally, "scandalizing them"), Jesus instructs Peter to pay the tax for both Peter and himself from the "stater" (a Greek coin equivalent to two didrachma or one shekel) he will find in the first fish he catches! The miraculous discovery of a coin in the mouth of the fish smacks of the kind of quaint tale often found in folk literature. Matthew is not clear about who it is that might be scandalized by failing to pay the temple tax. Presumably it is the Jewish community for whom the tax had important symbolic meaning.

It is more difficult to determine what this story might mean for the Christians of Matthew's community. On one level it teaches that taking care not to give needless offense to others should temper the use of one's freedom. Paul used a similar principle in his instructions to the Corinthians about the issue of eating meat offered to idols (see 1 Cor 8:1-13). For Matthew's Christians it might also suggest that even though Jesus taught that his disciples were not bound by the temple tax, he also was concerned not to offend other Jews who considered themselves obligated. Even after the nature of the tax had changed and in circumstances where some in Matthew's community were Roman citizens and therefore not obligated to the *fiscus Judaicus,* or "Jewish tax," these lessons were still valuable, especially for a community in growing tension with other Jewish groups.

◊ ◊ ◊ ◊

Matthew continues his concentration on themes of Christology and discipleship. The basis for the dignity and freedom of the community is the nature of the one who calls the community into being—Jesus, the Son of God. Yet this is not a reason for arrogance. The disciples, like their Master, must be always considerate of others—alert not to cause offense in the exercise of their freedom.

True Greatness Within the Community (18:1-35)

This is the fourth of Matthew's major discourses (see chaps. 5–7; 10; 13). It takes its initial inspiration from the parallel in Mark 9:33-37 where during the journey to Jerusalem the disciples "had argued with one another who was the greatest." Jesus admonishes them, "Whoever wants to be first must be last of all and servant of all." Matthew thoroughly revises this exchange, transforming the disciples' argument into a question and Jesus' response into a full-blown discourse on what it means to be "last of all and servant of all." Some of the content of the discourse is drawn from Mark 9:33-50 and Q material (cf. Luke 17:1-3; 15:3-7), but there is a significant amount of material unique to Matthew.

The structure of the discourse is debated. Six distinct segments make up its contents: (1) 18:1-5, concerning the "child"; (2) 18:6-9, concerning scandal to "one of these little ones"; (3) 18:10-14, the parable of the good shepherd; (4) 18:15-20, the procedure for handling disputes and the underlying authority of the community; (5) 18:21-22, Peter's question about the limits of forgiveness; (6) 18:23-35, the concluding parable of the merciless servant. Yet these are by no means independent units; they are linked into overarching themes. Some (see, e.g., Pesch 1966) consider the two parables, each ending with a decisive saying about the "Father in heaven," as the anchors for a two-part division: (1) 18:1-14, dealing with care for the vulnerable members of the community; (2) 18:15-35, dealing with alienation and forgiveness within the community.

The segment on procedures for handling disputes within the community (18:15-20), however, stands out within the discourse and may suggest a threefold division of the whole (for further discussion of the discourse's structure, see Davies and Allison 1991, 750-51; Thompson 1970, 238-52). As will be suggested below, Matthew may have seen the issue of expulsion as a necessary pastoral decision, but one to be tempered by the even more fundamental values of attentive pastoral care and an unlimited capacity for reconciliation.

This would result in the following structure for the discourse: (1) 18:1-14, on the need for humility and on pastoral care, especially for the vulnerable members of the community; (2) 18:15-20, the procedure for handling a recalcitrant member and the underlying authority of the community to do so; (3) 18:21-35, Jesus' teaching on unlimited forgiveness "from your heart." The first and third segments have a parallel structure, each concluding with a parable and a dominical saying. In the first half of the discourse the focus is on the "child" and the "little ones"; in the second half (including the middle segment on the errant member) the focus turns to one's "brother" in community (which the NRSV translates "member" for the sake of inclusion).

One other issue concerning the interpretation of this discourse is the question of whether it is addressed to the community in general or to its leadership. Both opinions have been proposed, but there is reason to suggest that Matthew is thinking of a core group within the community, if not its formal leaders. The addressees are not the "children" and not the "little ones," but rather the "strong." They are capable of placing obstacles rather than being impeded by them. Nor does the discourse directly address the erring member but rather those who have been offended and who are in a position to assemble the local church. The question about the limits of forgiveness is raised by the community spokesperson Peter, and Jesus' initial response is addressed to him (the "you" in 18:22 is singular; the final saying in 18:35 is addressed to the wider group with "you" in the plural).

The discourse as a whole, then, reveals Matthew's concerns about life within the community that gathers in Jesus' name. To what extent his choice of issues reflects tensions or concerns within the actual Matthean community is more difficult to determine, but cannot be ruled out (see Thompson 1970, 258-64).

◊ ◊ ◊ ◊

On the Need for Humility and Pastoral Care (18:1-14)

The opening segment begins with the disciples' leading question that sets the stage for the entire discourse: "Who is the greatest in the kingdom of heaven?" (18:1). The question flows from the previous scene where Jesus had told Peter that the disciples were children of the king (17:24-27). Matthew has thoroughly revised the parallel scenario in Mark where the disciples argue among themselves about who is the greatest (Mark 9:33-34). Typically Matthew portrays the disciples in a more favorable light than Mark, but Matthew's version is not without its implicit critique of the disciples' attitude. The key phrase "in the kingdom of heaven" will lead to an understanding of "greatness" that undercuts what those within a secular realm might expect (Brown 1984, 138-45).

Jesus sets a child in the midst of the disciples as a dramatic illustration of what greatness in the kingdom entails. In traditional Mediterranean culture the child was someone without status or power. If the disciples seek even to enter the kingdom of heaven, much less to find authentic greatness there, they must "change" (the Greek word *straphēte* implies a complete "turning around" or conversion, reminiscent of the Hebrew word for conversion, *shuv*) and become "like children"—that is, shed their pretensions and in a spirit of humility live and think in accord with the teaching of Jesus (this saying is similar to Mark 10:15 and may have been inspired by this text). Jesus himself exemplifies such childlike humility and, therefore, whoever welcomes such a child in Jesus' name welcomes him (18:5). The identification of Jesus with the seemingly weak and vulnerable members of the community is a recurring motif in Matthew (cf. 10:40; 25:31-46). The discourse that follows will illustrate what Jesus means; in each instance the disciples are asked to transcend their own self-absorption and be attentive to others.

The discourse now begins to focus on certain attitudes and concerns within the life of the community. The first deals with the problem of putting a "stumbling block" in front of "these little ones who believe in me" (18:6-9). Here the focus changes subtly from the "child" *(paidion)* as an example of humility to "little ones" *(mikroi),* who are symbolic of weak and vulnerable members of the community. The disciples are sternly warned not to place obstacles in the way of these members. The word *scandalize* is used as both a verb and a noun repeatedly in these verses. Literally it means to place an "obstacle" (the root meaning of the word *scandalon*) in front of someone; in the moral context of the discourse it apparently means some action or attitude on the part of others in the community that is destructive for these weaker members. Matthew does not define what these "obstacles" are, yet the fact that in verse 10 Jesus warns the disciples not to "despise" the "little ones" may suggest that placing an obstacle could include excessive rigor or moral arrogance as well as sinful and scandalous behavior. (Use of this same word elsewhere in Matthew suggests a range of meanings: e.g., lust [5:29-30]; taking offense at Jesus' ministry and teaching [11:6; 15:12]; scandal at not paying the temple tax even when not obligated [17:27]; and loss of faith in Jesus during the Passion [26:31, 33]).

The rhetorical admonitions to mutilate oneself rather than scandalize a little one give a sense of urgency and seriousness to Jesus' commands. Better for a disciple to enter "life" maimed than be thrown into the "hell of fire" (Gk.; literally, the "Gehenna of fire";

Gehenna or the Hinnon valley was a deep wadi south of Jerusalem and it becomes symbolic of hell; see also Matt 5:22, 29, 30; 10:28; 23:15, 33). As early as Origen, interpreters have wondered if the references to various parts of the body reflect an understanding of the community as a "body" in the manner of Paul's own famous metaphors in 1 Cor 12 and Rom 12. While this cannot be ruled out, it is more likely that Jesus' strong rhetoric catalogues various actions through which scandal might occur.

The disciples are also warned not to "despise" the "little ones," because "in heaven their angels continually see the face of my Father in heaven" (18:10). As reflected in the Qumran and other literature, first-century Judaism had a robust belief in protective or guardian angels (see Davies and Allison 1991, 770-73). Jesus' words assume there should be symmetry between life on earth and life in the heavenly realm: In heaven the guardian angels of the "little ones" are privileged to see the face of God and, therefore, the little ones themselves should not experience contempt within the community on earth (see the petition of the Lord's Prayer in 6:10, "Your will be done, on earth as it is in heaven" and the heavenly ratification of the community's decisions in 18:18). (Note: Verse 11, "The Son of Man came to save the lost" is missing in most manuscripts and is probably a later assimilation from Luke 19:11.)

The first major section of the discourse closes with the parable of the lost sheep (18:10-14). A version of this same parable is found in Luke 15:3-7, but its application is different. In Luke it is one of three great mercy parables that defend Jesus' mission of compassion for "tax collectors and sinners" (see Luke 15:1-2). Luke's parable concludes with an acclamation of joy over the lost sinner who is saved because the shepherd has gone beyond the boundaries of the community to find him. In Matthew, however, the parable drives home a lesson in pastoral care. The pastors of the community are to be attentive to those errant and weak members of the community who go "astray" and should actively seek them out. The motivation for this is absolutely fundamental in Matthew's theology: "So it is not the will of your Father in heaven that one of these little ones should be lost" (18:14). The original parable of Jesus may well have been inspired by Ezek 34 where the leaders of Israel are condemned for their failure as shepherds, allowing the sheep to become scattered and vulnerable to attack. God is the Good Shepherd who "will search for my sheep, and will seek them out. . . . I will rescue them from all the places to which they have been scattered" (Ezek 34:11-12). The backdrop of Ezek 34 reinforces the idea that the parable of the lost sheep—as well as the discourse as a whole—is directed to the leading members of the community and not just to the community as a whole.

On Handling a Recalcitrant Member (18:15-20)

The next major section begins with a procedure for dealing with a member of the community who "sins against you." (Some manuscripts omit the phrase "against you," which would change the offense from a personal injury to some sinful and intolerable action.) The focus moves from the "little ones," namely the weak and vulnerable members, to one's "brother" (NRSV: "another member"), that is, a peer in the community who has seriously sinned. This is the second time Matthew has used the term *ekklēsia* or "church" for the community (see above 16:18); it derives from the Hebrew notion of the *qahal* or "assembly" and here it obviously means the local church assembled to judge a particular case (see 18:17).

The procedure suggested is full of practical wisdom and is sensitive to the errant member, first attempting to correct the situation privately—a responsibility enjoined by Lev 19:17 ("You shall not hate in your heart anyone of your kin; you shall reprove your neighbor, or you will incur guilt yourself"). If that fails, the circle widens to include two or three witnesses, a step that also coincided with Jewish law (see Deut 19:15). And if that fails, the case is finally to be taken before the entire assembly for decisive action. This process is similar to that found in Qumran dealing with expulsion of a community member (see *1QS* v 24-vi 1).

If the offender refuses to listen even to the entire community, then the errant member is to be treated "as a Gentile and a tax collector" (18:17), that is, treated as a nonbeliever and no longer as a member of the community. This manner of describing the expulsion of the member is indirect and has some ambiguity. At other places in Matthew's Gospel "Gentiles" and "tax collectors" are code words for nonbelievers or outsiders, reflecting the essentially Jewish-Christian perspective of Matthew's tradition (see, e.g., 5:47; 6:7, 32; 9:10; 10:18; 11:19; 20:19). Yet at the same time, the reader of the Gospel cannot be unaware that within the narrative Gentiles and tax collectors are not infrequently the object of Jesus' ministry (e.g., 8:5-13; 9:9-13; 11:16-19) so that the phrase "let such a one be to you as a Gentile and a tax collector" may also suggest that the community's pastoral concern for the errant member does not completely end, even after the painful step of expulsion has taken place.

The subsequent sayings of Jesus in this section reveal the profound authority of the community from Matthew's perspective (18:18-20). What the community can "bind on earth" will be ratified in the heavenly realm (18:18). The authority of "binding and loosing" given earlier to Peter is now applied to the assembly as a whole (see above 16:19). Here the terms "binding and loosing" clearly refer to issues of membership and excommunication. And even if two members of the community "agree on earth about anything you ask"—a subtle plea for harmony—their prayer will be effective (18:19). And wherever even two or three of the community gather in Jesus' name, "I am there among them" (18:20). This is clearly the postresurrection conviction of Matthew's church; the promise of Jesus' abiding presence in the community recalls the name "Emmanuel" conferred on Jesus at his birth (1:23) and anticipates the final promise of the Risen Jesus to remain with the community in 28:20. The saying in 18:20 is reminiscent of rabbinic sayings about the *shekinah* or Divine Presence in the midst of the community (see especially the saying of Rabbi Hananiah ben Teradion in *m. 'Abot* 3:2: "But if two sit together and words of the law [are spoken] between them, the Divine Presence rests between them"). For Matthew, Jesus' presence in the midst of the community, even in moments of discord and painful decisions, becomes the embodiment of the Divine Presence and the guarantee of the community's authority.

On Unlimited Forgiveness (18:21-35)

The third segment of the discourse opens with Peter once again acting as spokesperson for the disciples (see especially 14:28; 15:15;

16:16; 17:24-27). He addresses Jesus reverently as "Lord" (see also 14:28, 30) and asks about the limits of forgiveness "if my brother sins against me" (the NRSV's "another member of the church" is not literal). This section continues the preceding section's concern about fellow community members ("my brother") but now shifts back to the discourse's primary emphasis on tolerant care and reconciliation. Peter suggests a limit—"seven times"—that is already extraordinarily generous (the number "seven" often has a symbolic meaning in Jewish numerology and can imply infinity). Jesus' reply explodes even that bounty: "Not seven times, but, I tell you, seventy-seven times" (18:22). The Greek term used, *hebdomēkontakis hepta,* could also be translated as "seventy times seven times" but, in any case, implies limitless forgiveness. Jesus' saying may also be a play on the words of Lamech, the descendant of Cain, who vows blood vengeance "seventy-sevenfold" (Gen 4:24).

The concluding parable, one unique to Matthew, anchors the call for limitless forgiveness in a theological conviction (18:23-35). The story of the king who decides to settle his accounts has certain fantastic features that smack of popular storytelling. The monarch begins his accounting with a "slave," a member of the royal household, who owes a staggering amount, "ten thousand talents." Ten thousand was the highest denomination in ancient accounting and Josephus reports that the entire yearly revenue from the Jewish tax was only six hundred talents! When the slave is unable to pay this amount, the king threatens to punish the slave by having the hapless debtor and his entire family and possessions sold. The slave appeals for more time to pay off his debt even though this, too, seems an act of fruitless desperation. The king is deeply moved by the plight of the slave (the verb *splangchnistheis*—literally a stirring of one's intestines—implies a profound emotional reaction), and instead of simply giving him more time he decides to forgive the "loan" (curiously Matthew uses "loan" [Gk. *daneion*] rather than "debt" [Gk. *opheilēma*] here).

Instead of being overwhelmed by his unbelievably good fortune, the slave goes out and acts brutally toward a fellow slave who owes him only "a hundred denarii" (by contrast, a single "talent" may have been equivalent to between six and ten thousand denarii!), by seizing the man by the throat, ignoring his plea for mercy, and casting him into prison. The rest of the slaves are greatly saddened by this display and report the merciless servant to the king. Judgment comes swiftly—the angry king condemns the slave for his lack of mercy and has him tortured and cast into prison until he should pay his original debt.

This vivid story and its concluding saying illustrate Matthew's fundamental theology of reconciliation: "So my heavenly Father will also do to every one of you, if you do not forgive your brother or sister from your heart" (18:35). The driving motivation for unlimited forgiveness within the community is imitation of God's own way of relating to humanity. Because the slave was already forgiven a staggering and unpayable debt by his king, he should have lived his life in memory of that inaugural grace. Matthew asserts an identical motivation in 5:43-48 where love of enemies is motivated by the realization that the Father in heaven "makes his sun rise on the evil and on the good, and sends rain on the righteous and on the unrighteous" (v. 45). Likewise, Matthew's emphasis on the threat of judgment for those who do not forgive echoes previous teaching in the Sermon: The disciple prays for forgiveness of debt "as we also have forgiven our debtors"—a codicil of the prayer amplified in the sayings that are appended to the prayer: "For if you forgive others their trespasses, your heavenly Father will also forgive you; but if you do not forgive others, neither will your Father forgive your trespasses" (6:14-15). For Matthew, the divine will remains the guiding ethical principle for the community, a divine will proclaimed in Jesus' teachings and embodied in his actions.

◊ ◊ ◊ ◊

Taken as a whole, this community discourse presents a remarkable portrayal of the virtues that Matthew's Gospel considered essential for the Christian community. The community, and in a special way its leading members, was to be characterized by a childlike humility, not seeking special status but willing to change their perspective and take on a new life. At all costs the community should not place obstacles in the way of weaker members or in any way despise them. Such "little ones" were held dear by God and were to be the object of the community's attentive pastoral care so that none would be lost. At the same time, the community had to deal fairly and decisively with those who seriously sinned against others in the community. Such errant members should be offered discrete opportunity to repent, but if they finally refuse all reasonable attempts on the part of the community, they had to be expelled. Because it is a community endowed with the presence of the Risen Christ, it could be confident that its decisions would be ratified by God. But even as the Gospel contemplates this painful step, Matthew's discourse returns to its fundamental theme of limitless forgiveness, a commitment to reconciliation based ultimately on the manner of God's own graciousness toward sinful humanity.

Teaching on Divorce and Remarriage (19:1-12)

Matthew punctuates the community discourse of chapter 18 with the same type of transitional formula he has used after each of Jesus' great discourses in the Gospel (see 7:1; 11:1; 13:53; 26:1). Now the journey to Jerusalem resumes (see 16:21 as Jesus and his followers leave Galilee and enter Judea, making their way down the eastern bank of the Jordan, the traditional route from Galilee to Jerusalem that enabled pilgrims to avoid Samaria.

The next two chapters have a certain "domestic" hue, as Jesus takes up issues of divorce and remarriage (19:1-12), children (19:13-15), a young man's quest for eternal life (19:16-22), possessions (19:23-30), and a mother's ambitions on behalf of her sons (20:20-28). Warren Carter suggests that Matthew may be interacting in these two chapters with elements of the patriarchal household, offering an alternate vision concerning husband-wife relations, the role of children, the dominant role of wealth in determining human worth, and uplifting Jesus' own model of service (Carter 1994).

In this first scene Matthew draws on Mark's parallel (10:1-12), but alters it in several significant ways: (1) He adapts the discussion on divorce to a more Jewish context than Mark's version, particularly by shifting the discussion to the grounds for divorce (cf. Matt

19:2//Mark 10:2) and by omitting the reference to the wife being able to initiate divorce (see Mark 10:12); (2) he rearranges the discussion so that the command of Genesis is stated first and the "concession" of Deuteronomy comes afterward; (3) he adds the follow-up exchange between the disciples and Jesus (19:10-12).

◊ ◊ ◊ ◊

The content of Jesus' teaching on divorce and remarriage is essentially the same as that already presented in the Sermon on the Mount (see 5:31-32). Here, however, it is in a narrative setting and Matthew presents us with the disciples' reactions to this demanding teaching. The lead question of the Pharisees is meant as a "test" (see the repeated use of this term [peirazō] in 4:1-11), clearly indicating the hostile intent of the leaders: "Is it lawful for a man to divorce his wife for any cause?" The addition of the phrase "for any cause" (contrast Mark 10:2) places the Matthean discussion in the context of rabbinical debates about the appropriate grounds for divorce as permitted by Deut 24:1-4. However, Jesus ignores the Pharisees' specific question and goes first to the will of God expressed in Genesis that the union of husband and wife is indissoluble. Two biblical texts are combined in Jesus' teaching: Gen 1:27, citing the essential complementarity of male and female as God's creation, and Gen 2:24, expressing the ideal of man and wife becoming "one flesh." What God has joined together, the husband (the probable referent of "man" in 19:6 since in Jewish tradition only the husband could initiate divorce) is not to separate.

Only after this fundamental principle is laid down is the text from Deut 24:1 dealt with, no longer introduced by Jesus as in Mark's version (see Mark 10:3), but by the Pharisees' question (19:7). The certificate allowing a husband to divorce his wife (and then for her to be free to remarry) was a concession because Israel (note: "you") was "hard-hearted" and not because it was the original and enduring will of God. Jesus' own magisterial saying that concludes the discussion reaches back to that original command of God: "I say to you, whoever divorces his wife, except for unchastity, and marries another commits adultery" (19:9). As discussed earlier (see 5:31-32), it is difficult to determine with precision the meaning of the exception clause in this verse (see Collins 1992, 104-45). The Greek term used, *porneia* (cf. 5:32, *logou porneias*), could mean either some sexual misconduct on the part of the wife, as the NRSV's "unchastity" renders it, or could refer to a marriage within the forbidden lines of blood relationship (see Lev 18:6-18). In the case of the former, the clause would refer to a serious circumstance that would mitigate Jesus' rigorous teaching; in effect, this would ally Jesus' teaching with the stricter rabbinical traditions such as that of Shammai that permitted divorce only in the case of adultery. If, however, the term *porneia* referred to a marriage within the forbidden bloodlines, such a marriage would be invalid under Jewish law and would not represent a true "exception" from Jesus' radical teaching forbidding divorce. In effect, Matthew would present the teaching of Jesus unchanged as it was already found in Mark's version where Jesus' prohibition of divorce is unconditional (see Mark 10:11). In this case, the "exception" clause would apply to cases where Gentile converts wishing to enter the community were in such forbidden and invalid marriages and would, in the light of Jesus' teaching, have to first separate before entering the community.

The disciples' dismay (19:10) shows that the teaching of Jesus forbidding divorce and remarriage was understood to be radical and demanding and, therefore, they conclude, "it is better not to marry." Jesus' comment pushes the discussion further, "Not everyone can accept this teaching, but only those to whom it is given" (19:11). Presumably "this teaching" (literally, "this word") refers to the immediately preceding statement of the disciples. Their comment appears on the surface to be ironic—"It is better not to marry"—but Jesus' reply takes their statement seriously. The Jewish law forbade castration (Lev 22:24; Deut 23:1), but Jesus uses this startling image to refer to those who forgo marriage "for the sake of the kingdom of heaven." In the light of the previous discussion with the Pharisees, this might include Christian women who were divorced by their husbands and yet, in obedience to Jesus' teaching, did not remarry. And, as subsequent Christian tradition would also interpret this saying, it might apply as well to missionaries and others in the community who chose not to marry in order to imitate the radical lifestyle of Jesus (see a hint of this in Matt 8:18-22 as well as in 19:29). The ordinary expectation in Judaism—and presumably in early Christianity as well—was that one would marry, but there is evidence in sectarian Jewish groups such as at Qumran or the Therapeutae that some remained celibate for the sake of a religious ideal.

◊ ◊ ◊ ◊

Jesus' teaching on divorce and remarriage is challenging, particularly for modern nuclear families where pressures on marriages are far more intense than they were in the traditional cultures known to Matthew's community. As in the Sermon on the Mount, the "righteousness" demanded appears to border on the heroic (see 5:20). Yet the teaching of the Matthean Jesus is first and foremost a profound support for the vocation of marriage; marriage fulfills the command of God that unites man and woman in an inseparable bond. In a society where the woman could be at the mercy of a husband who could write a certificate of divorce, even for seemingly insignificant offenses, Jesus' teaching also protects the rights of the woman by forbidding such divorce (and, even if the exception clause is a true exception, only in cases where there was substantial cause for a rupture). Jesus' teaching in this scene also reminds the community that the reign of God and its mission can demand the sacrifice of one's own interest, even conceivably, the possibility of marriage and family. At the same time, the Christian who has experienced a failed marriage can also keep in mind that within the narrative world of Matthew, Jesus' teaching is offered to weak and fallible disciples who struggle on the way to Jerusalem, a journey that will end only beyond death and resurrection. And the Jesus who lifts up extraordinary ideals before his followers is also the one who heals their weakness and forgives their sin.

Blessing the Children (19:13-15)

In a brief and vivid scene people bring children to Jesus for his blessing. Over the protests of the disciples, Jesus not only receives and blesses the children, but once again makes the child emblematic of what the kingdom of God means.

Matthew adapts the story already found in Mark (10:13-14), clarifying that the purpose for bringing the children to Jesus was to receive his blessing ("that he might lay his hands on them and pray" vs. Mark's unclear "that he might touch them"). Matthew omits the reference to Jesus' indignation at the disciples' protest, softening Mark's typical focus on their misunderstanding (19:13-14). Matthew also omits the saying in Mark 10:15 about receiving the kingdom of heaven like a child, perhaps since a similar declaration of Jesus has already been used in the community discourse (see above, 18:5).

The heart of this passage is Jesus' teaching that the children should not be hindered from coming to him because the kingdom of heaven belongs to them (19:14). Earlier, Jesus had admonished the disciples that unless they became like children they would not enter the kingdom of heaven (18:3), and that conviction is implicitly reasserted here. In first-century Mediterranean cultures, children had no status within the wider community. In Judaism itself a male child did not participate in religious practice until achieving adulthood at the age of twelve. But in Jesus' teaching the kingdom of heaven *belonged to* children and they had full access to Jesus. In this instance "children" are not simply symbolic of an attitude of child-like humility and openness to God's grace but may also reflect a practice within the early Christian community of allowing children to participate in the religious life of the assembly. Coupled with the previous discussion on divorce (19:1-12), this section of the Gospel continues to reveal a new perspective regarding inclusion within the community of those, such as women and now children, that traditional societies often considered vulnerable and without status.

The Rich Young Man and the Lure of Possessions
(19:16-30)

In the next set of scenes the focus of the Gospel remains on discipleship. There are three closely linked segments to this section: (1) the story of the rich young man (19:16-22); (2) Jesus' teaching about the lure of possessions (19:23-26); and (3) Jesus' hundredfold promise to the disciples about the future (19:27-30). The motif of possessions and the obstacle they pose to freely following Jesus is the link among all three.

◊ ◊ ◊ ◊

The Rich Young Man (19:16-22)

Adding to the string of instructions for various members of the household that weave through chapters 19–20 (see 19:1, above), a "young man" seeking life is offered challenging wisdom by Jesus (cf. Mark 10:17, "a man"; Luke 18:18, "a certain ruler").

In Matthew's version the young man asks what "good deed" he must do to obtain eternal life; an emphasis on good deeds is typical of this Gospel (see 5:20). Matthew also avoids the somewhat awkward exchange in Mark where the man calls Jesus "Good Teacher" only to have Jesus protest being called "good" (see Mark 10:18). For Matthew the issue is firmly fixed on seeking the good that ultimately is God alone (Matt 19:16-17). The way to that good is first of all to "keep the commandments"—an exhortation that fits neatly into Matthew's fundamental emphasis on fulfillment of Scripture (see above, 5:17).

The young man asks, "Which ones?" and Jesus' reply cites the second part of the Decalogue (see Exod 20:12-17; Deut 5:16-21). In comparison to Mark's list (10:19), Matthew omits "you shall not defraud" but, significantly, adds "you shall love your neighbor as yourself" (19:19). For Matthew, love of neighbor, coupled with love of God, fulfills the law and the prophets and is therefore an essential part of "keeping the commandments" (see 7:12; 22:39-40).

The young man "kept all these" (some manuscripts add, "from my youth"), but realizes he still lacks something (in Mark's version, Jesus is the one who tells the man he lacks something; see Mark 10:21). Jesus' reply drives home the point of the story: To be "perfect" the young man must sell his possessions and give the money to the poor, thereby gaining treasure in heaven, and then follow Jesus (19:21). The word for "perfect" is *teleios,* which derives from the Greek root *telos,* meaning the "end" or "goal." It could best be translated in this context as becoming "complete" or "whole" rather than implying static perfection. The same word was used earlier in the Sermon on the Mount where Jesus taught that loving one's enemy made one "complete" or "perfect" as God is perfect (see above, 5:43-48). In the context of the Sermon, Jesus' teaching about love of enemies is the climax in a series of "antitheses" that illustrate the "greater righteousness" for which the disciple must strive. Thus, being "perfect" is equivalent to becoming fully responsive to the will of God. In the story of the rich young man, "being perfect" means fulfilling the commandments in a radical way by selling one's possessions for the sake of the poor and following Jesus.

The challenge of Jesus' teaching is measured by the response of the young man, who leaves "grieving" because he had many possessions and could not break free (19:22). Matthew is consistent in portraying the cost of discipleship; earlier in the Gospel other disciples were also invited to "follow" Jesus and did so, leaving behind their possessions (see 4:18-22; 9:9; and the warnings in 8:18-22).

The Lure of Possessions (19:23-26)

Jesus' warning underscores the obstacle that riches pose for those who seek the kingdom of God (19:23). The proverbial saying about the camel and the eye of the needle repeats the warning. There is no basis for the frequent suggestion that the "eye of the needle" referred to a gate in the wall of Jerusalem. This indelible metaphor has force precisely because it expresses the seriousness of Jesus' teaching, even if with rhetorical exaggeration.

The prospect that the rich will have such difficulty in entering the kingdom of heaven deeply disturbs the disciples, perhaps reflecting the common wisdom that wealth was a sign of God's blessing. Yet Judaism also knew from practical experience the corrosive power of wealth and Jesus, in the manner of the prophets, was wary of how wealth could create a divided heart (see above,

7:24; see also Birch and Rasmussen 1978; Schrage 1988, 98-107; Wheeler 1995).

The Promised Reward (19:27-30)

Peter once again fills the role of spokesperson for the disciples. Here he bluntly asks Jesus what reward will belong to those who "have left everything and followed [Jesus]"—the essence of discipleship for the Gospel. "What then will we have?" is Peter's explicit request (not found in Mark's parallel, 10:28). In Matthew's version the eschatological nature of the disciples' reward is stressed. Those rewards will take place "at the renewal of all things"; *palingenesia* (literally "rebirth") is rare in the New Testament (see Titus 3:5) and refers in this context to the renewal of the world in the final age of salvation when "the Son of Man is seated on the throne of his glory." This latter image will be evoked again in Matthew to introduce the judgment parable of the sheep and the goats (25:31; see also the descriptions of the *parousia* in 24:27-31). At this decisive moment of future triumph the disciples will "sit on twelve thrones, judging the twelve tribes of Israel," a promise that echoes the Q saying found in Luke 22:30. The regathering of Israel at the end time was an expectation of some Jewish literature (see, e.g., *Pss. Sol.* 17:28), and Matthew had already hinted at this in the opening scene of Jesus' public ministry when the "light" of Jesus' messianic ministry dawns on the territory of "Zebulun and Naphtali," two of the tribes lost in the Assyrian invasion (see above, 4:13-16). For Matthew, therefore, the community established by Jesus was in essential continuity with Israel and represented its true hope for renewal.

In the final age the disciples will also receive a hundredfold of all they have left behind in order to follow Jesus (19:29). Matthew abbreviates Mark's version of the saying (cf. Mark 10:29-30) and by omitting Mark's reference to present reward ("now in this age") keeps a singular eschatological focus. The final saying that the "first will be last, and the last will be first" also refers to the reversal of fortunes expected for the end time; the followers of Jesus who have left all in this age will be abundantly rewarded in the future age. In Matthew's version it also serves as a transition to the parable of the laborers in the vineyard (see 20:1-16) and this same saying concludes the parable (see 20:16).

◊ ◊ ◊ ◊

Judaism's views on wealth were varied and generally pragmatic. While it could be seen as a sign of God's blessing and the reward of virtue (see, e.g., Deut 28:1-14), wealth also had the power to corrupt one's heart. The lust for wealth could lead to exploitation of the poor and the neglect or violation of one's covenant obligations, as the attacks of the prophets forcefully declared (see, e.g., the classic text of Amos 8:4-6). Jesus' teaching falls firmly within this prophetic tradition. For those who seek to fulfill God's will (i.e., to be "perfect"), wealth can sap their freedom and prevent them from following in the way of Jesus.

In the history of Christianity some have interpreted Jesus' words to the rich young man as offering a life of "perfection" or a more radical form of Christian life to a select few, such as monastics or vowed religious, while ordinary Christians, like the rich young man, may have to be content with simply fulfilling the fundamental commandments. Others have suggested that the Gospel contrasts the obligations of Judaism (i.e., keeping the commandments) with a more radical way of perfection represented by following Jesus. But neither of these interpretations is fully satisfying. The invitation to be "perfect" is also offered to the disciple of Jesus in 5:48, without any hint that it is meant for an elite group of Christians. Likewise, in 5:48 as well as in 19:21, the invitation to follow Jesus in a complete and radical way is viewed by Matthew not as an alternative to fulfilling the Jewish law but as its most faithful and complete expression (see also 10:8-11, 37-39). The teaching and example of Jesus embody the law and represent the full intent of God in revealing the law to Israel in the first place. A radical commitment to Jesus and his teaching, even though demanding single-minded devotion, is both a call and a grace ("for God all things are possible," v. 26) offered to all would-be followers of Jesus. Discipleship may in fact require an exacting cost in this age, but would be abundantly rewarded by God in the age to come. Apparently in the Matthean community, living a way of life that radically imitated the itinerant and self-sacrificing manner of Jesus was still a strong ideal (Luz 1995,110-12).

The Parable of the Landowner and the Laborers (20:1-16)

This parable, found only in Matthew, amplifies the theme of eschatological reversal presented in the preceding passage (see especially 19:27-30). The sayings of Jesus about the "first will be last, and the last will be first" frame the parable (19:30 and 20:16) and highlight its meaning in the context of Matthew's narrative.

◊ ◊ ◊ ◊

Like many of Matthew's special parables, the story is transparently allegorical. The vineyard was a traditional symbol for Israel (see especially the classical text of Isa 5:1-7) and Matthew will present another vineyard story in 21:33-46. Although the story itself does not directly state this, the reader can presume it is the harvest time since the landowner hires a number of day laborers to work in the vineyard. The story begins reasonably enough. At dawn a "landowner" (literally, the "head of the household") goes into the village marketplace to hire laborers and offers them the usual daily wage of one denarius; see 18:28 NRSV margin). The fact that the landowner himself hires the laborers (instead of his manager mentioned in 20:8) is somewhat unusual and begins to put the spotlight on the one who is the focus of this story. The landowner goes back to hire additional workers at different periods of the day (literally in the Greek "early in the morning," "noon," "the third hour" and, finally, "the eleventh hour"), tracking for the reader the long day of hard work. No specific wage is promised, only the landowner's word that he would pay "the usual wage" (literally, "what is just"; *dikaios,* the term so favored by Matthew; see, e.g., 1:19; 27:19). Curiously the laborers hired last, when asked why they are idle, reply that "no one has hired us"—an explanation that suggests they were willing to work but were ignored.

The parable breaks beyond the conventional pattern when at sundown the landowner sends his manager to gather the laborers and gives them their pay (payment was expected at the end of a day's labor; see Lev 19:13; Deut 24:14-15). The manager is instructed to give out the wages "beginning with the last and then going to the first"—words that alert the reader to the words of Jesus framing the parable. The laborers hired last receive a full day's pay of one denarius and when those hired first come for their wages, they expect to receive more and thus complain to the landowner when they receive pay equal to that of the other workers. The expression of their complaint is one of the keys to the parable's interpretation: "These last worked only one hour, and *you have made them equal to us* who have borne the burden of the day and the scorching heat" (20:12, emphasis added).

The landowner's reply is gracious (he addresses the laborer as "friend," 20:13; see also 22:12) but firm. The laborer received exactly what was agreed and was not treated unjustly. More important, the landowner is supremely free to do what he wishes with what belongs to him and therefore the laborers should not look on his generosity with an "evil eye" (the literal expression behind the NRSV's "envious"; see above 6:23). Therefore the parable ends with a firm emphasis not on conventional assumptions about a fair wage but on the sovereignty and generosity of the "lord of the vineyard" (the literal words of 20:8). He is the one who determines that the last shall be first and the first shall be last.

◊ ◊ ◊ ◊

Although the parable does not explicitly make this connection, it is quite possible that its stress on equality before God was directed at the Jewish-Christian members of Matthew's community. They were the ones who had labored long and hard in the vineyard (=Israel), yet latecomers, such as the sinners and Gentiles gathered by Jesus and the mission of the early community, seemed to enjoy the same status as those who had borne the heat of the day ("you have made them equal to us"). The lavish generosity of God toward sinners and Gentiles was not a reason for the "evil eye" of jealousy. Earlier scenes in the Gospel where the religious leaders protest Jesus' association with such social and moral outcasts imply a similar message (see 9:9-13; 11:16-19).

Prediction of the Passion and Instruction on Discipleship (20:17-28)

With the journey to Jerusalem nearing its end, Jesus, for a third time, solemnly predicts his Passion and resurrection. That announcement is immediately followed by a discordant response on the part of the disciples, drawing from Jesus further teaching on discipleship as service. This pattern of prediction-response-teaching is already found in Mark's narrative (cf. Mark 10:32-45; see also Matt 16:21; 17:22-23), but Matthew adds his characteristic nuances.

◊ ◊ ◊ ◊

The third Passion prediction is the most detailed, a terse summary of each major component of the entire Passion story with the Son of Man being "handed over," "condemned to death," "handed over to the Gentiles," "mocked," "flogged," "crucified" (more specific than Mark's "killed"), and finally "raised on the third day" (the same formulation as found in 16:21 and 17:23). Matthew's version is leaner than Mark's, and he omits the references to the disciples' reactions of amazement and fear (see Mark 10:32), probably part of his usual tendency to downplay Mark's harsher portrayal of Jesus' followers.

Response to Jesus' prediction of his suffering comes in the form of a request by the "mother of the sons of Zebedee." The "sons of Zebedee" (identified by Mark as "James and John," see Mark 3:17) are fairly prominent in Matthew's Gospel, being among the first disciples called by Jesus (4:21; see also 10:2), present at his transfiguration (17:1), and at Gethsemane (26:37). Their mother will also be present at the crucifixion in Matthew's account (27:56). In Mark's version the two disciples, James and John, approach Jesus directly; Matthew may have the mother make the request as a way of softening the discordant note of the disciples' request. As the story continues, Jesus will directly address them, not their mother (20:22). She requests that Jesus place her two sons in the two top positions of honor in his "kingdom," "one at your right hand and one at your left." In Matthew's narrative this request might seem to be a consequence of Jesus' own promise that in the end time the twelve would sit on thrones, judging the tribes of Israel (19:28).

Jesus' response is sober and continues with the teaching on the Passion begun with his solemn prediction. The disciples' crude attempt to ensure for themselves power and prestige, an ambition poorly masked by a mother's request, runs counter to the way of Jesus. In fact, the image of "sitting at my right hand and my left" may be ironically evoked in the Passion story where the two bandits crucified with Jesus are placed "one on his right and one on his left" (27:38). Matthew omits Mark's imagery about suffering as a "baptism" or immersion and focuses on the image of the "cup": "Are you able to drink the cup that I am about to drink?" (cf. Matt 20:22-23 and Mark 10:38-39; Matthew will refer to baptism as an initiation rite in 28:19 and, therefore, may have preferred to avoid this metaphorical use). Drinking from the cup as a metaphor for various forms of suffering endured by Israel was widely used, particularly in prophetic literature (e.g., Isa 51:17; Jer 25:15; 49:12; 51:7; Lam 4:21; *Mart. Isa.* 5:13; see the list of examples in Harrington 1991, 288-89). Jesus uses it here as another prediction of his impending Passion.

Jesus promises the sons of Zebedee that they will eventually "drink my cup," perhaps reflecting popular tradition known to Matthew (and Mark) about their martyrdom (the martyrdom of James is mentioned in Acts 12:2). As in Mark, Jesus tells the disciples that the granting of places of power is not his to give; God alone (in Matthew, "my Father") grants reward to those "for whom it has been prepared" (cf. 6:1, 4, 6, 18).

The anger of the other disciples is probably to be interpreted as jealous chagrin that they have been outmaneuvered rather than as virtuous indignation at the brothers' ambition (20:24). Jesus intervenes (note Matthew's "but" in 20:25) with corrective teaching directed to all the disciples, contrasting the oppressive exercise of power on the part of Gentile authorities with that which should characterize the followers of Jesus. The rulers of the Gentiles "lord it over" *(katakyrieuousin)* their subjects, and their "great ones" literally "exercise power over" them (*kataexousiazousin*, which the NRSV translates as being "tyrants over"). As in the community discourse of chapter 18, the intended audience for this teaching appears to be the leadership group within the community. Whoever among the disciples wishes to be "great" must be the "servant" *(diakonos)* of the others; whoever wishes to be first must be the "slave" *(doulos)*.

The concluding saying (20:28) recapitulates this entire section, including the Passion prediction at the beginning, and is the christological basis for the teaching about authority. The first part of the saying distills the entire mission of Jesus into the terminology of service: "The Son of Man came not to be served *(diakonēthēnai)* but to serve." The second half restates the fundamental purpose of Jesus' mission, but now in reference to his death: "to give his life a ransom for many." Here Matthew reaffirms the salvific nature of Jesus' death as the summit and expression of his entire mission (see 1:21; 8:17; 26:28). The Greek term *lytron* ("ransom") has as its original meaning the redemption of someone captive or enslaved (see, e.g., Exod 6:6 where God tells Moses he will "redeem" Israel from captivity). Jesus' redemptive suffering is a ransom "for many," the latter phrase evoking the image of the Suffering Servant of Isa 53:11-12. "Many" is not to be understood in a restrictive sense (i.e., only for some), but as an expansive expression signaling the broad impact of Jesus' redemptive mission.

◊ ◊ ◊ ◊

The third Passion prediction, and the teaching on discipleship that follows it, interprets both Jesus' mission and Christian practice in the light of the cross. Located at the conclusion of Jesus' journey to Jerusalem, the Passion prediction draws the reader forward in the narrative to the climactic events that will take place in the Holy City. The manner of Jesus' life and death serves as a challenge to the thoughtless ambitions of the disciples and as a clear contrast to the oppressive and exploitive power inflicted on Roman subjects by Roman authorities. Discipleship, therefore, is not simply a matter of an individual's following in the footsteps of Jesus but, in Matthew's perspective here (and in the community discourse of chap. 18), applies as well to the character of the community itself in its use of power and the mutual care of its members.

The Son of David Heals (20:29-34)

This last healing story in the Gospel concludes the journey of Jesus and his disciples to Jerusalem. Mark, too, had punctuated the journey with the dramatic story of the healing of Bartimaeus (10:46-52). The account in 20:29-34 is almost a doublet of a previous healing story in 9:27-31, yet it has a different purpose here, coming as it does at the end of the journey to Jerusalem. For one last time before the turbulent events in Jerusalem begin, Matthew reminds the readers of the extraordinary healing power and messianic authority of Jesus, the "Son of David." The plea of the blind men—"Lord, let our eyes be opened"—is an apt prayer and poignant conclusion for this section of the Gospel where discipleship instruction has been a strong motif.

◊ ◊ ◊ ◊

Matthew simplifies Mark's introduction to this story (cf. Matt 20:29-30 and Mark 10:46), omitting the details about entering Jericho and the presence of the disciples, and substituting "two blind men" for Mark's "Bartimaeus son of Timaeus, a blind beggar."

There are several instances in the Gospel where Matthew shows his preference for the number "two" (4:18, 21; 8:28; 9:27; 18:15-16, 19-20; 20:21, 24, 30; 21:2, 7) although the reasons for these changes are not always easy to determine. In this story, the change helps shift the focus subtly away from the identifiable character "Bartimaeus" and his determined pleas, to the power and compassion of Jesus as "Son of David" who comes to open the eyes of the blind, one of the signs anticipated for the end time (see, e.g., Isa 29:18; 35:5; also above, Matt 11:5).

The surrounding crowd's attempts to silence the blind men only serve to amplify their appeals to Jesus. They begin by crying out, "Lord, have mercy on us, Son of David," a plea that is repeated "even more loudly" in verse 31 (in some manuscripts the title "Lord" is omitted in the first cry in v. 30). Each of these phrases has resonance in Matthew's Christology. The term *kyrios* or "Lord" is an important title of reverence, often used in critical moments (e.g., 8:25; 14:30; 15:25). The prayer "have mercy on us" is an intense prayer used as a plea for rescue or healing (see

9:27; 15:22 [in both these stories coupled with "Son of David"]; 17:15). The title "Son of David" is favored by Matthew, appearing in the opening line of the Gospel (1:1) and used in contexts where the compassion and humility of Jesus the Messiah are on display (see the comments above, 9:27-31; see Senior 1997a, 53-57).

The concluding segment of the story links Christology to discipleship. Jesus hears the pleas of the two blind men, stands still, and calls them to him, "What do you want me to do for you?" (20:31). Their reply is an exquisite expression of "praying faith" (Held 1963, 284-88): "Lord, let our eyes be opened" (20:33). Matthew intensifies the emotional response of Jesus, noting that he is "moved with compassion" (the vivid participle *splangchnistheis* literally means a stirring of the intestines, the seat of the emotions in Semitic cultural understanding, and implies a strong emotional reaction; see also Matt 9:36; 14:14; 15:32; 18:27). Jesus "touched" their eyes and immediately they were able to see and they "followed" Jesus. As was already the case in Mark's version of the story, the healing of the men's blindness resulted not only in renewed sight, but in the determination to "follow Jesus," a decision all the more significant at this stage of the Gospel story.

◊ ◊ ◊ ◊

Matthew's story of the healing of the two blind men of Jericho comes at a major turning point in the Gospel narrative and aptly serves as a transition. Matthew again lifts up for the reader the icon of Jesus as the messianic healer—just as he had at the very beginning of Jesus' public ministry (see 4:23-25). Jesus is indeed the Son of David, the Lord, who has compassion on the multitudes and who can "open the eyes of the blind." Matthew's formulation of this phrase in the words of Isaiah is significant. The Gospel thereby reasserts the messianic authority of Jesus on the eve of his Passion. The magnificent vision of Isa 35 foresees in the end time that the desert will bloom and the blind and the deaf and disabled will be healed, and a way shall cut through the wilderness that will become the "Holy Way" on which the redeemed of the Lord will enter Zion "with singing."

IN THE HOLY CITY: CONFLICT, DEATH, RESURRECTION (21:1–28:15)

The Son of David Enters Jerusalem and the Temple (21:1-17)

The journey to Jerusalem, begun in 16:21, is now concluded and the movement of the story accelerates toward its climax in the death and resurrection of Jesus.

A significant structural change helps Matthew give this scene a dramatic flourish. What Matthew presents as one continuous sequence—entrance into the city (21:1-11) and entrance into the temple (21:12-17)—Mark divides into two separate incidents (see 11:1-10, 15-17). This is a result of Mark's framing the account of the temple cleansing with the curious incident of Jesus' cursing the fig tree (see 11:12-14, 20-26), a prophetic action that seems to be a commentary on the fate of the temple itself. In Matthew, however, Jesus' entrance into the temple is the climax of a triumphant procession that begins in Bethphage and ends in the temple court-yard.

Matthew also highlights fulfillment of Scripture, another characteristic motif. Most evident is the fulfillment quotation from Zech 9:9, but there are a number of other biblical allusions in this scene. Likewise, Matthew's trademark Christology is in evidence: Jesus is acclaimed as Messiah and as the humble Son of David who not only takes possession of his city and temple, but also heals the sick within the enclosures of God's house. All of this leads to consternation on the part of Jesus' opponents and acclamations of joy from the crowds and the "children."

◊ ◊ ◊ ◊

Matthew stages the beginning of the triumphant entry at the village of Bethphage, just over the eastern slope of the Mount of Olives. The reference to the Mount of Olives contributes to the eschatological aura of this entire scene. Zechariah 14:4 identifies the Mount of Olives ("which lies before Jerusalem on the east") as the location where the final struggle on the day of the Lord will take place.

Jesus prepares for his entry into Jerusalem by sending two disciples into the village to procure a donkey and a colt (21:2-3). The whole tone emphasizes Jesus' messianic authority—he commands the disciples; they do exactly as he says; and everything is as "the Lord" predicts. Matthew's curious and somewhat awkward reference to *two* animals (contrast Mark 11:4, "a colt") is obviously under the influence of the fulfillment quotation from Zech 9:9 ("riding on a donkey, on a colt, the foal of a donkey"). The Hebrew original probably referred to only one animal, with the second reference—"a colt, the foal of a donkey"—being simply an explication of the first. Matthew's having two animals is not necessarily a mistake, as some have suggested (e.g., Meier [1979, 21-22] who uses this as evidence that Matthew was not Jewish), but reflects the kind of literal exactness not uncommon in Jewish interplay with biblical allusions (see Stendahl 1968, 119; Hagner 1995, 594-95; Harrington 1991, 293). The fulfillment text itself (21:4-5) serves well Matthew's interpretation of this scene. Jesus' royal authority is in full view as this triumphant procession enters David's city and its temple. But this is a King like no other, one who is "humble" and mounted on common beasts of burden. To hold this focus, Matthew omits from the Zechariah quotation a phrase that spoke of the King as "triumphant and victorious" (Zech 9:9*b*).

In preparation for the procession, the disciples procure the animals and put their cloaks over them while a "very large crowd" (cf. Mark 11:8, "many") lay their cloaks on the road and pave it with branches cut from the trees. The scene is reminiscent of the royal acclamation given Jehu after he is anointed by the prophet Elisha in 2 Kgs 9:13. Crowds surround the procession, shouting praise to the "Son of David" (21:9, a title perhaps inspired here by Mark 11:10, "Blessed is the kingdom of our father David that is coming"). The words of praise are taken mainly from Ps 118:26 ("Blessed is the one who comes in the name of the LORD . . ."; see Mark 11:9). "Son of David" is clearly a messianic title for Matthew, so its presence in this scene of erupting triumph is apt. At the same time, Matthew frequently applies the title to Jesus in his role as healer and servant (see 9:27; 12:23; 15:22; 20:30; also 21:15), so it also fits here where Matthew stresses the humble character of Jesus' messianic identity.

The "whole city" of Jerusalem is "in turmoil" (literally, "shaken," 21:10), reminiscent of the distress of "all Jerusalem" and Herod at the news the Messiah had been born in Bethlehem (see 2:3). But the "crowds," who remain until this point generally favorable to Jesus, acclaim him as "the prophet Jesus from Nazareth in Galilee" (21:11). Matthew may imply that the crowds, too, see Jesus as a messianic figure, as the "prophet like Moses" foreseen in Deut 18:15, 18.

Matthew, following Mark's lead, situates the dramatic scene of the entry itself in the large enclosure of the Herodian temple where some of the commerce necessary for the temple liturgy took place (21:12-17). Here Greek and Roman coins, with their offensive images, could be changed into Tyrian and Jewish coins suitable for temple offerings (see Exod 30:11-16, which required the half-shekel offering). The selling of pigeons explicitly mentioned in Matthew was prescribed for certain sacrificial offerings (as in the case of a woman after childbirth; see Lev 12:6-8). Although historically much of this activity was necessary and hardly venal, the Gospel portrays Jesus as a fierce prophetic figure, purging the temple of all commercial transactions ("all who were selling and buying in the temple") and doing so in the name of God's word. Two texts are cited. The first, "My house shall be called a house of prayer," is from Isa 56:7. Matthew omits the phrase "for all the nations" still retained by Mark 11:17. While Mark's theology may foresee a "spiritual" temple ("not made with hands"; see Mark 14:58; on this see Donahue 1973, 103-38; Juel 1977, 143-57; Dunn 1991, 37-56) now identified with the Christian community itself, Matthew has no such perspective. The Jerusalem temple is the only temple and its fate would be sealed in the Jewish revolt, a fate Matthew seems to interpret as punishment for the rejection of Jesus (see 21:40-41; 22:7). The second part of the citation is from Jer 7:11, "but you are making it a den of robbers." From Matthew's perspective this is an apt quotation because Jeremiah excoriates Judah for its infidelities and predicts the destruction of God's house as punishment. Therefore Matthew views Jesus' prophetic action not simply as reform of the temple, but ultimately as a sign of its impending destruction due to the sins of the leaders and the people (see 24:1-2).

The remainder of the temple story is unique to Matthew (21:14-17). While Jesus is in the temple courtyard, the "blind and the lame" come to him to be cured (the verb *proselthon,* "to approach," is consistently used by Matthew to describe the supplication of the sick for healing from Jesus). In the account of David's taking of Jerusalem from the Jebusites, the "blind and the lame" are those "whom David hates" and the ones who are forbidden to "come into the house." In Lev 21:16-24, any Levite who had a physical disability, including the "blind or lame" (v. 18), was forbidden from offering the sacrifices. Such cultic boundaries are transcended when the blind and the lame approach Jesus and are healed by him inside the temple enclosure. Matthew may well see this as the penetration of Jesus' messianic work and authority (see 11:5, "the blind receive their sight, the lame walk") into the very center of Israel, fulfilling the hopes of such texts as Isa 35:1-10, which envision in the final days the healing of Israel and a triumphant march to Zion (including the blind and the lame; see Isa 35:5-6).

The reactions to Jesus' prophetic sign also have a familiar ring. The "chief priests and the scribes" become angry when they see the "amazing things" Jesus does and when they hear the acclamation of "children" in the temple, offering homage to the "Son of David." The children's praise of Jesus recalls his words in 19:13-15 that the kingdom of heaven belongs "to such as these" (see also 18:1-4). Typically, Jesus responds with a citation of Scripture, in this instance a quotation from Ps 8:2. As in 9:13 and 12:7, Jesus challenges the leaders to be aware of the Scriptures, which remain the authority and authentication for Jesus' actions.

The story ends abruptly when Jesus "left them" and went out of the city to the village of Bethany to spend the night (21:17). Bethany, a village on the eastern slope of the Mount of Olives, will enter the story again when Jesus stays at the house of Simon the leper and is anointed there for his burial by an anonymous woman (see 26:6-13).

◊ ◊ ◊ ◊

Matthew artfully weaves together several motifs in this dramatic scene. Jesus is filled with messianic authority but he is also a humble king. Jesus reverences the house of God and is zealous for its integrity, but the end of the temple and the dawning of the final era are also signaled. Jesus exhibits fierce prophetic energy in cleansing the temple of its commerce, but he is also the gentle healer and one acclaimed as Son of David by children. These multiple facets of Matthew's Christology also instruct the community about those virtues that must characterize Jesus' followers.

The Withering of the Fig Tree (21:18-22)

Situated between Jesus' prophetic action in the temple and his return on the next day is the strange story of the withering of the fig tree. Because Matthew has dissolved Mark's framework in which the cursing and subsequent withering of the fig tree become a symbolic commentary on the fate of the temple (see 21:1-17), this incident takes on a somewhat different meaning. The immediate point of the story is to further illustrate Jesus' messianic authority and the power of faith expressed in prayer. But the symbolic meaning of the fig tree as a preview of judgment against the temple and its leaders still lingers.

Many interpreters of this story, disturbed by its presentation of Jesus as condemning a hapless tree, speculate that its origin may have been in a parable such as that found in Luke 13:6-9 where a landowner threatens to cut down a barren fig tree. In the evolution of the gospel tradition such a parable may have been converted into a story in which Jesus becomes the principal character. In any case, Matthew finds the story in his primary source, Mark, and takes it at face value, while modifying some of its bizarre impression.

◊ ◊ ◊ ◊

As he returns to Jerusalem from Bethany, Jesus is hungry and goes to pick fruit from a fig tree by the roadside, but finds only leaves (21:19). Matthew's version of the story omits the enigmatic comment of Mark—"for it was not the season for figs"—a comment that makes Jesus' exasperation with the fruitless tree all the more puzzling. Matthew's reader can assume that it was the season for fruit (why else would Jesus look for it?) and, therefore, that this fig tree is barren. Consequently, Jesus condemns the fruitless tree and it "withered at once" (21:19)—evidence of Jesus' extraordinary power that in Mark's scenario has to be delayed until the following day (see Mark 11:20).

The disciples are amazed and ask how it was possible that the fig tree could "wither at once" (21:20). In Mark's version Peter remembers that Jesus had cursed the fig tree the day before and points out the now withered tree (11:21). Although Matthew often uses Peter as a spokesperson for the disciples, he passes up the chance to do so here. Jesus' answer turns the withering of the fig tree into a lesson on the power of faith. If the disciples had faith and did not doubt, they could not only wither barren fig trees but even move mountains (21:21). The point is extended to include the power of prayer that springs from such a faith: "Whatever you ask for in prayer with faith, you will receive" (21:22), an exhortation that echoes Jesus' previous teaching (see, e.g., 7:7-11).

Given the context, the question remains whether this story also holds a deeper symbolic meaning beyond an exhortation on faith and prayer. In 7:16-20 Jesus had already spoken of the fig tree in the context of bearing fruit: "Are grapes gathered from thorns, or figs from thistles? In the same way, every good tree bears good fruit, but the bad tree bears bad fruit. . . . Every tree that does not bear good fruit is cut down and thrown into the fire" (vv. 16, 19). Jeremiah uses an image that has striking resemblance to Matthew's story: "When I wanted to gather them, says the LORD, there are no grapes on the vine, nor figs on the fig tree; even the leaves are withered . . ." (Jer 8:13). Similarly, Hos 9:16 uses the image of a barren tree to describe judgment on Ephraim after earlier having spoken of finding Israel at its beginning "like the first fruit on the fig tree, in its first season" (Hos 9:10). Therefore, the image of the fig tree without fruit as a symbol for the infidelity of Israel and its leaders is not out of the question.

Placed as it is immediately after Jesus' prophetic action in the temple and his sharp exchange with the Jewish leaders (21:1-17), and coming immediately before a long series of parables and conflict stories that critique these same leaders (21:23–23:39), it is quite probable that Matthew saw the withering of the fig tree as a sign of the barren faith of the temple leaders and the fate that would befall the temple because of their failure.

◊ ◊ ◊ ◊

The basic message of this passage is consistent with Matthew's theology: The follower of Jesus is to live and act out of a profound faith in God. From this faith spring confident prayer and a sense of authority that imitates that of Jesus. Also present is a more problematic theological assertion of Matthew that foresees the destruction of the temple as God's punishment for the infidelities of Israel's religious leaders. As the biblical allusions to Jeremiah and Hosea demonstrate, this was not an exceptional perspective within the framework of Judaism itself. Serious infidelity provoked God's judgment, a judgment that could bring condemnation even to the sacred precincts of the temple itself.

John and Jesus (21:23-27)

This conflict story initiates a string of controversies and parables that stretch throughout Jesus' stay in the temple area (21:23–22:46) and will lead into the prophetic woes against the leaders in chapter 23. Matthew accepts this story virtually unchanged from Mark (11:27-33). The focus is on the authority of Jesus, an authority recognized by the crowds, but rejected by the leaders.

◊ ◊ ◊ ◊

Having returned to the city earlier in the morning (see 21:18), Jesus now enters the temple enclosure and begins to teach. Here he is confronted by the "chief priests and the elders of the people" (21:23); this group of leaders will be the major actors in the Passion story. The "chief priests" presumably include the high priest (whom Matthew will identify in the Passion story as Caiaphas, see 26:3) and the leading members of his entourage. The "elders of the people" is a more general category for those influential people with whom the high priest consulted and who in effect guided the local affairs of Jerusalem. Although the Romans directly ruled the province of Judea and therefore Jerusalem itself, they apparently left a great deal of day-to-day control in the hands of local leaders.

The lead question of the priests and elders reveals the fundamental point of the entire scene: "By what authority are you doing these things, and who gave you this authority?" "These things" presumably refers most immediately to the events of the previous day—Jesus' triumphant entry into Jerusalem and his prophetic action in the temple (21:1-17). The "chief priests and the scribes" had already reacted to the "amazing things" Jesus had done and to the acclamations of the children (21:15). More broadly, however, Jesus' "authority" (the Greek word *exousia* used here means "power" or "authority") has been a fundamental issue of the Gospel. On some occasions Jesus' "authority" is contrasted with that of the Jewish leaders (e.g., 7:29), and at other times different dimensions of his authority are affirmed (e.g., 9:6; 28:18) or transmitted to the disciples (9:8; 10:1). From the Gospel's point of view it is clear that the one who gives Jesus this authority is God (see, e.g., 3:17; 11:15-27; 17:5).

Jesus' counterquestion unmasks the insincerity of the leaders by linking the question of his authority with that of John the Baptist (21:25-27). He agrees to answer their question if they would first answer his about the Baptist—"Did the baptism of John come from heaven, or was it of human origin?" The leaders hesitate because if they admit that John's authority came "from heaven" (a typical euphemism for saying "from God") they have to explain why he was rejected; if they say it was not from God, they face the wrath of the crowds who revered John as a prophet.

Caught in the dilemma Jesus has set for them, the leaders choose to plead ignorance. So Jesus, too, refuses to answer their question. While the leaders' question about Jesus' authority and its origin receives no response, the reader of the Gospel has no doubt about the answer.

◊ ◊ ◊ ◊

The authority of Jesus as Christ and Son of God underwrites all of the ministry of Jesus and remains a fundamental affirmation of Matthew's Gospel. The question breaks the surface here as hostility against Jesus mounts and the Passion story is about to come into view. Once again, the fate of Jesus is linked with the fate of John. In Matthew's story the Jewish leaders play their stereotyped role as those who cannot read the signs of the times and therefore fail to see the hand of God in the words and actions of both John and Jesus.

The Parable of the Two Sons (21:28-32)

The parable of the two sons is unique to Matthew's Gospel. It connects with the previous scene because of its reference to the rejection of John the Baptist (21:32), and the setting in a vineyard (21:28) leads into the following parable of the vineyard. There is some confusion in the manuscript traditions concerning this parable. The order preferred by the NRSV has the first son refusing to go and afterward repenting of his decision. In some versions the order of the sons is reversed, with the first son saying "yes" but then not going into the vineyard. Such a change might be an attempt to have the order of the sons reflect salvation history, with Israel being first. There is also some confusion regarding the leaders' reply. In some versions where the first son repents, the leaders respond to Jesus' question about which son did the will of God by answering, the "afterward" son—presumably meaning the first son who later or "afterward" repented. Still other versions inexplicably have the leaders respond with the "second" son, despite the fact that this son did not go into the vineyard. This is due either to an error in the manuscript tradition or is meant to further underscore the bad will of the leaders. The NRSV order seems to be the most reliable version of the parable.

◊ ◊ ◊ ◊

Many of the parables unique to Matthew have a strong allegorical flavor, and that is the case here. The setting in a "vineyard" might suggest that a symbolic reference to Israel is intended (see above, 20:1-16; and the following parable of the vineyard, 21:33-44). The first son initially refuses to go into the vineyard but later "changed his mind" and goes. The second son, however, says the right thing but does not translate this into action. This is the type of hypocrisy Matthew's Gospel abhors and frequently levels such a charge at the Jewish leaders (see, e.g., 3:7-10; 7:21; 12:38-42; 15:7-8; 23:3-7).

The message Jesus draws from the story turns it into a pointed attack on the leaders. Like the first son, "the tax collectors and the prostitutes" who repent are going into the kingdom of God ahead of the religious leaders who, despite hearing John's message, refused to repent and believe in him. Matthew's description of John as one who came "in the way of righteousness [dikaiosynē]" fits perfectly into Matthew's perspective. "Righteousness" is a fundamental concept for Matthew's theology, expressing the whole spectrum of proper response to God, including repentance and good deeds. At the Jordan, Jesus himself had declared to John that he must "fulfill all righteousness" (see above, 3:15). Also typical is the assertion that those on the fringe of society—sinners, tax collectors, the sick, and even occasional Gentiles—respond more favorably to Jesus than the leaders themselves. A string of stories beginning with the Magi (2:1-12) and including such characters as the centurion of Capernaum (8:5-13), Matthew the tax collector (9:9-13), the Canaanite woman (15:21-28), and scores of the sick who reverently approach Jesus reaffirms the basic message of this parable.

The Parable of the Vineyard (21:33-46)

This parable has singular importance for Matthew's theology. Already in Mark's version (12:1-12), this story about an absentee owner of a vineyard who sends messengers to claim the fruits of the harvest from the tenants served as allegory on the history of salvation. Matthew builds on the Markan story and draws out its implications. A key factor is that the vineyard was a well-known symbol for Israel, based on the allegory of Isa 5:1-7 (see above, 20:1-16; 21:28-32). While there is no reason that the parable could not have originated with Jesus himself as a critique of the religious leaders or as an illustration of God's unrelenting attempts to save Israel, the parable as it now stands in Matthew has taken on later church concerns.

◊ ◊ ◊ ◊

Matthew begins by noting this is "another parable," in fact the second in a series of three, that Jesus addresses to the Jewish leaders (21:28-32, 33-46; 22:1-14). The story Jesus tells draws heavily on Isaiah's allegory about Israel. A "landowner" (Matthew's word is more exalted than Mark's "man"—already reflecting the story's identification of the landowner with God) plants a vineyard and protects it with a fence or hedge, digs a wine press for harvest time, and builds a watchtower to guard against theft as the grapes grow to maturity. All of these elements are found in Isaiah's story and reflect traditional farming practice in the region. The landowner is an absentee farmer and hires tenants to work the vineyard for him—also a typical situation in first-century Palestine.

The drama begins to unfold when "the harvest time had come" (21:34; cf. Mark 12:2, "when the season came"). Matthew's literal wording—"the time [kairos] of harvest was at hand [ēngisen]"—adds an eschatological flavor to the story. The verb engizō is frequently used to describe the approach of the kingdom of God (see 3:2; 4:17; 10:7) or of the end time (see 24:33). Likewise, the image of the harvest and the "time" for harvest can refer to the end of the world (8:29; 13:30). The momentous consequences of the tenants' actions further ratify the eschatological perspective hinted at here.

The owner of the vineyard sends his slaves to collect the produce of the vineyard. Matthew smoothes out Mark's somewhat awkward description at this point, ordering the messengers into two series (cf. Matt 21:34-36 and Mark 12:3-5). Each is met with violent opposition—beaten, stoned, and killed. In making two groups, Matthew may be thinking of the typical Jewish grouping of the Scriptures into the "former" (Joshua through Kings) and "latter" prophets (Isaiah through Malachi). In any case the rejection of the landowner's messengers certainly evokes the memory of the rejection of the prophets (see, e.g., the lament in Neh 9:26-31).

The procession of prophetic messengers prepares the way for the sending of the landowner's son and the catapulting of the story into a christological sphere. The parable situates Jesus in the line of the prophetic messengers to Israel but also affirms Jesus' unique status: He is not a slave, but the landowner's son and "heir" (21:38). The landowner's poignant statement, "they will respect my son" underscores the authority of the son while anticipating the drama's tragic outcome. The tenants decide to kill the son, too, hoping irrationally that his inheritance would fall to them. They seize the son, throw him out of the vineyard and kill him—all details that anticipate the death of Jesus. Matthew, in fact, reverses the order of Mark's description in order to have the son thrown outside of the vineyard before he is killed, bringing the fate of the son more closely in line with Jesus' death outside of Jerusalem (see 27:33; also Heb 13:12).

Judgment upon the tenants comes swiftly and decisively. Matthew's version again highlights the eschatological mood of this story by noting, "when the *Lord* of the vineyard comes . . ." (see 21:40 where the title *kyrios* has now replaced the word "owner"). Matthew also prepares for the confrontation that comes at the conclusion of the parable by having Jesus ask the question of the leaders and having them directly reply about their own fate, just as Jesus had done in the previous parable of the two sons (21:40-41; contrast Mark 12:9). The leaders' reply predicts an ominous punishment for the tenants because of their terrible crime: The Lord of the vineyard "will put those wretches to a miserable death, and lease the vineyard to other tenants who will give him the produce at the harvest time" (21:41). The phrase about giving "the produce at the harvest time" is found only in Matthew and reflects his typical concern with good deeds as the guarantor of authentic repentance (see 3:8, 10; 7:16-20; 12:33; 13:8; 21:19).

The parable concludes with a quotation from Ps 118:22-23 about the stone that was rejected by the builders becoming the cornerstone of the entire edifice. Matthew introduces the quotation with the words, "have you never read in the scriptures . . ." (21:42; see similarly 12:3, 5; 19:4; 22:31)—again reflecting the Gospel's fundamental conviction that the authority of the Scriptures underwrites all of the teaching and actions of Jesus. In this case Ps 118 is used to explain the paradox of Jesus' death. The "stone rejected" by the builders or leaders becomes the foundation or cornerstone of the building and this is in accord with God's own will (see, e.g., a similar use of Ps 118 in Acts 4:11 and 1 Pet 2:7).

Matthew intensifies the theology implicit in Mark and even goes beyond it by adding verse 43: "Therefore I tell you, the kingdom of God will be taken away from you and given to a people that produces the fruits of the kingdom." Matthew's insistence on good deeds—that is, "producing the fruits of the kingdom"—is familiar (see above, 21:41). What is new is the shift from the symbol of the vineyard to that of the "kingdom of God." Now the leaders are directly addressed and because they, like the tenants in the story, have rejected the son, the kingdom of God is taken from them and given to a fruitful people. In verse 44 Matthew adds a further word of judgment against the leaders that plays upon the "rock" theme of 21:42. This verse is missing in some manuscripts, but is probably authentic. The rejected stone is a "stumbling stone" that shatters those who oppose it—an image found in Isa 8:14-15 (a text also cited in Rom 9:33 and 1 Pet 2:8; in the latter case it also follows upon a citation of Ps 118:22-23). It is also a stone that will crush anyone it falls upon, a dire image that may be inspired by Daniel, where a stone cut out "not by human hands" shatters the statue and becomes a harbinger of the end time (Dan 2:34-35, 44-45).

The intent of these words of judgment against the Jewish leaders is confirmed by their own reactions (Matthew here identifies the leaders as "the chief priests and the Pharisees," the latter now taking their place with the temple-based priests [21:45]). They realize that through the parable Jesus was "speaking about them." They want to arrest him but hesitate for fear of the crowds who regard Jesus "as a prophet"—a note added by Matthew and one that recalls a similar description of the Baptist in 21:26.

◊ ◊ ◊ ◊

The allegory of the vineyard serves Matthew's Christology by placing Jesus in the context of salvation history. He follows in the line of the prophets that God sent to Israel but, as Messiah and Son of God, Jesus has a unique and decisive role. Even though Jesus will be rejected by those entrusted with the vineyard of Israel, his death will lead to resurrection, and the stone rejected will become the cornerstone of the entire edifice. Therefore Jesus' mission to Israel, including his death and resurrection, falls under the authority of the Scriptures.

Understanding the consequences of all this for the leaders who reject Jesus is another matter. Characteristic of Matthew's theology, serious sin bears consequences. Therefore the leaders responsible for the death of Jesus will suffer judgment. Here and elsewhere in his Gospel Matthew apparently interprets the calamity of the Jewish revolt and the destruction of Jerusalem as God's punishment for the death of Jesus (see 21:41; also 22:7; 27:24-25). Although such an interpretation may seem repugnant to us today, it is not an anomaly within the biblical and Jewish tradition. Jeremiah also predicted calamity for Jerusalem and its temple as God's punishment for infidelity (see, e.g., Jer 7:1-34, a passage already cited in part by Matt 21:13). Jesus' words here stand in that prophetic tradition (on early Christian attitudes to Jerusalem, see Walker 1996).

But the Matthean parable goes further, indicating that the leaders' rejection of Jesus also means a transfer of the vineyard from the unfaithful tenants to others. Determining who these "others" are is the difficult challenge of the parable. In 21:41, Matthew follows the lead of Mark in stating that the vineyard is taken from the leaders and given "to other tenants who will give [the Lord of the harvest] the produce at the harvest time." Here the meaning could simply be that unfaithful leaders will be replaced by faithful ones (for Matthew, those who do good deeds). But in verse 43, Matthew seems to move beyond this exclusively moral conclusion by asserting that the "kingdom of God" will be taken away from "the chief priests and the Pharisees" (the "you" identified in 21:45) and given to a "people" *(ethnei)* that produce the fruits of the kingdom.

For many interpreters this verse implies that in Matthew's perspective the privileged role of Israel as God's people now gives way to the Gentiles, or at least to the church made up of Jews and Gentiles who believe in Jesus. On the basis of this text, Wolfgang Trilling, for example, enunciated a classical thesis that Matthew foresees the church as a "new Israel," although the Gospel never uses that term (Trilling 1964). Sensitive to the Christian-Jewish dialogue and the consequences of a supersession theology, others have contended that the word *ethnos* can mean simply a "group" and in this context refers simply to other, faithful Jewish leaders to whom God will entrust responsibility for the vineyard of Israel. Therefore no transfer from Israel to the church or the Gentiles is foreseen at all (see Saldarini 1994, 58-63). This would not be the ordinary meaning of the term *ethnos,* however, and this interpretation may strain too much to avoid the difficulty of the text.

It is likely that Matthew does see the death and resurrection of Jesus as a decisive turning point in history, with God's people now entrusted to leaders drawn from the disciples of Jesus (and therefore reflected in Matthew's own community). These have been authorized by Jesus the Messiah and Son of God to proclaim the kingdom of God, and to them it belongs. Matthew does not set Gentile against Jew in this passage since many of his own community were Jewish Christians. But he does appear to see a cleavage looming between, on the one hand, the Jewish religious leaders who, in his view, are primarily responsible for the rejection of Jesus and the Christian message and, on the other, the disciples and the Christian community they will gather who are entrusted with the power to heal and teach in Jesus' name.

While such a theological position may have elements of a supersessionist perspective—that is, seeing Israel replaced by the Christian community—Matthew's perspective remains ambiguous. In turning to the "nations" at the end of the Gospel it is not clear that Matthew thereby considers the mission to Israel ended. Texts such as 23:39—"For I tell you, you will not see me again until you say, 'Blessed is the one who comes in the name of the Lord' "—may imply that Matthew still foresaw the inclusion of Israel in the story of salvation. In other words, despite growing bitterness and tension between Matthew's community and Pharisaic Judaism, the Gospel had not yet worked out a fully consistent and rigidly clear understanding of the place of Israel in the ongoing history of salvation.

The challenge for the modern reader of the Gospel is to understand Matthew's message in the context of his times and not to make absolute what remains uncertain in the biblical text. In any case Matthew's theology about Israel should be related to other

New Testament witnesses such as Rom 9–11 and interpreted in the light of our own contemporary experience where we see all too clearly the sad history of Christianity's relationship to Judaism.

The Parable of the Royal Wedding Feast (22:1-14)

This parable is drawn from Q (cf. Luke 14:15-24; *Gos. Thom.* 64), but the context in which Matthew has placed the parable and his characteristic editing give the story a very different cast than it has in Luke. A story about a banquet in Luke becomes in Matthew's version a royal wedding feast that a king gives for his son. In Luke's story the invited guests offer excuses to the man's servant for declining the invitation, but in Matthew the king sends two sets of servants who are violently rebuffed and even killed. In Luke the frustrated host opens his banquet to everyone who will come, especially the "poor, the crippled, the blind, and the lame" (Luke 14:21); in Matthew the angry king wreaks vengeance on those who rejected his invitation, destroying them and their city, and when the wedding feast is under way, the king comes to ensure that his guests are properly attired and punishes those who are not. These elements align Matthew's story with the previous two parables, each of which included a father-son relationship, varying responses to requests or invitations, and strong elements of judgment (see 21:28-32, 33-46).

◊ ◊ ◊ ◊

Matthew binds this parable into his narrative sequence by noting that Jesus "once more" spoke to "them" in parables. "Them" in this instance must be the "chief priests and the Pharisees" who were the target of the previous parable (21:45). Typical of Matthew, the entire parable illustrates a dimension of the kingdom of God (22:1; cf., e.g., 13:24, 31, 33, 44, 45, 47; 18:23; 20:1; 25:1).

The story itself tells of a king who gives a wedding feast for his son and sends out "slaves" to give a reminder call to all those who had been previously invited. The comparison of the kingdom of God to a banquet or feast is a traditional image, rooted in Jesus' own teaching and in the frequent meals that were part of his ministry (in Matthew, see chaps. 14; 16). Making the celebration a royal wedding feast for the king's son escalates the significance of the event and opens the parable further to both christological and eschatological significance.

The invited guests summarily refuse to come. Different from Luke's version (see Luke 14:18-20), there is scant attention to the excuses the guests give for not coming—the first call is simply rejected out of hand. So the king sends a second set of slaves to the same invited guests with a more urgent message that "everything is ready" (22:4) for the wedding banquet. This time they not only brush the invitation aside (22:5, "they made light of it . . ."), but some seize the king's slaves, mistreat them, and even kill them. The resemblance to the previous parable of the vineyard is striking and it is likely here, too, that Matthew intends the two sets of slaves sent to the invited guests to evoke the procession of prophetic messengers to Israel (see above, 21:35).

The king's reaction is fierce. He sends troops to destroy the murderers and burn their city (22:7). Although such a fate could simply be part of the story, it is quite possible that the parable reflects the historical memory of Jerusalem's fate when Roman troops destroyed the temple and city in 70 CE. Thus Matthew may be suggesting that the destruction of Jerusalem was God's judgment upon the leaders for their rejection of Jesus (see the discussion above, 21:33-46).

Declaring that the invited guests were "not worthy," the king now sends his slaves into the "main streets" (literally, the thorough-fares that presumably ran through the villages and out into the countryside, perhaps picking up an element present in Luke's version where the slaves are sent to "the highways and hedges," 14:21, 23, Gk.) telling them to invite "everyone you find" (22:9). The slaves do as they are told and fill the wedding hall with guests, including the "good and bad" (22:10). Here is another link to the preceding parable where the treachery of the tenant farmers results in the vineyard being taken from them and given to a people who will produce its fruits (see 21:41-43). In the current parable, the formerly invited guests are replaced by a new set of invitees. If the originally invited guests are the leaders of Israel who reject God's prophetic messengers and therefore suffer punishment and loss of their invitation, the newly invited guests are presumably Matthew's own community composed of Jews and Gentiles who respond to Jesus.

A new element is added to this parable that goes beyond the parable of the vineyard. When the wedding feast is filled with guests, including the "good and bad" (22:10), the king goes in to see the guests. He finds a guest who is not wearing a "wedding robe" and asks the man how he got in without wearing a wedding robe (the address "friend" has a certain ominous tone in Matthew; see 20:13; 26:50). The man is speechless and the king directs the attendants to bind him and throw him outside "into the outer darkness, where there will be weeping and gnashing of teeth" (22:13, typical Matthean descriptions of judgment; see 8:12; 13:42, 50; 24:22, 31; 25:30).

Matthew's addition to the parable expresses his characteristic theology. Even though called by God, the church remains a "mixed" reality including good and bad and stands under the same call to repentance and good deeds as Israel itself. This perspective came through strongly in the parable discourse (see, e.g., 13:24-30, 36-43, 47-50). So, too, is the threat of judgment on those who do not produce the fruits of repentance. Matthew does not define the meaning of the "wedding robe" that the hapless guest fails to wear, but it may have symbolic meaning, expressing repentance and a new life of good works. In other New Testament traditions, putting on new garments has a similar meaning (see, e.g., Gal 3:27; Col 3:12; Rev 3:4; 19:8).

The concluding saying captures a key message of the parable as a whole and sounds another characteristic note of Matthew's theology. "Many are called"—both within Israel and the Jewish-Christian community—"but few are chosen," because only those who respond to God's call with repentance and good deeds will be able to remain within the kingdom of God. Clearly Matthew does not consider the Christian community as a whole to be automatically replacing Israel as God's people—for both Israel and the Jewish-Christian community the criteria for authentic discipleship remains the same.

◊ ◊ ◊ ◊

This parable again presents the reader with Matthew's perspective on salvation history. God repeatedly offers Israel the opportunity for life with the kingdom but meets with rejection, especially on the part of the leaders. This negative response greeted the prophets of old, extended even to Jesus as God's son and to the messengers sent in his name. But if some in Israel and particularly its leaders refuse the invitation to the banquet, others are willing to respond more favorably. Thus, as Matthew's parable explains, the relative failure of the mission to Israel leads to new possibilities as both Jews and Gentiles now respond to the gospel. But this new situation should not lead to complacency on the part of the community. Only a life based on faith and good works will be acceptable for those who wish to live within the reign of God.

Taxes to Caesar (22:15-22)

This conflict story is the first of four encounters with the Jewish leaders that complete chapter 22 and lead to the woes of chapter 23. Matthew draws the story in its entirety from Mark (12:13-17), retaining its basic content, but intensifying the hostility of the leaders toward Jesus.

◊ ◊ ◊ ◊

Matthew ties this story to the preceding material by stating that the Pharisees who, along with the priests, were the targets of the previous three parables (21:28–22:10; see especially 21:45), "plotted to entrap" Jesus. The "taking counsel" or plotting of the leaders has an ominous sense to it, recalling their plot to destroy Jesus earlier in the Gospel (see 12:14; also 27:1; 28:12). They send some of their disciples, along with the "Herodians," to put Jesus on the horns of a dilemma by asking if it is lawful or not to pay taxes to the emperor (literally, to "Caesar"). The tax in question was the annual kēnson or "census"-based head tax levied by the Romans on all adults under their rule. To say "no" would be a public and dangerous repudiation of Roman authority. To say "yes" without qualification might seem too compliant for those who resented Roman hegemony. The "Herodians" are probably supporters of the Herodian dynasty, represented in the time of Jesus by both the ethnarch Herod Antipas, who ruled in lower Galilee, and Philip, who ruled in upper Galilee. Since they were dependent on Roman favor they would surely support taxation and therefore their presence in the story adds further tension to the dilemma pressed upon Jesus.

Matthew underscores the bad faith of the leaders. They elaborately praise Jesus (22:16) even as they attempt to entrap him. And Jesus himself is aware of their "malice" (the Greek term *ponēria*, meaning evil, a point added by Matthew, 22:18) and addresses them as "hypocrites," a term Matthew repeatedly uses of leaders whose words and actions do not coincide and whose evil intent is masked (see, e.g., 6:2, 5, 16; 7:5; 15:7; 23:13, 15, 23, 25, 27, 29; 24:51). He interprets their question as an attempt to put him to the "test," the same effort made by Satan in the desert (4:1, 3; see also 16:1; 19:3; 22:35).

Jesus asks to see a coin used to pay the tax, a Roman denarius, which was imprinted with a bust of Tiberius Caesar and bore the inscription in Latin, "Tiberius Caesar, august son of the Divine High Priest Augustus." Both the image of the emperor and the inscription would be offensive to observant Jews. Jesus turns the tables on the leaders by asking them whose image and whose inscription are on the coin. When they concede that both belong to the emperor, Jesus renders his famous aphorism: "Give therefore to the emperor the things that are the emperor's, and to God the things that are God's." In a single brilliant stroke Jesus silences his enemies, and they go away amazed at his answer (22:22). He answers their provocative question about paying the tax with an oblique answer—if the coin belongs to Caesar then it can be given to him. But Jesus immediately lays alongside this concession another more profound and more encompassing requirement: "[Give] to God the things that are God's." The comprehensive scope of "what belongs to God" makes it not a parallel with the concession to Caesar but a principle of commitment that moves far beyond civic obligation and even overrides it. The hostility of the leaders and their efforts to best Jesus only serve, for Matthew's Gospel, as a foil to highlight the wisdom and authority of Jesus the Messiah.

◊ ◊ ◊ ◊

This scene and particularly Jesus' proverbial response to the question of tribute to Caesar have often been interpreted as a theological principle regarding the relative powers of the civil and religious realm, or, particularly in an American context, as a basis for the separation of church and state. But it is unlikely that this text can be pushed too far in that direction. Jesus' response deftly permits the paying of taxes, even to a foreign power whose rule over Israel was illegitimate, while at the same time asserting the sovereignty of God that was the basis for Israel's ultimate freedom. Even though the leaders attempt to "test" Jesus by the political intimidation of their question, he will not submit to their ruse. In the context given, this is one more incident that contrasts the intransigence of the religious leaders with the authority and wisdom of Jesus.

Debate About Resurrection (22:23-33)

This and the following two encounters between Jesus and his opponents involve interpretation of Scripture. In this instance, Sadducees come forward to challenge Jesus about belief in resurrection, adding yet another group among the leaders who oppose Jesus. This story is also found in Mark (12:18-27), and Matthew absorbs it with only minor changes. The fact that it deals with Jesus' authoritative interpretation of Scripture makes it particularly compatible with Matthew's theology.

◊ ◊ ◊ ◊

Matthew emphasizes the cumulative force of the opposition against Jesus by noting that the Sadducees come to Jesus on "the same day" (22:23) as the previous debates involving chief priests, elders of the people, and the Pharisees. In Matthew's staging of the scene, this string of conflicts begins with Jesus' return to the city the day after his dramatic action in the temple (21:23) and continues through to Jesus' departure from the temple area at the beginning of chapter 24 (see 24:1). The Sadducees appeared earlier in Matthew's Gospel, paired with the Pharisees as implacable foes of Jesus (see 3:7; 16:1, 6, 11, 12). Historically, little is known for certain about the Sadducees (Saldarini 1988, 298-308). They are probably to be associated with elite priestly families of Jerusalem—the name *Sadducees* may derive from "Zadok" the high priest. Both Josephus (*Ant.* 18:14-16) and Acts 23:8 confirm what is asserted here, namely that the Sadducees did not accept a belief in resurrection because support for it could not be found in the Torah or Pentateuch. The Pharisees, on the other hand, made room for innovation in doctrine and, on the basis of such later texts as Dan 12:1-3, believed in resurrection. In this instance, as in others, Jesus would be closer to the Pharisaic position.

The question the Sadducees pose for Jesus is intended to challenge him just as the Pharisees had attempted with the previous question about paying taxes to Caesar (see 22:15-22). They first cite the teaching of Moses about the responsibility of a man to marry his brother's widow in order to provide her with offspring and not force her outside of the clan. This is the so-called levirite marriage (from the Latin word *levir* for "brother-in-law") based on Deut 25:5-10. The case the Sadducees pose is complicated: A woman has seven husbands in succession, all being faithful to the law of Deut 25:1-10. The bizarre story is reminiscent of that of Sarah in the book of Tobit who also survived seven husbands before her marriage to Tobias (see Tob 3:7-9). The Sadducees obviously intend to ridicule belief in resurrection by demonstrating its absurdity.

Jesus' response is decisive: The Sadducees are "wrong" because they know "neither the scriptures nor the power of God" (22:29). Jesus elaborates on each of these points, taking them in reverse order. The Sadducees overlook the power of God because resurrected life is different from ordinary life. In the resurrected life there is no marriage and the just are like "angels in heaven." This reflects traditional conceptions of resurrected life found in Judaism and in other New Testament texts. For example, 2 Bar 51:10 also speaks of the resurrected saints living "like angels." Paul describes the resurrected body as a "spiritual body" in contrast to the physical body of earthly life (see 1 Cor 15:42-49).

The Sadducees are also wrong about the Scriptures. Matthew uses a typical formulation to challenge their interpretation—"Have you not read . . . ?" (22:31; cf. 12:3, 5; 19:4; 21:16, 42) and intensifies the point of their misconception by stating "what was said *to you* by God" (emphasis added; contrast Mark 12:26, "how God said to him [Moses]"). Jesus cites Exod 3:6, 15-16 where God repeats to Moses that he is "the God of Abraham, the God of Isaac, and the God of Jacob." This is a text from the Pentateuch and therefore one the Sadducees should not have overlooked in their opposition to resurrection. Jesus' interpretation of the text implies that the patriarchs remain alive even after death because God is still in relationship to them. God is "God not of the dead, but of the living." This logic reflects traditional Jewish reflection among groups such as the Pharisees and later rabbinic traditions supporting resurrection. It is based not on a belief in the inherent immortality of the human soul, but on the power of God that is able to defeat death and sustain life despite all appearances to the contrary.

◊ ◊ ◊ ◊

While belief in resurrection is certainly an important assumption of Matthew's Gospel and one that anticipates the resurrection appearance stories at the conclusion of the narrative (see 27:62–28:20), the immediate concern of this conflict story is the contrast between Jesus and his opponents. Matthew signals this by his additions of the final verse where he notes that the crowds were "astounded" at Jesus' teaching (22:33) and at the beginning of the next scene where the Pharisees hear that Jesus had "silenced" the Sadducees (22:34).

The Great Commandment (22:34-40)

Matthew transforms Mark's story about a sincere scribe who asks wisdom of Jesus (12:28-34) into another round of conflict with the Pharisees over interpretation of the law. This passage has special importance for Matthew, reasserting as it does the Gospel's fundamental principle about the law.

◊ ◊ ◊ ◊

Matthew connects this passage with the preceding conflict about resurrection by noting that Jesus had "silenced the Sadducees" (22:34). Instead of Mark's character who is "one of the scribes,"

Matthew brings back on stage the Pharisees, the most prominent of Jesus' opponents in the Gospel. When they hear that Jesus had dispatched the Sadducees, the Pharisees "gathered together" *(synēchthēsan);* the word often has an ominous connotation in Matthew's narrative of gathering to plot against Jesus (see, e.g., 2:4; 22:41; 26:3; 27:17, 27; 28:12). It is possible that Matthew intends here an allusion to Ps 2:2, "The kings of the earth set themselves, and the rulers take counsel together *[synēchthēsan],* against the LORD and his anointed. . . ."

One of these Pharisee opponents, a "lawyer," poses a question "to test him." This is the only time Matthew's Gospel mentions a "lawyer" and, because the manuscript evidence is uncertain here, it is possible that this represents a later attempt of a copyist to harmonize Matthew with Luke 10:25. The addition of the phrase "to test him" transforms the whole atmosphere of what was a benign incident in Mark's version to yet another hostile attempt to trap Jesus (cf. 22:18 and earlier, 16:1; 19:3). The phrase recalls the efforts of Satan to lead Jesus astray in the desert test (4:1, 3) and further illustrates the profoundly negative character Matthew assigns to Jesus' opponents.

Using the deferential but surely ironic title "teacher," the lawyer asks Jesus, "Which commandment in the law is the greatest?" Later rabbinic tradition counted 613 individual commands in the law, all of which were to be respected and obeyed equally. Yet at the same time the rabbis also recognized that some commands were "weightier" than others. Various rabbinic texts discuss distillations of the law in summary statements such as Hillel's famed summary of the law in the Golden Rule (*b. Sabb.* 31a). The lawyer's challenge to Jesus may be intended to imply that he is unschooled in the law or that his answer will be incorrect.

Jesus' response is unfailingly respectful of tradition. He first cites Deut 6:5, "You shall love the Lord your God with all your heart, and with all your soul, and with all your mind" (22:37). This Old Testament text forms one version of the Shema or creed of Israel (see Deut 6:4-9), an expression of utter devotion to God and the Torah that stood at the heart of Jewish piety. Somewhat out of character, Matthew truncates the quotation, moving immediately to the command (cf. Mark 12:29). Matthew's formulation of the quotation brings it closer to the Hebrew in some respects (e.g., Matthew uses the preposition "*in* all your heart," which is similar to the Hebrew preposition *be*, whereas Mark's *ex* is identical to the Septuagint Greek). Both Mark and Matthew render the last phrase "with all your mind" while the Septuagint uses the term "power" *(dynamis)*.

Jesus characterizes this command as "the greatest" and "first" (22:38), but immediately goes on to speak of a second command that is "like it": "You shall love your neighbor as yourself" (22:39), a quotation of Lev 19:18 already cited in Matt 5:43 and 19:19. By adding "like it" Matthew's version brings the second command virtually to parity with the first.

Love of God and love of "neighbor" (originally referring to fellow Israelites with whom one was bound by the covenant) become not only the supreme expression of the law, but the guiding principle for its interpretation. This is the distinctive feature Matthew adds to the scene. Mark's material is omitted in which the scribe repeats with admiration Jesus' teaching and then concludes that love of God and love of neighbor are "much more important than all whole burnt offerings and sacrifices"—an answer that draws praise from Jesus (Mark 12:32-34). For Matthew, love of God and neighbor are the two commandments upon which "hang all the law and the prophets" (22:40). The phrase "the law and the prophets" was a traditional way of speaking of the Scriptures in their entirety (see above, 5:17; 7:12). Jesus' answer does not discount the law in any way or set the love command in tension with law observance. Rather, love of God and neighbor sums up the law. The individual commands "hang" or depend on this fundamental command for their ultimate meaning and purpose.

◊ ◊ ◊ ◊

Jesus' authority as Messiah is on display as he confounds yet another "test" engineered by his opponents—that messianic authority extends to interpretation of the Scriptures, as Matthew has repeatedly asserted throughout his Gospel. Jesus does not "destroy" the law and the prophets but as the Christ "fulfills" them.

Matthew illustrates what "fulfillment" of the law means by demonstrating Jesus' authoritative interpretation of the Scriptures. This was on dramatic display in the Sermon on the Mount, particularly in the antitheses where compassion, reconciliation, and love of enemy were the characteristic principles of Jesus' law teaching (see 5:21-48). Matthew also defended Jesus' healings and his mingling with sinners as expressions of obedience to the law (see 8:17; 9:13; 12:7). On the eve of his Passion and in the sacred precincts of the temple, the Matthean Jesus makes explicit what has been evident throughout the Gospel: All law "hangs" on the love command.

Whose Son Is He? (22:41-46)

This scene concludes the series of unrelenting conflicts between Jesus and his opponents that began with Jesus' entrance into Jerusalem and its temple (see 21:15, 23). While Mark's parallel has Jesus address a general and undefined audience, Matthew makes it a conflict with the Pharisees, connecting it with the previous scene by having the Pharisees still "gathered together" (22:41; see 22:34). In the preceding encounters, Jesus' opponents had first questioned him—now Jesus takes the initiative and confronts them.

◊ ◊ ◊ ◊

Matthew puts the christological issue clearly in play by having Jesus pose the key question directly to the Pharisees: "What do you think of the Messiah? Whose son is he?" (22:42; cf. Mark 12:35, where Jesus asks the crowds, "How can the scribes say that the Christ is the Son of David?"). The Pharisees respond by saying the Messiah is "the Son of David." The leaders' response is correct and, in fact, coincides with Matthew's own use of this title for Jesus (see 1:1; 9:27; 12:23; 15:22; 20:30, 31; 21:9, 15). Other biblical and Jewish texts spoke of the Messiah as emerging from the Davidic Messiah and therefore as "David's son" (see, e.g., Isa 11:1, 10; Jer 23:5; *Pss. Sol.* 17:21).

While "Son of David" is a legitimate messianic title, it still does not adequately describe the profound identity of Jesus. Jesus counters the Pharisees' response with yet another question. Jesus' fundamental argument is that the Messiah cannot be simply David's son if David himself, under the inspiration of God ("by the spirit"), calls the Messiah his "Lord" in the Psalms. As proof Jesus cites Ps 110:1, a passage repeatedly cited in the New Testament to affirm Jesus' exaltation at the right hand of God (see, e.g., Mark 16:19; Acts 2:34-35; 1 Cor 15:25; Heb 1:3; 8:1; 10:12). An essential assumption of Jesus' argument is that David is the inspired composer of the psalm and therefore it is David who is speaking when he says that God ("the Lord") speaks to "my Lord" (the newly enthroned king), "Sit at my right hand, until I put your enemies under your feet." Jesus interprets the psalm messianically as referring to the promised future liberator who would emerge from the Davidic dynasty.

If David calls the Messiah "Lord," then his identity is more than David's "son." Matthew's account leaves Jesus' original question unanswered—"Whose son is he?" The Pharisees are unable to give an answer and Matthew concludes this whole series of controversies with the comment, "Nor from that day did anyone dare to ask him any more questions" (22:46; see Mark 12:34). This, in fact, is the last conflict that Jesus has with his opponents outside of the Passion story. From now on he speaks only to the crowds and to his disciples (see 23:1).

◊ ◊ ◊ ◊

Like some great champion standing within the temple enclosure, the Matthean Jesus has trumped and silenced all of his opponents. Part of Matthew's purpose is to affirm for his readers that Jesus' wisdom and authority outshine the religious leaders. If, as seems likely, these leaders represent the opponents of Matthew's Jewish-Christian community, then the evangelist attempts to bolster the confidence of his own community.

But another, more profound assertion of Matthew's Gospel is left hanging in the air in this last scene. If Jesus is the Messiah, whose son is he? As a faithful Jew and the promised anointed one from the royal lineage of David (1:1-17), Jesus is indeed "Son of David." But the application of Ps 110, in which the Messiah is also called "Lord," reminds the reader of other, more profound titles applied to Jesus. Jesus is the "Lord" who exercises divine power over the raging sea (8:25; 14:28, 30). Jesus is the "Son of Man" who has authority on earth to forgive sins and to rule over the sabbath and who, after suffering and death, will come in triumph at the End of time. And he is God's beloved Son (3:17; 14:33; 16:16; 17:5) who enjoys extraordinary intimacy with God (11:25-27).

Prophetic Denunciation of the Scribes and Pharisees (23:1-39)

Following upon the series of conflicts with the religious leaders (21:14–22:46), Matthew presents Jesus, while still within the temple precincts, unleashing a bitter denunciation of "the scribes and the Pharisees"—addressed not directly to the leaders but to the "crowds" and "his disciples." The raw material for this prophetic speech comes in part from Mark 12:37-40 and from Q (see Luke 11:37-52; 20:45-47). Luke's version is a series of three woes against the Pharisees (11:42-44) and then four against the scribes (11:45-52). Matthew conflates these into a series of seven woes against the "scribes and Pharisees" (23:13-36).

The setting for the discourse is prompted by Mark's narrative. At the conclusion of his teaching in the temple, Jesus denounces the "scribes" for their pious pretensions, their hunger for status, and for their exploitation of widows (Mark 12:38-40). This prophetic denunciation is followed by a contrast scene in which Jesus praises the widow for giving all her possessions to the temple (12:41-44). Matthew omits the story of the widow but substantially expands Jesus' condemnation of the leaders into a full-blown discourse.

Some interpreters prefer to see 23:1-38 as a long preface to the apocalyptic discourse (24:1–25:46), thereby preserving the five-discourse format of the Gospel as a whole. But the emphatic change of scene in 24:1-3 (i.e., leaving the temple and going to the Mount of Olives) and the shift in audience from the "crowds and his disciples" (see 23:1) to his disciples alone (24:3) indicate that for Matthew the denunciations in chapter 23 form a separate, if not unrelated, passage. This attack on the scribes and Pharisees is not a discourse on the level of the other four, nor does it have the typical transition formula that concludes all the others (for chaps. 24–25, see 26:1). But within the framework of Matthew's story it is an opportunity to express judgment on the opponents for all of their hostility to Jesus. After this point, Jesus will no longer directly engage them in discussion. At the same time, in addressing this speech to the "crowds and disciples," Matthew also intends this to be a sober warning to the community.

The contents of the speech suggest a three-part division: (1) 23:1-12, an introductory section condemning the scribes and Pharisees for their hypocrisy and status seeking, coupled with an exhortation to the disciples; (2) 23:13-36, seven prophetic woes; (3) 23:37-39, a prophetic lament over the fate of Jerusalem.

The Scribes and the Pharisees (23:1-12)

Ironically, Jesus' bitter denunciation of the scribes and Pharisees begins with a concession that they "sit on Moses' seat" and therefore the disciples are to "do whatever they teach you and follow it" (23:2-3*a*). In later synagogue architecture the "seat of Moses" was a prominent chair symbolic of the teaching authority of the rabbi. For the period of Matthew's Gospel, and especially earlier in Jesus' own day, it is not certain whether a "seat of Moses" was part of the architecture, since most "synagogues" were not buildings dedicated to religious use alone, but shared other purposes. In any case, "seat of Moses" referred to the authority of the teacher whose interpretation of the tradition provided a link to Moses, the lawgiver and teacher par excellence. Is this text a remnant from a time when the Matthean community was still a minority group within the orbit of Judaism, retained here only as a reminder of the past? Or does this text suggest that at the time of the Gospel's composition Matthew's Jewish-Christian community had not yet made a definitive break with Judaism, and despite the Gospel's hostile estimation of the religious leaders, Matthew must still concede that the Jewish authorities are to be respected for their role as official teachers and interpreters of the Torah (Powell 1995, 419-35)? It is clear from what follows that this fundamental respect did not extend to particular points of their interpretation or to what Matthew considers their infidelity and "hypocrisy."

Jesus warns the disciples not to imitate the leader's actions for "they do not practice what they teach" (23:3; see also 5:19). A series of particulars follows, each of them echoing critiques found earlier in the Gospel. They "tie up heavy burdens" and impose them on the shoulders of others while they themselves do not lift a finger to bear them. Presumably this is directed to the rigors of Pharisaic law interpretation. As the demands of the Sermon on the Mount make clear, the Matthean Jesus, too, could present his disciples with a call to near heroic virtue, but the Gospel also describes the "yoke" of Jesus as "easy" and his "burden light" (11:30). Historically, the Pharisees were a lay reform movement that attempted to breathe new life into Judaism by extending into the life of the ordinary Jew the laws of purity usually reserved to the priests. Coupled with this attention to cultic purity (i.e., avoidance of contamination by contact with death or its presumed symptoms), the Pharisees also emphasized tithing and strict observance of the sabbath. These reforms were intended to renew Jewish piety and to provide a stronger sense of Jewish identity in the face of incursions by hellenistic culture. In many ways, Jesus shared the concerns of the Pharisees; however, he probably differed from them in giving less emphasis to cultic laws and sabbath observance. Coupled with Jesus' outreach to sinners, these differences are what Matthew sees as points of decisive contrast between Jesus and his opponents. At the time of the Gospel's composition, moreover, the Pharisees had become the dominant influence in post-70 CE Judaism; the tension between this normative Judaism and Matthew's own Jewish-Christian community no doubt added a level of bitterness to the historic differences between Jesus and his opponents.

The leaders are chastised for doing good deeds "to be seen by others" (23:5; see also 6:1). For this reason they make their phylacteries broad. "Phylacteries" were the small leather boxes, containing the text of the Shema (Deut 6:4-9) or other biblical passages, which were bound by leather straps to the forehead during prayer as a reminder of God's word (see the instructions in Deut 6:4-9; also Exod 13:9). The leaders also make the fringes or tassels on the corners of their garments long (see Num 15:38-39; Deut 22:12). These practices and identifying symbols are not condemned in themselves (Matt 9:20 and 14:36 mention that Jesus himself wore such tassels), but only the ostentatious nature of the leaders' piety (as in 6:1-18).

The leaders are also condemned as status seekers—those who love to have the place of honor at banquets, the best seats in the synagogue, and to be called "rabbi" (literally, "my great one," a term of respect later used especially for teachers). The examples are drawn from Mark 12:38-39, but Matthew alone criticizes the use of the title "rabbi." Only Judas will use this term in reference to Jesus and precisely at moments when his own treachery is in play (see 26:25, 49). Presumably "rabbi" was a term of honor within the Jewish community contemporary with Matthew and, consistent with his negative portrayal of the Jewish leaders, Matthew forbids its use in his own community.

In the direct exhortations that follow (23:8-12), the Gospel presents a radical view of relationships within the Christian community, in sharp contrast to the accusations of arrogance leveled against the religious leaders. In each instance relationships of status and power within a community are supplanted by a vision of equality before God (or Jesus himself; see 23:10). Thus the disciples are not to be called "rabbi" because they have "one teacher" and everyone else is a "brother [or sister]" (23:8). The NRSV uses the term "student" here for the purpose of inclusion, but the choice submerges part of Matthew's point: The Gospel affirms not only the subordinate relationship of the disciples to God or to Jesus (i.e., as students to one teacher), or both, but also the relationship among the disciples themselves (i.e., as equal "brothers" and sisters; see 12:46-50). Nor should anyone on earth be called "your father" since there is only "one Father—the one in heaven" (23:9). The term "father" (in Aramaic and Hebrew, *ab* or its diminutive, *abba*) was used in Judaism not only for a parent, but also as a term of respect and affection for a revered elder or teacher. There are to be no "fathers" in the Matthean community since it is not modeled on bloodlines or the patriarchal family; nor does any figure, even a powerful teacher, hold sway over the rest. Rather, all form a community of equals (i.e., "brothers and sisters") before God who alone is "Father." Matthew evidently considered "Father" to be a privileged address for God as indicated in Jesus' own prayers (see, e.g., 6:9; 11:25; 26:39, 47) and in numerous other references to God as "Father" in the Gospel. Nor are any to be called "instructors" (this is the only time the Greek word *kathēgētēs* is used in the NT; it has a connotation similar to "teacher") since the only instructor is the Christ (23:10).

The attitude of the disciple should be that of humility, not arrogance; therefore the greatest should be the servant and those who humble themselves will be exalted (23:11-12; reminiscent of Jesus' teaching in 18:1-4 and 20:24-28).

Prophetic Woes (23:13-36)

The second segment includes seven prophetic "woes" directed at the scribes and Pharisees, climaxing in a bitter denunciation of their hostile attacks on Jesus and his followers. Some of this material is from Q; in Luke 11:42-52 there are two sets of woes, three directed at the Pharisees and three at the lawyers. Matthew conflates this material into a set of seven against the "scribes and Pharisees." The rhetorical device of directing a "woe" against an erring opponent has roots in the Hebrew Scriptures, particularly in the prophetic writings (see, e.g., Isa 5:8-10, 11-14, 18-19, 20, 21, 22-24; 10:1-3; 28:1-4; 29:1-4; 30:1-3; 31:1-4; 45:9-10; Jer 13:27; 48:46; Ezek 16:23; Amos 5:18-20; 6:1-7; Mic 2:1-4). Most of the criticisms of the leaders echo earlier passages in the Gospel. Throughout these fierce denunciations the leaders are called "hypocrites" (23:13, 15, 23, 25, 27, 29; similarly 23:28; cf. 6:2, 5, 16; 7:5; 15:7; 22:18), a label that underscores the insincerity and lack of integrity that Matthew's Gospel seems particularly to abhor. Most of the practices listed here—tithing, attention to the laws of purity, discussions about oath taking—were apparently concerns of the historical Pharisees even though the Gospel stereotypes them in every instance as warped by hypocrisy and lack of proportion.

The leaders are accused of "lock[ing] people out of the kingdom of heaven" while not going in themselves (23:13). Matthew has used the image of "entering" the kingdom previously (see, e.g., 18:2). Unless one becomes humble like a child, one cannot even enter the kingdom, Jesus had warned (18:3). The act of closing off people from entering the kingdom also recalls the power of "binding and loosing" given to Peter (16:19) and the community (18:18). Jesus' discourse in chapter 18 had instructed the leadership of the Matthean community, in contrast to the behavior of the scribes and Pharisees, to exercise great care in seeking out the stray and expelling someone only after serious efforts to win over the erring member. Furthermore, the scribes and Pharisees carry on active proselytizing, but because they lead their converts astray they succeed only in creating a duplicate of their own vices, that is, "twice as much a child of hell as yourselves" (literally, "child of Gehenna," the valley south of Jerusalem where later Jewish traditions place the last judgment and which, in some NT texts, is portrayed as the place of eternal punishment). These bitter words may indicate that the Pharisees carried out active missionary work in the Diaspora, although historical evidence for such activity is scarce (McKnight 1991). Matthew may be referring here to competition for Gentiles sympathetic to Judaism who were already associated with the synagogues (the so-called "Godfearers").

The next two woes deal with oaths, another practice Matthew's Gospel condemns (23:16-22; cf. 5:34-35). Here Jesus condemns the attempts of the leaders to mitigate the obligations of their oaths through clever casuistry. They allege that one is not bound if an oath is taken "by the sanctuary," but bound if one swears by "the gold of the sanctuary"; not bound by an oath taken "by the altar," but bound if taken by the gifts on the altar, and so on. Jesus cuts through such devices and declares that any oath a person pretends to swear by some sacred object of the temple is an oath taken to God and therefore must be kept (23:22). The point is not to endorse oath taking, but to unveil once again the hypocrisy of the leaders. They are "blind guides" and "blind fools" because their own actions are a sham, and their example and teaching lead others astray.

The next woe is particularly illuminating. The scribes and Pharisees are accused of taking tithes on "mint, dill, and cummin" while neglecting the "weightier matters" of the law, "justice and mercy and faith" (23:23-24). Taking a tithe on produce for the support of the Levites at the temple was prescribed by the law (see Lev 27:30-33; Deut 12:17; 14:22); the extension of this to seasonings such as mint, dill, and cumin was a sign of the rigorous devotion of the Pharisees on this matter. What is noteworthy is that Jesus does not object to such devotion in itself but only when attention to these finer points is coupled with neglect of the weightier commands—"It is these you ought to have practiced without neglecting the others" (23:23). As is the case throughout this discourse, Jesus' language is vivid. To ensure complete cultic purity, the leaders are accused of straining the liquids they drink to make sure they would not be contaminated by consuming even a tiny unclean insect, although they end up swallowing a whole camel—an unclean animal to be sure (23:24; see Lev 11:4; Deut 14:7)!

The next two woes castigate the leaders because they attend to the "outside" of the cups and plates while the inside is full of "greed and self-indulgence" (23:25-26). The leaders are like "whitewashed tombs" (painted perhaps to avoid accidental contact and contamination; see Num 19:16), beautiful on the outside but full of "hypocrisy and lawlessness" on the inside (23:27-28). These accusations are reminiscent of the dispute about purity in 15:1-20 where Jesus had also accused the leaders of hypocrisy because they cared about externals to the neglect of inner integrity.

The final woe introduces a long and bitter accusation against the leaders as those who violently reject God's messengers (23:29-36). The leaders build memorial tombs for the prophets and the "righteous" that their ancestors had rejected and even killed (23:29-30). There is some evidence that at the time of Jesus such memorial tombs were constructed. In Judaism the tradition had developed that the prophets of old were not only rejected but in some instances killed. Matthew uses this tradition against the leaders; despite their disclaimers not to have taken part in the shedding of innocent blood they are "descendants" (literally, "sons") of those who murdered the prophets (23:31). As if taunting them to carry out their destined role, Jesus tells the leaders to "fill up, then, the measure of your ancestors" (23:32). The leaders are called "snakes" and a "brood of vipers"—as John the Baptist had labeled the unrepentant leaders at the baptism (3:7). Their murderous deeds will not escape the punishment of hell (i.e., "Gehenna"; see above, 23:15).

Jesus the prophet predicts the rejection and persecution his disciples will suffer at the hands of the leaders and declares bitter judgment on those who are guilty. While clear evidence of Jewish persecution of Christian missionaries is fairly sparse (see Hare 1967), it is not surprising that sporadic incidents may have occurred. No doubt the intensity of this "sibling" strife adds a special note of bitterness to this passage. Jesus declares that he sends to Israel "prophets, sages, and scribes" (23:34; see also Luke 11:49-51 [Matthew adds "sages" to Luke's list]). Each category of disciple sent on mission to Israel has a resonance in Matthew's Gospel. Jesus himself was a prophet who fearlessly proclaimed God's word and God's judgment to the leaders. Likewise, Matthew had portrayed Jesus as Wisdom incarnate (see 11:19) and now the disciples themselves are presented as the emissaries of "Wisdom." And the title of "scribe" seems to have a special place in Matthew's community (see 13:52). Like Jesus himself, these emissaries will encounter rejection, persecution, and even death (23:34). This rejection will bring judgment on the leaders who thereby, like their ancestors, become guilty of "innocent blood" (see 23:35). Matthew underscores this legacy of rejection, linking the leaders' sin to all of the innocent blood shed from the time of Abel, the first to be murdered in the biblical drama (Gen 4), to "Zechariah son of Barachiah." (There is confusion about the identity of Zechariah. Zechariah "son of Barachiah" was the OT prophet [Zech 1:1], but there is no evidence he was murdered "between the sanctuary and the altar" as Matthew claims [23:35]. That was Zechariah "son of . . . Jehoiada" mentioned in 2 Chr 24:20-27.) The guilt of all this innocent blood will be borne by "this generation," a designation for the leaders Matthew uses repeatedly in judgment texts (see 11:16; 12:39, 41; 16:4; 17:17; 24:34).

Lament over Jerusalem (23:37-39)

In the manner of Jeremiah, Jesus concludes his prophetic denunciation of the leaders with a lament over Jerusalem (see also Luke 13:34-35, who places this text during Jesus' Galilean ministry). After this Jesus will leave the temple and its city, returning only to celebrate the Passover with his disciples and then as a prisoner condemned to death.

The shift from a condemnation of the leaders to the fate of Jerusalem gives this passage an elegiac tone. Jerusalem is lamented as the city that "kills the prophets and stones those who are sent to it" (Zechariah, the last of the prophets mentioned by Jesus was himself stoned [see 23:35]). The bitter denunciations give way to poignant sadness as Jesus expresses his desire to have gathered the children of Jerusalem "as a hen gathers her brood under her wings," an image for God's provident care in the Hebrew Scriptures (e.g., Deut 32:11; Ruth 2:12; Pss 17:8; 36:7; 57:1; 61:4). But Jerusalem's refusal means that its "house" will be left desolate (23:38). Presumably this refers to the temple whose destruction by the Romans in 70 CE Matthew may view as punishment for the rejection of Jesus (see 22:7).

But the discourse concludes with yet another note. The house of Jerusalem will be desolate and not receive the messianic visitation *until* this city proclaims, "Blessed is the one who comes in the name of the Lord" (23:39). This is a quotation from Ps 118:26, the same acclamation that had greeted Jesus as he triumphantly entered Jerusalem (see 21:9). In Matthew's perspective, the rejection of Jesus by the leaders is indeed a grave sin, one that brings divine judgment. Yet the story of God's relationship to Israel is not concluded, and the day will come when Jerusalem will again receive its Messiah with shouts of praise.

◊ ◊ ◊ ◊

Viewed within the tradition of prophetic denunciations of Israel and its leaders, and set in the context of the tension between Matthew's community and other Jewish groups, this discourse is comprehensible as both a criticism of hypocritical religious leadership and a warning to Matthew's own community. Separated from these moorings, this text has often been used to feed anti-Semitism.

Ironically, however, this bitter passage should moderate the views of those who believe that Matthew's Gospel foresees a definitive turn from Israel to the Gentiles because of the rejection of Jesus. The lament that concludes this discourse implies that for Matthew the drama of Israel was not yet concluded—the day could still come when Jerusalem would again receive its Messiah as the crowds had done on that fateful day when Jesus first entered the Holy City.

The Apocalyptic Discourse (24:1–25:46)

The site of the magnificent Herodian temple across the Kidron valley from the Mount of Olives triggers Jesus' prediction about its destruction and, prompted by the disciples' question, leads to the discourse about the end time and the stance the community should take as it awaits the consummation of history. Such speculation was a typical theme of Jewish literature and many of the images and motifs found in the discourse have antecedents in biblical and other Jewish apocalyptic material (see Holman 1996).

The placement of the discourse at the conclusion of Jesus' teaching in the temple and immediately prior to the Passion story follows the Markan sequence (Mark 13). However, Matthew omits Mark's story of the widow (Mark 12:41-44), thereby fusing the apocalyptic discourse directly onto the previous condemnation of the scribes and Pharisees. The words of judgment against the leaders (23:1-36) and Jesus' prediction of judgment against the city of Jerusalem (23:37-39) already set the atmosphere for the great discourse, which itself begins with a prediction of the temple's destruction (24:1-2).

Matthew had anticipated some of Mark's apocalyptic material in the mission discourse, blending it with Q and his own material (cf. Matt 10:17-22a and Mark 13:9-13). The same pattern will hold here, particularly in the first part of the discourse where Matthew is more dependent on Mark (24:1-36; cf. Mark 13:1-32). Beginning with 24:37 and continuing on through 25:46, Matthew will draw on a series of sayings and parables of Jesus, some from Q and others unique to his Gospel. The profusion of this latter material and its strong Matthean stamp indicate that Matthew is particularly interested in the conduct of the community as it moves out into history.

Numerous divisions of the discourse have been proposed. Based on content, the following order is suggested: (1) 24:1-14, an introduction drawn primarily from Mark 13:1-13; (2) 24:15-31, a description of the signs and events leading up to the coming of the

Son of Man (drawn mainly from Mark 13:14-32); (3) 24:32–25:30, a series of sayings and parables instructing the disciples on the need for vigilance and fidelity while awaiting the End (composed mainly of Q materials and materials special to Matthew); (4) 25:31-46, a final judgment scene in which the Son of Man returns to judge "all the nations."

◊ ◊ ◊ ◊

The Fate of the Temple and Signs for the Beginning of the End Time (24:1-14)

Jesus leaves the temple behind, concluding the long segment of the Gospel that had begun in 22:23. No more will Jesus teach in the temple or engage the leaders in discussion. The prophetic condemnation of the leaders had been addressed to "the crowds and to his disciples" (23:1); now it is the "disciples" who approach Jesus and they alone will hear his words (24:1). In Mark's account a single disciple points out the magnificence of the temple to Jesus and four disciples (Peter, James, John, and Andrew) ask about the end time (Mark 13:1, 3), but in Matthew the entire community of the disciples gathers to hear Jesus' final instruction.

The disciples point to the magnificent Herodian temple, one of the true wonders of the ancient world. But its extraordinary beauty and majesty are no protection from judgment. With solemn authority, the Matthean Jesus predicts that not one stone of the temple would be left standing—"all will be thrown down." The prophets had warned that because of Israel's infidelity, even the temple would not be spared (see, e.g., Jer 7:1-15). And the prospect that the temple would be radically purified or even destroyed in connection with the messianic age was a current in Jewish tradition (Juel 1977, 169-210). Jesus' purification of the temple was itself a prophetic sign threatening the temple because of the sins of the leaders (see above 21:12-17). The parable of the vineyard (21:33-44) and the parable of the royal wedding (22:1-14) also raised the specter of divine judgment falling on Jerusalem and its leaders (see especially 22:7). In the Passion narrative Jesus' alleged threats against the temple would be the subject of false witness (26:61; 27:40).

Matthew situates the discourse on the "Mount of Olives," a location associated with the final judgment in Jewish tradition (24:3; see Zech 14:4). There Jesus sits as an authoritative teacher (cf. 5:1) and the disciples come to him "privately" to pose the question that will trigger the discourse. Matthew's formulation of the question is more precise than that in Mark and clearly separates the destruction of the temple from the end time itself (24:3; cf. Mark 13:4). The disciples ask, "When will this be [i.e., the temple's destruction], and what will be the sign of your coming and of the end of the age?" Jesus is clearly identified as the Son of Man who is to come and his *parousia* will mean the end of the age (i.e., "your" coming).

In response Jesus warns the disciples of events that are not the signs of the end time itself but only "the beginning of the birth pangs" (24:8). These chaotic events include false prophecy, external persecutions, and internal strife. The disciples should beware "that no one leads you astray" (24:4-5) by claiming to be messianic figures "in my name." Mark's version speaks of false prophets who claim "I am he," but Matthew refers to those who claim to be "the Christ" (cf. Mark 13:6; Matt 24:5). In the increasingly turbulent times leading up to the Jewish revolt of 66 CE, there were public figures who claimed a messianic role and Matthew may have this in mind (see, e.g., Josephus, *Ant.* 17:271-85). Matthew is concerned about members of the community being "led astray," a term that may refer to false teachers or prophets whose charismatic powers added allure to their false teaching (see similar concerns about those "led astray" in 18:12-13 and the critique of false prophets in 7:21-22). Matthew returns to these warnings in 24:23-26.

These "preliminary" signs also include chaos and turmoil—wars, famines, and earthquakes—calamities that often figure in Jewish apocalyptic literature as signs that accompany the approach of the end time (see, e.g., 4 Ezra 9:3-4; 13:31-32; Dan 2:28-29; 11:44; 2 Bar 27:6-7). The community will also suffer from dire persecution from without—being handed over to "affliction" (the Greek word *thlipsis* used here has a broader connotation than the word "torture" used by the NRSV) and death, and being "hated by all nations because of my name" (24:9). The word used for "nations" is *ethnos*, which generally refers to the "Gentiles" in

Matthew, but here and elsewhere may have a wider connotation as "peoples" or "nations" (in 10:18 Matthew rendered the same Markan parallel of 13:9 ["to them," i.e., governors and kings] as "to them and the Gentiles").

Matthew adds on to Mark's list of calamities the sufferings that arise *within* the community. Many will "fall away" (literally, be "scandalized") and "betray one another" and "hate one another." False prophets will lead people astray (see above 24:5). Because of "lawlessness" (*anomia*; see 7:23; 13:41; 23:28) the "love of many will grow cold" (24:12). This failure is one that resonates strongly with Matthew's perspective. To be "law-abiding" within the context of Matthew's Gospel entails faithful obedience to the law that finds its center or "hangs" on love of God and neighbor (see 22:40).

The disciple who endures these terrible sufferings will be saved (24:13). Later in the discourse Jesus will instruct his disciples further on what this "endurance" entails. Such sufferings are not without end, yet Matthew foresees considerable time before the end because of the mission task the community faces. Matthew adopts from Mark an important point of reference for all speculation about the end time: "This good news of the kingdom will be proclaimed throughout the world, as a testimony to all the nations; and then the end will come" (24:14; cf. Mark 13:10). Matthew's version is more emphatic about the universal scope of the mission: It will be proclaimed "throughout the world" and be a witness or testimony "to all nations." Only when the mission is completed will the travails end and the Son of Man return. This gives direction and urgency to the universal mission that Jesus will authorize at the conclusion of the Gospel (see 28:16-20).

The Sign of the Son of Man (24:15-31)

The next segment of the discourse describes the conditions and signs leading up to Jesus' triumphant return as the Son of Man. Matthew absorbs with only minor changes Mark's material, which itself is drenched in Old Testament allusions, particularly from the apocalyptic vision of Daniel (see Mark 13:14-27).

◊ ◊ ◊ ◊

The advent of the *parousia* will be signaled by an ominous sign that recalls the "desolating sacrilege" spoken of by Daniel (see Dan 9:27; 11:31; 12:11). By adding an explicit reference to Daniel and locating the desolating sacrilege "in the holy place," Matthew clarifies for the reader that the events in Daniel provide the analogy for this future sign (Matt 24:15; cf. Mark 13:14). In Daniel this "desolating sacrilege" referred to the statue or memorial that the Seleucid ruler Antiochus IV Epiphanes had placed on the altar in the temple in 167 BCE, a searing memory for Israel and one that had spurred the Maccabean revolt. This memorial was dedicated to the "lord of heavens"; using a play on words in Hebrew, this was derisively referred to in Daniel as the "abomination that desolates." In Mark's text Antiochus's sacrilege is intended to remind the reader of another similar horror, perhaps the threat of the Roman emperor Caligula to place his own image in the temple in 40 CE, a traumatic event in Jewish history thwarted at the last moment by Caligula's death, or, if Mark was composed after 70 CE, even Titus's destruction of the temple. Such unspeakable sacrileges will be among the calamities leading to the end time. Luke connects this metaphor with the siege of Jerusalem in 70 CE (see Luke 21:20), but Matthew has already placed the destruction of the temple in the past and it is not a proximate sign of the end time. The future event that deserves the title "desolating sacrilege" is left undefined and simply illustrates the level of terror and suffering that will precede the end time.

In the face of such calamities, the community is to respond urgently because the End is near (24:16-20). The text speaks of urgent flight as if escaping an immediate and terrible danger. Those in Judea should flee to the hill country, a traditional place of refuge. Those who happen to be on the roof or terrace of the house should not try to retrieve goods from inside; the laborer in the field should not turn back to get his outer garment. Such headlong flight will be especially trying for those who are pregnant or nursing. Poignantly, Jesus tells the disciples to pray that they do not have to flee in winter when the rains and the chill make travel all the more difficult. And in a detail unique to Matthew, may it not be "on a sabbath" (24:20), another hint that Matthew's Jewish-Christian community still maintained sabbath observance.

Jesus warns of "great suffering" (a phrase from Dan 12:1 LXX) that is unprecedented in the history of the world (24:21; see also Joel 2:2). If God had not shortened these sufferings no one would survive, but for the sake of the "elect" this time will be shortened. Matthew's Jewish sensitivity about direct reference to God is in evidence here, too; Mark refers explicitly to "the Lord" shortening the days; Matthew uses the "divine passive" (Matt 24:22; Mark 13:20). The notion of the "elect" or those especially chosen by God has deep roots in the Hebrew Scriptures (see, e.g., Deut 7:7-11). For Matthew, the term is used here to refer to the followers of Jesus. In the Lord's Prayer, the disciples were instructed to pray for deliverance from the "time of trial" (6:13) and here they are assured that God will hear that prayer.

Matthew returns to the warnings about false prophets who claim before the actual time that the Christ has returned (24:23-26; see above, 24:5). The repetition of these warnings suggests that some in the community were either claiming that the *parousia* had already taken place or that it was immediately imminent. In Matthew's perspective, however, the End could not come before the Christian mission was completed (24:14) and when it did come it would be so evident that no prophet would be needed to point it out. These "false Christs" and "false prophets" were using their charismatic powers to work signs intended to "lead astray" even the elect, but the community should heed Jesus' warnings and not be fooled. Jesus' triumphant return as the Son of Man will not occur in the recesses of the wilderness or hidden in a room, but will be as evident as the lightning that arches across the sky (24:26-27), or, in a more enigmatic metaphor, as clear as when the vultures hover over a carcass (literally the Greek refers to "eagles" but the ancient world considered the eagle and vulture to be associated; see similar imagery in Job 39:26-30: Hab 1:8).

Matthew now turns to the climactic moment of the *parousia* itself (24:29-31). To describe this final event that takes place "immediately after the suffering of those days," Matthew weaves together several Old Testament texts that speak of a cataclysm in the natural world: the darkening of the sun and moon, the stars falling from heaven, and the shaking of the "powers of heaven" (see especially Isa 13:10 but also Isa 34:4; Ezek 32:7; Joel 2:10, 31; 3:4; 4:15; Amos 8:9; Hag 2:6, 21). At last the "sign of the Son of Man" will appear in the heavens (24:30); this "sign" is not explained except that the reader already knows it will be unmistakable and self-evident. Isaiah speaks of a "sign" or "signal" that announces the end time, although no Old Testament text connects such a "sign" with the coming of the Son of Man (see Isa 11:12; 13:2; 18:3; 49:22). At the appearance of this sign, "all the tribes of the earth will mourn." The precise nature of this "mourning" is not completely clear. Perhaps the realization that the Son of Man is about to come strikes fear in human hearts in the face of inevitable judgment. Or, if Matthew alludes here to the mourning described in Zech 12:10-14, it may be a sign of repentance.

The actual moment of the Son of Man's triumphant return is described in the imagery of Dan 7:13, as he comes " 'on the clouds of heaven' with power and great glory" (24:30). The moment of the *parousia* is a moment of *gathering,* as the Son of Man sends out his angels with a loud trumpet call to summon the "elect" from the "four winds" and "from one end of heaven to the other." Earlier in the parable of the dragnet, Matthew also spoke of the angels involved at the end of the age, but there their task was to "separate the evil from the righteous" (13:49-50). The end-time scene in Matt 24:31 is reminiscent of Isa 27:12-13 where the Israelites, lost in Assyria and driven from Egypt, are summoned by a great trumpet call to return to worship "on the holy mountain at Jerusalem." The image of God gathering the scattered elect of Israel in the end time is a recurring Old Testament motif (see, e.g., Deut 30:3-4; Isa 11:11-12; Ezek 37:21; 39:27-29; Zech 2:6-12), which the Gospel now assigns to Jesus in his role as the triumphant Son of Man.

The Christian Stance While Awaiting the End Time (24:32-51)

The series of sayings and parables in this final section of the discourse describes the stance of vigilance and fidelity that the followers of Jesus are to maintain while awaiting the end time. Matthew takes his lead from the conclusion of Mark's apocalyptic discourse (see Mark 13:33-37), but greatly expands it with Q material and material unique to his Gospel.

◊ ◊ ◊ ◊

The exhortations begin with the "parable" of the fig tree whose lush green leaves blossom late in the spring and inevitably signal the approach of summer (24:32-33). The signs ("all these things") described in the previous sections of the discourse are, likewise, signals that the Son of Man (="he") is at the very gates of the city. The sense of urgency is accelerated: "This generation will not pass away until all these things have taken place" (24:34). Taken at face value this saying of Jesus seems to presume that his immediate disciples and their contemporaries ("this generation") will experience the *parousia,* a prediction that seems to run counter to other parts of the discourse that imply a delay before the end time (see, e.g., 24:14, 48). The following saying again discourages speculation about the precise time—no one except the Father knows the day or hour, not even the angels or the Son himself (24:36). Attempts to calculate the precise date and hour of the end time were common in the ancient world as they are today (see, e.g., Dan 7:25; 8:13; 9:27; 12:7, 11, 12). Therefore the sense of urgency in Jesus' words may be more rhetorical than predictive, a traditional quality of apocalyptic texts (Holman 1996, 134-37). The Gospel wants to emphasize that the return of the Son of Man is certain. Heaven and earth may pass away but Jesus' own words will not (24:35). The saying recalls the emphatic statement of 5:18, which assigned the same enduring quality to the validity of the Torah as proclaimed by Jesus.

The decisiveness of the *parousia* as well as its unpredictability are emphasized in the comparison to the days of Noah and the flood (24:37-44). Matthew draws this material from Q, but adds his own stamp to it (cf. Luke 17:26-36). By omitting the references to Lot and Sodom (see Luke 17:28-30), Matthew shifts the focus away from the purpose of the flood as an instrument of God's judgment to its unexpected and rapid appearance that left Noah's generation unprepared. People carried on normal life—eating, drinking, marrying—unaware that the flood was coming upon them and would call for extraordinary response. The coming of the Son of Man will be the same: catching some unaware as they work in the field or grind at the mill. Matthew's interest is clear as he injects into the Q material a saying from Mark: "Keep awake therefore, for you do not know on what day your Lord is coming" (24:42; cf. Mark 13:35).

The Parable of the Householder (24:43-44): The brief parable of the householder is from Q (24:43-44; cf. Luke 12:39-40). If the owner of the house had known in what part of the night the thief was coming he would have "stayed awake" to protect his house. The image of the *parousia* coming "as a thief" is found in other New Testament texts (see 1 Thess 5:2; 2 Pet 3:10; Rev 3:3; 16:15). Here, as in 24:42 and elsewhere in the Gospel, Matthew uses the verb *grēgorein* ("to stay awake") to describe the stance of active vigilance and readiness required for the coming of the *parousia* (see 25:13 and, in the Gethsemane account, 26:38, 40, 41).

The Parable of the Wicked and Faithful Slaves (24:45-51): Another parable contrasts faithful and wicked slaves (24:45-51; cf. Luke 12:41-46). The "faithful and wise" slave carries out his responsibilities while the master is away. And such a faithful servant will be blessed when the master returns and finds him "at work" (literally, "so doing"—*poiein*, the verb that Matthew has often attached to "doing the will of God" or "doing good deeds," a hallmark of discipleship in this Gospel; see, e.g., 3:8, 10; 5:19; 7:17, 18, 19, 21, 22, 24, 26; 12:33, 50; 19:16; 21:31, 43; 23:3). On the other hand, a wicked slave uses the opportunity of the master's apparent "delay" to mistreat his "fellow slaves" (Matthew adds the nuance of a "fellow" slave—a member of the community) and succumb to debauchery ("eats and drinks with drunkards"). As Jesus had warned, the master will return at an unexpected time and subject that slave to severe judgment. The text literally says the master will "cut him in pieces," which may simply be rhetorical exaggeration (i.e., how can he be placed with the hypocrites if he is also cut to shreds!) or be understood as "being cut off" or excluded from the community (see 18:15-17). The wicked and unfaithful slave is punished with the "hypocrites" where there will be "weeping and gnashing of teeth." "Hypocrite" is Matthew's favored term for describing those who are unfaithful (see above, 23:15, 23, 25, 27, 29) and "weeping and gnashing of teeth" evokes the abject misery of those who experience God's judgment (see 8:12; 13:42, 50; 22:13).

The Parable of the Wise and Foolish Virgins (25:1-13)

This parable is unique to Matthew, but echoes the conclusion of Mark's apocalyptic discourse (13:32-37) and a similar Q story about the servants who are alert for the return of their master from a wedding feast (Luke 12:35-38). Because the parable harmonizes with Matthew's theology and his style, it is likely he composed this story. As is often the case with Matthean parables, its moral point is communicated with a thinly veiled allegory.

There are a number of obscure aspects about Matthew's story. The setting is the awaited arrival of the bridegroom, but it is not certain whether he is coming to meet his betrothed at her father's house or, as is more likely, he is returning to his own home with his bride (it is there the "wedding banquet" will take place, 25:10). The bride is not mentioned at all in the story (although a later scribe added a reference to the bride in v. 1). From what is known of first-century Palestinian marriage customs, after the period of betrothal was completed the groom would go to his bride's family home to conclude the dowry arrangements and bring her to his own house or that of his family where a celebration would take place. Also uncertain is the role of the ten "virgins" (the Greek refers to *parthenoi;* the NRSV translation "bridesmaids" is not literal and assumes they are part of the bride's party). If the setting is the groom's house, they may be associated with his household or family. In any case, they are part of the wedding celebration and are to meet the groom with lighted lamps when he returns.

The parable wastes little time in illustrating the different attitudes among the ten virgins—five are "foolish" and five are "wise" (25:2). Matthew used these identical labels to contrast the wise man who built his home on rock and the foolish one who built on sand at the conclusion of the Sermon on the Mount (7:24-27). In the parable of the virgins, the contrasting reactions are the preparations each group makes for the awaited return of the groom. The foolish take no oil for their lamps while the wise take flasks of oil with them. When the bridegroom is delayed, all of the virgins become drowsy and fall asleep. Suddenly at midnight the signal is given that the groom is arriving and the procession is to meet him. When the virgins begin to trim their oil lamps (replacing the burned wicks and adding new oil?), the foolish realize they have no more oil. They ask the wise virgins for some, but they in turn calculate that there is not enough for everyone. Improbable as it may seem at midnight, the foolish virgins must go off to try to purchase more oil for their lamps.

Meanwhile the groom arrives and "those who were ready" (see the same word used in 24:44, "you also must be ready, for the Son of Man is coming at an unexpected hour") entered into the wedding feast (25:10). Then the door was "shut" so that no one else could enter. The foolish virgins finally arrive but they are too late. They cry out, "Lord, lord, open to us" but the groom rebuffs their last-minute pleas—"Truly . . . I do not know you" (25:11-12). This exchange is nearly identical to the warnings of Jesus at the conclusion of the Sermon on the Mount. Those who cry out "Lord, Lord" but fail to do the will of God are rejected by Jesus ("I never knew you; go away from me, you evildoers") and therefore cannot "enter the kingdom of heaven" (see 7:21-23).

Matthew drives home the lesson of the parable in its concluding verse: "Keep awake [*grēgoreite;* see the same verb in 24:42, 43] therefore, for you know neither the day nor the hour" (25:13). "Staying awake" is used metaphorically for a stance of thoughtful readiness in view of the certain but unknown hour of the *parousia*. All of the virgins "slept" (see 25:5), but the wise virgins had made preparations to be ready no matter when the bridegroom would arrive.

How far to push the allegorical dimensions of this parable has been debated. Matthew himself signals some key allegorical features. The bridegroom is surely intended to represent the Son of Man. The Hebrew Scriptures refer to God as the bridegroom who takes away Israel's barrenness and shame (see, e.g., Isa 54:1-8; Jer 31:32; Hos 2:1-20). In the New Testament, the image takes on eschatological tones, probably due to the motif of the end time as a wedding feast (see Mark 2:19-20; John 3:29-30; and the similar image of the community as the "bride" of Christ: 2 Cor 11:2; Eph 5:21-33; Rev 19:7; 21:2, 9; 22:17). That Matthew refers to the *parousia* of the Son of Man is clear from the overall context of the apocalyptic discourse where the parable functions as one of several exhortations to readiness in view of the *parousia*. Also, Matthew had already identified Jesus as the "bridegroom" earlier in the Gospel in a passage with strong eschatological tones (see 9:15). In the parable of the wedding feast (22:1-10), Matthew had also introduced wedding imagery as a way of speaking of the judgment that would befall not only those who violently rejected the original invitation by the king, but even those invited later who do not wear a wedding garment (22:11-14). In the story of the virgins, the "delay" of the bridegroom (25:5; see 24:48), the dramatic shout announcing his sudden arrival (25:6; see 24:31), and the address "Lord, lord" (25:11; see 7:21-23) all point to Jesus as the triumphant Son of Man coming at the *parousia*.

Likewise, the wise and foolish virgins represent the differing reactions within the community that will be evident at the final judgment. Matthew had already made this point in the parables of the weeds and wheat (13:36-43) and the parable of the dragnet (13:47-50). The parable of the wedding feast warned that some among the guests would come without a wedding garment, demonstrating that they were not properly prepared (22:11-14). The apocalyptic discourse, too, had anticipated that some in the community would not be ready for the sure but unexpected arrival of the Son of Man and would be led astray by false prophets (24:4-5, 11, 24) or by "lawlessness" and "love growing cold" (24:12).

However, to push this allegory further as some traditional interpretation has done, and to identify the "wise" with the Gentiles and the "foolish" with the Jews who rejected Jesus is not warranted by the text itself. Similarly, to give a precise meaning to the "oil" also seems perilous. A few rabbinic texts refer to "oil" as symbolic of good deeds (e.g., *Num. Rab.* 13:15-16; see Donfried 1974). While this would be convenient for Matthew's emphasis on doing good deeds as a way of readiness for the end time (see 24:46; 25:14-46), there is no clear evidence to support it in the text. Rather, the parable seems to work on a more generic basis: The wise virgins took steps to be ready for the coming of the groom; the foolish virgins did not. The results are that the wise virgins are invited to enter the wedding banquet while the foolish virgins are shut out. Matthew's use of the lamp imagery to make this fundamental point may be prompted by Prov 13:9, which warns that the "light of the righteous rejoices, but the lamp of the wicked goes out" (see also Job 18:5).

The Parable of the Talents (25:14-30)

The parable of the talents has similarities to Luke's parable of the nobleman (see Luke 19:11-17) and may, therefore, have originated as Q material (a later version of the story also appears in the *Gospel of the Hebrews*). More distant echoes are also found in Mark's brief parable of the man and his servants (13:34). Whatever its ultimate origin, Matthew has adapted the story to his own perspective and inserted it here in the apocalyptic discourse, giving the parable an allegorical cast similar to the preceding parable of the ten virgins.

◊ ◊ ◊ ◊

The story begins abruptly—"For it is as if . . ." (25:14). Matthew may have intended the more formal introduction to the parable of the ten virgins to serve as introduction to both parables ("Then the kingdom of heaven will be like this," 25:1). The setting for the story matches conditions in first-century Palestine. A man leaves on a long journey and places his property in the hands of trusted slaves or servants, a situation of absentee ownership reflected as well in the parables of the vineyard (21:33-43) and the wicked and faithful slaves (24:45-51). In this instance, the master entrusts money to a series of three servants, the amount calibrated according to each one's ability (25:15). This last point is important for the story—the master has not laid a burden on them, but has given each an amount suitable for them to take care of. The precise calculation of a "talent" is difficult; some suggest it was equivalent to the wages a laborer would accrue in fifteen years. As in the case of Matthew's parable about the unforgiving servant, the point is that a "talent" was a very large denomination, so even the slave who receives only one talent has been entrusted with a substantial responsibility (see 18:23-35).

The story reports no particular instructions on the part of the master as he departs on his journey. The first two slaves take decisive action. The one with five talents trades with them and makes five more talents; so, too, the one with two talents doubles the master's money. The slave with one talent, however, buries the money in the ground for safekeeping—a common practice in the ancient world for keeping valuables secure, and a much more prudent course of action than the slave in Luke's parable who simply wrapped the money in a napkin! (Luke 19:20).

With the return of the "master" (the Greek word is *kyrios*, a title that in the Gospel context takes on christological significance when applied to Jesus; see, e.g., 14:33), the story begins to display its eschatological meaning. The "master of those slaves" returns "after a long time" to settle accounts with them (25:19). Given the context for the parable, it is clear that the reader is to see the return of the master as signifying the *parousia* of the Son of Man. Matthew foresees that there may be a considerable amount of time or a "delay" before the End comes (see also 24:8; 25:5).

The settling of the accounts becomes a judgment scene. The first two slaves who had multiplied the master's money are abundantly rewarded, not only receiving praise from the Master—"well done, good and trustworthy slave"—but given additional responsibility ("I will put you in charge of many things") and invited to "enter into the joy of your master" (25:21, 23). As in the previous parable of the ten virgins, those who prove resourceful and trustworthy "enter" into the kingdom of God (see 25:10). By contrast, the slave who had received one talent and buried it in the ground receives condemnation and will be cast into the "outer darkness" (25:30; cf. with the fate of the foolish virgins in 25:11-12 who must remain outside). But the parable of the talents does not merely repeat the themes of the previous parables. The motivation of the condemned servant is significant. He judges that the master is a "harsh" man, "reaping where you did not sow, and gathering where you did not scatter seed" and therefore, out of fear, he decided to bury the talent. In his reply, the "master" concedes he has such sovereign power, but interprets the slave's fear as a sign that he is "wicked and lazy." If he were simply fearful of the master's authority and power, all the more reason to have invested the master's money.

The story ends with a decisive contrast between the two sets of slaves. The single talent of the lazy and wicked slave is given to the slave who had ten talents. In the end, the servants who dealt responsibly with the master's talents get to keep this bounty and receive even more (25:29), while those who were irresponsible will lose even the little they had and will be cast into the "outer darkness, where there will be weeping and gnashing of teeth" (Matthew's recurring portrayal of the suffering and frustration of those condemned; see 8:12; 13:42, 50; 22:13; 14:51).

Thus the parable of the talents joins ranks with the rest of the apocalyptic discourse in encouraging the community to be ready and alert for the return of the Son of Man (see 24:42, 43; 25:13; 26:38, 40, 41). This also means living in an active and responsible manner while awaiting the end time, doing good and using the gifts and opportunities God gives as indicated in the parable of the wicked and faithful slaves (24:45-51) and the parable of the talents. Thus Matthew's story is not simply an exhortation to develop one's talents in the manner of a self-development program—an interpretation often attached to this story (even the English word "talent" derives from this parable). Crucial to Matthew's perspective is the parable's eschatological dimension: The faithful disciple lives alert and active, following the commands of Jesus, while awaiting the final coming of the Son of Man and the consummation of the age.

Does this parable also imply a subtle critique of those within the wider Jewish community contemporary with Matthew who were wary of apocalyptic groups? Is Matthew, in other words, suggesting that those Jewish Christians among his community who had taken their God-given talents of the Torah and their Jewish heritage and incorporated them in a wider mission were doing what God intended, while other Jewish groups who chose to remain within a more defined ethnic and religious community were, in effect, burying the gift God had given them (see, e.g., Harrington 1991,

354-55)? In any case, the primary meaning of the parable is directed to the disciples who, within the framework of Matthew's narrative, are the sole recipients of this discourse (see 24:1-4) and stand first and foremost for the Christian community itself.

The Judgment of All the Nations (25:31-46)

This final portion of the apocalyptic discourse is one of the Gospel's most memorable passages (on the history of the interpretation of this parable, see Gray 1989). The passage is unique to Matthew and reflects his characteristic style and important motifs of his theology. The introduction, describing the return of the Son of Man and the overall cosmic scope of the scene in which "all the nations" are gathered before the Son of Man's "glorious throne," signals the climax of the entire apocalyptic discourse and sets this scene apart from the preceding sections.

◊ ◊ ◊ ◊

The scene begins with the triumphant return of the Son of Man (25:31). The description is strongly influenced by Dan 7:13-14— the Son of Man comes "in his glory," accompanied with "all the angels" to take his seat "on the throne of his glory." Earlier in the discourse Matthew had anticipated this scene when he described the actual moment of the Son of Man's return: " 'coming on the clouds of heaven' with power and great glory" and "send[ing] out his angels . . ." (see 24:30-31). And at other points in his narrative a similar scenario including the coming of the Son of Man, his glorious enthronement, the presence of angels, and a gathering of peoples is anticipated for the final judgment (see 13:41, "The Son of Man will send his angels, and they will collect out of his kingdom all causes of sin and all evildoers . . ."; 16:27, "For the Son of Man is to come with his angels in the glory of his Father, and then he will repay everyone for what has been done"; 19:28, "Truly I tell you, at the renewal of all things, when the Son of Man is seated on the throne of his glory, you who have followed me will also sit on twelve thrones, judging the twelve tribes of Israel").

"All the nations" are gathered before the Son of Man and here one encounters the first of several key elements in the scene that are significant for its interpretation (25:32). The use of the passive implies that the nations are gathered by God, perhaps implicitly through the instrumentality of the angels who accompany the Son of Man (as in 13:41 and 24:31). The problem is determining who are "all the nations." For many interpreters, the term *ethnos* in Matthew usually implies non-Jews or Gentiles (see, e.g., 4:15; 6:32; 10:5, 18; 12:18, 21; 20:19, 25). If this is the case, then the scene depicted is the judgment of the Gentiles or nonbelievers, not the Jews or the Christian community itself. But there are some cases where the term may have a more generic meaning as "people" (see, e.g., 21:43; 24:7, 9, 14; in the case of 21:43, Daniel Harrington, who otherwise argues strongly that *ethnos* means "Gentile," concedes that the term has a broader significance here, meaning "group of people"; see Harrington 1991, 303-4). In 25:32 the phrase used is "all the nations," which may indicate that here the term *ethnos* means "all peoples" (as in 24:9, 14 and 28:19), but still the ambiguity remains.

Matthew introduces the metaphor of the sheep and the goats to describe the sorting of the good from the bad at the final judgment, a recurring motif found in each of the parables within the apocalyptic discourse (25:32-33; see comments on the parable of the wise and foolish virgins above, 25:1-13). The Son of Man will act as a "shepherd," separating the sheep from the goats, putting the sheep at his right hand and the goats at his left. The image of the "shepherd" is a traditional biblical metaphor for pastoral leadership, and the Gospel also refers to "sheep" as the members of the community (2:6, "From you shall come a ruler who is to shepherd my people Israel"; 9:36, "He had compassion for them, because they were harassed and helpless, like sheep without a shepherd"; 18:12, the parable of the good shepherd; 26:31, " 'I will strike the shepherd, and the sheep of the flock will be scattered' "). The metaphor presumes a mixed flock of sheep and goats (a common sight in Middle Eastern herding) that are separated at the end of the day. The goats cannot endure the cold as sheep do and are usually sheltered, while the sheep can be allowed to pasture. Sheep seem to be the more treasured animal and is the term of choice for describing the community itself (as in 2:6 and 26:31) or the objects of Jesus' compassion (9:36 and 18:12). The sheep are placed in the honored position at "the right hand" and represent the saved, while the goats are consigned to the "left" and represent the condemned.

The shepherd image fades from view and the Son of Man is now referred to as the "king," reflecting Matthew's emphasis on the Davidic lineage of Jesus and his role as Messiah (see 1:1 and the repeated use of the "Son of David" title in Matthew; also 1:16; 2:2, 4; 21:4-5, 9; in the Passion narrative the title is used ironically of the condemned and crucified Jesus; see 27:11, 29, 37, 42). The Son of Man and royal Messiah now declares those on his right hand to be "blessed by my Father" and invites them to "inherit the kingdom prepared for you from the foundation of the world" (25:34). For Matthew the exalted Jesus serves as the mediator or channel of the Father's revelation and blessing (see 11:27; 28:18). In the parable of the dragnet, "angels" sort the good from the bad at the moment of judgment (13:49-50); but in the parable of the wheat and the weeds, the "Son of Man" is the one who sends the angels, after which the angels will "throw" the condemned "into the furnace of fire" while the righteous "will shine like the sun in the kingdom of their Father" (13:42).

The "righteous" performed acts of mercy and compassion toward the "least of these my brothers" (v. 40) while the condemned did not. For this reason the condemned will be consigned to eternal punishment while the righteous will enter into eternal life (25:46). The specific acts of mercy enumerated reflect classic biblical and Jewish categories of care for those in need: food for the hungry; drink for the thirsty; welcome for the stranger; clothing for the naked; care for the sick. Some of these virtuous acts are cited in the summary of Jesus' messianic work for John's messenger (11:5), and in Matthew's ongoing account of Jesus' public ministry (e.g., feeding the hungry, 14:13-21; 15:32-39). The mission discourse of Jesus also empowers the community to continue this merciful mission of Jesus (10:7-8), and acts of love toward neighbor are to have priority in interpreting the law (7:12; 22:34-40; 23:23). Visiting those imprisoned may, in fact, be the only unusual entry on the list and may reflect the circumstances of the early Christian community (see 10:16-20; on this issue, see Hare 1967).

Part of the mystery in interpreting this parable is that the righteous have performed, unaware, such acts of compassion toward *Jesus* himself. In each instance the "king" declares: "*I* was hungry and you gave me food. . . ." When the righteous protest their ignorance by asking "when" this happened, they are told that whatever they did for the "least of these my brothers" they did for him. (In the interests of inclusion, the NRSV translates this phrase as "the least of these who are members of my family," but the literal Greek phrase is *heni toutōn tōn adelphōn mou tōn elachistōn*—that is, "one of these least of my brothers.") Who are these "least of these my brothers" with whom Jesus so identifies? The word "brother" (sister) is frequently used in the Gospel to refer to fellow members of the community (see, e.g., 18:15, 17, 21, 35; 23:8; 28:10; this may be true in other instances as well: see, e.g., 5:22, 23, 24, 47; 7:3, 4, 5). The Greek term *elachistōn* ("least") is the superlative form of *mikros* ("small"), which is also used in the Gospel to refer to members of the community who are in need or who are vulnerable (see 18:6, 10, 14). In 11:11 the "least in the kingdom of heaven" (here the comparative, *mikroteros,* is used), that is, a follower of Jesus, is declared greater than John the Baptist.

Of special importance as a parallel is the reference to the "little ones" in the mission discourse. Jesus instructs the disciples that "whoever gives even a cup of cold water to one of these little ones *[mikrōn]* in the name of a disciple—truly I tell you, none of these will lose their reward" (10:42). The context for this saying is established in 10:40—"Whoever welcomes you welcomes me, and whoever welcomes me welcomes the one who sent me." The disciples sent on mission to proclaim the gospel represent and even embody the presence of Jesus, who himself in his own mission was the agent of God.

Based on these earlier texts in the Gospel, therefore, the term "least of these my brothers" probably refers to members of the Christian community and, even more specifically, to those who, by reason of their being sent on mission by Jesus, embody his presence. Taken on these terms, then, the parable declares that the "nations" will be judged on how they treat the "least" members of the Christian community, probably the Christian missionaries, because in treating these "least" with mercy or neglecting to do so, it is to so treat Jesus himself who identifies with these "least brothers" sent in his name.

Who then is being judged in this parable and on what basis? Most Christians read this scene as the last judgment for all peoples. Jesus assembles "all the nations" (including Jews and Gentiles) and judges them on their fidelity to the love command, a criterion that harmonizes with Jesus' own teaching in the Gospel. The fact that neither the righteous nor the condemned even knew they were encountering Jesus in the least of their brothers (and sisters) underscores the universality of the criterion for judgment. The "least" and Jesus' identification with them are not restricted to the Christian community alone but to all human beings in need. After instructions about the signs that will precede the final coming of Jesus as the Son of Man and warnings to be alert and ready for that decisive moment (24:1–25:30), the final judgment of all peoples is described in the parable of the sheep and the goats (25:31-46).

As attractive as this universal interpretation may be, there are reasons for concluding that, for Matthew, this scene may have a more restricted perspective. The term "all the nations" remains ambiguous, perhaps meaning "all peoples" including Jews and non-Jews, but with a strong case possible for interpreting it as "Gentiles." If this scene involves the judgment of the Gentiles, then Matthew's intent may have been to describe the judgment of the *community* by means of the preceding parables in 24:43–25:30. Matthew's fellow Christians are warned to be alert for the Son of Man's coming and to be "doing" good in order to be ready for that day of judgment. To fail to do so is to risk the fate of the wicked servant (24:51), the foolish virgins (25:11-12), or the slave who buried his master's talent (25:30). The judgment of *non-Christian Jews* who rejected Jesus may be implicit in the conclusion of chapter 23 where their "house" is left desolate until they are willing to receive the Messiah sent to them (23:38-39). The *Gentiles,* on the other hand, receive a special judgment of their own and that is what is described in 25:31-46. There is evidence in Jewish tradition that a separate judgment for Jews and Gentiles was expected, and Matthew may be assuming that tradition here (see Harrington

1991, 358-60, who notes that this also seems to be the view of Paul in Rom 2:9-10, "the Jew first and also the Greek"; and 1 Pet 4:17, which refers to judgment beginning with "the household of God").

But on what basis are "all the nations" to be judged? Even if one is convinced that "nations" here is more extensive than Gentiles or non-Christians, Matthew's wording suggests that a very specific context is highlighted as the basis for judgment. It is what the "nations" do to the "least of [Jesus'] brothers" that is decisive. The evidence is strong that Matthew thinks of this not as simply any human being in need, but as Christians in need and, perhaps more precisely, missionary Christians. How the peoples of the nations— Gentiles or perhaps Gentiles and Jews—treat those vulnerable members of the Christian community who go out to proclaim the gospel will be the basis for their judgment. The repeated insistence of both the righteous and the condemned that they were never aware of Jesus' identification with these "least brothers" suggests that Matthew is not basing the nations' judgment on whether they accept the gospel message as such, but more emphatically on whether the nations deal mercifully and compassionately with these vulnerable brothers. In other words, it is here at this moment of encounter with one of Jesus' disciples that the innate goodness and compassion of the peoples of the nations are tested before God. If they comply with Jesus' teaching about the love command, they will find mercy before God; if they neglect to do so, they are worthy of condemnation.

Here the more universal interpretation of the parable and the more restrictive context implied in Matthew's Gospel intersect. In both cases, fidelity to the love command—the heart of Jesus' teaching in Matthew—becomes the decisive criterion for divine judgment. Ultimately, Jew, Christian, and Gentile are all judged on the same basis. To illustrate this, Matthew's parable of the sheep and the goats may have selected one type of revealing situation when Gentiles (or non-Christians) encountered the vulnerable vanguard of the Christian community and had the opportunity either to deal with them compassionately and mercifully or to ignore their needs. In so doing, Matthew not only articulated a remarkable set of criteria for the ultimate judgment of the human person before

God, but also gave encouragement to the missionaries of his own community, reminding them that the Risen Jesus was present with them (see 28:20) and that the authority of God's judgment ratified their missionary courage (see 10:19-20).

◊ ◊ ◊ ◊

The apocalyptic discourse concludes the remarkable series of teachings that are a hallmark of Matthew's Gospel. The narrator's words in 26:1 note this: "When Jesus had finished saying *all these things* . . ." (emphasis added). All of the discourses are concluded and now the fateful events of the Passion will begin.

Matthew unambiguously identifies Jesus as the triumphant Son of Man who will return in glory at the end of the world. The final scene of the Gospel on a mountaintop in Galilee will promise that the Risen Christ—Jesus the Emmanuel (see 1:23)—remains present with the community until "the end of the age" (28:20). Yet, Matthew also foresees a final and decisive return of the triumphant Jesus as Son of Man who comes to judge the world and gather the elect.

Matthew's ethical concerns are also a characteristic feature of the apocalyptic discourse. To be prepared for the final day the community must be alert, because it does not know the precise time when the Son of Man will come. Being alert and ready are synonymous for Matthew with living faithfully, that is, actively doing good as Jesus had taught his disciples. So the faithful slave (24:45-51), the wise virgins (25:1-13), and the slaves who invest their master's talents (25:14-30) take the practical steps necessary in order to be ready. The final parable of the sheep and the goats (25:31-46) is the supreme expression of Matthew's ethical perspective in the Gospel. "All the nations" probably refers to Gentiles who do not yet know Jesus and certainly do not recognize him in the "least of these my brothers" they happen to encounter. The nations, too, will be judged on how they respond to those in need. If they instinctively follow the love command taught by Jesus and respond with mercy and compassion, then they, too, will enter into God's kingdom. As was the case in the Matthean parable of the two sons (21:28-32), action rather than proper words determines one's status before God.

The Passion of Jesus (26:1–27:56)

Matthew's narrative now reaches its climactic point with the final events of Jesus' life. With greater consistency than in any other major section of the Gospel, Matthew follows closely the content and narrative sequence of his major source, Mark (Mark 14–15; see Brown 1994, 40-46; Senior 1975, 1985). However, Matthew does add material in the body of the Passion story, such as the fate of Judas (27:3-10), Pilate's washing his hands and declaring his innocence (27:24-25), and the dramatic events that follow the death of Jesus (27:51-53). And, within scenes drawn from Mark, Matthew makes significant editorial adjustments, thereby stamping the narrative as a whole with his characteristic theological perspective.

The structure of the Passion story is based on a chronological and narrative sequence.

1. Matthew provides a prelude to the narrative in the opening scenes of 26:1-16: Two days before the Passover Jesus will once again announce his impending death at the very moment his opponents plot in stealth to destroy him. Judas's betrayal and the bold tenderness of an anonymous woman in Bethany provide ironic and jolting contrasts.

2. The next set of scenes, 26:17-35, revolves around the last Passover that Jesus celebrates with his disciples, providing another opportunity for Jesus to interpret the meaning of his impending death as well as predict Judas's betrayal and the denial and desertion by the rest of the twelve.

3. Following the Passover meal, Jesus and his disciples go to Gethsemane (26:36-46). There Jesus will pray intensely to be ready for the advent of his death. That moment arrives in the person of Judas, leading an armed band to arrest Jesus (26:47-56).

4. The scene now changes to the residence of the high priest where Jesus is interrogated and condemned to death (26:57-68) while, outside in the courtyard, Peter denies his discipleship (26:69-75).

5. Matthew adds the story of Judas's fate (27:3-10). When the disciple realizes that Jesus is condemned, he returns the blood money to the temple and then takes his own life. The money is retrieved by the priests and used to buy the potter's field.

6. The scene changes once again as Jesus is brought before Pilate for the Roman trial (27:11-31), eventually to be condemned to crucifixion.

7. Jesus is taken to Golgotha for his execution (27:32-56). There he is crucified, endures final mockery, and dies. His death triggers a series of extraordinary events.

The burial scene and the determination of the religious leaders to post a guard at the tomb (27:57-66) provide a transition from the Passion narrative proper to the empty tomb story and the resurrection appearances that will bring the Gospel story to its close.

◊ ◊ ◊ ◊

Prelude to the Passion (26:1-16)

Two sets of contrasting episodes open Matthew's Passion narrative and serve as a prelude or "overture" to the Passion narrative as a whole. The reader is informed by Jesus' solemn prediction of his Passion that the Gospel story has reached its climactic point and the moment of the "handing over" is at hand (26:1-2). Meanwhile the leaders plot in secret to arrest Jesus, unsure of when and how they can carry out their plan (26:3-5). In another set of contrasts, an anonymous woman of Bethany lovingly anoints Jesus' body for burial (26:6-13) while Judas, "one of the twelve," goes to the leaders and accepts payment for betraying Jesus (26:14-16).

◊ ◊ ◊ ◊

Matthew begins the Passion story with a formal introduction. In contrast, Mark's Passion story seems to emerge from the apocalyptic discourse, almost without seam (see Mark 13:37–14:1). Matthew concludes the apocalyptic discourse (chaps. 24–25) with the typical transition formula that marked the end of all the major discourses (see 26:1 for example). This time, though, he adds the phrase "all these things," signaling that Jesus' teaching ministry has come to its conclusion. This introductory statement is reminiscent of Deut 32:45 ("When Moses had finished reciting all these words to all Israel . . ."), as Moses completed his instruction of Israel and prepared for his death on Mount Nebo, within sight of the promised land (see Frankemölle 1974, 334, 369; Allison 1993, 192-94).

Instead of the narrator noting the time, as in Mark (14:1), the Matthean Jesus himself directly informs his disciples that after two days the Passover is coming "and the Son of Man will be handed over to be crucified" (26:2). Thus the Matthean Passion story begins with a fourth solemn prediction of the Passion (see 16:21; 17:22; 20:17). Jesus knows precisely what lies before him, even as his opponents debate when and how they can arrest him (26:3-5). This prediction is brief, speaking simply of the Son of Man being "handed over"—the passive voice of the word *(paradidōmi)* used to describe the betrayal and arrest of Jesus also implies God's own providence as the ultimate initiative behind the death of Jesus. No other details are included in this prediction other than the stark reminder that Jesus is "to be crucified" (see also 20:19). The Passion narrative itself will supply the story of what happens between the "handing over" and the crucifixion.

Both Mark and Luke refer to the dual feast of the Passover and "Unleavened Bread," but Matthew has condensed it into one designation (but see 26:17). The feast of Unleavened Bread was a spring festival that lasted seven days (Exod 23:14-15; 34:18). By the time of Jesus, it had been combined with Passover, the great pilgrimage feast that commemorated Israel's deliverance from Egypt and looked forward to the final redemption of Israel (Exod 12:1-20; Deut 16:1-8). Pilgrims would come from all over Israel and other regions of the Diaspora to celebrate the feast, greatly expanding the population of the city. In the chronology provided by Mark's account, the Passover began on Thursday evening after sundown. Since, according to Jewish understanding, a new day begins after sundown, the daylight hours of Thursday would be 14 Nisan and evening would be 15 Nisan. Matthew's account, following the Markan chronology, begins the Passion story with Jesus' prediction on Wednesday (26:2), two days (daylight Wednesday and daylight Thursday) before the Passover. The Last Supper, the arrest, and the interrogation of Jesus before the Sanhedrin all take place on Thursday evening (the beginning of Passover), and the trial before Pilate and the crucifixion occur on Friday, the day of the

Passover itself. John's chronology, by contrast, has Passover occur on Friday night/Saturday, with Jesus being executed on Friday afternoon before the Passover, at the very moment the Passover lambs were being slaughtered in the temple. There is a rush to have Jesus executed and buried before the beginning of the Passover festival, that is, by nightfall on Friday, the eve of the feast (see John 19:14, 31, 42).

While Matthew's use of Passover symbolism is subtle, Jesus' solemn reference to the feast ("you know . . .") in the opening lines of the Passion story and the attention given to the Passover meal where Jesus will speak of the meaning of his death suggest that Matthew wishes to evoke the motif of deliverance from oppression associated with Passover as a backdrop to Jesus' own death (see below, 26:17-29).

As Jesus informs his disciples about his impending death, the "chief priests and the elders of the people" gather in the palace of Caiaphas the high priest to plot in secret his arrest and execution. The conjunction *tote* ("then") as used by Matthew implies near simultaneity between these two events and heightens the irony that abounds here. Those who gather are the "chief priests and the elders of the people" (26:3). During Jesus' public ministry his main opponents were the Pharisees, but once the action moves to Jerusalem and particularly during the Passion, it is primarily the "chief priests and the elders" who lead the opposition (see already 21:15, 23, 45; and consistently in the Passion story: 26:14, 47, 51, 57, 58, 59, 62, 63, 65; 27:1, 3, 6, 12, 20, 41). When the leaders approach Pilate to post a guard at Jesus' tomb, the Pharisees will reemerge (see 27:62). The opponents gather in the palace of the high priest "Caiaphas" (26:3). Matthew, along with John, identifies Caiaphas, who was high priest from 18–36 CE, as the one who presides over Jesus' interrogation and condemnation (see 26:57-68; John 11:49; 18:12-28; Luke 3:2 mentions that John the Baptist begins his ministry "during the high priesthood of Annas and Caiaphas").

Matthew has consistently portrayed the religious leaders in an unfavorable light and that tendency is apparent here. The leaders conspire to arrest Jesus "by stealth" in order to kill him, but are concerned about the reactions of the crowds, especially during the

Passover festival, the same fear that gripped Herod in his desire to kill John the Baptist (14:5). Clearly, the plotting of the leaders is meant to be in contrast to the majestic comportment and prophetic knowledge of Jesus: While they plot his death, but fear doing it on the Passover, Jesus has already told his disciples that his death would take place as the feast approached (26:2).

The scene shifts somewhat abruptly to Bethany, a village near Jerusalem on the eastern slopes of the Mount of Olives (26:6-13), which Matthew had already identified as the place where Jesus lodged (21:17). Jesus is staying in the house of "Simon the leper." Neither Matthew nor Mark offers any further information about Simon or draws any inference from the fact that Jesus was the guest of a leper. In Luke's version of this story "Simon" is identified as a "Pharisee" (see Luke 7:36-50); in John's account the anointing takes place in the home of Lazarus, and Mary, Lazarus's sister, does the anointing (see John 12:1-8).

The focus of the scene is the gracious action of an anonymous woman who "approaches" Jesus (*proselthon*, Matthew's favored word for those who reverently approach Jesus for healing or supplication) and anoints his head with "very costly ointment" (26:7; Matthew simplifies Mark's description here, see Mark 14:3). The "disciples" are indignant at this "waste" and decry the fact that the ointment could have been sold and the proceeds given to the poor (26:8-9; in Mark 14:3 they are identified simply as "some" bystanders). The disciples' protest prompts Jesus to defend the woman and to interpret the meaning of her action. What she has done is a "good service" because she has anointed Jesus' body in preparation for his burial (26:10-12), a point ratified later in Matthew's narrative when the women who come to the tomb on Sunday do so simply "to see the tomb" (28:1), not to anoint Jesus' body as in Mark (16:1).

Jesus' words, "For you always have the poor with you, but you will not always have me," have been a focus of debate for centuries. In the context of this story, Jesus' statement counters the protest of the disciples that the proceeds of the ointment should have been sold for the poor rather than lavished on Jesus. Matthew's Gospel is unambiguous about Jesus' care for the poor. In the Sermon on the Mount, the disciples were taught to "give to everyone who begs from you" (5:42) and to give alms without hypocrisy (6:2-4). The rich young man was invited to sell his possessions and give the proceeds to the poor before following Jesus (19:21) and, in the Sermon, the disciples were also warned that they could not "serve God and wealth" (6:24). The judgment of the nations is based on their attention to "the least" who are in dire need (25:31-46). Therefore Jesus' statement, "You always have the poor with you," is not a fatalistic declaration that poverty is chronic and inevitable, but an observation that the opportunity to assist the poor is always at hand while the opportunity to offer Jesus, on the eve of his death, an act of gracious kindness is not.

Jesus continues with extraordinary praise for the woman's action: "Wherever this good news is proclaimed in the whole world, what she has done will be told in remembrance of her" (26:13). "This good news" probably refers to the missionary preaching of the community rather than to Matthew's story as such (although his addition of the word "this" leads some commentators to conclude Matthew is referring here to his own narrative as "gospel"). What is it about the woman's action that commands such praise? First of all, her "good deed" contrasts with the plotting of the religious leaders (26:3-5) and the betrayal by one of the twelve (26:14-16). These episodes frame the woman's action and illumine its beauty. Also, by anointing his body for burial, the woman reveals that she is fully aware of Jesus' destiny. In the scenes that follow, the disciples appear unprepared for the advent of Jesus' death even though he had repeatedly predicted the fate of the Son of Man. This anonymous woman of Bethany, however, is alert and takes action on Jesus' behalf—precisely the kind of stance praised in the parables of the apocalyptic discourse (see 24:42–25:30). The fact that she anoints Jesus "on his head" may also be a subtle sign that she wants to honor Jesus as the Messiah, just as the prophet Samuel anointed the future king David (1 Sam 16:12-13), or as the priest Zadok anointed Solomon (1 Kgs 1:39).

The Gospel remembers the woman's action as an act of gracious homage to Jesus before his death and as an act of alert discipleship.

For Matthew's Gospel, the presence of Jesus calls for extraordinary response, eclipsing all other obligations, even one as important as alms to the poor. In this sense, the anointing scene is reminiscent of Jesus' response to the disciples of John who complained that Jesus' disciples did not fast: While the bridegroom is present the guests cannot fast; the day will come when the bridegroom is "taken away" and then they can comply with the obligation to fast (see Matt 9:15).

The prelude concludes with another jolting contrast. At the very moment (*tote,* "then") the woman anoints Jesus in Bethany, Judas goes to the chief priests to barter for the betrayal of his Master. The poignancy of Judas and his failure grips Matthew's attention. In each episode where Judas appears Matthew intensifies the drama (see 26:20-25, 49-50) and he will add an entire scene dealing with the apostle's fate (27:3-10).

Here Matthew leads with the tragic notation, "one of the twelve" (26:14). Judas first appears in the Gospel in the mission discourse where he is listed as one of the twelve and as "the one who betrayed him" (10:4). Matthew puts the episode into direct address and depicts an exchange between Judas and the chief priests (cf. Mark 10–11). Judas's motivation is clearly venal since he asks for money in return for his act of betrayal (26:14). Earlier in the Gospel Jesus had warned about the corrupting influence of wealth (see 6:19-21, 24; 19:22, 23-26) and Judas now becomes a tragic exemplar of what can happen (similar to John 12:4-6).

The priests pay him on the spot "thirty pieces of silver," a significant detail that Matthew injects into the story. "Thirty pieces of silver" is the price to be paid to the owner of a slave who is gored by another person's oxen (Exod 21:32). The more immediate influence on Matthew's text is probably Zech 11:12, a somewhat enigmatic passage in which the "shepherd of the flock doomed to slaughter" is given wages of "thirty pieces of silver." Later the Lord directs the shepherd to cast the silver pieces "into the treasury in the house of the LORD" (11:13), a text that will be cited by Matthew in the story of Judas's fate (27:9-10). Thus, beginning with Judas's payment by the priests, Matthew again weaves an Old Testament backdrop into the story of Jesus, pointing to the divine plan that guides the Passion events. The pieces of silver become in Matthew's account "blood money," a sign of the collusion between Judas and the religious leaders, and ironically that money will eventually pass through the hands of Judas back to the temple and the priests, further implicating them in the death of Jesus.

The prelude concludes with the observation that "from that moment" Judas began to look for an "opportunity" to betray Jesus. The phrase "from that moment" *(apo tote)* was used earlier in the Gospel as a demarcation for significant turning points in the Gospel story. The *apo tote* in 4:17 comes in a transition scene that bridges the introduction to the Gospel and the beginning of Jesus' public ministry (see above 4:12-17); in 16:21 the same phrase occurs as Jesus begins the journey to Jerusalem and his teaching about the Passion (see 16:13-28). Here it marks the beginning of the Passion story, as Jesus solemnly declares that the day of his "handing over" is near and the plot against Jesus is set in motion. Ironically, Judas seeks an "opportunity" to betray Jesus; literally the word used is a "good moment" or *eukairian,* from the root word *kairos* used in reference to the end time (see 24:45) and by Jesus himself to refer to his approaching death (26:18). Thus the Gospel portrays both Jesus and Judas converging on a single fateful moment—Jesus toward his God-given destiny as the Son of Man and Judas as a tragic example of discipleship betrayed.

◊ ◊ ◊ ◊

The Last Passover (26:17-35)

Jesus' celebration of the Passover with his disciples is the centerpiece in a series of four brief scenes. As in the previous section, there is a brief introduction (26:17-19), and then a set of episodes that frame the central scene. Jesus' prediction of Judas's betrayal (26:20-25) and his prediction of denial by Peter and desertion by the rest of the disciples (26:30-35) form a poignant frame around the institution account, with its emphasis on Jesus' life-giving death and his covenant bond with the disciples (26:26-29).

◊ ◊ ◊ ◊

The opening scene (26:17-19) presents Jesus still firmly in command of the situation. On Thursday, at the beginning of the Passover festival on "the first day of Unleavened Bread," his disciples "approach" Jesus (Matthew uses his favored word *proselthon* to portray a reverential approach to Jesus) and ask where they are to prepare for the Passover meal (26:17). Before the destruction of the temple and while Passover was still one of the three great Jewish pilgrimage feasts (see Deut 16:16), the Passover meal had to take place within Jerusalem or its immediate environs (see Saldarini 1984). Pilgrims brought their Passover lambs to be slaughtered by the priests in the temple in the afternoon and the meal would take place after sundown that evening. The meal described in the synoptic Gospels does not refer to many of the characteristic elements of a Passover (e.g., the lamb or other traits of the Passover celebration) and thus raises the question whether historically this final meal with the disciples was in fact a Passover. In the Johannine chronology the meal could not have been a Passover since Jesus dies before the festival begins (see John 19:31, 42). However, by means of this introductory scene, Matthew clearly portrays the meal as a Passover and includes theological motifs associated with Passover in his presentation of Jesus' final words and gestures at the Last Supper.

Matthew omits some of the details found in Mark's account (e.g., the man carrying a water jar, Mark 14:13-14), focusing not on the uncanny prophetic knowledge of Jesus about what is to happen (see Mark 14:16, "[they] found everything as he had told them"), but on Jesus' majestic command and its immediate fulfillment. Jesus does not inquire where the guest room is (Mark 14:14), but the man in the city is told, "I will keep the Passover at your house with my disciples" (Matt 26:18). The mood is similar to the preparation for the entry into Jerusalem where Jesus had commanded the disciples to prepare for his dramatic procession into the Holy City (21:1-6).

An important Matthean nuance is found in Jesus' words: "My time is near" (26:18). The word for "time" here is *kairos*, a word used in the Gospel to refer to the end time (Matt 8:29; 13:30; 16:3; 21:34). The verb "is near" or "approaches" *(engizein)* is also consistently used to refer to the approach of the end time (3:2; 4:17; 10:7; 21:34; 24:32-33). Jesus' words give an eschatological aura to the Passion. Jesus' impending death and resurrection will be the decisive turning point that marks the beginning of the new age. Matthew's perspective on this is apparent when signs of the end time erupt at the very moment of Jesus' death (see 27:51-53). The Passion, therefore, is not simply a critical moment within the life of Jesus of Nazareth but a drama that compresses within itself the entire destiny of the world and the struggle of life over death.

As evening falls and the festival begins, Jesus "took his place" with the twelve disciples (26:20). Matthew's formulation here and at other points in the Passover scenes subtly emphasizes the bond of Jesus with the twelve (26:18, "with my disciples"; 26:29, "with you"). This is the last time the twelve will be together, a point recalled in the final scene of the Gospel where the "eleven" gather to greet the Risen Jesus (28:16).

The meal begins with Jesus' prediction that one of the disciples will betray him (literally, "hand over," the verb *paradidōmi* used throughout the Passion tradition for Jesus' betrayal; see above, 26:2), a tragic counterpoint to Matthew's emphasis on the bond of Jesus with his twelve disciples. The disciples are "distressed" or sorrowful at Jesus' prediction and one after another they respond, "Surely not I, Lord?" (26:22). Matthew adds the title "Lord," setting up a contrast with Judas's response (26:25). "Lord" is a strong confessional title in Matthew (see above, 14:30), underscoring the loyalty of the disciples toward Jesus. Even though weak and of "little faith," the Matthean disciples believe in Jesus and are obedient to him. Judas, by contrast, will address Jesus as "rabbi" (26:25; see also 26:49), a title in Matthew associated with Jesus' opponents (see 23:7). Earlier the disciples had been warned not to use the title "rabbi" (23:8) and twice Matthew prefers "Lord" as an address for Jesus rather than "rabbi" as in Mark's parallels (see 17:4; 20:33; also 21:10).

The Gospel makes clear that Judas's betrayal does not catch Jesus unaware. Jesus clearly predicts that the "one who has dipped his hand into the bowl with me will betray me" (26:23). The words are reminiscent of the lament in Ps 41:9: "Even my bosom friend in whom I trusted, who ate of my bread, has lifted the heel against me." The setting of the Passover meal underscores the tragedy of Judas's betrayal—he violates the bond of friendship and love implicit in discipleship and does so at the solemn moment when Israel celebrated its liberation from slavery and its birth as a covenant people.

The tragic figure of Judas poses the dilemma of divine sovereignty in juxtaposition with human freedom and responsibility. "The Son of Man goes as it is written of him . . ." (26:24)—a reaffirmation of the Gospel's fundamental perspective that Jesus is fully in accord with God's will expressed in the Scriptures ("as it is written"). Jesus' entire mission is to "fulfill" the law and the prophets (3:15; 5:17) and his obedience to his Father is a leitmotif of Matthew's narrative (see, e.g., 4:1-11; 11:27). The "handing over" of the Son of Man as signaled in the Passion predictions (17:22; 20:18-19; 26:2) is not a capricious accident of history but is the outcome of the divine will. At the same time, Judas has freely chosen to betray Jesus and sever the bonds of discipleship. Therefore Judas is deserving of the prophetic woe that Jesus directs at his betrayer: "Woe to that one by whom the Son of Man is betrayed! It would have been better for that one not to have been born" (26:24). Those tragic words of judgment catch the anguish of the scene and reinforce a consistent pattern in Matthew's Gospel. Matthew's concern for right action is matched by his warnings about judgment on those who willfully sin or act out of hypocrisy (see Marguerat 1981, who notes that judgment material concludes virtually all discourse material in Mathew). The apocalyptic discourse, in particular, had urged right action as the proper stance for the Christian as the end time approached (see especially 24:46; 25:14-30). Judas, therefore, becomes a negative example not only of flawed discipleship, but also of the tragic failure of those who do not respond at the advent of the *kairos*.

The scene closes with an exchange between Jesus and Judas, a dramatic touch not found in Mark (26:25; Matthew will do the same in 26:49-50). The betrayer follows the other disciples in asking, "Surely not I, Rabbi?" Jesus answers, "You have said so"—a response that ironically confirms the truth implicit in Judas's question, but without directly accusing him. Matthew may conceive the scene in such a way that Judas is dipping his hand in the bowl with Jesus at the very moment his question is posed (see above, 26:23). The enigmatic "you have said so" *(su eipas)* is the same as the responses Jesus gives the high priest (26:64) and Pilate (27:11) when they question him. In each instance Jesus' reply confirms the truth that the interrogator had posed in question form.

Jesus' words and gestures over the bread and the wine are the heart of this section (26:26-29). Matthew's account includes a number of details that are distinctive in comparison with Mark. Matthew balances the words over the bread and the cup, adding the explicit command "eat" with the bread (26:26) and the direct quotation, "Drink from it, all of you," over the cup (26:27). Some interpreters suggest that these changes reflect the impact of liturgical usage on Matthew's text. The use of direct address, however, and his making explicit elements that are only implicit in Mark are characteristic literary patterns in Matthew (see Senior 1975, 76-81). A more significant change is the addition of the phrase "for the forgiveness of sins" to the words over the cup (26:28; contrast Mark 14:24). Earlier in the Gospel Matthew had omitted this phrase when describing the purpose of John's baptism (3:2; cf. Mark 1:4). Matthew also uses the preposition *peri* (*"for* many") in place of Mark's *hyper*, a change that aligns this phrase more closely with the Septuagint (Greek) version of Isa 53:4, 10 where the servant is described as atoning for the sins of others. Finally, in 26:29 Matthew adds the phrase "with you," emphasizing the bond between Jesus and his disciples, one that will not be broken even by death.

There are several layers of meaning in this extraordinary scene (on the institution account, see Kodell 1988; Léon-Dufour 1987; LaVerdiere 1996). First of all, within the flow of Matthew's story the Supper functions as a final Passion "prediction," in which the meaning of Jesus' death is now stated by his own words and gestures in the setting of the Passover meal. The intent of Jesus' actions in taking the loaf, blessing it, and breaking it are expressed in his words—"this is my body," a "body" that stands on the brink of the Passion. Likewise, the taking of the cup—already identified as a symbol of Jesus' death (see 20:22; also 26:39)—and giving thanks is also explained as "this is my blood of the covenant, which is poured out for many for the forgiveness of sins." On a primary level of symbolism, therefore, the Matthean Jesus interprets the broken bread and the cup poured out as his body broken and his blood poured out as a death "for many." This salvific emphasis harmonizes with Matthew's overall theology. The name Jesus bears was interpreted in the infancy narrative as a sign of his mission to "save his people from their sins" (1:21). That salvific mission was also connected with Jesus' healings through the fulfillment citation of Isa 53:4, "He took our infirmities and bore our diseases" (Matt 8:17). Matthew applied the role of the servant to Jesus by means of another fulfillment quotation from Isa 42:1-4 in 12:17-21. And, in 20:28, the Matthean Jesus stated his entire mission in servant terminology: "The Son of Man came not to be served but to serve, and to give his life a ransom for many." The liberation of the dead from their graves at the moment of Jesus' death further ratifies this salvific interpretation of Jesus' mission (see 27:51-53).

Other layers of meaning are woven into the scene. The setting of a meal with Jesus and his disciples recalls the great feeding stories that took place earlier in the Gospel (see above, 14:13-21; 15:32-39). The nearly identical actions in which Jesus offers a prayer of blessing over the food (a typical component of Jewish prayer) along with gestures of blessing, breaking, and distributing the elements connect these two feedings with the final meal of Jesus with his disciples. The feedings of the multitudes themselves trigger biblical memories of the Exodus and the miraculous manna (Exod 16) as well as the prophetic ministries of Elijah and Elisha who also miraculously fed the hungry (1 Kgs 17; 2 Kgs 4:42-44). The gathering of multitudes for an abundant meal also projects forward in history by tapping into Israel's anticipation of the final eschatological banquet (Isa 25:6-9). Jesus' words at the conclusion of the institution account vigorously reaffirm this eschatological perspective. Jesus declares that he will "never again drink of this fruit of the vine until that day when I drink it new with you in my Father's kingdom" (26:29). Matthew intensifies this Markan text by adding the phrases "never again" *(ap' arti)*, which intensifies Mark's "no longer" *(ouketi),* and "with you," which emphasize both the breaking of the fellowship bond through death ("I will *never again* drink of this fruit of the vine . . .") and the certainty of fellowship renewed in the eschaton (*"with you* in my Father's kingdom"). The Last Supper, as well as its anticipation in the previous two feeding stories, also clearly connects with the eucharistic experience of the Christian community.

The Passover context of the Last Supper further supports this ensemble of motifs and perspectives. This pilgrimage feast celebrated Israel's past liberation from slavery through the Exodus and the forging of the covenant between God and Israel in the wilderness. At the same time, it served as an anticipation of God's future and definitive redemption of Israel. In the context of Matthew's Gospel, Jesus' final Passover with his disciples expresses the ultimate meaning of his mission of salvation and forges a new covenant in his blood (26:28). The reference to "my blood of the covenant" is probably inspired by Exod 24 where Moses pours half of the blood of slaughtered oxen on the altar and then sprinkles the rest on the people declaring, "See the blood of the covenant that the LORD has made with you in accordance with all these words" (Exod 24:8). Blood as a symbol of life expresses the covenant between God and Israel. The Christian tradition incorporated into Matthew's Gospel portrays the death of Jesus as a definitive renewal of the covenant, reaffirming God's salvific intent and promising future liberation (some manuscript traditions insert the word "new" before "covenant" in 26:28). Against this backdrop of covenant theology, the betrayal by Judas and the denial and flight by the rest of the disciples take on even more poignant meaning.

Matthew's portrayal of the last Passover of Jesus and his disciples closes with a final scene in which Jesus predicts the denial of Peter and abandonment by the rest of the disciples (26:30-35). Together with the prediction of Judas's betrayal (26:20-25), it forms a poignant frame of discipleship failure around the institution account. As Jesus and his disciples leave the house where they celebrated Passover and go to the Mount of Olives, they sing the Hallel, the traditional psalms of praise that conclude the Passover meal (Pss 114–118). Jesus breaks the spell by predicting, "You will all become deserters because of me this night . . ." (26:31). Literally, Jesus says that all of the disciples will be "scandalized" or "find Jesus an obstacle" (the root meaning of the Greek verb *scandalizomai* used here). Matthew's formulation emphasizes that Jesus himself is the obstacle ("in me"). Earlier in the Gospel Jesus had responded to the messengers from John by declaring, "Blessed is the one who takes no offense at me" (11:6). The people of Nazareth had also been "scandalized" in Jesus or "found him an obstacle" (13:57; NRSV: "took offense at him"), as did the Pharisees, because of his declaration about purity (15:12). Now it will be the turn of the disciples themselves to find Jesus and his way an "obstacle."

Matthew seals Jesus' prediction of crisis for the community with a citation from Zech 13:7, "I will strike the shepherd, and the sheep of the flock will be scattered" (26:31). Earlier Matthew had used this image of shepherd and a scattered flock to underscore Jesus' compassion for the crowds (9:36; see also 15:24). Coupled to the prediction of the community's breakdown is a promise of renewal: "But after I am raised up, I will go ahead of you to Galilee" (26:32). This promise is fulfilled in the final scene of the Gospel where the Risen Christ appears to the "eleven" in Galilee (see 28:16-20). Galilee was the place where the disciples were first called (4:18-22) and where Jesus had empowered the twelve for their mission (10:1-42). The promise to "go ahead of you to Galilee," therefore, gives the resurrection appearances the aura of a restoration of the disciples following their denial and flight.

The text now turns its focus to Peter, consistent with Matthew's attention to this representative disciple throughout his Gospel. Peter boldly declares that even though "all become deserters because of you [literally, "become scandalized in you"; note Matthew once more adds the emphatic words "in you"], I will never desert you [literally, "be scandalized"]" (26:33). Jesus in turn predicts that Peter will deny his master three times before the cock crows. Peter, however, intensifies his bravado: "Even though I must die with you, I will not deny you" (26:35). All of the disciples join in Peter's brave words. The irony of this scene becomes apparent to the reader in the immediately following set of scenes when Peter and the disciples sleep rather than pray (26:36-46) and flee at the moment of the arrest (26:56), and when Peter denies with an oath he even knows Jesus (26:69-75). Earlier in the narrative, Peter had earned a severe rebuke from Jesus when he had attempted to silence Jesus' prediction of the Passion (16:22-23). Matthew consistently portrays Peter as one capable of deep faith and tragic failure (see, e.g., 14:28-31).

◊ ◊ ◊ ◊

The ensemble of Passover scenes is rich in Matthean theology. The evangelist again portrays Jesus as fully aware of his impending death, deliberately preparing for his final Passover, and using the meal to proclaim the meaning of his life-giving death. That meaning reaches back to the wellsprings of Israel's Passover theology and forward into the community's own liturgical experience and eschatological hopes. At the same time, Jesus prophetically foretells the destiny of the community, as it, too, will undergo a passion of failure and death before it experiences the renewal of the resurrection.

The exemplary role of the Passion story is also in evidence here. The profound integrity of Jesus' obedience to his Father's will stands in sharp contrast to the treachery of Judas and the weakness of the disciples. Despite Jesus' pointed warnings, Peter and the rest of the disciples succumb to false bravado and are not alert for the moment of crisis when it falls upon them in the garden at the moment of Jesus' arrest.

Gethsemane: The Handing Over of the Son of Man (26:36-56)

Jesus and his disciples leave the site of the Passover meal and go to "a place called Gethsemane," presumably situated on the way to the Mount of Olives. Here Jesus will pray intensely in preparation for his "handing over" (26:36-46), and here Judas and his opponents will effect his arrest (26:47-56).

Matthew draws the sequence and most of the content of these scenes from Mark (14:32-52), but a host of subtle editorial changes leave a characteristic stamp on the material. In the prayer scene Matthew edges the spotlight away from Mark's focus on the weakness of the disciples to a more intense concentration on Jesus' repeated prayer in the face of his onrushing *kairos*. In the arrest scene, Matthew underlines Jesus' majesty even at a moment of abject humiliation as well as his typical motif of scriptural fulfillment.

◊ ◊ ◊ ◊

Jesus' Prayer in Gethsemane (26:36-46): Matthew subtly puts Jesus in the lead—he comes with the disciples to Gethsemane (26:36, cf. Mark 14:32, "They went . . ."). "Gethsemane" means "olive press" in Hebrew and may have been on the way to the Mount of Olives (26:36; Luke 22:39 situates the prayer on the Mount of Olives; John 18:1 speaks of a "garden" that was "across the Kidron valley," which runs between Jerusalem and the Mount of Olives). Jesus deploys the disciples in a curious way: Most of them are to sit at a distance while he takes "Peter and the two sons of Zebedee" farther away to pray (26:36-37). Matthew's wording may be a subtle allusion to Gen 22:5 where Abraham instructs his servants to stay back while he and Isaac go a distance away to pray. The *Akedah Isaak* or "binding of Isaac" was a favored motif in rabbinic Judaism that stressed the exemplary faith of Abraham and the willing sacrifice of Isaac, and Matthew may wish to alert the reader that Jesus embodies both the faith of Abraham and the sacrificial spirit of Isaac.

This trio of disciples (Peter and the "sons of Zebedee," that is, James and John; see 10:2) were among the first called by Jesus (see 4:18-22) and were the privileged witnesses of the transfiguration (17:1-8). Peter, of course, figures prominently in Matthew's Gospel. This same set of disciples also exhibited a lack of comprehension concerning Jesus' Passion. Peter had protested Jesus' first Passion prediction (16:22) and the Sons of Zebedee had interceded on their behalf to win positions of power in Jesus' reign, a move that prompted Jesus to say, "You do not know what you are asking," and to predict that they would "drink [my] cup" (20:20-23).

Jesus' mood gives the scene a foreboding character. He begins "to be grieved and agitated" and expresses his distress in the words of a lament psalm, "I am deeply grieved, even to death . . ." (26:38; see Pss 42:4-5; 43:5). The phrase "even to death"—not found in the psalm—intensifies the lament and binds it to the Passion story.

Jesus implores the disciples to "remain here, and stay awake with me" (v. 38). Typically Matthew underscores the personal bond between Jesus and his disciples by adding the phrase "with me" (cf. Mark 14:34; see above, 26:20). Jesus moves forward and throws himself prostrate (literally, "on his face," Matt 26:39; cf. original Greek of Mark 14:35, "on the ground")—a phrase that connotes deep respect or even adoration (see Gen 17:3, 17; Num 14:5; 2 Sam 9:6; 1 Kgs 18:39).

Jesus' exhortation to "stay awake" gives an eschatological tone to the Gethsemane prayer (26:38, 40-41). The need to "watch" (literally, "stay awake") recalls the eschatological discourse of chapters 24–25 where a series of parables and sayings had warned the disciples to be alert for the coming of the end time (see the explicit injunction to "stay awake" in 24:42-43; 25:13). The saying of Jesus in 26:18 had interpreted the impending Passion as the *kairos,* the opportune eschatological moment that called for decisive and alert response (see also 26:16). The Gethsemane scene further specifies the *kairos* as the precise moment when Judas, the one who would "hand over" Jesus, approaches and sets in motion the events leading to Jesus' death (see 26:45-46). Jesus' prayer, therefore, is the immediate preparation for the fateful event toward which the Gospel narrative has been moving since the first Passion prediction at Caesarea Philippi (16:21).

Matthew constructs three distinct prayers. The first two are in direct address and the third is reported as "saying the same words" (26:44). In the first two prayers Jesus addresses God as "my Father," a rendition of Mark's more intimate and archaic "Abba, Father" (26:39, 42; Mark 14:36; on this Aramaic address for God see Senior 1984, 73-77). "Father" is a preferred address for God in Matthew's Gospel, used some fifty-three times in the Gospel compared to six in Mark. This metaphor serves Matthew's Christology, which both portrays Jesus as "Son of God" who enjoys extraordinary intimacy with God (see particularly 11:25-27) and as one who is obedient to the will of the "heavenly Father" (see, e.g., 7:21; 12:50).

In the Sermon on the Mount Jesus had instructed the disciples to pray in this same manner, addressing God as "Our Father" and being committed to doing God's will (6:9-10). The wording of the Gethsemane prayer is strongly reminiscent of the Lord's Prayer. Both the address "my Father" and the phrase "your will be done" recall for the reader Jesus' instruction on how to pray, a teaching he himself now carries out (see 6:9-10; 26:39, 42).

The prayer of Jesus is at once a prayer for deliverance from death and a resolute commitment to God's will, a profound paradox that gives the Gethsemane scene its haunting appeal. The realization that Jesus' death is inevitable seems to mount as the wording of the prayers progresses from "if it is possible, let this cup pass from me" in the first prayer to, in the second, "if this cannot pass unless I drink [the cup], your will be done."

Meanwhile, the disciples are unable to sustain their watchfulness and succumb to sleep. Mark's account is much more emphatic about the failure of the disciples than that of Matthew. Mark enumerates the three times Jesus comes to find the disciples sleeping (Mark 14:37, 40, 41); Matthew, by contrast, enumerates Jesus' threefold return to prayer (26:39, 42, 44). Matthew also omits Mark's comments, "Simon, are you asleep?" (14:37) and "They did not know what to say to him" (14:40).

Yet the failure of the disciples to "stay awake" in watchfulness for the approach of the *kairos* remains part of Matthew's account. The disciples are exhorted to "stay awake with me" (26:38) at the beginning of the scene and Peter is chided for sleeping after the first prayer, "So, could you not stay awake with me one hour?" (26:40). They are found still sleeping after the second and third prayers (26:43, 45). The disciples' failure is attributed to "weakness" of the flesh, even though their "spirit" is willing (26:41). The disjuncture "flesh"/"spirit" in this context does not refer to a division between "body" and "soul," but to two dimensions of the human being, one "spiritual" and willing that is in tension with another that is "fleshly" and weak. Such notions of an inherent struggle within the human body-spirit were commonplace in Jewish literature and have echoes in Paul's ethical perspective (see, e.g., Rom 7:14-25). Such a portrayal fits well with Matthew's designation of the disciples as of "little faith" (see above 6:30; 8:26; 14:31; 16:8; 17:20).

The point of Jesus' exhortations to the disciples is clear: They are to be awake and pray "that you may not come into the time of trial" (literally, the *peirasmon* or "test"). This is another link to the Lord's Prayer where Jesus instructed the disciples to pray that they would not enter "into the test" (*peirasmon;* NRSV: "time of trial," 6:13). The "test" foreseen here is most probably the cataclysmic struggles of the end time such as depicted in the eschatological discourse (see, e.g., 24:9-13, 15-24), sufferings that even the elect could not endure without God's deliverance (see 24:22). Within the framework of the Passion narrative, the impending suffering and death of Jesus are a foretaste of the struggle between good and evil that will engulf the community itself within the arena of history.

The scene concludes with Jesus returning to the still-sleeping disciples, now through prayer resolute in the face of the onrushing "hour" (26:45-56). Matthew's formulation draws a tight line between the fateful *kairos* or "hour" and the arrival of Judas: "My time *[kairos]* is near *[engys]*," 26:18; "Behold the hour is at hand *[ēngiken]*," 26:45; "Behold my betrayer is at hand *[ēngiken]*," 26:46.

For Matthew, Judas becomes the instrument that "hands over" the Son of Man to sinners and triggers the fateful events of the Passion.

The Arrest of Jesus (26:47-56): While Jesus is still speaking, his words are fulfilled as Judas and a "large crowd" come on the scene. Judas, "one of the twelve," is now publicly associated with an armed band sent from "the chief priests and the elders of the people" (26:47). The collusion that began the Passion narrative with the plot of the leaders and Judas's offer of betrayal now comes to fruition (see 26:3-5, 14-16).

Matthew interjects an exchange between Judas and Jesus at the moment of his famed kiss of betrayal, the sign Judas had given to the armed band. A kiss between disciple and master was a sign of respect and friendship. As Judas comes forward to kiss Jesus he formally greets him, "Greetings, Rabbi!" (26:49). The reader of Matthew is aware of Jesus' teaching not to use this title (23:8) and of Judas's own words at the moment Jesus had predicted his betrayal ("Surely not I, Rabbi?" 26:25). In Mark's version, the crowd seizes Jesus as soon as Judas has planted his betrayer's kiss. But Matthew has Jesus speak first, subtly underscoring Jesus' full awareness of what is taking place (26:50). In the Greek text Jesus' words are terse and somewhat obscure, although the fundamental meaning is clear. It could be translated as an ironic question, "Friend, why are you here?" Or in the NRSV's translation as a permissive: "Friend, do what you are here to do." Or, perhaps, most literally, as, "Friend, this [i.e., the kiss of betrayal] is what you are here for." Because Jesus had already predicted Judas's betrayal at the Last Supper, his words here are a confirmation, perhaps ironic, that Jesus is fully aware of what his failed disciple is about to do. Only "then," Matthew notes, does the crowd seize Jesus and arrest him (26:50).

In Mark's version "one of those who stood near" draws a sword and cuts off the ear of the high priest's slave (14:47). This appears to be someone from the armed mob and not a disciple. In an atmosphere of mayhem and confusion the swordbearer wounds the slave—contrasting with the calm majesty of Jesus who reproaches the crowd that comes against him as a robber, "with swords and clubs" (Mark 14:48; on this see Senior 1984, 82-83). Matthew, however, clearly identifies the one who draws the sword as "one of those with Jesus" who deliberately "put his hand on his sword, drew it" and attacked the high priest's slave (26:51; note that Luke 22:49-50 and John 18:10 also identify the attacker as a follower of Jesus; in John's account the culprit is "Simon Peter"). This affords Jesus the opportunity to reject the use of violence on his behalf. The one with the sword is told to "put your sword back into its place; for all who take the sword will perish by the sword" (26:52). This latter part has the flavor of a proverb and is similar to a saying in Rev 13:10, "If you kill with the sword, with the sword you must be killed." The content and spirit of Jesus' words resonate with the Sermon on the Mount where Jesus had taught the disciples to "not resist an evildoer" (5:38-39) and to love one's enemy (5:43-44).

Matthew reaffirms that the Passion is not an accident of fate but the fulfillment of the divine will expressed in the Scriptures. If deliverance from arrest and death were the only issue, Jesus could have appealed to his Father and have dispatched to him "more than twelve legions of angels" (26:53), a number that may play off the number of the twelve apostles Jesus had chosen. But the intent of Jesus is to "fulfill the scriptures" that "say it must happen in this way" (26:54). The immediate inspiration for this emphasis on scriptural fulfillment is probably Mark 14:49 (see Matt 26:56), but its taproot sinks deep into Matthew's overall theology. As expressed in the "fulfillment quotations" throughout the Gospel and in a programmatic text such as 5:17 ("Do not think that I have come to abolish the law or the prophets; I have come not to abolish but to fulfill"), Matthew presents the entire mission of Jesus as bringing to fruition God's will as expressed in the Scriptures (Senior 1997b). Here no specific text of scripture is cited. Earlier, at the Last Supper, Jesus had quoted Zech 13:7 in reference to the striking of the shepherd and the scattering of the sheep, a moment that might seem to refer in particular to the moment of the arrest and the resulting flight of the disciples. Yet reference to scriptural fulfillment here and, even more clearly, in 26:56 probably has a broader sweep. Applied not simply to the moment of the arrest, but to the entire Passion drama, it evokes not any specific text but the whole span of the Scriptures, which for the Matthean community speak as one prophetic voice pointing to the Messiah Jesus.

The scene concludes with Jesus directly addressing the armed crowd (26:55-56). Matthew adds "at that hour" (26:55, *en ekeinē tē hōra*)—reinforcing the earlier statement of Jesus that the moment of the arrest was the fateful "hour" (26:45), the anticipated *kairos* (26:18), when the Passion actually begins. In contrast to their stealth and violence, Jesus himself had openly faced his opponents, teaching in the temple, yet they had not attempted to seize him then. Jesus' challenge recalls his bold teaching in the temple precincts that had silenced his enemies (21:23–22:46) and the leaders' fear of arresting him because the crowds revered him (21:45; 26:3-5). "But all this," Jesus declares, "has taken place, so that the scriptures of the prophets may be fulfilled" (26:56). This declaration of scriptural fulfillment has its parallel in Mark 14:49

("But let the scriptures be fulfilled"), but Matthew has amplified this statement. The formula is similar to those that introduce the other "fulfillment quotations" in the Gospel (see, e.g., 1:22; 2:15; 4:14; 12:17; 21:4), except that, in this case, no specific quotation is cited and the formula is stated not by the narrator of the Gospel but by Jesus himself. Not unlike 26:54, this statement of the Matthean Jesus has a "programmatic" character, wrapping all of the events of the Passion in the mantle of scriptural fulfillment. Although the arrest of Jesus is the immediate context, the pivotal role of the arrest as the predicted moment of Jesus' "hour" when he would be handed over and, therefore, as the trigger for all the sufferings Jesus would endure, places this scene at the heart of the Passion. "All this," therefore, refers not simply to the arrest, but to the Passion as a whole.

As if driving home the sureness of Jesus' prediction, at that very moment the disciples desert him and flee (26:56). Warned at the Last Supper (see 26:31-35) and failing to prepare through watchful prayer, the disciples fall prey to the terror of the Passion—an anticipation of the travails that would tear at the community in the arena of history (see especially 24:3-13).

◊ ◊ ◊ ◊

The Gethsemane scenes are a strong blend of Christology and exhortations concerning discipleship. On the brink of his arrest, Jesus displays his unbroken integrity and deep bond of obedience with the Father. When the "hour" of the Passion comes in the form of Judas and an armed band, Jesus remains the majestic teacher and one filled with prophetic knowledge despite submitting to arrest. All of what he does and all that will occur fulfill the Scriptures.

The disciples, on the other hand, become an object lesson for the community. They "sleep" rather than stay alert in prayer and, when the armed band arrives, one of them chooses the way of violence and all of them desert their Master. Throughout the Passion the Gospel provides sober lessons for the reader on the cost of discipleship.

Jesus Before the Council (26:57–27:2)

Those who had seized Jesus in Gethsemane now lead him to Caiaphas the high priest where there is a gathering of "the scribes and the elders" (26:57). Here Matthew clusters three interwoven episodes: (1) the interrogation by the high priest and the council and the mockery that follows it (26:57-68); (2) Peter's denial of Jesus (26:69-75); and (3) the council's final condemnation of Jesus (27:1-2). Given Matthew's attention throughout his Gospel to the rejection of Jesus by the Jewish leaders, this scene of formal condemnation takes on particular significance for his Gospel. Historically it is likely that this encounter between Jesus and the Jerusalem leaders was not a formal trial as such, but at best a hearing or strategy session in which the leaders reviewed their complaint against Jesus and prepared for their meeting with the Roman governor who had the power of capital punishment. In the development of the gospel tradition this scene took on more and more of a juridical cast, similar to that of the Roman trial that follows (on this see the thorough discussion in Brown 1994, 328-97).

◊ ◊ ◊ ◊

Interrogation by the High Priest and the Council (26:57-68): Matthew identifies the high priest as "Caiaphas" (see 26:3) and includes "the scribes and the elders" as those arrayed against Jesus (26:57; cf. Mark 14:53, "all the chief priests, the elders, and the scribes"). Note that in 27:1 Matthew refers to "all the chief priests and the elders of the people"; apparently the evangelist thought of the assembled leaders as loosely including priests, scribes, and elders. The Pharisees, the leading opponents in the body of the Gospel, return after the death of Jesus in Matthew's special material about placing a guard at the tomb (see 27:62). Matthew also reintroduces Peter who follows Jesus "at a distance" and goes into the courtyard of the high priest and sits with the guards "to see how this would end" (26:58; in contrast to Mark's colorful detail, "warming himself at the fire," 14:54). The reference to Peter, of course, prepares for the denial scene that will follow (26:69-75), and his intent "to see how this would end" recalls the disciple's bravado at the Supper and Jesus' prediction that he would fail (26:33-35).

Matthew immediately underscores the bad faith of the proceedings, as the chief priest and the "whole council" seek "false" testimony against Jesus (26:59). Despite a parade of such witnesses, none of them are apparently credible. Finally "two" witnesses come forward with the claim, "This fellow said, 'I am able to destroy the temple of God and to build it in three days' " (26:60-61). The enumeration of "two" witnesses aligns the proceedings with Jewish law that demanded two witnesses in capital cases (Deut 17:6). Also they testify not that Jesus said he "will destroy" the temple as in Mark's version (14:58) but that he is "able to" destroy the temple. Likewise the statement does not refer to the contrast between a temple "made with hands" and one "not made with hands" as in Mark, but simply to "the temple of God."

Although Matthew may still want to imply that this testimony against Jesus is false, his formulation moves it in a more plausible direction (note that he also omits Mark's observation that their testimony "did not agree," 14:59). Their accusations now become an ironic affirmation of Jesus' messianic power that is "able to" destroy the temple of God and rebuild it in three days. Earlier in the Gospel, Jesus had entered the temple as the humble yet triumphant Messiah and disrupted its activity, citing the prophetic judgment of Jer 7:11 (see 21:1-17). Subsequently the "chief priests and the elders of the people" had challenged Jesus' authority to do such things, but he refused to answer them (21:23-27). And, at the beginning of the apocalyptic discourse, Jesus had predicted that "not one stone [of the temple] will be left here upon another; all will be thrown down" (24:2). Although the Gospel does not cite any statement of Jesus' predicting that he himself *would* destroy the temple (allowing the testimony of the witnesses to be considered false), Matthew's Christology would not hesitate to assert that the Messiah Jesus *could* destroy it and restore it. There is evidence that Jewish tradition associated a possible destruction and restoration of the temple as one of the cataclysmic events of the messianic era (see Juel 1977, 169-210; Sanders 1985, 77-90). In fact, Matthew linked the ultimate destruction of the temple with the death of Jesus, seeing it as divine judgment for the rejection of Jesus (see above, 21:40-41; 22:7). Although no restoration of the Jerusalem temple is foreseen in Matthew's theology, some early Christian traditions identified the Risen Christ or the community founded on Christ the cornerstone as the new spiritual "temple" (e.g., John 2:21; Eph 2:19-22; 1 Pet 2:4-8; see further, Walker 1996).

The high priest now enters directly into the proceedings. He demands that Jesus respond to these charges, but Jesus remains silent—a possible allusion to the figure of the Suffering Servant who remained silent before his accusers (see Isa 53:7). This leads the high priest to the definitive question, "I put you under oath before the living God, tell us if you are the Messiah, the Son of God" (26:63). Matthew intensifies this moment by having the high priest put Jesus under oath. The high priest's question includes two of the Gospel's most important titles for Jesus: the "Messiah" or "Christ" and "Son of God." Jesus' identity as the promised "Messiah" has been affirmed literally from the first line of the Gospel (see 1:1, 17, 18). The title "Son of God" is a key christological title in Matthew's Gospel, expressing not only Jesus' identity as the Davidic Messiah (and, therefore, "Son of God"), but also expressing Jesus' extraordinary bond with the Father (see 11:25-27; also 3:17; 17:5) and his power over the demonic (see 8:29). More than any other title in Matthew, "Son of God" affirms the transcendent authority of Jesus and thus appears in key confessional contexts (see 14:33; 16:20, where it is also coupled with "Messiah").

Jesus' response is identical to that given to Judas at the Last Supper; the connotation of "You have said so" confirms the truth implicit in the interrogator's own question (26:64; see 26:25). Jesus continues, making further claims about his identity. He solemnly affirms ("But I tell you . . .") that "from now on" the leaders will see "the Son of Man seated at the right hand of Power and coming on the clouds of heaven" (26:64). This affirmation, found already in Mark (14:62) and likely to have been a traditional formulation, is a blend of Ps 110:1 ("The LORD says to my lord, 'Sit at my right hand until I make your enemies your footstool' ") and Dan 7:13 ("I saw one like a son of man coming with the clouds of heaven"). In Matthew, as in Mark, the "Son of Man" title is used in reference to the rejection and humiliation of Jesus (8:20; 11:19; 12:40; 17:12, 22-23; 20:18) as well as for his anticipated authority on earth (9:6; 12:8) and his triumphant return as judge at the end time (10:23; 13:41; 16:27-28; 24:27, 30, 37, 39, 44; 25:31). It is the latter function of Jesus as triumphant judge at the end time that is cited here in the context of the trial. Despite humiliation as one who stands as a prisoner under interrogation, Jesus will "from now on" confront his opponents as the triumphant Son of Man. Matthew's emphatic "from now on" heightens the eschatological aura of the Passion story and may find its confirmation in the signs of the end time that break out at the moment of Jesus' death (27:51-53; also 28:2) and particularly in the Risen Jesus' appearance to the eleven at the conclusion of the Gospel (28:16-20).

The high priest brands Jesus' answer as "blasphemy" (see 26:65) and tears his garment, a dramatic gesture that can express mourning (see, e.g., Lev 10:6; 2 Kgs 19:1) or anguish at misuse of the divine name (*m. Sanh.* 7:5; similarly in Acts 14:14 Paul and Barnabas tear their garments to protest the attempts of the Lycaonians to worship them as divine beings). Blasphemy in its strictest sense meant abuse of the divine name but was applied more widely to anything considered an insult to God. Jesus' claim to be "Son of God" may have fallen under the latter category. In any case, Matthew clearly presents Jesus' religious claim to be Messiah, Son of God, and triumphant Son of Man as the direct cause for his condemnation by the Jewish leaders. Caiaphas puts the question to the council and their response is that Jesus deserves death (26:66). Matthew stops short of calling this a formal judgment (in contrast to Mark 14:64 who notes that they judge Jesus—*katakrinan auton*); that moment comes in the morning when the leaders reassemble and "take council" against Jesus (27:1).

Perhaps to portray the leaders in an even more negative light Matthew implies that it is the leaders themselves who begin to torment and mock Jesus (26:67-68; in Mark's version [14:65] "some" begin to abuse Jesus and in Luke this is done by "the men who were holding Jesus" [Luke 22:63]). This scene may also invoke the image of the servant (see Isa 50:6; 53:3-5). The leaders mock

Jesus for his messianic claims, taunting him to name those who struck him (an element added by Matthew, 26:68).

Peter's Denial (26:69-75): Peter's denial of his discipleship stands in vivid contrast with Jesus' bold confession before the high priest. Matthew skillfully accentuates the gravity of Peter's failure through the staging of the scene. A string of accusers comes forward, beginning with "a servant-girl" (26:69), then a second servant-girl who shares her suspicions with bystanders (26:71; in Mark 14:68 it is the same woman who made the first accusation), and finally the bystanders themselves who accuse Peter in chorus (26:73). Peter himself retreats under this assault, beginning where he is seated "outside in the courtyard" of the high priest's residence (26:69; Matthew once again omits Mark's detail about Peter warming himself at the fire), then moving "out to the porch," and finally leaving the scene altogether when he realizes the enormity of what he has done (26:75).

Both the accusations directed against Peter and the vehemence of his denials seem to mount in intensity. The first servant says, "You also were with Jesus the Galilean" (in contrast to Mark's more unusual designation, literally, "the Nazarene, Jesus," 14:67). To this first accusation, Peter feigns ignorance, "I do not know what you are talking about." Matthew adds that he denied it "before all of them," emphasizing the public character of Peter's denial with a phrase used earlier by Jesus in the Gospel to encourage public confession of discipleship (see 5:16; 10:32-33). The second maid announces to the bystanders that Peter was "with Jesus of Nazareth" (cf. Mark 14:69, "This man is one of them"), subtly emphasizing the bond with Jesus in words reminiscent of the Last Supper scene (see 26:18, 29, 36, 38, 40). This time Peter denies his link to Jesus "with an oath" (26:72), an ominous step in a Gospel that forbade oath taking (5:33-37) and portrayed such characters as Herod (14:7), the scribes and Pharisees (23:16-22), and Caiaphas (26:63) as swearing by oaths. In the third accusation the bystanders reassert their accusation that Peter was "one of them" because his accent betrays him, a conclusion Matthew apparently deduces from Mark's formulation, "you are a Galilean" (Matt 26:73;

Mark 14:70). Peter's final denial is the most vehement one of all, as he "began to curse, and he swore an oath" saying, "I do not know the man!" (26:74).

At this poignant moment, Peter hears the cock crow and recalls Jesus' prediction at the Last Supper (see 26:34). Crushed by the enormity of his failure, the disciple leaves the porch of the high priest's residence and goes outside to weep—"bitterly," Matthew adds (26:75).

Consistent with his portrayal throughout the Gospel, Matthew accentuates the weakness of Peter just as he had accentuated the prominence of his role as leader and spokesperson for the disciples. Peter's repeated and vehement denial of his discipleship stands in painful contrast with his status as the first disciple called (4:18), his confession at Caesarea Philippi (16:16), and his privileged role as witness to the transfiguration (17:1-8). In drawing out the collapse of Peter, Matthew demonstrates the consequences of failing to heed Jesus' warnings to Peter and the other disciples that they should be watchful and alert in the face of the test the Passion would bring (25:13; 26:31-35, 37-38, 40-41).

The Council's Condemnation (27:1-2): In Mark's version, this morning assembly is merely a "consultation" (15:1) since the council had already made a formal judgment condemning Jesus the night before (14:64). Matthew, however, presents this episode as the conclusion of the trial that lasted through the night, interrupted by the mockery of Jesus (26:67-68) and the denial of Peter (26:69-75).

Now "all the chief priests and the elders of the people" literally "take counsel" against Jesus in order "to put him to death." Earlier in the Gospel, Matthew uses the phrase "take counsel" to describe sessions in which Jesus' opponents plot to take hostile actions against him (12:14; 22:15; 28:12; similarly, 27:7). Their decision in hand, the leaders have Jesus bound and lead him away in order to "hand him over" to Pilate the Roman governor. This sequence of events literally fulfills the Passion prediction made by Jesus earlier in the Gospel, once again affirming the prophetic knowledge of Jesus (see 20:18-19).

◊ ◊ ◊ ◊

As is often the case in the Passion narrative, Matthew weaves together motifs of Christology and discipleship. The confrontation between Jesus and the Jewish leaders highlights his authority as Christ, Son of God, and Son of Man and serves as a review and confirmation of the Gospel's estimation of Jesus. The hostility of the leaders whereby they reject Jesus' claims and even label them blasphemous serves as a foil to Jesus' self-proclamation. The parallel contrast between Jesus' fearless confession of his identity and Peter's abject and public denial of his discipleship serves as a sober warning to the community. The abuse directed at Jesus is a preview of the travails the community will face as it carries out its mission to the world. Attentive listening to Jesus' words and alert prayer are needed for the disciple to withstand the assaults of evil.

The Fate of the Betrayer (27:3-10)

Matthew may have developed the account of Judas's death on the basis of a tradition circulating in the early community (see Senior 1975, 343-97). Acts 1:15-20 also reports on Judas's death, but in a very different manner. According to Acts, Judas had purchased a field with the money earned by betraying Jesus, but had a tragic accident—falling "headlong" his body is shattered and the field soaked with his blood. In this manner the field became known as Hakeldama ("Field of Blood") and the whole tragedy fulfills the warnings of Pss 69:26 and 109:8. While Matthew's account also revolves around the origin of the name "Field of Blood" and asserts scriptural fulfillment, all of the other details are different. Judas commits suicide after being seized by remorse and flinging the blood money into the temple. The chief priests use the "blood money" to purchase a "potter's field" for the burial of strangers, thereby unwittingly fulfilling a prophecy of "Jeremiah."

To a certain degree, Matthew develops this story on the basis of material he derives from his major source, Mark. At the Last Supper Jesus had predicted a dire fate for Judas (Matt 26:20-25; Mark 14:17-21), just as he had predicted the denials of Peter and abandonment by the rest of the disciples (Matt 26:31-35; Mark 14:27-31). Mark's story illustrates the fulfillment of all of those predictions except that of Judas's fate. Matthew, in a sense, completes the picture by describing not only the flight of the disciples and the denial of Peter, but also the fate of Judas. This interest in Judas harmonizes with Matthew's editing of earlier scenes where he adds a reference to the "thirty pieces of silver" (26:15) and pointed dialogue at the moment of Jesus' prediction (26:25) and at the arrest (26:49-50). Peter and Judas, in effect, illustrate the stark difference between the destinies of two flawed disciples.

◊ ◊ ◊ ◊

Matthew inserts the Judas story just at the moment Jesus is formally condemned by the council: Judas actually "sees" that Jesus is condemned to death (27:3; cf. 27:1-2). The story about Judas becomes something of an aside by the narrator during the time Jesus is being led from the house of the high priest to Pilate.

Jesus' condemnation strikes remorse in Judas. The verb Matthew uses is not the usual term for "repentance" *(metanoiein)*, but a word that implies a "change of mind" *(metameletheis)*, suggesting perhaps that Judas's disposition is something less than full repentance. He brings back to the chief priests and elders the thirty pieces of silver that they paid him to betray Jesus (26:14-16) and declares that he has "sinned by betraying innocent blood" *(haima athoon,* 27:4). This introduces one of Matthew's major interests in this scene, namely the recognition that the Jewish leaders bear responsibility for shedding the innocent blood of Jesus. A similar note was already struck by Matthew in chapter 23, where Jesus accuses the leaders of bearing responsibility for shedding "righteous blood" *(haima dikaios),* from the blood of Abel the "righteous" until the blood of Zechariah (cf. above, 23:35-36). Later Pilate will declare to the leaders and people, "I am innocent of this man's blood" (27:24).

The chief priests and elders rebuff Judas ("What is that to us?") and ironically conclude with the same phrase Pilate will use toward them: "See to it yourself" (27:4; cf. 27:24). With that Judas succumbs to despair, casting the coins into the temple and going out to hang himself. The story does not end there, as Matthew's focus continues to fix on the Jewish leaders. The chief priests and elders admit their complicity by conceding that the pieces of silver are "blood money" and should not be placed in the temple treasury

(27:6). They therefore decide to use the money to purchase "the potter's field as a place to bury foreigners" (27:7). This, Matthew explains, is the reason the field "to this day" has been called "Field of Blood," thereby invoking the tradition that may be the taproot of this story.

The story's strange combination of betrayal, silver coins cast into the temple, the purchase of a potter's field, and a burial place for strangers finds coherence in the unusual fulfillment text that concludes the story (27:9-10). Matthew's introduction to the quotation—"then was fulfilled"—is reminiscent of 2:17 where another quotation from "Jeremiah" is cited in connection with the slaughter of the innocents. While in all the other fulfillment quotations Matthew underscores the purposefulness of the action ("in order to fulfill"), in these two quotations that adhere to sinful and tragic actions, the sense of fitting purpose is less assertive. God's providence guides these events, too, but in a more mysterious and opaque fashion.

The quotation itself is a free adaptation of Zech 11:12-13: "So they weighed out as my wages thirty shekels of silver. Then the LORD said to me, 'Throw it into the treasury'—this lordly price at which I was valued by them. So I took the thirty shekels of silver and threw them into the treasury in the house of the LORD." Matthew adapts the wording to fit the Gospel context: It is not Zechariah's shepherd who casts the coins into the treasury, but "they" (i.e., the priests and elders), and the price is set by "some of the sons of Israel"; and in Matthew's version, the price is set not on the shepherd's head but on "him" (i.e., Jesus). Curiously, although the text is from Zechariah, Matthew attributes it to *Jeremiah*. Two things may have prompted this. First of all, Matthew favors the mood and words of Jeremiah, particularly his critique of Israel's leaders (see above, 21:13; also 16:14; Knowles 1993). Second, in some manuscripts the Hebrew text of Zech 11:13 has the word "potter" *('yôṣēr)* instead of "treasury" *(ôṣâr)*, a curious play on words that may have inspired Matthew to connect this quotation about the "thirty pieces of silver" with the story of the potter's field in Jer 18–19, thereby justifying the citation of the prophet's name and mood. Particularly in Jer 19 there is a connection with the "potter" and the purchase of a field that will be used for burials.

◊ · ◊ · ◊ · ◊

The tragic account of Judas's death serves Matthew's christological interests by demonstrating that the prophetic utterance of Jesus about the fate of his betrayer is realized. At the same time, this story is a sober warning to the reader about the consequences when someone called to be a disciple of Jesus squanders that gift through greed, betrayal, and despair. Peter, too, failed in his discipleship but, unlike Judas, he remembers the words of Jesus and weeps tears of remorse and repentance.

On another level, this story continues Matthew's sharp critique of the religious leaders. In Matthew's perspective they exhibit bad faith at virtually every turn—opposing Jesus through his ministry, plotting his arrest, and falsely condemning him. Despite their protests to Judas, they themselves admit complicity by picking up the "blood money" and using it to purchase the potter's field. All of these strange and tragic events, Matthew asserts, are enveloped by scriptural fulfillment and thus advance God's plan of salvation.

The Trial Before Pilate (27:11-31)

Matthew returns to the flow of the narrative suspended during the story of Judas's fate (see 27:2): Jesus now stands before Pilate the Roman governor. As is the case throughout the Passion narrative, Matthew follows closely the narrative sequence and much of the content of Mark's account, but leaves his characteristic imprints on the story.

For Matthew this scene represents the culmination of a critical choice that had been building since the beginning of the Gospel. Now the Jewish leaders—and under their influence the people themselves—will solemnly and fatefully reject their "king" Jesus.

The Roman trial scene includes three episodes: (1) 27:11-14, an initial interrogation by Pilate; (2) 27:15-26, the choice between Barabbas and Jesus that leads to Jesus' condemnation; (3) 27:27-31, the mockery of Jesus by the Roman soldiers.

◊ ◊ ◊ ◊

Jesus Before Pilate (27:11-14): Having concluded their own interrogation of Jesus and judging him worthy of death (27:1-2), the chief priests and elders take Jesus to the Roman governor, Pontius Pilate. Because the province of Judea was under direct Roman control, Roman authorities held judicial power. Although the Gospels give equal weight to the Jewish proceedings, presenting them as a "trial," it is most likely that only Pilate could decide a capital punishment case. Pilate, who served as governor of Judea from 26 to 36 CE, had probably come up to Jerusalem from the coastal city of Caesarea Maritima, where the governor usually resided, to exercise control during the Passover feast. Matthew offers no information about the site for the Roman trial, but it was probably in Herod's former palace in the upper part of the city.

Now Jesus stands as an accused criminal before the Roman governor—the vivid scene recalls Jesus' warnings to the disciples in the mission discourse that they, too, would be "dragged before governors and kings" (10:18). The interrogation begins abruptly with Pilate posing a key question to Jesus: "Are you the King of the Jews?" (27:11). The Jewish leaders had challenged and mocked Jesus for his claim to be the "Messiah" (26:63-68). Pilate poses a similar question, but in secular terms (i.e., "King of the Jews"; see also 2:2; 27:29, 37). Jesus responds to Pilate somewhat enigmatically: "You say so," an answer that seems to confirm the assertion implicit in the governor's question, just as Jesus had "confirmed" the questions of Judas in 26:25 and the high priest in 26:64. From the perspective of Matthew's Gospel, Jesus *is* "King of the Jews," but in a manner not comprehended by the religious or civil authorities.

If Jesus responds to the governor in a veiled fashion, he offers no answer at all to the accusations of the chief priests and elders (27:12). Matthew underscores this silence of Jesus. When Pilate asks him again to respond to the cascade of accusations, Jesus offers no response, "not even to a single charge" (cf. Mark 15:5), a silence that leaves the governor "greatly amazed" (27:14). It is likely that Matthew wants to evoke here the image of the suffering servant who stands silent before his accusers (Isa 53:7) and whose bearing causes kings to be amazed (Isa 52:14-15). Earlier in the Gospel

Matthew had portrayed Jesus' healing ministry as a fulfillment of the servant's work (see Matt 8:17, which cites Isa 53:4) and applied Isa 42:1-4 to Jesus' humble comportment (Matt 12:17-21).

Barabbas or Jesus: The Condemnation of the King of the Jews (27:15-26): This is a scene to which Matthew gives particular attention. First of all he emphasizes the stark choice between Jesus the Messiah and Barabbas, a "notorious prisoner." Second, he adds special material that lifts the choice of Barabbas over Jesus to a solemn moment with fateful consequences for salvation history. The custom of releasing a prisoner on the feast of Passover has no historical corroboration outside of the Gospels. Yet it could have been a practice of Roman largesse timed with the liberation feast of Passover (see Brown 1994, 814-20).

The terms of that choice are highlighted by a series of editorial changes Matthew introduces. First of all, he identifies Barabbas as "a prisoner, called Jesus Barabbas" (27:16). This ancient and well-attested reading (now accepted by the NRSV) makes the comparison with "Jesus called the Christ" all the more acute (on the textual history, see Senior 1975, 238-40). Matthew puts it precisely in those terms in 27:17. Similarly, Matthew repeats the terms of the choice throughout the scene: In 27:15 he uses the word "whom they *wanted*" (*ēthelon;* cf. Mark 15:6, "for whom they asked"); in 27:17, "Whom do you *want* [*thelete*] me to release for you, Jesus Barabbas or Jesus who is called the Messiah?" (cf. Mark 15:9, "Do you want me to release for you the King of the Jews?"); in 27:20 the leaders persuade the crowd "to ask for Barabbas and to have Jesus killed" (cf. Mark 15:11, "to have him release Barabbas for them instead"); and in 27:21 adds, "Which of the two do you want [*thelete*] me to release for you?" (not found in Mark's parallel).

Matthew portrays the religious leaders as the protagonists in the scene and Pilate as a vacillating judge vainly attempting to blunt their accusations. The editorial comment that Pilate realized Jesus had been handed over "out of jealousy" (27:18) suggests that the governor knew the charges against Jesus were bogus. The governor concedes only after repeated, failed attempts to dissuade the crowds and when he realizes that a riot is about to break out (27:24). Matthew intensifies the contrast between the leaders and Pilate by adding the curious scene with Pilate's wife (27:19). While the governor sits on the *bēma* or judgment seat in preparation for sentencing, his wife sends word that he should "have nothing to do with that innocent man, for today I have suffered a great deal because of a dream about him." For Matthew's Gospel dreams are a medium of divine messages, such as those received by Joseph and the Magi in the infancy narrative (see 1:20; 2:12, 13, 19-20). Pilate's wife learns in her dream that Jesus is a "righteous man" and is tormented by the prospect of his condemnation. The Greek word used is *dikaios,* whose primary meaning in Matthew's Gospel is "just" or "righteous"; Joseph is termed a "just" or "righteous" man in that he chose not to expose his wife as unfaithful (1:19) and Jesus, in his first words in the Gospel, tells the Baptist that he must "fulfill all righteousness" (*dikaiosynē,* the noun form, 3:15). Thus the term "just" with its connotation of faithful fulfillment of the law is an apt one to describe Jesus.

This unusual intervention, combined with Pilate's own attempts to have the crowd choose Barabbas, enables Matthew once again to put the Jewish leaders in a bad light while stressing Jesus' innocence. At the very moment that Pilate's wife, a Gentile, attempts to intercede on Jesus' behalf, the religious leaders persuade the crowd "to ask for Barabbas and to have Jesus killed" (27:20). Pilate's repeated attempts to have them choose Jesus fail, and he asks in seeming frustration, "Then what should I do with Jesus who is called the Messiah?" Then "all of them"—leaders and crowds— call for Jesus' crucifixion (27:22). In a final and futile exchange, Pilate asks, "Why, what evil has he done?"—a question drenched in irony from the vantage point of the Gospel that views Jesus as the embodiment of justice and one who had performed the "works of the Messiah" (see 11:2-6)—but their response is even more intense: "Let him be crucified!" (27:23).

In a gesture drawn from Jewish tradition, Matthew portrays Pilate washing his hands with water to declare he is not responsible for condemning Jesus: "I am innocent of this man's blood; see to it yourselves" (27:24). The symbolic gesture of washing one's hands in order to declare one's innocence for the unjust shedding of blood has several biblical precedents (see, e.g., Ps 26:6-10; Isa 1:15-16). A text that may have directly influenced Matthew's composition of this scene is Deut 21:1-9, which describes the procedure to be followed when a murder has taken place. The leaders of the surrounding villages where the crime was committed are to come together, sacrifice a heifer, and wash their hands over the slain animal, while declaring, "Our hands did not shed this blood, nor were we witnesses to it. Absolve, O LORD, your people Israel, whom you redeemed; do not let the guilt of innocent blood remain in the midst of your people Israel" (Deut 21:7-8). Pilate, therefore, absolves himself of any responsibility for Jesus' death and places the matter in the hands of the leaders and the crowds—"See to it yourselves" (27:24)—ironically using the identical words of the priests and elders to Judas when they rejected his return of the blood money (27:4).

The response of the leaders and the crowds to Pilate's gesture has become one of the Gospel's most notorious passages: "Then the people as a whole answered, 'His blood be on us and on our children!' " (27:25). Two elements of this passage are key for its interpretation: (1) the precise meaning of "the people as a whole" and (2) the significance of the people's statement, "His blood be on us and on our children!"

Up until this point in Matthew's narrative, the "crowds," in contrast to the religious leaders, have been neutral or even favorable in their response to Jesus. They follow Jesus (4:25; 8:1; 14:13; 19:2; 20:29), are "astounded" at his teaching (7:28), "glorify" God when he cures the paralytic (9:8), and marvel at his exorcisms and healings (9:33-34; 15:31). When Jesus enters Jerusalem, the crowds offer him homage and shout out their praises (21:8, 9, 11). The leaders are afraid to arrest Jesus openly, because the crowds revere him as a prophet (21:46; 26:5). But during the Roman trial the stance of the crowd changes under the influence of the religious leaders who persuade them to ask for Barabbas and to have Jesus condemned (27:20). Matthew, therefore, does not absolve the crowds, but places the major blame on the leaders who, throughout the Gospel, have been consistently hostile toward Jesus.

When the reader comes to the crucial text of 27:24-25, therefore, it is the combined force of leaders and people that takes responsibility for the death of Jesus. This is the sense of the Greek phrase *pas ho laos* (literally, "all the people"), which the NRSV accurately translates as "the people as a whole." Matthew no longer uses the term *ochlos,* "crowd," but *laos,* a collective term used in the Gospel to refer to people as a whole (see, e.g., 1:21, "for he will save his *people* from their sins" or the repeated phrase, "elders of the *people*").

Their declaration—"His blood be on us and on our children"— also has biblical precedent as an expression of responsibility for the shedding of blood (see similar phrases in Lev 20:9-16; Josh 2:19-20; 2 Sam 1:16). In 1 Kgs 2:33 the unjust murder of Abner and Amasa brings condemnation to the house of Joab: "Their blood [shall] come back on the head of Joab and on the head of his descendants . . . forevermore." Of particular importance is the warning of Jeremiah directed at "all the officials and all the people" (26:12) that if they kill him "you will be bringing innocent blood upon yourselves and upon this city and its inhabitants . . ." (26:15).

For Matthew, therefore, the leaders and the people—"the people as a whole"—take responsibility for shedding the "innocent blood" of Jesus. Matthew may have understood this "responsibility" from several points of view. First of all, through the motif of "innocent blood" Matthew views the rejection and death of Jesus as one more instance in the history of the rejection of prophetic messengers sent by God to Israel. This was the message of the parable of the vineyard where the tenants reject and abuse the servants and ultimately kill the son (21:33-44), and of Jesus' accusations against the scribes and Pharisees whom he accuses of rejecting and killing the prophets and messengers sent to them with the result that "upon [them] may come all the righteous blood shed on earth, from the blood of righteous Abel to the blood of Zechariah son of Barachiah . . ." (23:29-36). This latter text introduces the motif of "righteous" or "innocent" blood, which Matthew carries over into the Passion story through the device of Judas's betrayal. The money Judas used to betray "innocent blood" is ultimately picked up by the leaders and used to purchase the potter's field (see 27:3-10). At the trial

Pilate declares he is not responsible for Jesus' "blood" while "the people as a whole" accept responsibility.

From another vantage point, Matthew sees in this fateful moment a decisive turning point in salvation history. In the parable of the vineyard, Matthew noted that the rejection and death of the "son" would result in "the kingdom of God [being] taken away from you and given to a people that produces the fruits of the kingdom" (21:43). This rejection is enacted in the Passion story when the leaders and people choose Barabbas over Jesus and call for his crucifixion. This is part of a process that will culminate in the final scene of the Gospel where the mission previously restricted to Israel (10:5; 15:24) is now directed to "all nations" (28:19).

The question remains—how definitive is this statement of responsibility on the part of "the people as a whole"? Some have suggested that the phrase "on us and *on our children*" implies a temporal limit of one generation (see Fitzmyer 1965, 667-71). Matthew probably interpreted the destruction of Jerusalem and the temple as God's judgment for the rejection of Jesus and therefore considered that generation as absorbing the terrible consequences (see above, 21:41; 22:7). Even if Matthew did not envisage such a temporal limit to the people's words in 27:25, it is highly unlikely that he was thinking of a blanket condemnation of all Israel for all time. The "people as a whole" represents all those who did not accept Jesus and who, under the sway of their leaders, were opposed to Matthew's Jewish-Christian community. Matthew surely saw his own community as faithful to the covenant and the law as taught by Jesus the Messiah and therefore as a continuation of Israel. Even those who had rejected Jesus still might experience a conversion of heart (see 23:38-39).

The scene ends on a subdued note as Pilate accedes to their wishes, releasing Barabbas "for them" and having Jesus flogged and handed over to crucifixion (27:26).

The Mockery of Jesus (27:27-31): Similar to the end of the Jewish "trial" where Jesus was mocked for claims of being a prophet, so here also he is tormented by his captors for his pretensions to royal status. In this instance "the soldiers of the governor" (27:27) bring the condemned prisoner to the governor's "headquarters" (literally, the "pretorium"), probably Herod's former palace or, less likely, the Antonium fortress adjacent to the northwest corner of the temple enclave. Matthew notes that the "whole cohort"—at full strength six hundred men—gathers around Jesus.

Matthew's editing of the scene found already in Mark (15:16-20) emphasizes its brutality. Jesus is "stripped" (27:28, a detail not explicitly mentioned in Mark) and enrobed with a "scarlet" robe. Mark 15:17 refers to a "purple" robe, the color of royalty; Matthew's "scarlet" is the color of the robes worn by ordinary Roman troops and intensifies the irony of the scene. Matthew also alters the sequence of the soldier's torture found in Mark, adding the "reed" scepter and having them escalate from mock homage (crowning with thorns, the reed scepter, kneeling before him and hailing him as king) to physical abuse (spitting on him and beating him with the scepter).

The soldiers' actions frame the Roman trial scene with the motif of Jesus' kingship. The scene had begun with Pilate asking Jesus if he were "the King of the Jews" (27:11) and concludes with the Roman soldiers mocking the now condemned Jesus as "King of the Jews" (27:29). Given Matthew's repeated affirmation of Jesus' identity as royal Messiah throughout the Gospel, the irony in the trial scene is acute.

◊ ◊ ◊ ◊

Throughout the Gospel Matthew has stressed that Jesus and his mission "fulfill" the Scriptures and are in accord with God's intent. Therefore, the rejection of Jesus by the religious leaders and, ultimately, by the Jerusalem crowds in concert with their leaders was a painful paradox for Matthew's Jewish-Christian community. From the Gospel's perspective, Jesus clearly was the royal Messiah and Son of God and, therefore, preeminently "King of Israel" and "King of the Jews"—even though he exercised that sovereignty in a manner far different from any earthly monarch. Yet Jesus' own people and their leaders failed to recognize his identity. Nevertheless, Matthew sees all of this tragedy falling under the plan of God and within the prophetic knowledge of Jesus. God's judgment for the failure of the people came in the form of the Jewish war and the resulting destruction of Jerusalem and its temple.

This sober theology is a difficult perspective for the modern reader to absorb within the context of Christian faith. Even more problematic are Matthew's words in 27:25—"His blood be on us and on our children"—a text that has been used repeatedly in Christian history and with disastrous consequences to justify persecution of Jews. The modern interpreter is responsible for understanding the limits of Matthew's perspective within the temporal and cultural context of the Gospel.

Crucifixion and Death (27:32-56)

The Passion story reaches its climax with the crucifixion and death of Jesus. Matthew continues to follow the narrative sequence and virtually all of the content of Mark's account. But Matthew's strong Christology, particularly his portrayal of Jesus as obedient Son of God, his emphasis on scriptural fulfillment, and his conviction that the death and resurrection of Jesus form a turning point in salvation history, add important new features to the Passion story.

This portion of the narrative can be divided into three episodes: (1) the way of the cross and the moment of crucifixion (27:32-37); (2) the mockery of Jesus on the cross (27:38-44); and (3) the death of Jesus (27:45-56).

◊ ◊ ◊ ◊

The Way of the Cross and the Moment of Crucifixion (27:32-37): Matthew's description of the way of the cross and the moment of crucifixion itself is sober and spare. After finishing their mockery of Jesus, the governor's soldiers lead Jesus out to be crucified (27:31-32). The traditional site for public executions was outside the city walls and Matthew is aware of this; in the parable of the vineyard, the son was taken "outside" the vineyard to be killed (21:39).

The soldiers impound "a man from Cyrene named Simon" to carry the cross for Jesus. Matthew omits the bit of information Mark offers about Simon (cf. Mark 15:21, "who was coming in from the country, . . . the father of Alexander and Rufus"). The suggestion is overly subtle that Matthew omitted the reference to Simon's coming in from the countryside because it may have implied that he was working on the sabbath. Matthew routinely omits narrative details found in Mark and that is the case here. Neither Mark nor Matthew seems to emphasize the exemplary character of Simon's action as a type of discipleship, but Luke does so (cf. Luke 23:26, "and they laid the cross on him, and made him carry it behind Jesus").

The procession ends at "a place called Golgotha," a Hebrew word that Matthew translates as "Place of a Skull" (27:33). No information is given as to whether this name was applied to the site because executions took place there or because it was shaped like a skull. Once arrived, the soldiers offer Jesus wine to drink, "mixed with gall," but after tasting it he refuses to take it (27:34). The drink was probably intended to be a mild narcotic offered to the condemned prisoner, but Matthew sees a deeper significance here. He changes Mark's "mixed with myrrh" (15:23) to "mixed with *gall*," aligning it with Ps 69:21: "They gave me poison for food, and for my thirst they gave me vinegar to drink." This psalm is one of the "lament" psalms, in which God's servant pours out his heart in the midst of torment. Matthew uses this and another lament, Ps 22, as important backdrops for the crucifixion scene.

The moment of crucifixion itself is passed over quickly in a subordinate clause ("and when they had crucified him . . .") and the attention of the text falls on another point of scriptural fulfillment. The soldiers divide up Jesus' clothes "by casting lots," the first of several allusions to Ps 22 in Matthew's account: "They divide my clothes among themselves and for my clothing they cast lots" (Ps 22:18; some manuscripts incorporate this quotation in the text as another of Matthew's fulfillment quotations, but it is probably a later insertion).

Having completed their gruesome task of attaching Jesus to the cross, the soldiers "sat down there and kept watch over him"

(27:36). Matthew's formulation emphasizes the watchful presence of the soldiers. Peter had taken up a similar posture in the courtyard of the high priest: "He sat with the guards in order to see how this would end" (26:58). And, after Jesus' death, Mary Magdalene and the "other Mary" would keep vigil, "sitting opposite the tomb" (27:61). The soldiers, therefore, become observant witnesses of the momentous events that are about to take place and, under the impact of Jesus' death, these same soldiers "who were keeping watch over Jesus" would acclaim him as "God's Son" (27:54).

Matthew also notes that a placard was attached to the cross over Jesus' head, inscribed with the charge against him: "This is Jesus, the King of the Jews" (27:37). The title recalls the preceding trial scene where Jesus' identity as "King of the Jews" had been the focus of Pilate's questions and the soldiers' mockery (27:11, 29).

The Mockery of Jesus on the Cross (27:38-44): For the third time in the Passion story Jesus is subjected to derision and mockery (see above, 26:67-68; 27:27-31). Flanking Jesus are two crucified "bandits" (this is a good translation of the Greek word *lēstai*, which suggests something more than a generic criminal and yet less than a revolutionary). The fact that Jesus is associated with bandits is probably meant to be part of the humiliation heaped by the authorities on the "King of the Jews." There may also be a level of irony here in that Jesus had deliberately associated with "sinners" during his public ministry and provoked the ire of his opponents for doing so (see, e.g., 9:10-11; 11:18-19).

A procession of mockers pass by the cross (27:39-44). A first group passes by "shaking their heads" as they fling their taunts at Jesus, a curious gesture that is another allusion to Ps 22: "All who see me mock at me; they make mouths at me, they *shake their heads*" (v. 7, emphasis added). Their words of mockery recall the accusation made against Jesus in the hearing before the high priest (see 26:61). There, as here, the taunt is directed at Jesus' supposed claims to messianic authority over the temple. The mockers add the words, "Save yourself!" (27:40). The challenge to "save yourself" is both ironic and paradoxical in that earlier in the Gospel Jesus had instructed his disciples, "For those who want to save their life will lose it, and those who lose their life for my sake will find it" (16:25). The term "save" *(sōson)* has a profound meaning in Matthew's Gospel, used in the infancy narrative to interpret Jesus' very name and to describe his mission as "saving" his people from their sins (1:21). In moments of distress, the disciples had cried out to Jesus to "save" them (see 8:25; 14:30) and the verb is used in healing stories to describe the full effect of Jesus' miraculous healings (see, e.g., 9:21, 22) or to refer to salvation more generically (see, e.g., 10:22; 16:25; 19:25; 24:13, 22; 27:49).

Matthew extends the words of the mockers: "If you are the Son of God, come down from the cross" (27:40). In the temptation story, the devil had twice introduced his attempts to lure Jesus with the identical phrase, "If you are the Son of God . . ." (4:3, 6). In this context, the title "Son of God" connotes the fidelity of Jesus the Messiah to God's will—the precise point of Jesus' retorts to the demon (see 4:4, 7, 10). In the crucifixion scene the demonic presence is felt once again, but this time in the guise of the mockers who attempt to lure Jesus from the cross: "Come down from the cross." However, the reader is fully aware that Jesus is destined for the cross and that Jesus' death is in accord with the Scriptures (see, e.g., 26:54, 56).

The "chief priests," "scribes," and "elders" form the second set of mockers (27:41-43). Their taunts, too, attempt to separate Jesus from the cross and challenge his identity as God's Son. Their words "he saved others; he cannot save himself" also have ironic echoes with the discipleship saying of Jesus earlier in the Gospel (see 16:25). From Matthew's vantage point, precisely in "losing" his life on the cross, Jesus will "save his people from their sins" (see 1:21; 26:28). Just as the first set of mockers had recalled a charge from the hearing before the Sanhedrin, the religious leaders hurl at Jesus an accusation from the Roman trial: "He is the King of Israel; let him come down from the cross now, and we will believe in him." Where Pilate and the soldiers had referred to Jesus as "King of the Jews" (27:11, 29, 37), the religious leaders use the more religiously charged term "King of *Israel*." "Jews" is simply an ethnic designation; "Israel" connotes the religious identity of the people chosen by God and therefore "King of Israel" has strong messianic implications.

Matthew alone adds a final verse to the mockery: "He trusts in God; let God deliver him now, if he wants to; for he said, 'I am God's Son' " (27:43). This is an adaptation of a quotation from Ps 22:8, "Commit your cause to the LORD; let him deliver—let him rescue the one in whom he delights!" But it also recalls Wis 2:18 (which itself probably alluded to Ps 22:8): "For if the righteous man is God's child [literally, "son"], he will help him, and will deliver him from the hand of his adversaries." Matthew portrays Jesus not only as the suffering Israelite in the psalm of lament, but as the righteous or just man portrayed in the Wisdom of Solomon who is mocked for his trust in God and suffers greatly because of it, yet is ultimately vindicated by God (on the influence of the "suffering just man" motif on the Passion story, see Marcus 1995, 206-12).

Matthew notes that even the bandits who were crucified with Jesus join in taunting him, a possible allusion to Ps 69:9: "The insults of those who insult you have fallen on me." By concluding this scene with an emphasis on the vindication of Jesus' trust in God as God's Son, Matthew prepares the reader for the climactic death scene where Jesus will die with the words of Ps 22 on his lips and have his faith vindicated by the spectacular signs that erupt at the moment of his death.

The Death of Jesus (27:45-56): The dramatic scene of Jesus' death begins with the onset of "darkness . . . over the whole land" from noon until three in the afternoon (27:45, literally from the "sixth" to the "ninth" hour). Matthew gives an apocalyptic atmosphere to this momentous hour; his Gospel had already portrayed the end time as one in which "the sun will be darkened, and the moon will not give its light" (Matt 24:29, citing Joel 2:10). The description here of darkness spreading "over the whole land" from noon until three o'clock echoes Amos 8:9, "On that day, says the Lord GOD, I will make the sun go down at noon, and darken the earth in broad daylight," as well as Exod 10:22 where God instructs Moses to stretch out his hand and darkness descends "in all the land of Egypt."

At "about three o'clock" Jesus "cried out," using the opening words of Ps 22. Following the lead of Mark, Matthew first cites the text in Aramaic or Hebrew (the textual variants make it difficult to decide which) and then translates it: "My God, my God, why have you forsaken me?" (Ps 22:1). This extraordinary lament psalm describes in vivid detail the suffering and isolation of the Israelite who prays to God in the midst of distress. This psalm may have been used in connection with the Passion story in the earliest stages of the tradition prior to Mark's Gospel (on this, see Brown 1994, 1455-65; Senior 1985, 129-30).

Matthew expands the role of Ps 22 both by absorbing Mark's citations and adding additional ones—for example, the words of the mockers in 27:43. Yet Matthew's use of the psalm may be more fundamental than this. Matthew's version of the death scene seems to imply that Jesus recites the psalm at the very instant of his death. He cries out the opening verse of the psalm in 27:46 moments before he expires. And, at the very instant of death, Matthew states that Jesus "cried *again*" (27:50), not only using the adverb "again" to imply that Jesus repeated his previous "cry," but employing the verb *kraxas,* the word for "crying out" found repeatedly in Ps 22 to describe the lament of the psalmist (see Ps 22:2, 5, 24). In the spirit of the psalm, Jesus prays to his Father even in the midst of abject desolation, remaining the obedient Son of God to the end.

Jesus' faithful prayer does not impress the bystanders. Some of them, either through ignorance or, more likely, continuing the derision of Jesus, interpret his call "*Ēli, Ēli*" ("My God, My God") as a call for Elijah to rescue him. One of them runs to get a sponge soaked in vinegar (probably common wine) for Jesus to drink; thereby another allusion to Ps 69 may enter the story—"They gave me poison for food, and for my thirst they gave me vinegar to drink" (Ps 69:21). Others from the group, however, stop the man, wanting to see if "Elijah will come to *save [sōson]* him" (27:49). Matthew's formulation again utilizes the vocabulary of Ps 22 (see 22:5, 8, 21) and a word found in the previous mockeries (see above, 27:40, 42; cf. Mark 15:36, "to take him down").

Matthew describes the instant of Jesus' death in stark terms. Jesus cried out once again the psalm of lament in a loud voice and "breathed his last" (27:50). Literally, the Greek text states "he yielded up his spirit" *(aphēken to pneuma)*. This is a thoroughly Jewish way of describing the moment of death; the human person who is both "dust" and "spirit" *(pneuma)* yields back to God the life breath God had originally given (see, e.g., the reference to death in precisely these terms in Eccl 12:7 and Ps 104:27-30). For Matthew, Jesus dies fittingly, reciting the prayer of the just sufferer and obediently yielding his spirit to God.

Thus the evangelist casts the whole first part of the crucifixion scene in accord with the lament portion of Ps 22. Jesus, who is stripped, surrounded by malefactors, and mocked, dies with his voice raised to God in a prayer of tortured faith (Ps 22:1-21). Similarly the second half of the crucifixion scene (Matt 27:51-56), with its mood of muted triumph, will draw on the second half of the lament psalm, which speaks of God's vindication of the sufferer's trust and the exaltation of that trust throughout the nations and even into the reaches of sheol (see, e.g., Ps 22:22-31).

In Mark's version, after Jesus dies, the curtain of the temple is torn in two and the centurion who observes the manner of Jesus' death acclaims him as Son of God (Mark 15:38-39; on Mark's death scene, see Senior 1984, 121-32). In Matthew, the death of Jesus instantly (note "at that moment," 27:51) triggers a series of extraordinary events, beginning with the tearing of the temple curtain, then an earthquake, the splitting of rocks, the opening of tombs, and the emergence of "saints" who enter the Holy City and appear to "many." In response to this string of "happenings" the centurion and his companions acclaim Jesus.

All of these events are tied together (all are linked by *kai*, "and . . .") and lead to the acclamation by the soldiers, a point Matthew explicitly makes by stating that their witness of the "earthquake and what took place" prompted both their "fear" and their confession of Jesus as Son of God (27:54; cf. Mark 15:39). Thus the tearing of the curtain of the temple (probably referring to the great curtain or veil that shrouded the entrance to the innermost sanctuary or "Holy of Holies") continues in one great seismic event that shakes the earth, splits the rocks, and opens the tombs to free the dead. All of this is described in the passive voice, probably the so-called divine passive implying that God is the ultimate source of these events that serve as a vindication of Jesus' faithful death.

Matthew draws a straight line from the death of Jesus to the liberation of "the holy ones" or "saints" who had been "asleep" within their tombs, but now experience resurrection. This redemptive power of Jesus' death fulfills the promise implicit in Jesus' name (1:21), which is demonstrated in his healings (8:17), is foretold at the Last Supper (26:28), and is now extended to the realm of the dead. However, this affirmation creates a problem narratively and perhaps even doctrinally for Matthew in that the resurrection of the saints and their appearances in the Holy City seem to occur before Jesus' own resurrection and inaugural appearances to the women and the eleven (28:1-10, 16-20). To offset this, Matthew notes somewhat awkwardly that the risen saints emerge from the tombs and begin their appearances only "after his resurrection."

The signs that accompany Jesus' death also serve Matthew's apocalyptic interpretation of Jesus' death and its harmony with the Scriptures. In the apocalyptic discourse Jesus had linked the destruction of the temple with the events leading to the end time (24:1-2); the tearing of the temple curtain, now linked with other apocalyptic signs in 27:51-53, implies an act of judgment against the sanctuary. Earthquakes, splitting of rocks, and opening of tombs are all events found in biblical and noncanonical Jewish texts as typical apocalyptic events (see, e.g., Judg 5:4; 2 Sam 22:8; Pss 68:8; 104:32; Joel 4:14-17; 4 Ezra 9:2-3; 2 Bar 32:1; *1 Enoch* 1:3-9).

Two texts that may have had direct influence on the formulation of 27:51-53 are Dan 12:1-2 and Ezek 37:11-14 (see Senior 1987, 272-94). Daniel 12:1-2 refers to the raising of the dead at the end time: "There shall be a time of anguish, such as has never occurred since nations first came into existence. But at that time your people shall be delivered, everyone who is found written in the book. *Many of those who sleep in the dust of the earth shall awake . . ."* (emphasis added). The vision of the dry bones in Ezek 37 has even more striking parallels to Matthew's text, particularly the reference to the "opening of graves" and the procession of the raised dead back "to the land of Israel" (Ezek 37:12). The famous Ezekiel panel in the third-century CE Dura-Europos synagogue frescoes indicated that the event in Ezekiel was interpreted messianically in later Judaism and Matthew's own application of the text to the death of Jesus would reflect a similar tradition (Senior 1976, 312-29). By portraying the impact of Jesus' death in colors drawn from these apocalyptic biblical texts, Matthew affirms that the death and resurrection usher in the final age of salvation and that all of these events fulfill the promise of the Scriptures.

The scene concludes with the testimony of witnesses (27:54-56). When the centurion and "those with him, who were keeping watch over Jesus" (see above, 27:36) see the events that happen after Jesus' death they are "terrified" and acclaim: "Truly this man was God's Son!" (27:54). Ironically, the Roman soldiers who had crucified Jesus become the first group to testify to God's vindication of Jesus. By his formulation in 27:40, 43, Matthew accentuated Jesus' trust in God and his claim to be God's Son as the underlying issue of the crucifixion scene. God's response to Jesus' death by the series of apocalyptic signs and now through the confession of the centurion and his companions (Matthew adds these to the list of witnesses; cf. Mark 15:39) vindicates that trust and confirms the identity of Jesus as God's Son.

Matthew also notes the presence of "many women" who had followed Jesus from Galilee, and "provided for him" (literally, "served him," using the quasi-technical term for discipleship, *diakonein*; see above, 20:28). The list of names is slightly different from that found in Mark. Matthew refers to "the mother of the sons of Zebedee" rather than to "Salome" (see above, 20:20-21). Mary Magdalene and "the other Mary [Mary the mother of James and Joseph]" will be witnesses to the burial (27:61) and the empty tomb (28:1). In 13:55 Matthew lists "James and Joseph" among the "brothers" of Jesus. It seems unlikely that Matthew identifies "Mary the Mother of James and Joseph" (or the "other Mary" as he refers to her in 27:61 and 28:1) with Jesus' own mother. Even though Matthew describes these women as "looking on from a distance," he probably includes them in a positive way with those who confess Jesus as Son of God. Matthew notes they are "there" at Golgotha (27:55; cf. Mark 15:40) and will present them as observant witnesses to the burial (27:61) and the first to encounter the Risen Jesus (28:9-10).

◊ ◊ ◊ ◊

From the vantage point of the Gospel, Jesus' obedient death and his trust in God are fully vindicated through the signs that erupt at the moment of Jesus' death and through the impact on the soldiers and faithful women who testify that Jesus is indeed the Son of God. The allusion to Scripture throughout these scenes—particularly the lament psalms 69 and 22, as well as the influence of Dan 12:1-2 and Ezek 37—affirms once again that Jesus' entire mission fulfills the Scriptures.

The crucifixion scenes also express Matthew's view of Jesus' death as redemptive. Through the death of Jesus, the dead are liberated from their tombs, and the salvific mission of Jesus, implicit in his very name and enacted in his ministry of healing, comes to its most powerful expression.

And, finally, Matthew's interpretation of these scenes also serves his view of what we might call "salvation history." For Matthew, the death and the resurrection of Jesus usher in the final age of history in which salvation will be effected. As signs of the end time erupt on Golgotha, Jesus' rejection as Messiah by the leaders and the "people as a whole" is thwarted, God's judgment against the Jerusalem temple is anticipated, and a new people who acclaim Jesus as Son of God begin to appear. Matthew lays the groundwork for the final words of Jesus in the Gospel when the Risen Jesus will extend the mission of the disciples to the ends of the earth and the End of time (see 28:16-20).

Vigil at the Tomb (27:57-66)

These two scenes, the burial of Jesus (27:57-61) and the setting of a guard at the tomb (27:62-66), serve as a transition between the events of Jesus' Passion and death, and the resurrection. The story of the setting of the guard at the tomb is special to Matthew and represents his typical perspective on the enduring and futile opposition of the religious leaders against Jesus.

◊ ◊ ◊ ◊

The Burial of Jesus (27:57-61): When "evening" arrives, Joseph of Arimathea comes on the scene. Matthew differs from Mark in his overall characterization of Joseph. In Mark, Joseph is a "respected member of the council, who was also himself waiting expectantly for the kingdom of God" (Mark 15:43). In Matthew's version, Joseph is a "rich man . . . who was also a disciple of Jesus" (27:57). Likewise, the exchange with Pilate is also different. In Mark, Joseph summons up his courage and asks Pilate for the body of Jesus. But Pilate hesitates, first wondering if Jesus was already dead and verifying it with the centurion before releasing the body to Joseph (Mark 15:43-45). In Matthew's story, there is no hesitation: Joseph asks Pilate for the body of Jesus and permission is immediately given (27:58).

Matthew's description of the burial itself also has subtle differences from Mark's version. Joseph takes the body, wraps it in a "clean linen cloth," lays it in "his own new tomb, which he had hewn in the rock," rolls a "great" stone to the door, and departs (27:60; cf. Mark 15:46). In each detail Matthew follows through on his description of Joseph as a "rich" disciple—the tomb is new and belongs to Joseph personally, the stone is "great," signifying an appropriately large tomb.

Along with Matthew's typical economy in narrative detail, one suspects that these changes are also intended to make a point. In Mark's version the stance of Joseph may have some degree of ambiguity. Although he does a good deed for Jesus and is "waiting expectantly for the kingdom of God" (15:43; similar to the good scribe in Mark 12:34), he is also identified as "a respected member of the council" and not as a full disciple of Jesus. In Matthew's story Joseph *is* a disciple, albeit a "rich" one, and his actions on behalf of Jesus are decisive and unhesitating. Being "rich" has ambiguous status in Matthew's Gospel as illustrated in the story of the rich young man for whom the lure of wealth is an obstacle to following Jesus (19:16-26). Jesus warns the disciples that the rich will have difficulty entering the kingdom of heaven (19:23-26). Yet there is some evidence that Matthew's community may have included prosperous members (e.g., Matthew consistently inflates amounts of money found in Mark's parallels and in general refers more frequently to gold, silver, and other types of coins; see Kingsbury 1986, 97-98) and perhaps the evangelist uses Joseph as an example of a rich disciple who unhesitatingly risks exposure to the authorities out of devotion to the crucified Jesus. This devotion of Joseph will also contrast sharply with the unyielding hostility of the "chief priests and the Pharisees" in the following story (see 27:62-66).

The scene concludes with a reference to "Mary Magdalene" and the "other Mary" (identified in 27:56 as "Mary the mother of James and Joseph") who are "sitting opposite the tomb" (27:61). This posture, reminiscent of the watchful stance of the soldiers near the cross of Jesus (see 27:36, 54), alerts the reader to the witness role these same two women will play in the discovery of the empty tomb (28:1). The women also serve as a thread that runs from the conclusion of the crucifixion account where they, among others, stand faithfully by to witness Jesus' death (27:55-56), through the burial, and on into the discovery of the empty tomb and the first encounter with the Risen Christ (28:9-10).

The Setting of a Guard (27:62-66): The story of the setting of a guard at the tomb of Jesus is unique to Matthew (on this text, see Senior 1992, 1433-48).

After a long hiatus the "Pharisees" return as one of the major sources of opposition to Jesus (see above, 23:39), here allied with "the chief priests" (27:62). During Jesus' public ministry the "Pharisees," along with the "scribes," were his implacable opponents; during the Passion story that role fell to the "chief priests and elders of the people." Now both sets of opponents gather before Pilate to ask for a guard to seal the tomb.

The opponents unwittingly prepare for the story of the Resurrection by recalling Jesus' own prediction that "after three days I will rise again" (27:63; see 16:21; 17:23; 20:19). They also anticipate the heart of the Christian proclamation by their fear that Jesus' disciples "will tell the people, 'He has been raised from the dead' " and that such a message would have a great impact (27:64). The opponents, of course, judge Jesus to be an "impostor" (27:63) and the disciples as likely to steal Jesus' body from the tomb (26:64). The story no doubt anticipates the kind of counterarguments to Christian claims about the resurrection that Matthew's community had heard from their Jewish opponents (see below, 28:15).

Pilate continues to play the somewhat cynical and laconic role he had in his dealings with the religious leaders in the course of the Roman trial. The leaders are told, "You have a guard of soldiers; go, make it as secure as you can" (27:65; literally, "as you know how"). In view of the empty tomb story that follows, and the panic-stricken confusion of the guard, the reference to "[making] the tomb secure by sealing the stone" (27:66) is an ironic note, demonstrating the completely futile efforts of the opponents to thwart God's will regarding Jesus.

◊ ◊ ◊ ◊

Both of these stories help the reader move from the dramatic and poignant events of the Passion to the triumphant resurrection scenes. In the crucifixion scene the explosive events following the death of Jesus led to the confession of the centurion and his companions and to the faithful witness of the women at the cross. That homage continues now in the burial scenes through the devotion of Joseph of Arimathea, a rich disciple who gives his own tomb for Jesus' burial, and through the continuing presence of the women who witness the events. But the opposition to Jesus that was constant during his public ministry and led to his death also resurfaces here in the persons of the Pharisees and chief priests who brand Jesus an "impostor" and mock his claim that he would rise from the dead.

The Empty Tomb (28:1-15)

Matthew begins the Gospel's account of the resurrection with the discovery of the empty tomb as in Mark's Gospel (28:1-8; Mark 16:1-8), but goes far beyond it, adding an appearance of the Risen Jesus to the women (28:9-10) and the story about the bribing of the guards (28:11-15). All of this prepares for the final scene of the Gospel where Jesus appears to the "eleven" in Galilee (28:16-20).

◊ ◊ ◊ ◊

The Discovery of the Empty Tomb (28:1-8): At dawn on Sunday morning—that is, after the conclusion of the sabbath (which ran from Friday sundown to Saturday sundown) and on "the first day of the week"—the two Marys who had witnessed the burial (27:61) now come "to see the tomb" (28:1), part of their continuing homage to Jesus. In Mark's version the women come to *anoint* Jesus (Mark 16:1), but Matthew had already emphatically described the anointing of Jesus by the woman in Bethany as a burial anointing (see 26:12).

Matthew omits Mark's details of the women's concern about the stone sealing the tomb and their discovery that it had already been rolled back, because he will describe the very moment of the unsealing of the tomb in vivid apocalyptic detail (Matt 28:2-3; cf. Mark 16:3-4). Although none of the canonical Gospels attempt to describe the actual moment of resurrection, Matthew's Gospel edges toward it. There is a "great earthquake" and an "angel of the Lord" descends from heaven, rolls back the stone, and sits on it. The angel's appearance is "like lightning" and his clothing "white as snow." In Mark's account a "young man" sitting inside the tomb serves as the heavenly messenger (16:5), but in Matthew this role is taken by an "angel of the Lord." In the infancy narrative an "angel of the Lord" had appeared to Joseph in dreams to interpret the meaning of Mary's pregnancy and to give Joseph his charge to protect the mother and child (1:20-23; 2:13, 19). The angel will perform a similar function for the women at the tomb.

The angel's appearance completely neutralizes the guards put there by Jesus' opponents; they "shake" and they become "like dead men" (see 28:4). Matthew extends into the empty tomb story the apocalyptic atmosphere that erupted at the moment of Jesus' death (see above, 27:51-53). The resurrection of Jesus coincides with the advent of the new and final age of salvation. The awesome events that followed Jesus' death, with special emphasis on the "earthquake," also provoked "terror" in the soldiers guarding the cross, just as the events at the tomb do (the word *phobos* implies "fear" or "awe" and the term *seismos,* or "earthquake," is used in both texts; see 27:54 and 28:4). However, the guards at the tomb do not confess Jesus as Son of God but remain under the sway of the leaders (see 28:11-15).

The angel soothes the women's fear and interprets the meaning of the empty tomb for them: "I know that you are looking for Jesus who was crucified. He is not here; for he has been raised, as he said. Come, see the place where he lay" (28:5-6). The reference to Jesus' own predictions about his resurrection recalls the Passion predictions made earlier in the Gospel (16:21; 17:22-23; 20:18-19). The angel also commissions the women to go "quickly" and tell the disciples that "he has been raised from the dead, and indeed he is going ahead of you to Galilee; there you will see him. This is my message for you" (28:7).

In Matthew's account the angel urges the women to go "quickly," anticipating their eager departure at the end of the scene (28:8). They are to alert the disciples (Matthew omits any specific reference to Peter; cf. Mark 16:7) to the resurrection and to the promised encounter in "Galilee." In Mark 16:7 the promise is based on Jesus' words: "as he told you"; in Matthew the promised encounter is part of the heavenly message: "This is my message for you." The original ending of Mark's Gospel did not include a final resurrection appearance of Jesus with his disciples, leaving open the possibility that the encounter promised in the empty tomb story may refer to the return of Jesus at the *parousia* rather than resurrection appearances (see Mark 16:1-8; on this, see Lincoln 1995, 229-51). But there is no ambiguity in Matthew's version. The fact that Matthew will narrate the appearance of Jesus to the eleven in Galilee gives the angel's instructions urgency and focus. The disciples are to assemble in "Galilee," the region where Jesus' mission had begun and a place that symbolized for Matthew the universal scope of the church's mission (see 4:12-17, "Galilee of the Gentiles").

Obedient to the angel's instructions, the women leave the tomb "quickly" and "run" to tell the disciples (see 28:7, 9). Their emotions of "fear" or "awe" *(phobos)* and "great joy" are appropriate for those who have experienced a theophany and heard the Easter message (in contrast to the ambiguity many interpreters see in the fear and silence of the women in Mark's story; cf. Mark 16:8; see, e.g., Lincoln 1995).

Appearance of the Risen Jesus to the Women (28:9-10): In a scene unique to his Gospel, Matthew reports a first appearance of the Risen Jesus to the two women as they set out on their way to alert the disciples. Although there are some similarities to John's account of the appearance to Mary Magdalene (John 20:14-18), it is likely that the present form of Matthew's story is a composition of the evangelist.

Jesus greets the women in a normal fashion (see a similar typical greeting on the part of Judas in the garden, 26:49). They approach the Risen Jesus in a reverent, worshipful manner; the verb *proselthon* is used throughout the Gospel to describe the approach of the sick or other petitioners to Jesus (see, e.g., 8:2, 5, 19, 25; 9:14, 20, 28; 13:10, 36; 15:30; 17:14; 18:21; 19:16; 20:20; 21:14; 26:7). Here the word is coupled with the gesture of clasping his feet and "worshiping" him (*prosekynēsan;* see above, 14:33); "clasping his feet" expresses profound obeisance and underscores that this is not a ghost, emphasizing the identification of the Risen Jesus with Jesus of Nazareth.

Jesus' instructions to the women virtually repeat that of the angel at the tomb: They are not to be afraid, but are to go and tell "my brothers" to go to Galilee where they will see Jesus (28:10; cf. 28:7). The address "my brothers" echoes earlier passages in the Gospel where the disciples of Jesus were described as the "family" of Jesus, as well as the manner in which community members were to address one another (see 12:46-50; 18:15, 16, 17, 21, 35).

In Luke's account, the women who discover the empty tomb and report it to the disciples are met with skepticism and their testimony must be confirmed by Peter (see Luke 24:1-12). In Matthew's version, however, these same women were present at the crucifixion, witnessed the burial, discovered the empty tomb, were commissioned by an "angel of the Lord" and now, most extraordinary of all, meet the Risen Jesus on their way to the disciples. Their authority as bearers of the resurrection message is unchallenged and the eleven apostles will gather in Galilee as they had been instructed (28:16-20).

The Bribery of the Guards (28:11-15): This scene, unique to Matthew, provides the sequel to the leaders' futile attempt to thwart the resurrection story by setting a guard at the tomb (see 27:62-66) and serves as a foil to the exemplary response of the women in the previous two episodes. At the very moment the women are on their way with the Easter message to the disciples, "some of the guard" who had been posted at the tomb and were overwhelmed by the fearsome appearance of the angel (28:4) go into the city to report to the chief priests "everything that had happened" (28:11).

The chief priests form a council with the elders and decide to bribe the soldiers with "a large sum of money" (28:12). Their action recalls a similar ploy in paying Judas to betray Jesus (see above, 26:14-16; 27:3-10). The soldiers are instructed to spread a false story about what happened at the tomb; the suggestion that the disciples had stolen the body from the tomb was the same excuse the leaders had used earlier in pressing Pilate to give permission for a guard (27:64). The leaders promise to protect the soldiers if the story's report of their having fallen asleep reaches the ears of the governor.

The entire episode presents the leaders in the worst possible light. They not only refuse to listen to the soldiers' report of what had happened at the tomb (28:11), but create a false explanation for the empty tomb that, Matthew notes, "is still told among the Jews to this day" (28:15). No doubt this comment reflects the experience of Matthew's own community in its polemical encounters with other non-Christian Jewish groups. The Gospel's explanation for the empty tomb is presented with the sure authority of an "angel of the Lord," whereas the story that Jesus' dead body was stolen by the disciples is concocted by discredited religious leaders. The generic reference to "the Jews" rather than to a specific leadership group is unusual in Matthew and seems to imply a growing distance between his own mixed community of Jews and Gentiles and other Jewish groups.

◊ ◊ ◊ ◊

The tomb stories continue Matthew's dual focus on Christology and discipleship in this part of the narrative. Jesus' triumph over death is proclaimed by an "angel of the Lord" at the empty tomb, confirming the vindication already signaled in the events that erupted at the cross. This resurrection marks the beginning of the final age of the world.

The two women, Mary Magdalene and "the other Mary," are exemplary disciples whose fidelity to the crucified and buried Jesus is rewarded when they receive the resurrection message at the tomb, are commissioned to bring the good news to the disciples, and encounter the Risen Jesus himself.

By contrast, the Jewish leaders demonstrate once again the stereotyped role Matthew's Gospel confers on them. They bribe the guards to lie about their experience at the tomb and spread a story that attempts to undermine the truth of the resurrection message.

All of these scenes help prepare for the finale of Matthew's Gospel when the eleven disciples, now alerted by the women's report, gather in Galilee and are commissioned by the Risen Jesus to spread the gospel message to the ends of the earth.

THE FINALE (28:16-20)

Matthew concludes his narrative with a resurrection appearance story unique to his Gospel. Jesus' promise at the Last Supper to "go ahead" of the disciples "to Galilee" (26:32), the message of the angel to the women at the empty tomb (28:7), and the Risen Jesus' own instructions to the women (28:10) are now fulfilled in this majestic mountaintop scene.

Most of the language and content is Matthean and it is likely that the evangelist composed this scene as the finale to his Gospel and as a summary of some of its most fundamental motifs. While John 21 reports resurrection appearances in Galilee, none of them are similar to Matthew's text. The appearance to the eleven in Mark 16:14-20 has probably been influenced by Matthew's account but remains quite different in setting and content. Interpreters are divided about what literary models or influences stand behind this text (see Hubbard 1974). The apocalyptic vision of Dan 7:14 is one likely influence, with its description of the exaltation of the "Son of Man," the impact on "all peoples, nations, and languages," and the promise of an everlasting kingship. Others have compared this scene to the mountaintop theophany in Exod 19–20 or to commissioning texts such as that of Cyrus in 2 Chr 36:23 where Israel is sent home from exile.

The text falls into two major segments: (1) 28:16-18, the appearance of the Risen Jesus to his disciples and the assertion of his authority; (2) 28:19-20, the commission of Jesus to his disciples and the promise of his abiding presence.

◊ ◊ ◊ ◊

The "eleven" disciples obey the message presumably transmitted by the two women, and go to Galilee (28:16). Unlike Luke, who is eager to have the symbolic number of the "twelve" reconstituted (see Acts 1:15-26), Matthew leaves the number incomplete, thereby reminding the reader of the tragic failure of Judas (see above, 27:3-10). The disciples go to a "mountain," an important setting in this Gospel for moments of revelation and teaching (see 4:8; 5:1; 15:29; 17:1; see Donaldson 1985).

There they encounter the Risen Jesus (28:17, "When they saw him . . ."). The disciples respond with reverence, "worshiping" him (Matthew's typical word *proskynein;* see 14:33; 28:9). Curiously, however, Matthew notes "but some doubted." The Greek phrase *hoi de edistasan* is ambiguous. The verb *distazō* implies doubt or hesitation in the face of challenge, as in Peter's response when confronted with the strength of the wind and waves as he walks on the water (see 14:31, "Why did you doubt *[edistasas]*?"). The phrase *hoi de edistasan* leaves it unclear whether *all* of the disciples doubted, or whether only *some,* since it could be translated either way. Given Matthew's portrayal of the disciples as of "little faith" (see above, 6:30; 8:26; 14:31; cf. 17:20), the text may be asserting that the disciples worshiped Jesus, yet remained weak and hesitant in this moment of their first encounter with the Risen Christ.

Their hesitation may be the reason Matthew portrays Jesus as "approaching" them (see 28:18); here he uses his characteristic word *proselthon,* often used in the healing stories to describe the reverent approach of the sick to Jesus (e.g., 8:2, 5, 25; 9:20, 28; 15:30; 17:14; 21:14). Now the Risen Jesus himself approaches his hesitant disciples to reveal his full authority and to commission them. The declaration that "all authority in heaven and on earth has been given to me" recalls the text of Dan 7:14 ("To him was given dominion and glory and kingship, that all peoples, nations, and languages should serve him. His dominion is an everlasting dominion that shall not pass away, and his kingship is one that shall never be destroyed.") and thereby affirms Jesus' identity as the exalted Son of Man. The Jesus who suffered and was humiliated has now been fully vindicated by God. In the apocalyptic discourse the triumphant return of the Son of Man at the end time was a recurring motif (see 24:30-31, 37, 39, 44; 25:31). In Matthew's perspective, the final age began with the moment of Jesus' death and resurrection (see 27:51-53; 28:2-3) and now the exalted Son of Man returns as promised in an anticipation of the final *parousia.* This is what Jesus himself had warned Caiaphas during the Passion, *"From now on* you will see the Son of Man seated at the right hand of Power and coming on the clouds of heaven" (26:64).

The power and authority of the Risen Jesus stand behind the mission now entrusted to the disciples. Several elements are compressed in Jesus' words:

1. They are to "go . . . and make disciples of all nations" (28:19). The term "make disciples" *(matheteusate)* is the verb form of Matthew's favored term "disciple" (both the ideal "scribe" and Joseph of Arimathea were described as ones who had "been discipled"; 13:52; 27:57). Now the disciples themselves are to call and instruct followers of Jesus in the same manner they themselves had experienced (see 4:18-22 and the mission discourse of chap. 10).

Previously the mission of Jesus and the disciples was restricted to "the lost sheep of the house of Israel" (10:5; 15:24) and, except for rare encounters with individual Gentiles, Matthew's description of the mission of Jesus observed that restriction. Now, however, the disciples are sent to "all nations." The precise meaning of this extension is a major point of debate for interpreters (see Hare and Harrington 1975, 359-69, and Meier 1977, 94-102). Does the term "all nations" include Israel as one among many peoples, and therefore mean that, along with the continuing mission to Israel, Matthew's community is also to reach out to Gentiles? Or does the term "nations" refer exclusively to Gentiles and therefore imply that the mission to Israel has ceased and now Matthew's community will go only to Gentiles? While in Matthew the word *ethnē* ("nations" or "peoples") usually refers to "Gentiles," there is some ambiguity (see above, 25:31-46). In 28:19 Jesus does not explicitly forbid the mission to Israel, in contrast to the prohibition of the Gentile and Samaritan missions in 10:5. Matthew may present these words of the Risen Jesus as a turning point in the mission history of his community when their efforts would be concentrated on including Gentiles without, however, forbidding a continuing mission among Jews. That turn to the Gentiles was prompted by the relative failure of the mission among Matthew's fellow Jews and, more important for Matthew, by the eschatological authority of the Risen Jesus. Jesus' new commission to the eleven, therefore, fulfills the vision he spoke of after encountering the centurion's extraordinary faith in Capernaum: "Many will come from east and west and will eat with Abraham and Isaac and Jacob in the kingdom of heaven, while the heirs of the kingdom will be thrown into the outer darkness, where there will be weeping and gnashing of teeth" (8:11-12).

2. The disciples are to "baptiz[e] them in the name of the Father and of the Son and of the Holy Spirit" (28:19). This appears to be a liturgical formula imported from Matthew's community (see a similar early Christian Trinitarian formula in *Did.* 7:1-3). What were varied references to "Father," "Son," and "Holy Spirit" throughout the Gospel (for the latter, see 1:18, 20; 3:11, 16; 10:20; 12:28, 32; 22:43) are now drawn together into a fuller expression of the Christian experience of the divine presence. The instruction to the disciples is not only to make new disciples, but to incorporate them into the community through baptism. While Matthew does not refer to any explicit Trinitarian concepts earlier in the Gospel, his interest in the "church" as a corporate entity is clear (see, e.g., 16:17-19; 18:15-20).

3. Finally, the disciples receive a charge of "teaching them to obey everything that I have commanded you" (28:20). The authority of Jesus as teacher was first asserted in the Sermon on the Mount (chaps. 5–7) and continued in the major discourses throughout the Gospel. Matthew also strongly emphasized obedience to Jesus' commands (see, e.g., 5:17-20; 7:24-27). In the mission discourse "teaching" was not listed among the list of actions the disciples were empowered to do (see 10:7-8), but at the finale of the Gospel when the teaching of Jesus has been fully expressed (note: "*everything* I have commanded you"), the disciples are so commissioned.

The appearance concludes with Jesus' promise to remain with the community: "And remember, I am with you always, to the end of the age" (28:20). This recapitulates the promise implicit in Jesus' God-given name "Emmanuel" ("God with us"; cf. 1:22-23) and is reasserted in the community discourse ("For where two or three are gathered in my name, I am there among them," 18:20). In the mission discourse, Jesus had also affirmed his identification with the messengers sent in his name (10:40-42) and, in the final judgment parable, the "Son of Man" had stated his abiding presence with the "least" (25:31-46). Matthew, therefore, presents a different conception of the community's relationship to the Risen Christ than the other Gospels. For Mark, the community apparently still awaits the return of the Risen Jesus as exalted Son of Man at the *parousia* (Mark 16:7). In Luke and John, the Risen Jesus ascends (or in John's Gospel, is "lifted up" in exaltation) to God and sends the Spirit or Paraclete who remains with the community. For Matthew, however, the Risen Jesus himself is the equivalent to the divine presence within the community as it moves out into history. Matthew thus ratifies the authority, content, and scope of the community's mission by rooting it in the commands and abiding presence of the Risen Jesus.

◊ ◊ ◊ ◊

The finale of the Gospel recapitulates major aspects of Matthew's Christology and ecclesiology. Jesus is acclaimed as the Risen Christ and exalted Son of Man. The vindication of his obedience and trust as God's Son, already signaled at the moment of his death (27:51-

54) and at the empty tomb (28:1-10), is also now triumphantly proclaimed on the mountaintop as the Risen Jesus is worshiped by his disciples. At the same time Jesus' unique authority as teacher and interpreter of the law is confirmed.

Matthew's portrayal of discipleship and the authority of the community are also ratified here. Despite the disciples' hesitant faith, they are commissioned to make disciples of "all nations" and to baptize. They are also to teach everything commanded by Jesus. The opposition to Jesus that coursed through the Gospel and climaxed in the Passion story has proved futile. Now the mission entrusted to the community by Jesus will extend to "all nations" until "the end of the age."

SELECT BIBLIOGRAPHY

WORKS CITED IN THE TEXT
(EXCLUDING COMMENTARIES)

Allison, Dale C., Jr. 1993. *The New Moses: A Matthean Typology.* Minneapolis: Augsburg/Fortress.

Barth, Gerhard. 1963. "Matthew's Understanding of the Law." In *Tradition and Interpretation in Matthew,* edited by Günther Bornkamm, Gerhard Barth, Heinz Joachim Held, 58-164. Philadelphia: Westminster.

Barton, Stephen C. 1994. *Discipleship and Family Ties in Mark and Matthew.* SNTSMS 80. Cambridge: Cambridge University Press.

Bauer, David R. 1995. "The Kingship of Jesus in the Matthean Infancy Narrative: A Literary Analysis." *CBQ* 57:306-23.

Betz, Hans Dieter. 1995. *The Sermon on the Mount.* Hermeneia. Minneapolis: Fortress.

Birch, Bruce C., and Larry L. Rasmussen. 1978. *The Predicament of the Prosperous.* Philadelphia: Westminster.

Brown, Raymond E. 1965. "The Pater Noster as an Eschatological Prayer." In *New Testament Essays,* 217-53. New York: Doubleday.

———. 1977. *The Birth of the Messiah.* Garden City, NJ: Doubleday.

———. 1984. *The Churches the Apostles Left Behind.* New York: Paulist.

———. 1994. *The Death of the Messiah: From Gethsemane to the Grave.* Anchor Bible Reference Library. New York: Doubleday.

Brown, Raymond E., Karl Donfried, and John Reumann, eds. 1973. *Peter in the New Testament: A Collaborative Assessment by Protestant and Roman Catholic Scholars.* Minneapolis: Augsburg; New York: Paulist.

Cahill, Lisa Sowle. 1987. "The Ethical Implications of the Sermon on the Mount." *Interpretation* 41:144-56.

Carter, Warren. 1994a. *What Are They Saying About Matthew's Sermon on the Mount?* New York: Paulist.

———. 1994b. *Households and Discipleship: A Study of Matthew 19–20.* JSNTSup 103. Sheffield: JSOT.

Charlesworth, James H., ed. 1994. *The Lord's Prayer and Other Prayer Texts from the Greco-Roman Era.* Valley Forge, PA: Trinity Press International.

Collins, Raymond F. 1992. *Divorce in the New Testament.* Collegeville, MN: Liturgical Press, Michael Glazier.

Davies, W. D. 1964. *The Setting of the Sermon on the Mount.* Cambridge: Cambridge University Press.

Dodd, C. H. 1961. *The Parables of the Kingdom.* New York: Scribner's.

Donahue, John R., S.J. 1973. *Are You the Christ? The Trial Narrative in the Gospel of Mark.* SBLDS 10. Missoula: University of Montana Press.

————. 1988. *The Gospel in Parable.* Philadelphia: Fortress.

Donaldson, T. L. 1985. *Jesus on the Mountain.* JSNTSup 8. Sheffield: JSOT.

Donfried, Karl. 1974. "The Allegory of the Ten Virgins (Matt 25:1-13) as a Summary of Matthean Theology." *JBL* 93:415-28.

Dunn, James D. G. 1991. *The Partings of the Ways Between Christianity and Judaism and Their Significance for the Character of Christianity.* Philadelphia: Trinity Press International.

Evans, C. A. 1989. *To See and Not Perceive: Isaiah 6:9-11 in Early Jewish and Christian Interpretation.* JSOTSup 64. Sheffield: JSOT.

Fitzmyer, Joseph A. 1965. "Anti-semitism and the Cry of 'All the People' (Mt. 27:25)." *TS* 26:667-71.

————. 1974. "The Aramaic *qorbân* Inscription from Jebel Hallet et-Tûri and Mk 7:11/Mt 15:5." In *Essays on the Semitic Background of the New Testament,* 93-100. London: Chapman; Missoula, MT: Scholars Press.

Frankemölle, Hubert. 1974. *Jahwebund und Kirche Christi.* NTabh 10. Munich: Aschendorff.

Gerhardsson, Birger. 1966. *The Testing of God's Son (Matt 4:1-11 & Par).* Coniectanea Biblica New Testament Series 2:1. Lund, Sweden: CWK Gleerup.

Gray, S. W. 1989. *The Least of My Brothers: Matthew 25:31-46: A History of Interpretation.* SBLDS 114. Atlanta: Scholars Press.

Hare, Douglas R. A. 1967. *The Theme of Jewish Persecution of Christians in the Gospel According to St. Matthew.* SNTSMS 6. Cambridge: Cambridge University Press.

Hare, Douglas R. A. and D. J. Harrington. 1975. " 'Make Disciples of All the Gentiles' (Mt 28:19)," *CBQ* 37:359-69.

Harner, Philip B. 1975. *Understanding the Lord's Prayer.* Philadelphia: Fortress.

Held, Heinz Joachim. 1963. "Matthew as Interpreter of the Miracle Stories." In *Tradition and Interpretation in Matthew,* edited by Günther Bornkamm, Gerhard Barth, and Heinz Joachim Held, 165-300. Philadelphia: Westminster.

Holman, Charles L. 1996. *Till Jesus Comes: Origins of Christian Apocalyptic Expectation.* Peabody, MA: Hendrickson.

Howell, David B. 1990. *Matthew's Inclusive Story: A Study in the Narrative Rhetoric of the First Gospel.* JSNTSup 42. Sheffield: Sheffield Academic Press.

Hubbard, B. J. 1974. *The Matthean Redaction of a Primitive Apostolic Commissioning: An Exegesis of Matthew 28:16-20.* SBLDS 19. Missoula, MT: Society of Biblical Literature and Scholars Press.

Hummel, Reinhart. 1963. *Die Auseinandersetzung zwischen Kirche und Judentum im Matthäusevangelium.* Munich: Kaiser Verlag.

Jeremias, Joachim. 1963. *The Parables of Jesus.* New York: Scribner's.

Juel, Donald. 1977. *Messiah and Temple: The Trial of Jesus in the Gospel of Mark.* SBLDS 31. Missoula, MT: Scholars Press.

Kiley, Mark. 1994. "The Lord's Prayer and Matthean Theology." In *The Lord's Prayer and Other Prayer Texts from the Greco-Roman Era,* edited by James H. Charlesworth, 15-27. Valley Forge, PA: Trinity Press International.

Kingsbury, Jack Dean. 1969. *The Parables of Jesus in Matthew 13: A Study in Redaction Criticism.* Oxford: Clarendon.

———. 1975. *Matthew: Structure, Christology, Kingdom.* Philadelphia: Fortress.

———. 1979. "The Figure of Peter in Matthew's Gospel as a Theological Problem." *JBL* 98:67-83.

———. 1986. *Matthew.* Rev. ed. Proclamation Commentaries. Philadelphia: Fortress.

Klassen, William. 1984. *Love of Enemies: The Way to Peace.* OBT. Philadelphia: Fortress.

Knowles, M. 1993. *Jeremiah in Matthew's Gospel: The Rejected-Prophet Motif in Matthean Redaction.* JSNTSup 68. Sheffield: JSOT.

Kodell, Jerome. 1988. *The Eucharist in the New Testament.* Zacchaeus Studies. Wilmington, DE: Michael Glazier.

LaVerdiere, Eugene. 1996. *The Eucharist in the New Testament and the Early Church.* Collegeville: Liturgical Press, Pueblo.

Léon-Dufour, Xavier, S.J. 1987. *Sharing the Eucharistic Bread: The Witness of the New Testament.* New York: Paulist.

Lincoln, Andrew T. 1995. "The Promise and the Failure: Mark 16:7, 8." In *The Interpretation of Mark: Studies in New Testament Interpretation,* edited by William R. Telford, 229-52. Edinburgh: T & T Clark.

Luz, Ulrich. 1994. *Matthew in History: Interpretation, Influence, and Effects.* Minneapolis: Fortress.

————. 1995. *The Theology of the Gospel of Matthew.* New Testament Theology. Cambridge: Cambridge University Press.

McKnight, Scot. 1991. *A Light Among the Gentiles: Jewish Missionary Activity in the Second Temple Period.* Minneapolis: Fortress.

Marcus, Joel B. 1995. "The Old Testament and the Death of Jesus: The Role of Scripture in the Gospel Passion Narratives." In *The Death of Jesus in Early Christianity,* edited by John T. Carroll and Joel B. Green, 205-33. Peabody, MA: Hendrickson.

Marguerat, Daniel. 1981. *Le Jugement dans l'évangile de Matthieu.* Geneva: Labor et Fides.

Meier, John P. 1975. "Salvation-History in Matthew: In Search of a Starting Point." *CBQ* 37:203-15.

————. 1976. *Law and History in Matthew's Gospel: A Redactional Study of Mt. 5:17-48.* AnBib 71. Rome: Biblical Institute Press.

————. 1977. "Nations or Gentiles in Matthew 28:19?" *CBQ* 39:94-102.

————. 1979. *The Vision of Matthew: Christ, Church and Morality in the First Gospel.* Theological Inquiries. New York: Paulist.

————. 1994. *A Marginal Jew.* Vol. 2. New York: Doubleday.

Neirynck, Frans. 1990. "Synoptic Problem." In *The New Jerome Biblical Commentary,* edited by Raymond E. Brown, 587-95. Englewood Cliffs, NJ: Prentice Hall.

Orton, David E. 1989. *The Understanding Scribe: Matthew and the Apocalyptic Ideal.* JSNT 22. Sheffield: Sheffield Academic Press.

Overman, J. Andrew. 1990. *Matthew's Gospel and Formative Judaism: The Social World of the Matthean Community.* Minneapolis: Fortress.

Perkins, Pheme. 1994. *Peter: Apostle for the Whole Church.* Columbia: University of South Carolina Press.

Pesch, Wilhelm. 1966. *Matthäus der Seelsorger: Das neue Verständnis der Evangelien dargestellet am Beispiel von Matthäus 18.* Stuttgarter BibelStudien 2. Stuttgart: Verlag Katholisches Bibelwerk.

Petuchowski, Jakob J., and Michael Brocke. 1978. *The Lord's Prayer and Jewish Liturgy.* New York: Seabury.

Piper, John. 1979. *"Love Your Enemies": Jesus' Love Command in the Synoptic Gospels and the Early Christian Paraenesis.* SNTSMS 38. Cambridge: Cambridge University Press.

Powell, Mark Allan. 1995. "Do and Keep What Moses Says (Matthew 23:2-7)." *JBL* 114:419-35.

Przybylski, Benno. 1980. *Righteousness in Matthew and His World of Thought.* SNTSMS 41. Cambridge: Cambridge University Press.

Richardson, Peter. 1996. *Herod.* Columbia: University of South Carolina Press.

Saldarini, Anthony J. 1984. *Jesus and Passover.* New York: Paulist.

———. 1988. *Pharisees, Scribes and Sadducees in Palestinian Society. A Sociological Approach.* Wilmington, DE: Michael Glazier.

———. 1994. *Matthew's Christian-Jewish Community.* Chicago: University of Chicago Press.

Sanders, E. P. 1985. *Jesus and Judaism.* Philadelphia: Fortress.

Schottroff, Luise. 1995. *Lydia's Impatient Sisters.* Louisville: Westminster/John Knox.

Schrage, Wolfgang. 1988. *The Ethics of the New Testament.* Philadelphia: Fortress.

Senior, Donald. 1975. *The Passion According to Matthew: A Redactional Study.* BETL 39. Louvain: Louvain University Press.

———. 1976. "The Death of Jesus and the Resurrection of the Holy Ones (Mt 27:51-53)." *CBQ* 38:312-29.

———. 1984. *The Passion of Jesus in the Gospel of Mark.* Passion Series 2. Wilmington, DE: Michael Glazier.

———. 1985. *The Passion of Jesus in the Gospel of Matthew.* Passion Series 1. Collegeville, MN: Liturgical Press.

———. 1987. "Matthew's Special Material in the Passion Story." *ETL* 63:272-94.

———. 1992. "Matthew's Account of the Burial of Jesus Mt 27:57-61." In *The Four Gospels 1992: Festschrift Frans Neirynck,* edited by F. Van Segbroeck, C. M. Tuckett, G. Van Belle, and J. Verheyden, 1433-48. Leuven: Leuven University Press.

———. 1996. *What Are They Saying About Matthew?* New York: Paulist.

———. 1997a. *The Gospel of Matthew.* IBT. Nashville: Abingdon.

———. 1997b. "The Lure of the Formula Quotations: Re-Assessing Matthew's Use of the Old Testament with the Passion Narrative as Test Case." In *The Scriptures in the Gospels,* edited by C. M. Tuckett, 65-115. BETL 31. Leuven: Peeters.

Stendahl, Krister. 1968. *The School of St. Matthew and Its Use of the Old Testament.* Philadelphia: Fortress.

Swartley, Willard M., ed. 1992. *The Love of Enemy and Nonretaliation in the New Testament.* Louisville: Westminster/John Knox.

Thompson, William G. 1970. *Matthew's Advice to a Divided Community. Mt. 17, 22–18, 35*. AnBib 44. Rome: Biblical Institute Press.

Trilling, Wolfgang. 1964. 3rd rev. ed. *Das Wahre Israel: Studien zur Theologie des Matthäus Evangeliums*. STANT 10. Munich: Kösel-Verlag.

Van Segbroeck, F. 1972. "Les citations d'accomplissement dans l'évangile selon Matthieu d'après trois ouvrages récents." In *L'évangile selon Matthieu: Rédaction et Théologie*, edited by M. Didier, 107-30. BETL 29. Gembloux, Belgium: Duculot.

Walker, Peter W. L. 1996. *Jesus and the Holy City: New Testament Perspectives on Jerusalem*. Grand Rapids, MI: Eerdmans.

Weaver, Dorothy Jean. 1990. *Matthew's Missionary Discourse. A Literary Critical Analysis*. JSNTSup 38. Sheffield: JSOT.

Wheeler, Sondra Ely. 1995. *Wealth as Peril and Obligation: The New Testament on Possessions*. Grand Rapids, MI: Eerdmans.

Wilkins, Michael J. 1995. 2nd ed. *Discipleship in the Ancient World and Matthew's Gospel*. Grand Rapids, MI: Baker.

COMMENTARIES ON MATTHEW
(BOTH CITED AND NOT CITED)

Boring, M. Eugene. 1995. "The Gospel and Letters of Matthew." In *The New Interpreter's Bible*, edited by Leander E. Keck et al., 87-505. Vol. 8. Nashville: Abingdon. — An extensive commentary geared for preaching and church-related contexts.

Davies, W. D. and Dale C. Allison Jr. 1988. ICC. Vol. 1, *Matthew I-VII*. Edinburgh: T & T Clark. — A massive commentary, based on the Greek text, that offers a thorough review of scholarship and tackles theological as well as historical issues.

———. 1991. ICC. Vol. 2, *Matthew VIII-XVIII*. Edinburgh: T & T Clark.

———. 1997. ICC. Vol. 3, Matthew XIX-XXVII. Edinburgh: T & T Clark.

Garland, David E. 1993. *Reading Matthew: A Literary and Theological Commentary on the First Gospel*. New York: Crossroad. — Part of a series designed to guide the reader through the literary and theological continuities of the Gospel.

Gundry, Robert H. 1994. 2nd ed. *Matthew: A Commentary on His Handbook for a Mixed Church Under Persecution*. Grand Rapids, MI: Eerdmans. — This evangelical commentary represents a more conservative historical approach to the Gospel and offers detailed commentary on Matthean literary style.

Hagner, Donald. 1993. *Matthew 1–13*. WBC 33a. Dallas: Word. — Written from an evangelical perspective, this thorough commentary takes a more traditional approach to the authorship and historical background of the Gospel.

———. 1995. *Matthew 14–28*. WBC 33b. Dallas: Word.

Hare, Douglas R. A. 1993. *Matthew. Int.* Louisville: John Knox. — Designed for pastors and preachers, this commentary emphasizes the theological message of Matthew.

Harrington, Daniel J., S.J. 1991. *The Gospel of Matthew.* Sacra Pagina. Collegeville: Liturgical Press. — A commentary that concentrates on the Jewish background of Matthew's Gospel, suitable for a broad but informed audience.

Luz, Ulrich. 1989. *Matthew 1–7: A Continental Commentary.* Minneapolis: Augsburg Fortress. — A masterful commentary that remains only partially translated for an English-speaking audience. Luz comments on the text of Matthew and traces the history of the interpretation of key passages.

Overman, J. Andrew. 1996. *Church and Community in Crisis: The Gospel According to Matthew.* The New Testament in Context. Valley Forge, PA: Trinity Press International. — In accord with the goal of this series, this commentary emphasizes the relationship of Matthew's Gospel to its context in first-century Judaism.

Wainwright, Elaine Mary. 1995. "The Gospel of Matthew." In *Searching the Scriptures: A Feminist Commentary,* edited by Elizabeth Schüssler Fiorenza, 2:635-77. New York: Crossroad. — A brief commentary that views Matthew from a feminist perspective.

INDEX